soggy
sneakers

UPDATED
Fourth Edition

A Paddler's
Guide to Oregon's
Rivers

Pete Giordano and the
Willamette Kayak and Canoe Club

THE MOUNTAINEERS BOOKS

THE MOUNTAINEERS BOOKS
*is the nonprofit publishing arm of The Mountaineers,
an organization founded in 1906 and dedicated to the exploration,
preservation, and enjoyment of outdoor and wilderness areas.*

1001 SW Klickitat Way, Suite 201, Seattle, WA 98134

Third edition 1994. Fourth edition: first printing 2004, second printing 2007, third printing 2008, fourth printing 2009, updated fifth printing 2012

Distributed in the United Kingdom by Cordee, www.cordee.co.uk

Manufactured in the United States of America

Project editor: Kate Rogers
Copy editor: Heath Silberfeld
Cover design: Karen Schober
Interior design: Peggy Egerdahl
Layout Artist: The Mountaineers Books
Mapmaker: Moore Creative Designs
Cover photograph: Stone/Yvette Cardozo

Library of Congress Cataloging-in-Publication Data
Giordano, Pete.
   Soggy sneakers: a paddler's guide to Oregon's rivers/Pete Giordano and the Willamette Kayak and Canoe Club.–4th ed.
    p. cm.
   Rev. ed. of Soggy sneakers/Willamette Kayak and Canoe Club. 3rd ed. c1994.
   Includes bibliographical references and index.
   ISBN 0-89886-815-7 (pbk)
    1. Canoes and canoeing—Oregon–Guidebooks. 2. Rivers—Recreational use–Oregon—Guidebooks. 3. Oregon–Guidebooks. I. Title: Paddler's guide to Oregon's rivers. II. Willamette Kayak and Canoe Club. III. Title.

GV776.O6S63 2004
917.95–dc22
2003025513

ISBN (paperback): 978-0-89886-815-9
ISBN (ebook): 978-1-59485-382-1

contents

Map Overview and Legend   11
Acknowledgments   12
Preface   13
Introduction   14
How to Use This Book   15
River Safety   18
River Etiquette   23
River Preservation   24
River Runs at a Glance   25

REGION 1: NORTH COAST RIVERS

Grays River, Washington
   1. Grays River: South Fork to Highway 4 34
Nehalem River
   2. Nehalem River: Spruce Run County Park to Nehalem Falls 35
   3. Salmonberry River: Beaver Slide Road to Nehalem River 38
Kilchis River
   4. Kilchis River: Confluence of North Fork and South Fork to Little
      South Fork 40
Wilson River and Tributaries
   5. Devil's Lake Fork Wilson River: Near Milepost 29 to Jones Creek
      Forest Camp 42
   6. North Fork Wilson River: Confluence with West Fork to Jones
      Creek Camp 43
   7. Wilson River: Jones Creek Camp to Milepost 15 44
   8. Wilson River: Milepost 15 to Milepost 8 Boat Ramp 45
   9. Jordan Creek: Headwaters to Wilson River 47
Trask River and Tributaries
   10. North Fork Trask River: North Fork of North Fork Trask River
      to Bridge 48
   11. Trask River: Fish Hatchery to Upper Peninsula Boat Ramp 49
Nestucca River
   12. Nestucca River: Rocky Bend Campground to Blaine 50
Siletz River and Tributaries
   13. North Fork Siletz River: Boulder Creek to South Fork Siletz
      River 51
   14. Siletz River: Elk Creek to Buck Creek 53
   15. Siletz River: Buck Creek to Moonshine County Park 54
   16. Siletz River: Moonshine County Park to Sam Creek Bridge 55
   17. Drift Creek: North Creek to Covered Bridge 56

Alsea River and Tributaries
18. South Fork Alsea River: Hubert McBee Memorial Park to Rock
Quarry Weir 57
19. Alsea River: Mill Creek Park to Tidewater 60
20. Drift Creek: Meadow Creek to Lower Bridge 61
Siuslaw River and Tributaries
21. Siuslaw River: Milepost 3 to Swisshome 62
22. Lake Creek: Deadwood Creek to Tide 64

REGION 2: SOUTH COAST RIVERS

West Fork Millicoma River
23. West Fork Millicoma River: Henrys Falls to Stonehouse Bridge 68
South Fork Coos River
24. South Fork Coos River: Johnson Beach to Milepost 6 70
South Fork Coquille River
25. South Fork Coquille River: 16-Mile Bridge to Milepost 3.2 71
26. South Fork Coquille River: Powers to Baker Creek 74
Elk River
27. Elk River: Butler Creek to Fish Hatchery 75
Chetco River
28. Chetco River: Chetco Gorge 77
Smith River and Tributaries, California
29. North Fork Smith River: 13 Miles above Gasquet to Gasquet 79
30. Middle Fork Smith River: 6 Miles above Patrick Creek
to Patrick Creek 80
31. Middle Fork Smith River: Gasquest to above Oregon Hole
Gorge 81
32. Middle Fork Smith River: Oregon Hole Gorge 82
33. South Fork Smith River: Upper Bridge to South Fork Gorge 82
34. South Fork Smith River: South Fork Gorge to Bridge 83

REGION 3: SOUTHERN OREGON RIVERS

Umpqua River and Tributaries
35. Jackson Creek: 7 Miles above Cover Camp to
Cover Camp 86
36. Jackson Creek: Cover Camp to NF 31 Bridge 87
37. Cow Creek: Reuben Road to West Fork of
Cow Creek 89
38. Cow Creek: West Fork of Cow Creek to Union Creek 91
39. South Umpqua River: Campbell Falls to Three C Rock 91
40. South Umpqua River: Three C Rock to Milepost 22 93
41. South Umpqua River: Milepost 22 to Days Creek 94
42. South Umpqua River: Canyonville County Park to
Lawson Bar 95

43. Copeland Creek: NF 300 Bridge to North Umpqua River 96
44. Canton Creek: 6.5 Miles above Steamboat Creek to Steamboat Creek 98
45. Steamboat Creek: Steamboat Falls to Canton Creek Campground 99
46. North Umpqua River: Boulder Flat to Gravel Bin 100
47. North Umpqua River: Steamboat to Cable Crossing 101
48. North Umpqua River: Idleyld Park to Winchester 103
49. North Umpqua River: Winchester to River Forks Park 105
50. Calapooya Creek: Nonpareil to Driver Valley Road 106
51. Umpqua River: River Forks Park to Scottsburg 106
52. Umpqua River: Sawyers Rapid 108

Rogue River and Tributaries

53. North Fork Rogue River: Natural Bridge to Woodruff Campground 108
54. North Fork Rogue River: Takilma Gorge 111
55. North Fork Rogue River: River Bridge Campground to North Fork Reservoir 112
56. North Fork Rogue River: Mill Creek Falls to Lost Creek Lake 114
57. Middle Fork Rogue River: Butte Falls Road to Lost Creek Lake 115
58. Big Butte Creek: Butte Falls Picnic Area to Crowfoot Road 116
59. Grave Creek: 6 Miles to Confluence with Rogue River 117
60. Rogue River: Above Nugget Falls to Gold Hill Boat Ramp 119
61. Rogue River: Grave Creek to Foster Bar 120
62. Illinois River: Oak Flat to Oak Flat 122

REGION 4: UPPER WILLAMETTE AND MCKENZIE DRAINAGES

Upper Willamette River and Tributaries

63. Brice Creek: Upper NF 22 Bridge to Champion Creek 126
64. Brice Creek: Champion Creek to Cedar Creek Camp 130
65. Layng Creek: Rujada Campground to above Wildwood Falls 131
66. Row River: Wildwood Falls to Dorena Lake 131
67. Row River: Dorena Dam to BMX Park 132
68. Hills Creek: Upper Reaches to NF 2118 Bridge 133
69. Salt Creek: McCredie Springs to Kitson Springs Road Bridge 134
70. Salmon Creek: 1.5 Miles above NF 2408 Bridge to Fish Hatchery Road Bridge 135
71. Christy Creek: NF 1926 Bridge to North Fork of the Middle Fork Willamette River 137
72. North Fork of the Middle Fork Willamette River: Miracle Mile through The Gorge 138
73. North Fork of the Middle Fork Willamette River: Bottom of The Gorge to Westfir 139
74. Fall Creek: Gold Creek to Bedrock Campground 140
75. Fall Creek: Bedrock Campground to Fall Creek Reservoir 141

76. Fall Creek: Fall Creek Dam to Jasper County Park 142
77. Winberry Creek: Winberry Campground to Fall Creek Reservoir 143
78. Middle Fork Willamette River: Oakridge to Lookout Point Lake 144
79. Middle Fork Willamette River: Dexter Dam to Jasper County Park 146
80. Willamette River: Jasper County Park to Alton Baker Park 147

McKenzie River and Tributaries

81. South Fork McKenzie River: Above French Pete Campground to Cougar Reservoir 148
82. Blue River: Quentin Creek to Blue River Lake 151
83. Quartz Creek: Milepost 7.5 Bridge to Milepost 2 Bridge 151
84. McKenzie River: Olallie Campground to Paradise Campground 153
85. McKenzie River: Paradise Campground to Finn Rock 154
86. McKenzie River: Finn Rock to Leaburg Dam 155
87. McKenzie River: Leaburg Dam to Hendricks Bridge Wayside 156
88. McKenzie River: Hendricks Bridge Wayside to Hayden Bridge 157
89. McKenzie River: Hayden Bridge to Armitage Park 158

Mohawk River

90. Mohawk River: Gate on Mohawk Road to Hileman Road Bridge .. 160

REGION 5: MID-WILLAMETTE VALLEY

Marys River

91. Marys River: Blodgett to Philomath 162

Calapooia River

92. Calapooia River: 22 Miles above Holley to Bridge 13 Miles above Holley 162
93. Calapooia River: Bridge 13 Miles above Holley to Bridge 4 Miles above Holley 166
94. Calapooia River: Bridge 4 Miles above Holley to McKercher Park 167
95. Calapooia River: McKercher Park to Brownsville 168

Mill Creek

96. Mill Creek: Upper Bridge to Mill Creek County Park 168
97. Mill Creek: Buell County Park to Sheridan 170

South Fork Yamhill River

98. South Fork Yamhill River: Grand Ronde to Sheridan 171

South Santiam River and Tributaries

99. Moose Creek: Cub Creek to South Santiam River 172
100. Canyon Creek: 7-Mile Bridge to South Santiam River 173
101. Wiley Creek: Upper Bridge to Middle Bridge 175
102. Crabtree Creek: North Fork Bridge to Larwood Park 176
103. Crabtree Creek: Larwood Park to South Santiam River 177

104. Thomas Creek: Hall Creek to 5-Mile Bridge 178
105. Thomas Creek: 5-Mile Bridge to Hannah Bridge 180
106. South Santiam River: Mountain House to Foster Lake 180
107. South Santiam River: Foster Dam to Jefferson 182

Middle Santiam River and Tributaries

108. Quartzville River: Above Gregg Creek to Galena Creek 184
109. Quartzville River: Galena Creek to Green Peter Lake 185
110. Middle Santiam River: NF 2041 to Green Peter Lake 186
111. Middle Santiam River: Green Peter Dam to Foster Lake 188

North Santiam River and Tributaries

112. Breitenbush River: Cleator Bend Campground to Detroit
     Reservoir 189
113. Little North Santiam River: Old Mine to Three Pools (Opal Creek) .. 190
114. Little North Santiam River: Salmon Falls to Elkhorn Valley
     Recreation Site 192
115. Little North Santiam River: Elkhorn Valley Recreation Site
     to Mehama 193
116. North Santiam River: Bruno Mountain Road to Detroit Lake 195
117. North Santiam River: Big Cliff Dam to Packsaddle
     County Park 196
118. North Santiam River: Packsaddle County Park to Mill City 197
119. North Santiam River: Mill City to Mehama 198
120. North Santiam River: Mehama to Stayton 199

REGION 6: LOWER WILLAMETTE VALLEY AND CLACKAMAS RIVER

Silver Creek

121. Silver Creek: Silver Falls State Park to Silverton Reservoir 202

Abiqua Creek

122. Abiqua Creek: Abiqua Falls to Abiqua Road 204

Butte Creek

123. Butte Creek: Fault Line to Oregon 213 205

Molalla River and Tributaries

124. Table Rock Fork of the Molalla River: Second Bridge to Gravel Pit ... 207
125. Molalla River: Copper Creek to Table Rock Confluence 208
126. Molalla River: Table Rock Fork Confluence to Turner Bridge 209
127. Molalla River: Turner Bridge to Glen Avon Bridge 210
128. Molalla River: Glen Avon Bridge to Feyrer Park 212
129. Molalla River: Feyrer Park to Oregon 213 Bridge 213

Clackamas River and Tributaries

130. Nohorn Creek: Nohorn Creek to Peg Leg Falls 213
131. Collawash River: Elk Lake Creek to Bridge 5.5 Miles from
     Mouth 215
132. Collawash River: Bridge 5.5 Miles from Mouth to Two Rivers
     Picnic Area 217

133. Roaring River: 3.2 Miles above Clackamas River to Clackamas River 218
134. North Fork Clackamas River: 3.75 Miles from North Fork Reservoir to North Fork Reservoir 220
135. Eagle Creek: Fish Hatchery to Snuffin Road 222
136. Eagle Creek: Snuffin Road to Eagle Creek Road 223
137. Clear Creek: Metzler Park to Redland Road Bridge 224
138. Clackamas River: June Creek Bridge to Collawash River ... 225
139. Clackamas River: Collawash River to Sandstone Road Bridge 226
140. Clackamas River: Three Lynx Power Station to North Fork Reservoir 228
141. Clackamas River: Milo McIver State Park to Barton Park ... 230
142. Clackamas River: Barton Park to Carver 231
143. Clackamas River: Carver to Clackamette Park 232

REGION 7: COLUMBIA GORGE

Sandy River and Tributaries

144. Salmon River: Wilderness Trailhead to Arrah-Wanna Road 235
145. Bull Run River: Bull Run Road Bridge to Dodge Park 237
146. Sandy River: McNeil Campground to Lolo Pass Road Bridge 238
147. Sandy River: Zigzag to Marmot Bridge 239
148. Sandy River: Marmot Bridge to Marmot Diversion Dam 240
149. Sandy River: Marmot Diversion Dam to Revenue Bridge 241
150. Sandy River: Revenue Bridge to Dodge Park 243
151. Sandy River: Dodge Park to Oxbow Park 243
152. Sandy River: Oxbow Park to Lewis and Clark State Park 244

Hood River and Tributaries

153. Lake Branch Fork Hood River: Divers Creek to West Fork Hood River 245
154. West Fork Hood River: Lake Branch Fork to East Fork Hood River 247
155. East Fork Hood River: Sherwood Campground to Oregon 35 Bridge 248
156. East Fork Hood River: Dee to Tucker Bridge 250
157. Hood River: Tucker Bridge to Hood River Marina 251

Klickitat River, Washington

158. Little Klickitat River: Esteb Road to Klickitat River 252
159. Klickitat River: Yakama Indian Reservation to Klickitat Salmon Hatchery 254
160. Klickitat River: Klickitat Salmon Hatchery to Leidl Campground 255
161. Klickitat River: Leidl Campground to Icehouse Public Access 256
162. Klickitat River: Icehouse Public Access to Rivermile 5 257

White Salmon River and Tributaries, Washington

163. Trout Lake Creek: Guler Road Bridge to River Road Bridge 258

164. White Salmon River: Warner Road Bridge to Green Truss Bridge 260
165. White Salmon River: Green Truss Bridge to BZ Corner 261
166. White Salmon River: BZ Corner to Husum 263
167. White Salmon River: Husum to Northwestern Park 264

Little White Salmon River, Washington

168. Little White Salmon River: Fish Hatchery to Columbia River 265

Wind River and Tributaries, Washington

169. Trout Creek: NF 43 Bridge to Pacific Crest Trail Bridge 267
170. Wind River: Stabler to High Bridge 268
171. Wind River: High Bridge to Columbia River 270

Rock Creek, Washington

172. Rock Creek: 1.5 Miles above Steep Creek to 3.5 Miles below Steep Creek 271

Washougal River and Tributaries, Washington

173. Stebbins Creek: South Fork and North Fork Confluence to Washougal River 272
174. West Fork Washougal River: West Fork Bridge to Washougal River 274
175. Washougal River: Prospector Creek to Stebbins Creek 276
176. Washougal River: Doc's Drop to Dougan Falls 277
177. Washougal River: Dougan Falls to Salmon Falls 278
178. Washougal River: 10-Mile Bridge to above Washougal 279

REGION 8: CENTRAL OREGON RIVERS

Deschutes River and Tributaries

179. Metolius River: Source to Lake Billy Chinook 282
180. Crooked River: Lone Pine Bridge to Crooked River Ranch 285
181. Crooked River: Crooked River Ranch to Lake Billy Chinook 287
182. White River: Barlow Crossing to Keeps Mill 288
183. White River: Keeps Mill to Wamic–White River Bridge 289
184. White River: Wamic–White River Bridge to Tygh Valley 290
185. Deschutes River: Wickiup Dam to Pringle Falls 291
186. Deschutes River: Pringle Falls to Big River Campground 294
187. Deschutes River: Big River Campground to Benham Falls 294
188. Deschutes River: Upper Benham Falls 295
189. Deschutes River: Aspen Campground to Lava Island Falls 296
190. Deschutes River: Lava Island Falls to Meadow Camp Picnic Area 297
191. Deschutes River: Meadow Camp Picnic Area to Mount Bachelor Village 298
192. Deschutes River: Bend to Tumalo State Park 300
193. Deschutes River: Tumalo State Park to Cline Falls State Park 301
194. Deschutes River: Cline Falls State Park to Lower Bridge 303
195. Deschutes River: Lower Bridge to Lake Billy Chinook 304

196. Deschutes River: US 26 Bridge to Sherar's Falls 306
197. Deschutes River: Sherar's Falls to Columbia River 308

Klamath River
198. Klamath River: Keno Dam to John C. Boyle Reservoir 310
199. Klamath River: John C. Boyle Power Plant to Copco Lake 311

REGION 9: EASTERN OREGON RIVERS

John Day River and Tributaries
200. North Fork John Day River: Route 52 Bridge to Dale 316
201. North Fork John Day River: Dale to Monument 318
202. North Fork John Day River/John Day River: Monument to Service
Creek 321
203. John Day River: Service Creek to Clarno 322
204. John Day River: Clarno to Cottonwood 324
205. John Day River: Cottonwood Bridge to Columbia River 326

Snake River and Tributaries
206. Donner und Blitzen River: Blitzen Crossing to Page Springs 328
207. Powder River: Milepost 20.5 to Cable Tram (Milepost 34) 330
208. Jarbidge River/Bruneau River: Murphy Hot Springs to Bruneau 332
209. Grande Ronde River: Tony Vey Meadows to Red Bridge
State Park 334
210. Grande Ronde River: Red Bridge State Park River to Hilgard
Junction State Park 335
211. Grande Ronde River: Hilgard Junction State Park to Riverside
City Park 337
212. Grande Ronde River: Riverside City Park to Elgin 338
213. Grande Ronde River: Elgin to Palmer Junction 339
214. Wallowa River/Grande Ronde River: Minam to Troy 340
215. Grande Ronde River: Troy to Boggan's Oasis 343
216. Grande Ronde River: Boggan's Oasis to Snake River
(Heller Bar) 344
217. Snake River: Hells Canyon Dam to Heller Bar 345

Owyhee River and Tributaries
218. East Fork Owyhee River: Garat Crossing to Three Forks 348
219. Owyhee River: Three Forks to Rome 350
220. Owyhee River: Rome to Leslie Gulch 353

Coastal Surf Kayaking
Coastal Access Overview (16 Areas) 358

Other Rivers to Explore   362
Index   380
Bibliography   382
Appendix A: River Flow Information   383
Appendix B: Whitewater Boating Organizations   383

how to use this book

Most of the known river runs in Oregon are described in this book. They are grouped into nine chapters organized around the seventeen drainage basins of the state. Multiple runs on one river are listed beginning upstream and heading downstream. All river runs reported in this book were run by the authors.

General river descriptions are given for major rivers and river systems. Each run begins with an information block that lists **class** designation, **flow** in cubic feet per second (cfs), **gradient** in feet per mile (fpm), **length** in miles, **character** of the surroundings (the most significant topographic, geographic, and/or scenic features), and **season** in which the river can be run. Because the class designation of a river varies depending upon the flow, multiple information-block entries, separated by semicolons, are given for some runs. Detailed information on some of these information-block categories and how they are used in this book is given later in this section.

Following the information block is a description of the run. The character of the river is described, as well as the rapids and landmarks that are found on the run. Unless otherwise indicated, "right" and "left" are used with respect to an observer looking downstream (river right and river left). Each run concludes with short sections on **hazards, access,** and **gauge** information (no gauge information is given for the surf sections in Region 10: Coastal Surf Kayaking).

The maps in this book show the principal rivers and roads, the sections for which runs are described, the locations of access points, and such major landmarks as campgrounds and towns. Although the main shuttle roads are shown, it is intended that a state road map be used with this book. (For more information on maps, see the end of this section.)

The appendices include important additional information. Appendix A lists the various sources for river flow information. Appendix B lists some of the whitewater boating organizations in Oregon. These organizations provide an invaluable voice in the ongoing battles over how our rivers and streams are and will be used. Through clinics, workshops, and trips, they provide information and training on safety and paddling skills. Best of all, they put people in touch with a great bunch of paddlers and open the door to a rich agenda of river activities.

Following are definitions of some of the categories used in this book.

Class. The class designations indicate the class of the majority of the run, according to the American Whitewater Affiliation International Scale of River Difficulty, as listed below. If the water temperature is below 50 degrees Fahrenheit, the American Whitewater Affiliation states that the river should be considered one class more difficult than normal. If only one or two spots are more difficult than the majority of the run, the class of these spots is given in parentheses—for example, South Santiam as 4(5+) or Lower McKenzie as 1(2). The letter T is given after the number designation for a run that is predominantly technical in nature, and the letter P indicates that at least one portage is mandatory.

Class 1. Moving water with a few riffles and small waves. Few or no obstructions. (Still water and class 1 are sometimes subdivided by water speed: Class A, standing or slow-flowing water, not more than 2.5 mph; Class B, current between 2.5 and 4.5 mph, but back-paddling can effectively neutralize the speed; Class C, current more than 4.5 mph, thus back-paddling cannot neutralize the speed of the current, and simple obstacles may occur that require a certain amount of boat control.)

Class 2. Easy rapids with waves up to 3 feet and wide clear channels that are obvious without scouting. Some maneuvering is required.

Class 3. Rapids with high, irregular waves often capable of swamping an open canoe. Narrow passages that often require complex maneuvering. May require scouting from shore.

Class 4. Long, difficult rapids with constricted passages that often require precise maneuvering in very turbulent waters. Scouting from shore is often necessary, and conditions make rescue difficult. Generally not possible for open canoes, except experts. Boaters in covered canoes or kayaks should be able to Eskimo roll.

Class 5. Extremely difficult, long, and very violent rapids with highly congested routes that nearly always must be scouted from shore. Rescue conditions are difficult, and significant hazard to life may result in event of a mishap. Ability to Eskimo roll in kayaks and canoes is essential.

Class 6. Difficulties of class 5 carried to the extreme of navigability. Nearly impossible and very dangerous. For teams of experts only, after close study and with all precautions taken.

Flow. The rate of flow, which is normally measured at the gauge location, is reported in cubic feet per second (cfs). The flow may differ significantly upstream or downstream of the gauge, depending upon flow in any tributaries. Where necessary, flows are estimated by the authors.

Gradient. The average gradient of the run is the elevation change over the length of the run, in units of feet per mile (fpm). The letters PD are used to indicate that a run is primarily *pool drop* in nature—that is, relatively flat stretches are connected by relatively steep sections in which most of the elevation changes occur. The letter C is used to indicate that a run is primarily *continuous* in nature; that is, the elevation change is relatively uniform over its length.

Season. The time of year that a river can normally be run is related to the weather and the type of source for the river. Following are the classifications used in this book:

Year-round. There is adequate water all year for boating. The sources of these rivers are generally impounded or spring-fed.

Dam-controlled. The flow of these rivers is controlled by dams or irrigation diversions, but there is no requirement for minimum flow. Water may be shut off or reduced to less than runnable flows by the controlling agency.

Rainy. Runnable levels are reached after several days of rain. Many of the rivers of western Oregon are in this group, with a season from about October to April.

Snowmelt. Most of the water comes from melting snow in the spring and early summer. Such rivers are at high elevations or in eastern Oregon.

Rainy/snowmelt. The water is received from both rain and snow. The rivers are runnable after a few days of good rain and into early summer because of melting snowpack.

Hazards. The most difficult rapids are described, and some suggestions are made about how they can be approached or portaged. Other hazards, such as sweepers, weirs, and dams, are also mentioned.

Access. Directions to the river, primary and optional put-ins and take-outs, and directions on running the shuttle are described.

Gauge. Where applicable, the location of the river gauge and the agency for obtaining the flow are given. When possible, the authors' opinion of *high runnable*, *low runnable*, and *optimum* flows are provided. Further information is available from the sources listed in Appendix A.

Maps. This book's maps are intended to be used with a state road map. The *Oregon Atlas and Gazetteer* is probably the most useful single collection of maps for boaters in Oregon. It is extremely useful for locating all the runs and shuttle routes and is available at most bookstores. California and Washington versions of this publication are similarly useful.

For smaller streams and national forest service roads, the U.S. Forest Service maps are useful. All the roads in the national forests in Oregon and Washington were renumbered in 1982, and the maps have been republished. National forest maps are available from the Pacific Northwest Region Field Office (319 SW Pine Street, Portland, OR 97208) or from any of the national forest headquarters offices throughout the state.

U.S. Geological Survey (USGS) topographical maps are indispensable for exploratory boating. However, their coverage of Oregon's whitewater country is not extensive, and many of the maps are at least 20 to 30 years old. The 7.5-minute USGS maps with 40-foot contour intervals are the ones to obtain. Many sports stores, bookstores, and libraries carry some topographical maps.

Ender anyone? Upper Quartzville River. (Pete Giordano)

river safety

The run descriptions in this book reflect the general character of a river, but the character can change dramatically in the course of a day, a season, or a year. Thus, while this book is a guide to the rivers and what to expect, it must in no way be regarded as the exact description of what you will find on a particular day. Each boater must accept personal responsibility for finding out what lies around the next corner—and for possessing sufficient skills to cope.

Persons running rivers are responsible for their own safety. This book is offered only as a guide. Neither the authors nor the publisher are responsible or liable for any loss of life or property that may befall others running the rivers.

A Note About Safety

Safety is an important concern in all outdoor activities. No guidebook can alert you to every hazard or anticipate the limitations of every reader. Therefore, the descriptions of roads, runs, and natural features in this book are not representations that a particular place or excursion will be safe for your party. When you follow any of the runs described in this book, you assume responsibility for your own safety. Under normal conditions, such excursions require the usual attention to traffic, road and river conditions, weather, terrain, the capabilities of your party, and other factors. Keeping informed on current conditions and exercising common sense are the keys to a safe, enjoyable outing.

The Mountaineers Books

People run rivers for different reasons; some seek a relaxing aesthetic experience, others seek adventure or challenge. Many seek a combination of the two. For whatever reasons you choose to boat, your river-running experience will be more fun and more rewarding if done safely. On any river, even apparently small ones, the price of ignorance or carelessness can be anything from lost or damaged equipment to personal injury or the loss of life.

A large part of safe boating lies in identifying potential dangers. Prevention is the key, not just reacting to a hazardous situation already in motion. Recognizing potential hazards requires experience. Boating clubs offer the novice a way other than trial and error to acquire that experience and learn boating safety. Clubs normally have people who teach boating and are willing to share their experiences and instill safe boating practices. Many clubs provide instruction in boat handling (for a listing of boating organizations, see Appendix B). Another way to learn boating skills and safety is in classes offered by city parks and recreation departments, community colleges, the Red Cross, or the YMCA. Many of the books in the Bibliography at the back of this book discuss safety, rescue techniques, and safety equipment.

The Safety Code of the American Whitewater Affiliation, slightly condensed, is reprinted here with permission. Read it carefully.

T. R. Torgersen

I. ***Personal Preparedness and Responsibility***
1. Be a competent swimmer with ability to handle yourself underwater.
2. Wear a life jacket.
3. Wear a solid, correctly fitted helmet.
4. Keep your craft under control. Control must be sufficient to stop or reach shore before reaching danger. Do not enter a rapids unless you are reasonably sure that you can run it safely or swim it without injury.
5. Be aware of river hazards and avoid them. The following are the most frequent killers:
   A. High water. The river's power and danger, and the difficulty of rescue, increase tremendously as the flow rate increases. It is often misleading to judge river level at the put-in. Look at a narrow, critical passage. Be aware that sun on a snowpack, hard rain, or a dam release may greatly increase the flow.
   B. Cold. Cold quickly drains strength and robs the ability to make sound decisions. Dress to protect yourself from cold water and weather extremes. When the water temperature is less than 50 degrees Fahrenheit, a wetsuit or drysuit is essential. Next best is wool or pile clothing under a waterproof shell. In the latter case, also carry matches and a complete change of clothes in a waterproof bag. If, after prolonged exposure, one experiences uncontrollable shaking or loss of coordination, or has difficulty speaking, one is hypothermic and needs assistance.
   C. Strainers. These include brush, fallen trees, bridge pilings, and any other obstacle that allows river current to sweep through but pins boats and boaters against it. The water pressure on anything trapped this way can be overwhelming. Rescue is often extremely difficult. Pinning may occur in fast current with little or no whitewater to signal the danger.
   D. Dams, weirs, ledges, reversals, and holes. When water drops over an obstacle, it curls back on itself, forming a strong upstream current that can hold boats or swimmers. Some holes make for sport; others are proven killers. Hydraulics around human-made dams are especially dangerous. Despite a benign appearance, such water can trap a swimmer. Once trapped, a swimmer's only hope is to dive below the surface, where downstream current is flowing beneath the reversal.
   E. Broaching. When a boat is pushed sideways against a rock or log by strong current, it may collapse and wrap. Kayakers and decked canoe paddlers especially may become trapped and drowned. To avoid pinning, throw your weight downstream and lean downstream toward the obstacle. This allows the current to slide harmlessly underneath the hull of your craft.
6. Boating alone is not recommended. The preferred minimum is three craft.
7. Be honest with yourself about your boating ability. Do not attempt waters beyond that ability.
   A. Develop paddling skills and teamwork to match the river you plan to boat. Attempts to advance too quickly compromise safety and enjoyment.

B. Be in good physical and mental condition. Make adjustments for loss of skills due to age, health, or fitness. Explain any health limitations to your fellow paddlers.

8. Be practiced in self-rescue, including escape from an overturned craft. The ability to Eskimo roll is strongly recommended.

9. Be trained in rescue skills, CPR, and first aid, with special emphasis on recognizing and treating hypothermia.

10. Be suitably equipped. Wear shoes that will protect your feet during a bad swim or a walk for help. Carry a knife, a whistle, and waterproof matches. If you wear eyeglasses, tie them on and carry a spare pair. Do not wear ponchos, heavy boots, or anything that will reduce your ability to survive a swim.

11. Individual paddlers are ultimately responsible for their own safety and must assume sole responsibility for the following:
   A. The decision to participate on any trip.
   B. The selection of appropriate equipment.
   C. The decision to scout any rapids and to run or portage according to their best judgment.
   D. The continual evaluation of their own and their group's safety, voicing concerns when appropriate. The willingness to speak with anyone whose actions on the water are dangerous.

The Ten Essentials: A Systems Approach

Following is the revised version of the Ten Essentials that one should carry for safety and for emergencies, including in watercraft. The Ten Essentials have evolved from a list of individual items to a list of functional systems. The classic list has been expanded in the systems approach to include hydration and emergency shelter.

1. Navigation (map and compass)
2. Sun protection (sunglasses and sunscreen)
3. Insulation (extra clothing)
4. Illumination (headlamp or flashlight)
5. First-aid supplies
6. Fire (firestarter and matches/lighter)
7. Repair kit and tools (including knife)
8. Nutrition (extra food)
9. Hydration (extra water)
10. Emergency shelter

The Mountaineers

II. Boat and Equipment Preparedness

1. Test new and unfamiliar equipment before trusting it on a river.
2. Be sure craft is in good repair before starting a trip. Eliminate sharp projections that could cause injury during a swim.
3. Install flotation bags in noninflatable craft, securely fixed and designed to displace as much water as possible. Inflatable craft should have multiple air chambers and should be test-inflated before launching.

4. Paddles or oars should be strong and of adequate size for controlling the craft. Carry sufficient spares for the length and type of trip.
5. Outfit your craft safely. Be certain there is absolutely nothing to cause entanglement when coming free from an upset craft, such as a spray skirt that will not release or will tangle around legs, life jacket buckles or clothing that might snag, canoe seats that lock on shoe heels, foot braces that fail or allow feet to jam under them, flexible decks that collapse on the boater's legs when trapped by water pressure, baggage that dangles in an upset, loose ropes in the craft, or badly secured bow and stern lines (painters).
6. Provide ropes to allow you to hold onto your craft in case of upset and so that it may be rescued. Following are the recommended methods:
   A. Kayaks and covered canoes should have grab loops attached to bow and stern. A stern painter, or line, 7 or 8 feet long may be used if properly secured to prevent entanglement.
   B. Open canoes should have bow and stern lines (painters) consisting of 8 to 10 feet of ¼- or ⅜-inch rope. These lines must be secured in such a way that they are readily accessible but cannot come loose accidentally. Attached balls, floats, and knots are not recommended.
   C. Rafts and dories should have taut perimeter grab lines threaded through the loops that are usually provided. Rafts should have flip lines for righting in case of upset.
7. Respect rules for craft capacity and know how these capacities should be reduced for whitewater use. When running rapids in open canoes, do not carry more than two paddlers.
8. Carry appropriate repair materials: cloth repair tape for short trips, complete repair kit and tools for wilderness trips.

III. Group Preparedness and Responsibility

1. Organization. A river trip, except an instructional or commercially guided trip, should be regarded by all participants as a common adventure. Participants share the responsibility for the conduct of the trip, and each is responsible for judging his or her own capabilities.
2. River conditions. Each member of the group should have a reasonable knowledge of the difficulty of the run. Be aware of possible rapid changes in river level and how these changes can affect the difficulty of the run. Secure flow information. If the trip involves important tidal currents, secure tide information.
3. Participants. Determine if the prospective boaters are qualified for the trip. All decisions should be based on group safety and comfort. Difficult decisions regarding the participation of marginal boaters must be based on total group strength.
4. Equipment. Plan so that all necessary group equipment is present on the trip: 50- to 100-foot throw rope, first-aid kit with fresh and adequate supplies, extra paddles, repair materials, and survival equipment if appropriate. Check equipment as necessary at the put-in, especially life jackets, boat flotation, and any items that

could prevent complete escape from the boat in case of an upset.

5. Organization. Keep the group compact, but maintain sufficient spacing to avoid collisions. If the group is large, divide into smaller groups, each with appropriate boating strength and a designated leader and sweep.
   A. The lead paddler. Set the pace and do not get in over your head. Never run blind drops. When in doubt, stop and scout.
   B. Keep track. Each boat keeps the one behind it in sight, stopping if necessary. Know how many people are in your group and take head counts regularly. Less-skilled paddlers should stay near the center of the group.
   C. Courtesy. Do not cut in front of a boater running a drop. Always look upstream before leaving eddies to run or play. Never enter a crowded drop or eddy when there is no room.
6. Float plan. If the trip is into a wilderness area, or for an extended period, file plans before leaving with appropriate authorities or with someone who will contact authorities after a certain time. It may be wise to establish checkpoints along the way where people could be contacted if necessary. Knowing the location of possible help and preplanning could speed rescue.

IV. Guidelines for River Rescue

1. In case of an upset, recover if possible with an Eskimo roll. Evacuate your boat immediately if there is imminent danger of being trapped against logs, brush, or any other form of strainer.
2. If you swim, hold onto your craft. It has much flotation and is easy for rescuers to spot. Get to the upstream end so the craft cannot crush you against obstacles.
3. Release your craft if this improves your safety. If rescue is not imminent and water is numbingly cold, or if worse rapids follow, strike out for the nearest shore.
4. When swimming in shallow or rocky rapids, use a backstroke with your legs downstream and feet near the surface. If your foot wedges on the bottom, fast water will push you under and hold you there. Get to slow or very shallow water before trying to stand or walk. Look ahead. Avoid possible entrapment situations: rock wedges, fissures, strainers, brush, logs, and extreme hydraulics. Watch for eddies and slack water and be prepared to use them to your advantage. Use every opportunity to work toward shore.
5. If others spill, help the boaters first. Rescue boats and equipment only if it can be done safely.
6. The use of rescue lines requires training. Never tie yourself into either end of a line without a reliable quick-release system.

V. Universal River Signals

1. Stop: Arms extended horizontally or paddle held horizontally.
2. Help/emergency: Three blasts on whistle, or wave arm or paddle vertically above head.
3. All clear (come ahead): Paddle or arm held vertically.

river etiquette

Etiquette on the river means treating other people as you would like to be treated and keeping the environment as clean and natural as you would like to find it on future trips. Landowners' rights, paddling and rowing etiquette, and camping conservation should be recognized and practiced. Run descriptions make note of private land when it affects the river runner; pay attention to these warnings and respect private property rights. It is possible that historic granting of passage means the private property is okay to use until misused—in other words, use can be withdrawn at any time.

Paddling and rowing etiquette involves all watercraft. Kayakers who stop at surfing waves should be aware of and yield to others paddling downstream. Rafters and drifters should be alert for smaller boats. Be courteous on the river.

Camping conservation is important. On long trips in fragile river environments, carry and use a fire pan if you have campfires. Pack out excess coals and ashes. For less impact on the wilderness, use a gas stove.

Pack out your camping garbage, including bottle caps, cigarette butts, burnt aluminum foil, and orange peels. Buried human waste decomposes within 2 to 3 weeks, but toilet paper may last a year or longer, so pack out all toilet paper or burn it in your campfire. Do not bury it.

You river runners who are independent and enjoy wilderness, accept your responsibility.

Kim Hummer

Ready to head into the unknown by Jason Rackley

river preservation

Much has changed for river protection in Oregon since the printing of the second edition of *Soggy Sneakers* in 1986. Then, sections of only four rivers were included in the federal Wild and Scenic River system. In 1988 that all changed. Thanks to the vision and energy of Oregon Rivers Council founder Bob Doppelt, Senator Mark Hatfield, the forest planning process, and the popular support of the conservation community, Congress passed the 1988 Oregon Rivers Omnibus Bill. This unprecedented legislation included sections of forty Oregon rivers and encompassed more than 1700 miles. Additionally, sections of five rivers were designated to be studied for future inclusion in the Wild and Scenic River system. For perspective, other than the Alaska Lands Act, the next largest river protection bill in history included only parts of three rivers in California.

More was yet to come. In November of that year, Oregon voters added parts of eleven rivers to the State Scenic Waterways system, thanks to an initiative sponsored by fifty-five conservation, sporting, outdoor recreation, religious, and business organizations. By adding 573 miles, this initiative doubled the river miles protected by the State Scenic Waterways system. Nearly $1,000 in proceeds from the sale of *Soggy Sneakers,* Second Edition, was donated to the Oregon Rivers Council and the State Scenic Waterways initiative to help get these historic efforts off the ground.

Also in 1988, an historic ruling by the Oregon Supreme Court stated that the most important use for water in a State Scenic Waterway is for fish, wildlife, and scenic values. This decision affects the water rights to those streams and rivers. As a result, a process is underway for evaluating the minimum flows required in the State Scenic Waterways to protect their values.

Since 1990, under pressure from the Oregon Rivers Council, the U.S. Forest Service and other state and federal agencies have begun focusing on the concept of managing river basins instead of just river sections. This is clearly the way of the future. We must still work to protect stream segments using the Wild and Scenic Rivers Act and the State Scenic Waterways system, as well as other tools at our disposal. However, no part of any river is protected or preserved if its upstream drainages are not protected. With the decline of the northern spotted owl, old-growth forest ecosystems, and anadromous fish runs, it is becoming clear that only ecosystem-wide measures can protect an ecosystem.

Fortunately, managers are finally looking at the big picture instead of attempting to manage and protect rivers piecemeal. Rivers receive their water from precipitation throughout their drainage basins. The character of a river, and its flows, vegetation, and wildlife, are dependent upon the entire basin. Because all are interconnected, it is not enough to protect any one species or characteristic, and we must continue to strive for the health of the entire system. To fall into the trap of saving only whitewater, an owl, or a flower would be a huge step backward.

Michael Becerra

river runs at a glance

*Indicates whether it is both possible and feasible to run the section in a raft. Some of these runs are rarely done in rafts due to difficult access, small size of the river and the difficulty of the rapids.

Run #	River	Section	Class	Rafts?*	Page #
1	Grays River	South Fork to Highway 4	4-4+(5)	Yes (Experts)	34
2	Nehalem River	Spruce Run County Park to Nehalem Falls	3	Yes	35
3	Salmonberry River	Beaver Slide Road to Nehalem River	3(4)	Yes	38
4	Kilchis River	Confluence of North Fork and South Fork to Little South Fork	2+(3)	Yes	40
5	Devil's Lake Fork Wilson River	Near Milepost 29 to Jones Creek Forest Camp	3+(4)	Yes	42
6	North Fork Wilson River	Confluence with West Fork to Jones Creek Camp	3	Yes	43
7	Wilson River	Jones Creek Camp to Milepost 15	2+; 3; 4	Yes	44
8	Wilson River	Milepost 15 to Milepost 8 Boat Ramp	2+(3); 3(3+); 3+(4)	Yes	45
9	Jordan Creek	Headwaters to Wilson River	3-3+	No	47
10	North Fork Trask River	North Fork of North Fork Trask River to Bridge	2+; 3	Yes	48
11	Trask River	Fish Hatchery to Upper Peninsula Boat Ramp	3	Yes	49
12	Nestucca River	Rocky Bend Campground to Blaine	3(4, 5)	Yes	50
13	North Fork Siletz River	Boulder Creek to South Fork Siletz River	3-4+(5)	Yes	51
14	Siletz River	Elk Creek to Buck Creek	3; 4	Yes	53
15	Siletz River	Buck Creek to Moonshine County Park	3(4); 4(5)	Yes	54
16	Siletz River	Moonshine County Park to Sam Creek Bridge	1; 2	Yes	55
17	Drift Creek (Siletz River Tributary)	North Creek to Covered Bridge	3(4)	Yes	56
18	South Fork Alsea River	Hubert McBee Memorial Park to Rock Quarry Weir	2; 3	No	57
19	Alsea River	Mill Creek Park to Tidewater	1(2)	Yes	60
20	Drift Creek (Alsea River Tributary)	Meadow Creek to Lower Bridge	3	Yes	61
21	Siuslaw River	Milepost 3 to Swisshome	1+(2+)	Yes	62
22	Lake Creek	Deadwood Creek to Tide	2+(3); 3(4)	Yes	64
23	West Fork Millicoma River	Henrys Falls to Stonehouse Bridge	3(4)	Yes	68

25

Run #	River	Section	Class	Rafts?*	Page #
24	South Fork Coos River	Johnson Beach to Milepost 6	3	Yes	70
25	South Fork Coquille River	16-Mile Bridge to Milepost 3.2	4(5), T; 4+(5)	No	71
26	South Fork Coquille River	Powers to Baker Creek	2+(4)	No	74
27	Elk River	Butler Creek to Fish Hatchery	3-4+	Yes	75
28	Chetco River	Chetco Gorge	3(4, 5)	Yes	77
29	North Fork Smith River, CA	13 Miles above Gasquet to Gasquet	3; 5	Yes	79
30	Middle Fork Smith River, CA	6 Miles above Patrick Creek to Patrick Creek	4(5)	Yes	80
31	Middle Fork Smith River, CA	Gasquet to above Oregon Hole Gorge	2+; 3	Yes	81
32	Middle Fork Smith River, CA	Oregon Hole Gorge	4; 5	Yes	82
33	South Fork Smith River, CA	Upper Bridge to South Fork Gorge	3(4)	Yes	82
34	South Fork Smith River, CA	South Fork Gorge to Bridge	4; 5	Yes	83
35	Jackson Creek	7 Miles above Cover Camp to Cover Camp	4(5)	No	86
36	Jackson Creek	Cover Camp to NF 31 Bridge	3(4)	No	87
37	Cow Creek	Reuben Road to West Fork of Cow Creek	3(4)	No	89
38	Cow Creek	West Fork of Cow Creek to Union Creek	2+(3)	No	91
39	South Umpqua River	Campbell Falls to Three C Rock	3(4+); 4(5)	Yes	91
40	South Umpqua River	Three C Rock to Milepost 22	3(4)	Yes	93
41	South Umpqua River	Milepost 22 to Days Creek	2+(4)	Yes	94
42	South Umpqua River	Canyonville County Park to Lawson Bar	2(3)	Yes	95
43	Copeland Creek	NF 300 Bridge to North Umpqua River	4+(5)	No	96
44	Canton Creek	6.5 Miles above Steamboat Creek to Steamboat Creek	3(5); 4(5)	Yes	98
45	Steamboat Creek	Steamboat Falls to Canton Creek Campground	4(5)	No	99
46	North Umpqua River	Boulder Flat to Gravel Bin	2 to 4	Yes	100
47	North Umpqua River	Steamboat to Cable Crossing	3(4)	Yes	101
48	North Umpqua River	Idleyld Park to Winchester	2+(3)	Yes	103
49	North Umpqua River	Winchester to River Forks Park	2	Yes	105
50	Calapooya Creek	Nonpareil to Driver Valley Road	3+(4)	No	106
51	Umpqua River	River Forks Park to Scottsburg	1(2)	Yes	106
52	Umpqua River	Sawyers Rapid	2+(3)	Yes	108

#	River	Run	Rating		Page
53	North Fork Rogue River	Natural Bridge to Woodruff Bridge Campground	3+(5)	No	108
54	North Fork Rogue River	Takilma Gorge	4+	Yes	111
55	North Fork Rogue River	River Bridge Campground to North Fork Reservoir	3(4)	Yes	112
56	North Fork Rogue River	Mill Creek Falls to Lost Creek Lake	4+	No	114
57	Middle Fork Rogue River	Butte Falls Road to Lost Creek Lake	5	No	115
58	Big Butte Creek	Butte Falls Picnic Area to Crowfoot Road	3+(4)	No	116
59	Grave Creek	6 Miles to Confluence with Rogue River	3	No	117
60	Rogue River	Above Nugget Falls to Gold Hill Boat Ramp	4-	Yes	119
61	Rogue River	Grave Creek to Foster Bar	3+	Yes	120
62	Illinois River	Oak Flat to Oak Flat	4+(5)	Yes	122
63	Brice Creek	Upper NF 22 Bridge to Champion Creek	4+(5)	No	126
64	Brice Creek	Champion Creek to Cedar Creek Camp	4(5)	No	130
65	Layng Creek	Rujada Campground to above Wildwood Falls	3(4); 4(5)	Yes	131
66	Row River	Wildwood Falls to Dorena Lake	2+(4); 3(4+)	Yes	131
67	Row River	Dorena Dam to BMX Park	3	Yes	132
68	Hills Creek	Upper Reaches to NF 2118 Bridge	4(5); 5	No	133
69	Salt Creek	McCredie Springs to Kitson Springs Road Bridge	3(4); 4(4+)	No	134
70	Salmon Creek	1.5 Miles above NF 2408 Bridge to Fish Hatchery Road Bridge	3+(4+); 4-(5)	No	135
71	Christy Creek	NF 1926 Bridge to North Fork of the Middle Fork Willamette River	5; 5+	No	137
72	North Fork of the Middle Fork Willamette River	Miracle Mile through The Gorge	4+(5); 5	No	138
73	North Fork of the Middle Fork Willamette River	Bottom of The Gorge to Westfir	3;4	Yes	139
74	Fall Creek	Gold Creek to Bedrock Campground	3; 3+	Yes	140
75	Fall Creek	Bedrock Campground to Fall Creek Reservoir	3(4); 4(5)	Yes	141
76	Fall Creek	Fall Creek Dam to Jasper County Park	2(3)	Yes	142
77	Winberry Creek	Winberry Campground to Fall Creek Reservoir	3+(5)	No	143
78	Middle Fork Willamette River	Oakridge to Lookout Point Lake	2+	Yes	144
79	Middle Fork Willamette River	Dexter Dam to Jasper County Park	2	Yes	146
80	Willamette River	Jasper County Park to Alton Baker Park	2(3)	Yes	147

Run #	River	Section	Class	Rafts?*	Page #
81	South Fork McKenzie River	Above French Pete Campground to Cougar Reservoir	3(4-); 4(5)	No	148
82	Blue River	Quentin Creek to Blue River Lake	4(5)	No	151
83	Quartz Creek	Milepost 7.5 Bridge to Milepost 2 Bridge	3+(4)	No	151
84	McKenzie River	Olallie Campground to Paradise Campground	3	Yes	153
85	McKenzie River	Paradise Campground to Finn Rock	2+	Yes	154
86	McKenzie River	Finn Rock to Leaburg Dam	2(3)	Yes	155
87	McKenzie River	Leaburg Dam to Hendricks Bridge Wayside	2	Yes	156
88	McKenzie River	Hendricks Bridge Wayside to Hayden Bridge	2	Yes	157
89	McKenzie River	Hayden Bridge to Armitage Park	1	Yes	158
90	Mohawk River	Gate on Mohawk Road to Hileman Road Bridge	2(3-)	No	160
91	Marys River	Blodgett to Philomath	1+(2)	No	162
92	Calapooia River	22 Miles above Holley to Bridge 13 Miles above Holley	3(4)	No	162
93	Calapooia River	Bridge 13 Miles above Holley to Bridge 4 Miles above Holley	3	Yes	166
94	Calapooia River	Bridge 4 Miles above Holley to McKercher Park	2	Yes	167
95	Calapooia River	McKercher Park to Brownsville	1	Yes	168
96	Mill Creek	Upper Bridge to Mill Creek County Park	3(4)	No	168
97	Mill Creek	Buell County Park to Sheridan	2-	Yes	170
98	South Fork Yamhill River	Grand Ronde to Sheridan	2(3)	Yes	171
99	Moose Creek	Cub Creek to South Santiam River	3(4+)	No	172
100	Canyon Creek	7-Mile Bridge to South Santiam River	5	No	173
101	Wiley Creek	Upper Bridge to Middle Bridge	4(5-)	No	175
102	Crabtree Creek	North Fork Bridge to Larwood Park	3 T; 4	No	176
103	Crabtree Creek	Larwood Park to South Santiam River	2-	Yes	177
104	Thomas Creek	Hall Creek to 5-Mile Bridge	3(4)	Yes	178
105	Thomas Creek	5-Mile Bridge to Hannah Bridge	2+	Yes	180
106	South Santiam River	Mountain House to Foster Lake	4(5+)	No	180
107	South Santiam River	Foster Dam to Jefferson	1 ; 2(4)	Yes	182
108	Quartzville Creek	Above Gregg Creek to Galena Creek	4+(5+); 5(5+)	No	184
109	Quartzville Creek	Galena Creek to Green Peter Lake	4; 5	Yes	185

#	River	Run	Difficulty		Page
110	Middle Santiam River	NF 2041 to Green Peter Lake	3(4)	No	186
111	Middle Santiam River	Green Peter Dam to Foster Lake	4	No	188
112	Breitenbush River	Cleator Bend Campground to Detroit Reservoir	4	Yes	189
113	Little North Santiam River	Old Mine to Three Pools (Opal Creek)	4(5)	No	190
114	Little North Santiam River	Salmon Falls to Elkhorn Valley Recreation Site	2(3)	Yes	192
115	Little North Santiam River	Elkhorn Valley Recreation Site to Mehama	3(4)	Yes	193
116	North Santiam River	Bruno Mountain Road to Detroit Lake	3(4); 3+(4)	Yes	195
117	North Santiam River	Big Cliff Dam to Packsaddle County Park	3+(5)	Yes	196
118	North Santiam River	Packsaddle County Park to Mill City	2+(3); 3; 4	Yes	197
119	North Santiam River	Mill City to Mehama	2; 3	Yes	198
120	North Santiam River	Mehama to Stayton	2-	Yes	199
121	Silver Creek	Silver Falls State Park to Silverton Reservoir	4(5)	No	202
122	Abiqua Creek	Abiqua Falls to Abiqua Road	2(3)	No	204
123	Butte Creek	Fault Line to Oregon 213	3(4-)	No	205
124	Table Rock Fork of the Molalla River	Second Bridge to Gravel Pit	3(4)	No	207
125	Molalla River	Copper Creek to Table Rock Confluence	3(4)	Yes	208
126	Molalla River	Table Rock Fork Confluence to Turner Bridge	3(3+)	Yes	209
127	Molalla River	Turner Bridge to Glen Avon Bridge	3; 4	Yes	210
128	Molalla River	Glen Avon Bridge to Feyrer Park	2	Yes	212
129	Molalla River	Feyrer Park to Oregon 213 Bridge	1+	Yes	213
130	Nohorn Creek	Nohorn Creek to Peg Leg Falls	3+–4(5)	No	213
131	Collawash River	Elk Lake Creek to Bridge 5.5 Miles from Mouth	4(5)	No	215
132	Collawash River	Bridge 5.5 Miles from Mouth to Two Rivers Picnic Area	3(4); 3+(5)	Yes	217
133	Roaring River	3.2 Miles above Clackamas River to Clackamas River	4	No	218
134	North Fork Clackamas River	3.75 Miles from North Fork Reservoir to North Fork Reservoir	4–4+(5)	No	220
135	Eagle Creek	Fish Hatchery to Snuffin Road	3(4+)	No	222
136	Eagle Creek	Snuffin Road to Eagle Creek Road	3+(5)	No	223
137	Clear Creek	Metzler Park to Redland Road Bridge	2+(3)	No	224

Run #	River	Section	Class	Rafts?*	Page #
138	Clackamas River	June Creek Bridge to Collawash River	3+(4); 4	No	225
139	Clackamas River	Collawash River to Sandstone Road Bridge	4(5+)	Yes	226
140	Clackamas River	Three Lynx Power Station to North Fork Reservoir	3(4)	Yes	228
141	Clackamas River	Milo McIver State Park to Barton Park	2+	Yes	230
142	Clackamas River	Barton Park to Carver	2	Yes	231
143	Clackamas River	Carver to Clackamette Park	2	Yes	232
144	Salmon River	Wilderness Trailhead to Arrah-Wanna Road	2+(3)	Yes	235
145	Bull Run River	Bull Run Road Bridge to Dodge Park	3	Yes	237
146	Sandy River	McNeil Campground to Lolo Pass Road Bridge	4+	No	238
147	Sandy River	Zigzag to Marmot Bridge	2; 3	Yes	239
148	Sandy River	Marmot Bridge to Marmot Diversion Dam	2+(4)	Yes	240
149	Sandy River	Marmot Diversion Dam to Revenue Bridge	4	Yes	241
150	Sandy River	Revenue Bridge to Dodge Park	2+-3	Yes	243
151	Sandy River	Dodge Park to Oxbow Park	2+(3)	Yes	243
152	Sandy River	Oxbow Park to Lewis and Clark State Park	1	Yes	244
153	Lake Branch Fork Hood River	Divers Creek to West Fork Hood River	4+	No	245
154	West Fork Hood River	Lake Branch Fork to East Fork Hood River	4(5)	Yes (Advanced)	247
155	East Fork Hood River	Sherwood Campground to Oregon 35 Bridge	4+-5	Yes	248
156	East Fork Hood River	Dee to Tucker Bridge	3(4); 4	Yes	250
157	Hood River	Tucker Bridge to Hood River Marina	3; 4-	Yes	251
158	Little Klickitat River, Washington	Esteb Road to Klickitat River	4+	No	252
159	Klickitat River, Washington	Yakama Indian Reservation to Klickitat Salmon Hatchery	3; 4	Yes	254
160	Klickitat River, Washington	Klickitat Salmon Hatchery to Leidl Campground	3	Yes	255
161	Klickitat River, Washington	Leidl Campground to Icehouse Public Access	2	Yes	256
162	Klickitat River, Washington	Icehouse Public Access to Rivermile 5	2+; 3	Yes	257
163	Klickitat River, Washington	Guler Road Bridge to River Road Bridge	3(4)	No	258
164	Trout Lake Creek, Washington	Warner Road Bridge to Green Truss Bridge	4(5)	Yes (Expert)	260
165	White Salmon River, Washington	Green Truss Bridge to BZ Corner	4+; 5	Yes (Expert)	261
166	White Salmon River, Washington	BZ Corner to Husum	3+(4)	Yes	263

#	River	Run	Class	Scout	Page
167	White Salmon River, Washington	Husum to Northwestern Park	2+	Yes	264
168	Little White Salmon River, Washington	Fish Hatchery to Columbia River	5	No	265
169	Trout Creek, Washington	NF 43 Bridge to Pacific Crest Trail Bridge	5	No	267
170	Wind River, Washington	Stabler to High Bridge	4+; 5	Yes (Expert)	268
171	Wind River, Washington	High Bridge to Columbia River	4(5)	Yes (Expert)	270
172	Rock Creek, Washington	1.5 Miles above Steep Creek to 3.5 Miles below Steep Creek	4–4+(5)	No	271
173	Stebbins Creek, Washington	South Fork and North Fork Confluence to Washougal River	5(5+)	No	272
174	West Fork Washougal River, Washington	West Fork Bridge to Washougal River	4(5)	No	274
175	Washougal River, Washington	Prospector Creek to Stebbins Creek	4+(5)	No	276
176	Washougal River, Washington	Doc's Drop to Dougan Falls	5	Yes (Expert)	277
177	Washougal River, Washington	Dougan Falls to Salmon Falls	3-(4); 5	Yes	278
178	Washougal River, Washington	10-Mile Bridge to above Washougal	3(4); 4	Yes	279
179	Metolius River	Source to Lake Billy Chinook	3(4)	Yes	282
180	Crooked River	Lone Pine Bridge to Crooked River Ranch	3(4); 4(5)	Yes	285
181	Crooked River	Crooked River Ranch to Lake Billy Chinook	3(4)	Yes	287
182	White River	Barlow Crossing to Keeps Mill	3(4)	No	288
183	White River	Keeps Mill to Wamic–White River Bridge	3+(4); 4-(4+)	No	289
184	White River	Wamic–White River Bridge to Tygh Valley	3(4)	No	290
185	Deschutes River	Wickiup Dam to Pringle Falls	1(4)	Yes	291
186	Deschutes River	Pringle Falls to Big River Campground	1(2)	Yes	294
187	Deschutes River	Big River Campground to Benham Falls	1(5+)	Yes	294
188	Deschutes River	Upper Benham Falls	5+	No	295
189	Deschutes River	Aspen Campground to Lava Island Falls	2(3)	Yes	296
190	Deschutes River	Lava Island Falls to Meadow Camp Picnic Area	4 to 6; 6	Yes (Expert)	297
191	Deschutes River	Meadow Camp Picnic Area to Mount Bachelor Village	4; 5	Yes (Expert)	298
192	Deschutes River	Bend to Tumalo State Park	3+(4); 4(4+)	No	300
193	Deschutes River	Tumalo State Park to Cline Falls State Park	3	No	301

Run #	River	Section	Class	Rafts?*	Page #
194	Deschutes River	Cline Falls State Park to Lower Bridge	3	No	303
195	Deschutes River	Lower Bridge to Lake Billy Chinook	4 to 4+	Yes (Advanced)	304
196	Deschutes River	US 26 Bridge to Sherar's Falls	3	Yes	306
197	Deschutes River	Sherar's Falls to Columbia River	3	Yes	308
198	Klamath River	Keno Dam to John C. Boyle Reservoir	3+	Yes	310
199	Klamath River	John C. Boyle Power Plant to Copco Lake	4(5)	Yes	311
200	North Fork John Day River	Route 52 Bridge to Dale	3+(5)	Yes	316
201	North Fork John Day River	Dale to Monument	2+; 3	Yes	318
202	North Fork John Day River/John Day River	Monument to Service Creek	1+; 2-	Yes	321
203	John Day River	Service Creek to Clarno	1+(2)	Yes	322
204	John Day River	Clarno to Cottonwood	2(3)	Yes	324
205	John Day River	Cottonwood Bridge to Columbia River	2(5+)	Yes	326
206	Donner und Blitzen River	Blitzen Crossing to Page Springs	3(3+)	No	328
207	Powder River	Milepost 20.5 to Cable Tram (Milepost 34)	3(4)	No	330
208	Jarbridge River/Bruneau River	Murphy Hot Springs to Bruneau	4(6)	Yes	332
209	Grande Ronde River	Tony Vey Meadows to Red Bridge State Park	3(4+)	Yes	334
210	Grande Ronde River	Red Bridge State Park to Hilgard Junction State Park	2; 2+	Yes	335
211	Grande Ronde River	Hilgard Junction State Park to Riverside City Park	2(3+); 3(4)	Yes	337
212	Grande Ronde River	Riverside City Park to Elgin	1	Yes	338
213	Grande Ronde River	Elgin to Palmer Junction	2(3); 2(4)	Yes	339
214	Wallowa River/Grande Ronde River	Minam to Troy	2; 3	Yes	340
215	Grande Ronde River	Troy to Boggan's Oasis	2; 2+(3)	Yes	343
216	Grande Ronde River	Boggan's Oasis to Snake River (Heller Bar)	2(4); 3(4)	Yes	344
217	Snake River	Hells Canyon Dam to Heller Bar	3(5)	Yes	345
218	East Fork Owyhee River	Garat Crossing to Three Forks	3+(6)	No	348
219	Owyhee River	Three Forks to Rome	4(5)	Yes	350
220	Owyhee River	Rome to Leslie Gulch	3(4)	Yes	353

North Coast Rivers

Region 1

Grays River, Washington

1 Grays River
South Fork to Highway 4

Class: 4–4+(5)	Length: 5 miles
Flow: 500–700 cfs	Character: isolated canyon
Gradient: 68 fpm, PD	Season: rainy

The Grays River is located in the far southwest corner of Washington, and for this reason advanced boaters often overlook it. First-time boaters on the Grays will be pleasantly surprised to find big, powerful rapids set in a beautiful basalt gorge. At most flows, pools are present after all the big rapids, but the rapids often contain sharp rocks and other hazards. At high flows, the rapids can be very pushy and large holes develop in several of the biggest rapids.

The run begins with about 0.5 mile of class 2 followed by a class 3+ with swirling currents directly below the road bridge. If this rapid looks and feels big, be ready for some excitement downstream. Just downstream of the bridge, the river drops over two riverwide ledges. The first ledge develops a sticky hydraulic at high flows but can be run with momentum on the left or by boofing on the right. The second ledge has two narrow slots that can be danger-ous for swimmers. Scout both ledges on the right. After several fun class 3–4 rapids in a beautiful gorge, the walls peel back as you approach Superbowl. Superbowl consists of a steep slide into a big hole. Trying to miss the hole can be difficult, so make sure you have some speed. Scout/portage on the left.

A short boulder garden separates Superbowl from the next big rapid, Picnic. This long class 5 rapid begins with a difficult boulder slalom and finishes with

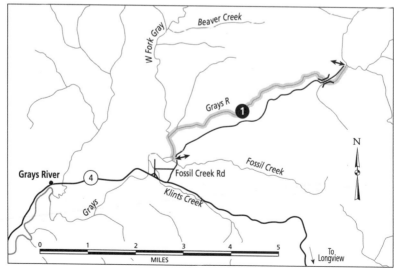

a plunge through several large holes. The current tends to push boaters into the left wall at the bottom, but a good recovery pool lies below the rapid. The entrance can be snuck with difficulty by carrying boats down the left bank and sliding into the river from a large boulder. The gorge walls at the bottom of the rapid make portaging impractical, so plan on running this rapid. Just around the corner is Broken Paddle, the last big rapid. The hole at the bottom is deceptively sticky, so scout carefully from the right.

After a couple more fun rapids, the canyon becomes more open and the river flattens out for the last couple of miles. One interesting note: Just above the take-out, the river becomes braided as it weaves its way through the remnants of a large flood that shifted the river channel. Picking the best channel through this maze is difficult, but the right channel seems to be the clearest.

Hazards

The riverwide ledge shortly below the road bridge, Superbowl, Picnic, and Broken Paddle should be scouted. Hiking out from the river would be very difficult in places.

Access

From Longview, Washington, travel west on Washington 4 for about 35 miles and, just before the bridge over the Grays River, turn north on Fossil Creek Road. The take-out is at a sharp bend in the road where the river comes into sight.

To reach the put-in, continue north on Fossil Creek Road another 5 miles and put in just above the confluence with the South Fork, about 0.25 mile after crossing the river.

Gauge

Visual. The level can be estimated using the Naselle River, which is a short distance west of the Grays. The Naselle River at Naselle is currently available via the Internet (see Appendix A). The Grays is usually a little higher than the Naselle. The level can also be estimated at the bridge before the put-in.

Pete Giordano

Nehalem River

2 Nehalem River
Spruce Run County Park to Nehalem Falls

Class: 3	Length: 14 miles
Flow: 2000–8000 cfs	Character: forested
Gradient: 16 fpm, C	Season: rainy

The Nehalem River flows westward from the northern Coast Range to the Pacific Ocean, and is among the largest rivers in the Coast Range. In earlier times many logs were floated down the Nehalem from the lush forests where they were cut. The terrain along the river is rugged, with very few inhabitants, and in places the hills rise 1200 feet above the river. One freight train per day still makes the round trip from Portland to Tillamook on the coast, following a 1910 route along the Salmonberry and Nehalem Rivers.

Spruce Run County Park, at the put-in, is a pleasant place with very few visitors in winter and spring. Below the put-in, the run is fairly straight-forward for the first mile to Little Falls, a small riverwide ledge. For the next 6 miles below Little Falls, the river consists of long flat stretches with occasional class 2 waves. At mile 7, the gradient increases and the river narrows in a long curve to the left through a scenic gorge with some class 2 waves.

The next river mark is at mile 8 where the Salmonberry River enters from the left. A short distance farther is Salmonberry Drop, the largest rapids on this section. At low water this drop contains a violent hole. Portage/scout on the right or from a small eddy on the left. Several other good class 3 rapids are separated by stretches of quiet water between here and the take-out. At moderate flows, many play spots are found in the river. At high water, the hydraulics become powerful, and many of the play spots are washed out. Nehalem Falls (class 3–4, depending on water level) can be run as a finale. The Falls, not a true waterfall, is formed by the river pinching between a concrete fish ladder and a basalt wall. The hydraulics in the rapid can be pushy, and the runout is turbulent.

Hazards
Salmonberry Drop should definitely be scouted. This drop cannot be seen from the road, but can be recognized from the river by a large rock at least 10 feet high on the right at the head of the rapids. The main chute can develop a violent hole at low water. Nehalem Falls, just below the normal take-out, can be scouted from the river on either side or by hiking through the park.

Access
To reach the put-in, take US 26 west from Portland to the Nehalem River, 5 miles west of the highway summit. About 1 mile farther west, turn south on a secondary road or proceed another mile west on US 26 to Elsie and take the road south. In either case, Spruce Run County Park is about 6 miles beyond the turnoff. An alternate put-in is located approximately 7 miles farther downstream and about 150 feet upstream of the Salmonberry River confluence. This divides the run into the lower 7-mile class 3 rapids and the upper 7-mile class 1–2 rapids.

The same road becomes rough and unpaved as it continues along the river to the take-out at Nehalem Falls Campground. An alternate take-out for those who run Nehalem Falls is near the bridge, less than 0.5 mile downstream. Boaters wishing to avoid the class 3 rapids can use the take-out above the confluence with the Salmonberry River.

Gauge
Located near Foss. The Nehalem River at Foss gauge is currently available on the Internet (see Appendix A). Flow is unregulated.

Rob Blickensderfer and WKCC Editors

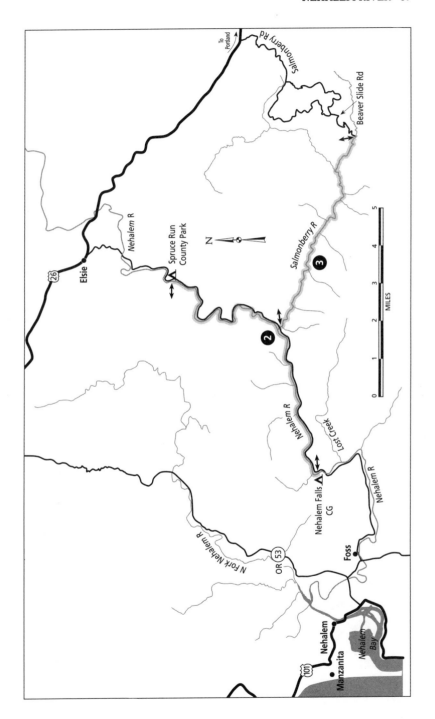

3 Salmonberry River
Beaver Slide Road to Nehalem River

Class: 3(4)	Length: 10 miles
Flow: 500–2000	Character: forested
Gradient: 70 fpm, C, PD	Season: rainy

First the good news: The Salmonberry River is a great intermediate run with a lot of great rapids and beautiful scenery. Now the bad news: The long shuttle and steep road to the put-in combine to make any run on the Salmonberry a long day, and they usually reduce the frequency of Salmonberry trips.

The Salmonberry River is located in an isolated canyon just north of the more popular Wilson River. Access is limited to a few places, which makes hiking out of the canyon difficult in the event of an emergency. A currently

Lush forests along the North Fork Salmonberry River (Pete Giordano)

(as of 2012) inactive railroad parallels the length of the run and is the best option if considering hiking out of the canyon. Views of the canyon rim some 1000 feet above the river are plentiful from the river.

From the put-in at the bottom of Beaver Slide Road, the river consists of continuous class 3 rapids that are pleasantly technical at low water and a consistent flush at high water. At the confluence of the North Fork Salmonberry about 1.5 miles from the put-in, the river broadens, short pools develop between rapids, and the rapids begin to develop bigger hydraulics. Two significant rapids are found within a mile of the North Fork confluence. The first rapid, a class 3+, is a long boulder garden just upstream of a railroad tunnel. Scout on the left. The second rapid, Chew-Chew(class 4), is about 0.5 mile downstream just after Bathtub Creek, which enters on the left. Chew-Chew begins with a steep drop over some boulders and finishes with a few pushy waves and holes. Most people choose to punch several holes on the far left or to boof the large boulder in the center. Scout/portage on the right.

Below Chew-Chew, the river continues through several fun class 3–3+ rapids until it gradually flattens out. Some great views of the canyon are found in this section. The rapids pick up again as boaters approach the takeout. Take out under the new (2012) road bridge on river right. It's about 200 feet upstream of the confluence with the Nehalem River.

Hazards

Wood and other debris from the railroad could be dangerous anywhere along the run but especially in the first 1.5 miles. Scout Chew-Chew. Beaver Slide Road is very steep and can be very slick when wet. Four-wheel drive is recommended, although a high-clearance vehicle might be okay if the road is dry.

Access

Bring a good map to prevent getting lost on the shuttle. To reach the put-in, take Salmonberry Road south from US 26. Salmonberry Road is about 0.5 mile west of milepost 30. Stay straight at the 4-way intersection about 1.2 miles from US 26. Turn left at the sharp turn about 4.4 miles from the highway. Turn left at the three-way intersection just over 8.5 miles from the highway, and after about a mile begin the long descent down Beaver Slide Road to the river.

To reach the takeout return to US 26 and travel west. Turn south about 0.75 mile west of milepost 21 on US 26 and continue south along the river to the bridge over the Salmonberry River.

Gauge

None. Generally, if the Wilson River is over 3000 cfs (Wilson River at Tillamook gauge), there will be enough water. The Salmonberry River drops quicker than the Wilson River, so it is usually better when the Wilson gauge is rising.

Pete Giordano and WKCC Editors

Kilchis River

4 Kilchis River
Confluence of North Fork and South Fork to Little South Fork

Class: 2+(3)	Length: 6.5 miles
Flow: 300–800 cfs	Character: forested
Gradient: 45 fpm, PD–C	Season: rainy

Beautiful clear green water, small waterfalls cascading in from steep banks, moss-laden trees, and few signs of civilization characterize this scenic coastal stream. The run begins with several class 2 drops pushing around blind corners, with an abundance of eddies to catch. This section offers nice play spots and surfing waves. Toward the middle of the run are several 3-foot ledges. All the obvious chutes are runnable, but be sure to check for logs in the drops before committing yourself.

At about mile 3.5, the gradient increases and the river becomes more constricted. This section cannot be seen from the road but can be lined or portaged. Two good class 3 rapids in here can be run without scouting by eddy hopping. Soon the gradient eases and the river splits around several islands. At about mile 5 is a tricky drop. Here the river narrows and pours over a basalt ledge. The route seems clear but should be scouted. A large diagonal hole at the bottom loves to give the unwary open boater a twist (and often a swim). The remainder of the trip is a pleasant class 1+–2.

Hazards
The ledge at about mile 5 should be scouted. Otherwise be sure to keep an eye out for logs. At high water, this narrow run becomes a little more pushy, but new surfing spots appear, and the major rapids are no more difficult.

Access
Take US 101 north from Tillamook to Kilchis River Road. Drive upriver about 3 miles and turn right across the river. Continue on this road about 2 miles past the end of the pavement until it crosses a sizable creek (Little South Fork Kilchis River). The take-out is on the left just above the confluence of the Little South Fork with the Kilchis River. It is advisable to walk to the river to ensure recognition of the take-out on the way down.

To reach the put-in, drive another 6.5 miles up the bumpy potholed road to a fork in the road. Take the small road left down toward the river. Follow this road as far as you dare. Lower your boat down the steep slope to the river.

Gauge
None exists. Generally there will be enough water when the Wilson River gauge is over 1100 cfs and rising, but there is no consistent correlation. The

Kilchis falls quicker than the Wilson. When the Wilson is too high to run, the Kilchis is a good alternative.

Alex McNeily and Paul Norman

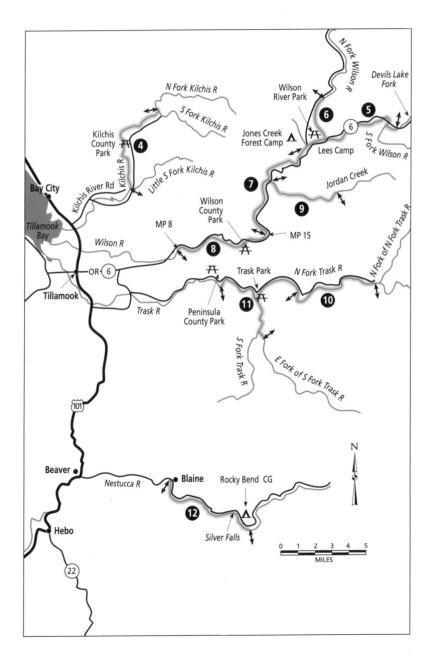

Wilson River and Tributaries

5 Devils Lake Fork Wilson River
Near Milepost 29 to Jones Creek Forest Camp

Class: 3+(4)	Length: 5 miles
Flow: 300–1000 cfs	Character: forested
Gradient: 75 fpm, C	Season: rainy

This is a great little run, just an hour from Portland. It shares the emerald water and lush coastal forest that make this and the rest of the Wilson River runs so beautiful. Significant ledge drops are mixed with steep, continuous whitewater. Oregon 6 follows the Devils Lake Fork and the Wilson and crosses the latter three times but does not intrude. Even if flows are too low on the Devils Lake Fork, the flow on the Wilson may be sufficient.

Put in at the normal put-in if there's enough water and you will be rewarded with a fast, continuous class 2–3 ride down to the confluence with the South Fork of the Wilson. If flows are too low, put in at the next bridge 0.5 mile downstream on the Wilson River, where the volume is approximately double. (The Devils Lake Fork joins the South Fork to form the Wilson River just above this highway bridge at milepost 28.)

Once on the Wilson, the action picks up. First one encounters a class 3 rapids followed by class 3+ Elk Creek Drop. Elk Creek Drop is a ledge drop with a boulder in the center and a rock wall at the bottom. Scout on the right and, normally, run on the right. Class 2+ water follows as one passes under the second highway bridge. The highway is on river right for the next 5 miles.

About 2 miles below the put-in, the river becomes braided into multiple channels. This area is clearly visible from the road. The middle channel is best. About 4 miles into the run is another multiple channel section. A short way downstream where a few homes are visible from the river is the start of the Lees Camp community. Keep off this private property. About 0.5 mile farther downstream, the North Fork Wilson River enters from the right. The remaining 1 mile of the run includes mostly class 2 water, but there is one class 3 drop just above the take-out at Jones Creek Forest Camp. Take out under the Jones Creek Forest Camp bridge or 100 yards downstream on the right.

More adventurous boaters can put in 1.2 miles upstream from the usual put-in. This additional section adds some tougher rapids. Most notable are a series of rapids, visible from milepost 29 high above the river, which include unimaginatively named The Big One and The Little One. These are class 4+ at lower levels and class 5 at higher flows. Check for logs, and keep in mind that road construction has resulted in sharp rocks in these rapids.

The uppermost put-in contains several tight rapids including Coffin Corner, which could be class 5 at high water. This upper section also usually contains wood and other debris.

Hazards

Elk Creek Drop should be scouted before beginning the trip or from the river as logs could make this rapid very dangerous. Be especially alert for logs in the braided sections of the river.

Access

The Wilson River Highway, Oregon 6, follows the river. The normal put-in is between mileposts 28 and 29 on Oregon 6 at the bridge over the Devils Lake Fork. The turnout is on the south side and a trail leads to the river. Alternate put-ins are 0.5 mile downstream at milepost 28 at the bridge over the Wilson River, 2 miles upstream at the Drift Creek Bridge (from Oregon 6 between mileposts 29 and 30, take Drift Creek Road to the bridge), or 2.6 miles upstream at the bridge over the Devils Lake Fork.

To reach the take-out, continue downstream to milepost 23 where the Jones Creek Forest Camp road crosses the Wilson River. Parking is available on the north side of the river.

Gauge

Currently available via the Internet (Wilson River at Tillamook) (see Appendix A). Because this section is so far from the gauge, the minimum gauge reading is about 3200 cfs. Optimal flows are 3400 to 4000 cfs on the gauge. Flows on the Wilson change quickly so do not rely on 12-hour-old gauge readings.

Laurie Pavey, Alex McNeily, Paul Norman, and WKCC Editors

6 North Fork Wilson River
Confluence with West Fork to Jones Creek Forest Camp

Class: 3	Length: 3 miles
Flow: 500 cfs	Character: forested
Gradient: 80 fpm, C	Season: rainy

If you are looking for a short run with continuous rapids, the North Fork Wilson River is a good choice. The flow is fast, so the run can be completed quickly on cold snowy days, but abundant play waves, holes, and eddies invite a longer stay.

Boaters can extend the run by putting in farther upstream on either the West Fork or the North Fork. The North Fork is more interesting and has more gradient (estimated at 140 fpm). Scout the river from the road to decide whether you want to do this, and pay particular attention to logs, which are a major hazard in this narrow upper section. An interesting plunge drop about 0.3 mile above the confluence with the West Fork deserves a scout. The upstream landmark for this drop is a smaller plunge drop.

About 1.5 miles below the West Fork confluence, after a nice waterfall comes in from the left bank, are several ledges that deserve caution because rocks and trees regularly slide into the river from the steep right bank. It is possible to scout and portage on the left. After the ledges you pass the houses of Lees Camp. This is a private area with a private road and is not an alternate access. Watch out for a nasty midstream boulder on a right turn.

Below Lees Camp the North Fork merges with the main Wilson River, which then splits into channels where the positions and status of logs and debris are subject to change. It is 1 mile to the take-out from here. Powerlines cross the river just above the Jones Creek Rapid, a fun series of waves, which can be scouted from the bridge at the take-out. Below Jones Creek Rapid is a good take-out path a little below the bridge on river right.

Hazards
Watch for strainers at the ledges halfway through the run.

Access
The road to Jones Creek Forest Camp, the take-out, is at milepost 23 on Oregon 6. The road to the camp crosses the Wilson River, and the Jones Creek rapid is visible from the bridge. This is the take-out; leave shuttle vehicles at the parking area across the bridge or a short distance downstream on the road along river right.

To reach the put-in, continue on Jones Creek Road 0.2 mile and take the first right turn. The North Fork road roughly follows the river, but you will not always see it. Take a left at the first fork (at 1.4 miles) and a right at the second (1.7 miles). It is 3 miles to the put-in from the take-out. Sometimes there are directional signs at forks and intersections to help you find your way, but do not count on them.

Gauge
None exists. If it looks like enough water at the confluence with the West Fork, it is probably runnable. If the Wilson gauge is over 2000 cfs, enough water is probably present, but a gauge reading over 3000 cfs is usually better.

Linda Starr and WKCC Editors

7 Wilson River
Jones Creek Forest Camp to Milepost 15

Class: 2+; 3; 4-	Length: 8 miles
Flow: 1200 cfs; 2300 cfs; 7000 cfs	Character: forested
Gradient: 35 fpm, PD	Season: rainy

On this run, the Wilson River is relatively narrow as it winds between basalt rock walls. At medium flow, most rapids are pool drop and eddies directly below major rapids are turbulent with eddies of their own. The river curves frequently, pushing curling rapids off rock walls. Many small tributaries and cascading streams join the Wilson on this run, so the volume increases as the run progresses.

The usual put-in is directly under the Jones Creek Forest Camp bridge, or about 100 yards downstream along a dirt road with campsites on river right.

The first several miles have warm-up class 2 rapids. At about mile 2.5, an island divides the river. Most of the water flows through the right channel over a steep, rocky boulder garden. Scout from the island.

Below the island, the river narrows into a gorge. This section is extremely turbulent at high water and excitingly turbulent with good drops at medium levels. Several log bridges cross the river at the beginning and end of the gorge section (at miles 3 and 4.8). After the second log bridge, Jordan Creek enters on the left. At medium levels, play spots are common throughout the gorge and below Jordan Creek. The take-out is on a rock ledge on the left, before a right bend in the river. Look for parked shuttle cars.

The Wilson is a popular winter steelhead fishing stream; minimize your contact with the many anglers along this section. Do not play in their fishing holes.

Hazards

The river can rise from a mild run to a hair-raiser within 3 to 4 hours, so beware of fast runoff. The gorge section consists of several blind corners with no place to land or to scout from the river, so check the gorge from the road during the shuttle. Check for logs jamming the drops.

Access

Oregon 6 parallels the Wilson River throughout this run. The put-in at Jones Creek Forest Camp is at milepost 23 on Oregon 6. The road to the forest camp crosses the Wilson.

The take-out is opposite milepost 15 on Oregon 6. Park on a small turnout overlooking a rocky ledge. The carry from the river is not too difficult.

Gauge

Currently available via the Internet (Wilson River at Tillamook) (see Appendix A). Minimum flow is 1200 cfs. Optimal flows are 1500 cfs to 2500 cfs.

Kim Hummer

8 Wilson River
Milepost 15 to Milepost 8 Boat Ramp

Class: 2+(3); 3(3+); 3+(4)	Length: 7 miles
Flow: 900–1000 cfs; 1200–2300 cfs; 2600–7000 cfs	Character: forested
Gradient: 26 fpm, PD	Season: rainy

The Wilson River flows through some beautiful sunless canyons where spectacular hues of green and yellow lichens cover the trees and rocks. The clean white bark of the young alder trees contrasts with the large green Sitka spruces and red maples. Before the trees leaf out in the spring, young saplings and flowers can be seen growing from the thick moss of the tree limbs. This beauty can be enjoyed by boaters drifting in the glassy reflective pools and flat water between the rapids. Oregon 6, never more than 0.5 mile from the river, and the homes overlooking the river do not detract from the scenery. One does not realize that the drifting speed is 4 to 7 miles per hour until one looks through the crystal-clear water to see the colored rocks flashing by. This run becomes more difficult as the flows increase above 1500 cfs. Beginner boaters will want to use the put-in at milepost 12 to avoid the harder rapids upstream.

SECTION 1: MILEPOST 15 TO MILEPOST 12, 3.5 MILES, CLASS 3(3+)

The put-in has a set of nice waves that are perfect for warming up. After about 0.5 mile of short class 2+ rapids, the river begins to drop more steeply. This is a good time to stop and scout for logs in the Narrows—class 3+ at moderate flows—because a swim at the first drop might mean a swim through the narrow slot, which is only about 6 feet wide. Scout and/or portage on the right.

About 1 mile farther downstream, a small creek enters on river left near a wonderful ledge play wave that is about 20 feet wide. Just below is the second major rapid on this run. Here you will find a rock garden with room-size boulders scattered across the river. About halfway through this rapid, you may eddy out on river right to scout the steeper part of the drop. The usual run at moderate flows is in the middle-right channel to avoid the large hole at bottom right. Beyond, the river is filled with fun play spots interspersed with quiet water.

SECTION 2: MILEPOST 12 TO MILEPOST 8, 3.5 MILES, CLASS 2

This section is a great run for beginners with beautiful scenery and fun, playful rapids at moderate flows. Although only 3.5 miles long, the run feels much longer and is good for cold, short winter days. Immediately below the put-in, the river enters an especially scenic part of the canyon. Farther along, a nice chute occurs between narrow rock walls spanned by a small bridge. Below, a gauge is located on river right just above a small boulder garden. About 0.5 mile farther, look for a red log cabin on the right followed by boat skid rails, the take-out.

Hazards

Section 1: The Narrows should be scouted every trip because logs in the slot would be a major problem. The big boulder rapid should be scouted at least the first time down. *Section 2:* None in particular.

Access

The Wilson River Highway, Oregon 6, follows the river. The upper put-in is opposite milepost 15. Park on a small turnout overlooking a rocky ledge. The lower put-in is at milepost 12 just upstream of the highway bridge. Park in the dirt area on the north side of the highway.

The upper take-out is at milepost 12 just upstream of the highway bridge. The lower take-out is located just west of milepost 8 at a wide turnout with a drift-boat skid launch.

Gauge

See the Wilson River, Jones Creek Forest Camp to Milepost 15 run.

Lloyd Likens, Laurie Pavey, and WKCC Editors

9 Jordan Creek
Headwaters to Wilson River

Class: 3-3+	Length: 7.5 miles
Flow: 150–500 cfs	Character: forested
Gradient: 70 fpm, C	Season: rainy

Anyone who has run the Wilson River has driven by Jordan Creek. This tight technical creek is a great introduction to creek boating and can be run after a good rain or when the Wilson is over 7 feet. Lots of maneuvering and tight turns are required. Many of the drops are blind and rather precipitous and possibly blocked by logs. At low water, you will find several ledges with narrow slots, and at high water big holes are common. From the uppermost put-in, you are immediately confronted with a sharp 5-foot ledge in a small granite gorge. This ledge is very difficult to scout at river level and almost impossible to portage, and it develops a nasty hole at high water. Because of this, many boaters choose to put in somewhere downstream of the gorge. Below the gorge, fun, technical ledge drops are interspersed with calmer sections of river. The last mile of the run cannot be seen from the road and contains several big rapids. The scenery is excellent throughout the run, despite the presence of the road. Take out at the confluence with the Wilson, or continue down the Wilson for a few more good rapids.

Hazards
The biggest hazards are overhanging brush and logs. At flows on the Wilson over 10,000 cfs, large holes develop and pools between rapids shrink. Several of the biggest rapids can be seen from the road and are good indicators of the difficulty of the run.

Access
From Oregon 6, which runs along the Wilson River, proceed upstream along Jordan Creek on good gravel and dirt logging roads, crossing the creek several times and paralleling the entire run. This road is washed out 5 miles upstream of the Wilson (2008). The uppermost put-in is just below a small, narrow waterfall in a granite gorge. Because of the washout, this put-in requires a 1.5 to 2-mile hike. If you do not want to run the difficult drop within the gorge, put in anywhere along the road downstream.

Take out on Oregon 6 where Jordan Creek meets the Wilson River, or continue downstream along the Wilson a few miles.

Gauge
None exists. On a rising Wilson River gauge, Jordon Creek is usually runnable if the flow on the Wilson gauge is above 3000 cfs. On a falling Wilson River gauge, Jordan Creek is usually runnable if the Wilson gauge is above 5000 cfs.

Alex McNeily, Paul Norman, and WKCC Editors

Trask River and Tributaries

10 North Fork Trask River
North Fork of North Fork Trask River
to Bridge

Class: 2+; 3	Length: 8 miles
Flow: 500 cfs; 1500 cfs	Character: forested valley
Gradient: 52 fpm, C	Season: rainy

The North Fork Trask River flows through second-growth coastal forest and drains an area of steep ridges punctuated by high rock walls, canyons, and frequent waterfalls. The upper half of this scenic run contains most of the significant rapids, including three drops approximately 3 miles from the put-in. The second of these drops is a riverwide basalt ledge with the flow pouring over the right side. Shortly downstream is a rapid formed by a landslide. Scout/portage on the left. A significant boulder garden can be found downstream from the landslide rapid. Rock gardens and small play spots are plentiful. While rapids are less frequent on the lower half of the run, the road and river part company, providing a sense of isolation as well as a difficult hike out if problems arise.

The 4.3-mile section from the take-out to Trask Park has not been run by the authors but has been run by others. The gradient is 37 fpm, continuous. About 0.4 mile upriver from Trask Park is a difficult 8-foot drop through basalt that should be scouted on the shuttle if this section is to be run. The location of this drop is marked by a basalt outcropping above the road on river right and follows a sharp right bend in the river.

Hazards

All the significant rapids can be scouted from the river.

Access

Roughly 1 mile south of Tillamook on US 101, go east on Long Prairie Road for 3.2 miles. Immediately after crossing the river, turn right on Trask River Road. (Boaters traveling west on Oregon 6 from Portland can turn south onto Trask River Road 2 miles before reaching Tillamook.) Proceed 10 miles upriver to the North Fork Road, 0.2 mile before Trask Park. Turn left and travel 3.5 miles on this dirt road to a prominent fork. The take-out is reached by traveling 0.7 mile down the right fork, crossing the bridge, and going upriver about a hundred yards.

To get to the put-in, return to the fork and travel 7.8 miles upriver on the left fork. A second fork is encountered; bear right and go several hundred yards to the put-in at the confluence of the North Fork of the North Fork Trask River with the Middle Fork of the North Fork Trask River.

Gauge

Currently available via the Internet (Trask River Above Cedar Creek) (see Appendix A). The minimum recommended flow on this gauge is 1600 cfs with optimal gauge flows at 2000 to 3000 cfs.

Steve Cramer, Cliff Ryer, and Craig Colby

11 Trask River Fish Hatchery to Upper Peninsula Boat Ramp

Class: 3	Length: 6.7 miles
Flow: 1000 cfs	Character: forested; residential
Gradient: 30 fpm, C	Season: rainy

The run begins just below the hatchery on the East Fork of the South Fork Trask River and passes through a lightly populated valley. The gradient is steepest in the first 2 miles, with several tight twisting drops. The last of these is recognized by the remains of a log bridge hanging over the river 50 yards downstream. Scout the drops for debris.

After the confluence with the North Fork at mile 2.2, the gradient lessens but still provides interesting rapids and play spots. At mile 3.5 a busy class 2 rapids on a left bend leads immediately to a class 3 ledge drop with a reversal that must be punched. Paddlers in kayaks or decked single canoes (C-1s) should not be surprised when they disappear briefly in this hole. The remaining run is enjoyable class 2 water.

Several more miles of whitewater downstream from the take-out have been run in open canoes. The rapids are lesser except for a very tight class 3 chute, known as Dan's Hole, that should be scouted or portaged on the right and is visible from the road. An alternate skid-rail launch is available to drift boats about 1.5 miles above the Upper Peninsula boat ramp.

Hazards

Drops at roughly 0.5 mile and 2 miles should be scouted. The drop at 3.5 miles can be seen from the road.

Access

About 1 mile south of Tillamook on US 101, go east on Long Prairie Road for 3.2 miles. Immediately after crossing the river, turn right on Trask River Road. (Boaters traveling west on Oregon 6 from Portland can turn south onto Trask River Road several miles before reaching Tillamook.) The take-out is 6.1 miles upriver at the Upper Penninsula boat ramp on the right.

To reach the put-in, continue upriver 6.1 miles, passing Trask Park and the North Fork Trask River, to a fork in the road. Take the road on the left over the South Fork of the Trask. The put-in is located several hundred yards up this road just before the fish hatchery. Elk are frequently seen near the road during the shuttle.

Gauge

Currently available via the Internet (Trask River Above Cedar Creek) (see Appendix A).

Steve Cramer and Cliff Ryer

Nestucca River

12 Nestucca River
Rocky Bend Campground to Blaine

Class: 3(4, 5)	Length: 8 miles
Flow: 1000–2500 cfs	Character: forested; private property
Gradient: 50 fpm, C	Season: rainy

The Nestucca River, a State Scenic Waterway, drops relentlessly through a lush scenic forest into a small valley into which a few small farms are squeezed. Some stretches are uniform in gradient, others are pool drop. Much can be seen from the road.

On this run, the river flows through about half national forest lands and about half private lands. The rights of property owners along the river became a major issue in 1991 when kayakers were arrested for trespassing while scouting the class 5 rapids. The issue is not yet resolved. Do not use private lands to scout or portage around the rapids.

If one chooses to put in at Rocky Bend Campground, the first 1.5 miles include a class 4 rapids followed by Silver Falls (class 5) and another class 4 rapids. A fast rock garden then leads to a private log bridge. Areas surrounding this stretch of river are posted "No Trespassing". The landowners have indicated that they believe it is not possible to scout or portage below the high water mark and that they aim to prosecute to the full extent of the law anyone found trespassing. For these reasons it is best to avoid paddling this section of river unless one is comfortable boat scouting and running class 5 water.

An alternate put-in that avoids private property is found near mile 12 (as measured from Hwy 101 in Beaver). It has room for perhaps one or two vehicles on the side of the road. Enjoyable class 2 and 3 rapids can be found downstream of this put-in.

Hazards

In the upper 1.5 miles: the above-mentioned class 4 and 5 rapids, which cannot be scouted from the road and probably not from the river. From the lower put-in: Three Rocks Rapids, class 3+, at MP 9.5 and a big ledge drop (almost river wide with a serious reversal) at MP 7.

Access

The Nestucca River may be reached from the coast on US 101 at the town of Beaver, about 16 miles south of Tillamook. At Beaver take paved County Road 858 east along the river. The take-out is 6.3 miles from Beaver near the community of Blaine. Look for a parking turnout where the road is quite near the river. A large school-like house sits nearby across the road.

To reach the put-in, continue upstream to either a wide spot in the road approximately 6 miles upstream from the take-out, or Rocky Bend Campground, 8 miles upstream.

From the Willamette Valley, the river may be reached by driving west on the paved road out of Carlton, which is on Oregon 47 north of McMinnville. After 13 miles, pass Meadow Lake, the headwaters of the Nestucca River, and continue to the desired put-in.

Gauge
Available via the Internet (Nestucca near Beaver) (see Appendix A). Low flow is about 1000 cfs, 1600 cfs is good.

Rob Blickensderfer and WKCC Editors

Siletz River and Tributaries

13 North Fork Siletz River
Boulder Creek to South Fork Siletz River

Class: 3–4+(5), P	Length: 5 miles
Flow: 700 cfs	Character: forested; clear-cut
Gradient: 65 fpm, PD	Season: rainy

This is a short but fun section of the Siletz, containing significant whitewater. All major drops can be easily portaged and can be seen from the road.

A mile from the put-in is a smooth ledge that can develop a riverwide dangerous hydraulic. It is normally run on the right. Ten minutes later is Bombshell, a class 4 mini-gorge on a hard right bend next to the road. Scout during the shuttle. Several miles farther is a narrow chute that drops into an even narrower chute between two badly undercut walls. A portage is recommended. However, this spot makes a good take-out as the remaining mile to the confluence with the South Fork is class 1 and 2.

Hazards
The first ledge, the gorge rapids, and the undercut chute mentioned above offer difficulty. These are serious class 5 at levels above 7.5 feet on the gauge.

Access
From the Central Willamette Valley, travel west on Oregon 20 and turn north on Kings Valley Highway (Oregon 223). Drive 6.4 miles north on Oregon 223 and turn left onto Hoskins Road. From here, follow the Luckiamute River, staying on the main road. Stay right at the bridge at mile 14.9 (from Oregon 223) and left at the bridge at 15.4 miles (staying south of the Valsetz Lake Bed). Cross the South Fork Siletz at mile 26.6 and continue 0.5 mile to the take-out at the North Fork–South Fork confluence.

To reach the put-in, drive up the South Fork Siletz and take the first left. Take the next left in an ugly clear-cut and follow the North Fork to the put-in. The best put-in for lower water runs is about 100 yards up Boulder Creek (5.4 miles from the South Fork turnoff) on river right.

Gauge

Just 5.5 feet on the gauge located at Siletz is not too boney. If you drive this far and the river is too high for your tastes, try the South Fork Siletz, the Luckiamute, or the Valley of the Giants section of the North Fork Siletz (yes, it has been run.)

Eric Brown, Arthur Koepsell, and Chopper

14 Siletz River Elk Creek to Buck Creek

Class: 3; 4	Length: 4.5 miles
Flow: 1000 cfs; 3500 cfs	Character: forested; roadless
Gradient: 20 fpm, PD	Season: rainy

The river canyon here is extremely beautiful and remote. Once on the river, a boater has no contact with the road. The diversity of the rapids on this class 3 run gives intermediate boaters the chance to experience some interesting paddling. There are short ledge drops, fast constricted chutes, and broad V slicks leading to standing waves below.

This run begins anywhere one can get a boat to the river below Valsetz Falls. At the falls, the river squeezes through a basalt plug and plunges 70 feet within a few hundred yards. This awe-inspiring section of the river is absolutely unrunnable—but fun to view. Therefore, this run description begins 1 mile below Valsetz Falls, at Elk Creek. Boaters choosing to put in between the falls and Elk Creek will find a class 5 put-in and two rapids that are class 3 and 4 at medium flows. Below Elk Creek the gradient drops and allows boaters to enjoy the plentiful play spots, solitude, and scenery. Take out at the Buck Creek bridge.

For a longer day's paddle, many boaters combine this run with parts of the next run (see the Siletz River: Buck Creek to Moonshine County Park run). The bridge above Silache Rapid offers a possible take-out for those not yet ready for class 4 Silache Rapid. The road upstream of Moonshine County Park is a private logging road open for public use only on weekends.

Hazards
The first two rapids are the trickiest. The remoteness of the river dictates caution, since a broken paddle or boat would lead to a tough hike out.

Access
From US 101 in Newport, take US 20 7 miles east to Toledo. Turn north on OR 229 to Siletz. Proceed 8 miles east on E Logsden Road to Logsden. From the Willamette Valley, Logsden is reached by taking US 20 west from Interstate 5 near Albany to Blodgett; at Blodgett, turn north on Summit Highway and continue through Summit to Nashville. In Nashville, turn right on Rock Creek Road and proceed to Logsden. From Logsden, head north on Moonshine County Park Road. About 5 miles upstream of the Park, the road crosses the river at the head of Silache Rapid. Two miles farther upstream, the road forks. The right fork leads to the take-out at Buck Creek.

To reach the put-in, return to the fork and turn right, taking the left fork. Continue upstream for about 6 miles to the first and only place where the road meets the river, at Elk Creek bridge. This is the best put-in and avoids Valsetz Falls upstream.

To have a look at the falls, continue up the road for 1 mile. A small road to the right leads to the falls. At the head of the falls, some cable crosses the river, but there is no last eddy for unsuspecting boaters floating downstream to the falls.

Gauge

Located at Siletz (see the Siletz River: Buck Creek to Moonshine County Park run). A level of 4.5 feet provides adequate water. At 7.5 feet, the rapids are faster and more plentiful, but no more difficult.

Lance Stein

15 Siletz River
Buck Creek to Moonshine County Park

Class: 3(4); 4(5)	Length: 6.5 miles
Flow: 1600 cfs; 4500 cfs	Character: second growth; canyon
Gradient: 40 fpm, PD	Season: rainy

Of the 50 or more miles of boatable water on the Siletz River, this stretch has the most whitewater. Several possible put-ins vary the run's distance from 3 to 12 miles. At flows above 8 feet on the gauge, the river is swift, and a 12-mile run from Elk Creek to Moonshine County Park is an easy day. Buck Creek is the normal put-in and provides about 2.5 miles of warm-up class 2 rapids before Silache (Sil-at-chee) Rapid, the most difficult stretch on this run.

The steel bridge about 2 miles from the put-in marks the beginning of Silache Rapid. The hardest parts of Silache can be seen from the road on the way to the put-in. At low water, Silache is a class 3 to class 4 rock garden with very distinct pools between drops. At moderate levels of 6 to 8 feet on the gauge, the pools become shorter and Silache turns into a long class 4 rapid that requires a boater to dodge rocks and holes. Above 8 feet on the gauge, Silache becomes a mile-long rapid with big waves and complex currents. The route through Silache straightens out, but the holes are large and the hydraulics powerful. As the flow increases, fewer and fewer eddies are available. At flows above 10 feet, expect the river to carry you through huge breaking waves and into big holes. Staying upright at high flows becomes very important, as there is little time to adjust your line.

Good surfing spots are plentiful below Silache. The rapids again tend to be pool and ledge drop. Two locations are of note. About 2 miles above the take-out is a gravel quarry on the side of the road opposite the river. At this spot the river narrows into a rock-sided gorge called Quarry Drop. At the beginning of Quarry Drop are several holes on the right. These holes can be challenged or avoided by keeping left. The last hole, the biggest, is not noticeable from upstream. The second location of note is about 1 mile below the second bridge where the river is divided by a gravel island. The left channel has the most water and, although rocky, is the normal route. The right channel falls over about a 4-foot ledge.

Boaters who remember the beautiful set of surfing waves and play holes on the left at the beginning of Moonshine County Park will be disappointed to learn that the river changed course here during the floods of 1996 and 1997 and now flows in the right channel. However, one can still enjoy a boat shower at the base of the falls, just across the river from the take-out. At low flows, many steelhead anglers will be on the river. Please be courteous to them.

Hazards
During the drive to the put-in, scout Quarry Drop near the gravel pit about 2 miles upstream from Moonshine County Park, as well as Silache Rapid and a few of the ledge drops.

Access
The shuttle road follows the river along most of this run. Follow directions to Logsden given in the Siletz River: Elk Creek to Buck Creek run. From Logsden, follow Moonshine County Park Road upriver about 3.5 miles to the park entrance. Turn left and go 0.5 mile to the take-out at the park.

To reach the several optional put-ins, follow the gravel logging road that parallels the Siletz River. Please be careful on this road. It is a private road open for public use only on weekends. Continued access for boaters and anglers is dependent upon responsible use. Some boaters put in at the bridge marking the start of Silache Rapid or below Silache. The usual put-in is under the bridge over the Siletz River near Buck Creek. To reach that bridge, drive about 7 miles upstream from Moonshine County Park. Just after the road crosses Buck Creek, take the right fork and continue 400 yards to the bridge over the Siletz River.

Gauge
Located at Siletz. Currently available via the Internet (Siletz River at Siletz), the River Forecast Center in Portland (see Appendix A), the weather radio, or local newspapers. Minimum flow for boating is about 4.5 feet; 6 feet is very nice. See the description for flows above 8 feet.

Kim Hummer, Rick Starr, and WKCC Editors

16 Siletz River
Moonshine County Park to Sam Creek Bridge

Class: 1; 2	Length: 7 miles
Flow: 400 cfs; 2000 cfs	Character: rural; roaded
Gradient: 12 fpm, C	Season: rainy

This is a pleasant and scenic run for beginning kayakers and intermediate open canoers. It is usually runnable in late spring or early fall when most of the other coastal rivers are too low to navigate. Numerous small rapids, shallow riffles, eddies, and a few small surfing waves provide enjoyable and easy boating. An occasional tree in the river is usually included. The river passes under the highway bridge about midway through the run. The second bridge (concrete) helps locate the take-out at the boat ramp on the left.

Hazards
At high water, the large standing waves that develop in some places could swamp an open canoe.

Access
The take-out is 5.5 miles upstream from the town of Siletz on East Logsden Road (for directions to Siletz, see the Siletz River: Elk Creek to Buck Creek run). At Sam Creek Road, cross the river and park on the left in the lot adjacent to the boat ramp.

For the put-in, see the directions to the take-out for the Siletz River: Buck Creek to Moonshine Run. From the parking area, it is a short carry to a nice pool put-in.

Gauge
See the Siletz River: Buck Creek to Moonshine County Park run.

Rob Blickensderfer

17 Drift Creek (Siletz River Tributary) North Creek to Covered Bridge

Class: 3(4) T	Length: 8 miles
Flow: 400 cfs	Character: forested; canyon
Gradient: 31 fpm	Season: rainy

Drift Creek is a small Coast Range stream that flows through a scenic forest, including 5 miles of old timber, and into Siletz Bay. The river is very beautiful, with large trees draped in moss and lichens and with many huge boulders, some as large as a house. In places the channel is very narrow—just enough to get a boat through.

The run starts in a small valley with a fairly gentle gradient but soon flows into a steep-sided, narrow canyon with a gradient of 95 fpm. This is followed by a lower-gradient section below the canyon, which is followed by another steep, narrow canyon. It is important to remain alert at all times because logs could block almost any drop. If the water is much higher than 400 cfs, some of the channels and drops might be easier, but scouting from a boat might be more difficult. No signs of civilization appear until the last mile or so, which reveals a few buildings and fields and a view of the road. The last mile is flat water.

Hazards
Several twisting rapids could be blocked by logs. Portages may be difficult depending on the water level. This run is in an isolated, steep canyon. Climbing out to the road would be difficult if not impossible.

Access

A couple miles south of Lincoln City, look for a sign for Drift Creek. Go 1.6 miles to a T intersection and take a right, continuing about 0.3 mile (past a fork to the left) to a bridge across Drift Creek. A good parking area is located on the left across the bridge.

To reach the put-in, go back and take the fork passed just before the bridge. Stay on NF 19, a paved road. Turn right at a T intersection after about 5 miles. From here the road is gravel and goes generally downhill. Follow the signs to Drift Creek Camp. The put-in is at the first bridge crossing Drift Creek.

Gauge

None exists. With the Siletz gauge at 5.1 feet, Drift Creek was estimated at 400 cfs. For a close estimate of the flow see Pat Welch's Flow Page (Drift Creek, Siletz) (see Appendix A).

Al Grapel, Bob Metzger, and WKCC Editors

Alsea River and Tributaries

18 South Fork Alsea River
Hubert McBee Memorial Park to Rock Quarry Weir

Class: 2; 3	Length: 6 miles
Flow: 400 cfs; 1000 cfs	Character: forested; logging
Gradient: 45 fpm, PD	Season: rainy

The South Fork Alsea River is a narrow stream runnable only during or shortly after substantial rains. It runs through the scenic coniferous forests of the Coast Range, although recent logging and road building have encroached upon its beauty. Many logs in, above, or under the water have accumulated in recent years.

The upper 2 miles, down to the third concrete bridge, are a leisurely class 2 run with several small play spots at higher water levels. Around the corner below the third bridge is a drop that begins a 0.5-mile stretch of fairly continuous rapids. This stretch is a technical class 3 at lower water and a dynamic class 3 with chutes and twisting turns at high flow. The last third of the run flattens out somewhat but is punctuated by three steeply sloping ledges and several play spots.

Hazards

Since the South Fork is a small seasonal stream, boaters must constantly be on the lookout for brush, low-hanging trees, and sweepers.

Many trees occur in the river. Eddies at the take-out are small, big enough for 1 or 2 boats. Use caution if paddling beyond the take-out near the rock quarry, as large broken concrete blocks with exposed reinforcing rods may be encountered. There are remnants of a weir that was sited immediately downstream of the gravel storage area road.

Access

From the town of Alsea, located on Oregon 34 about 25 miles southwest of Corvallis, turn south onto the paved road with a sign pointing toward Lobster Valley. One mile from Alsea, turn left on South Fork Road toward Alsea Falls. The take-out is 2.9 miles from Alsea at a small turnout opposite the access road to an ODOT gravel storage area, immediately downstream of a small quarry.

Upriver, approximately 6.5 miles from Alsea, the road crosses the river. This is the bridge mentioned in the description as the third from the top and is an optional put-in. The put-in at Hubert McBee Memorial Park is 8.7 miles from Alsea. This park may also be reached by driving west from Alpine, which is just west of Oregon 99W near Monroe. A look at Alsea Falls, a short distance upstream, is always interesting.

Gauge

None exists. A reading on the main Alsea gauge at Tidewater can be used for a rough guide. A reading of 7 feet (which corresponds to about 400 cfs on the South Fork) is minimum for an acceptable run. A reading of 7.5 feet and above provides a delightful run. The upper gauge limit has not been established. Currently available via the Internet (Alsea River at Tidewater) or by calling the River Forecast Center in Portland (see Appendix A). Several local papers also carry the gauge reading, but the time of the reading should be noted since the river level can change rapidly.

Dan Valens

Class 5 whitewater (Pete Giordano)

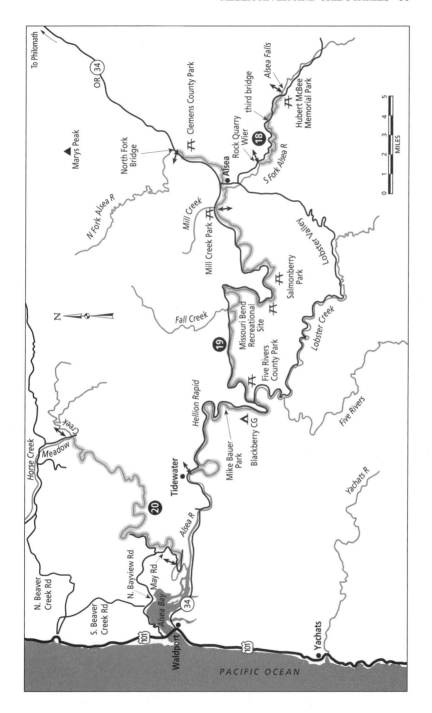

19 Alsea River
Mill Creek Park to Tidewater

Class: 1(2)	Length: 32 miles
Flow: 500–2000 cfs	Character: rural
Gradient: 7 fpm, PD	Season: rainy

The main stem of the Alsea River provides a number of runs that are used by numerous drift boat anglers, as well as beginning canoers and kayakers. The river usually becomes too low in the summer to negotiate in anything but a swimsuit and inner tube. Any of numerous possible runs can be designed between the river access points described below. The milepost markers are along Oregon 34; river distances are greater than the road miles.

The 9 miles from the put-in at Mill Creek Park to Missouri Bend Recreation Site include several surfing waves at high water and rocks at low water. The 12 miles from Missouri Bend to Five Rivers is the most isolated section. It is relatively flat except for a class 2- technical rapid about 1 mile below River Edge Recreation Site. At milepost 26.7, Fall Creek, a major tributary, enters from the right. At Five Rivers Junction (milepost 20.1), Five Rivers, the largest tributary of the Alsea, enters from the left.

The next 5 miles include a nice combination of class 1 drops, eddies, and pools. Opposite Blackberry Campground is a small rocky shelf. The deepest slots are along the right third. At milepost 15.6, Rock Crusher Rapid has a fast class 1 lead-in on a right curve, followed by a clean chute with waves at the bottom. Part of the river flows left at the head of the lead-in. Stay in the right channel.

The biggest rapid on the Alsea, Hellion Rapid (milepost 14.9), class 1–2, has swamped unwary drift boaters. The rapid tends to push boats to the right onto exposed rocks. Below the bridge on a side road at milepost 13.2, the river is fairly flat and makes a 3-mile loop away from the highway. The last access is just above the town of Tidewater (milepost 10); the tidewater continues to Alsea Bay and Waldport.

Hazards
None in particular.

Access
From Interstate 5 near Albany, take US 20 or Oregon 34 west past Corvallis to Philomath, and take Oregon 34 to Alsea. The first put-in is 2 miles west of Alsea at the boat ramp in Mill Creek Park, in Benton County (milepost 38.3).

To reach the lowermost take-out, continue west on Oregon 34 to 0.4 mile before the town of Tidewater. The take-out is at a "Road to River" sign at a side road at milepost 10.4 that provides access at the head of Tidewater.

Other accesses include Campbell Park (milepost 34.7), Salmonberry Park (milepost 33.1), Missouri Bend Recreation Site (milepost 31.2), River Edge Recreation Site (milepost 23.1), an unimproved boat ramp (milepost 20.5) a short distance above Five Rivers Junction that is a good place to launch paddle craft, a Siuslaw National Forest boat ramp (milepost 19.4), Blackberry Campground (milepost 17.7), the bridge at Mike Bauer Campground, a possible access for paddle craft at milepost 16.5, an unimproved access at Rock Crusher Rapid (milepost 15.6) where the driveway entrance is at an opening in the guardrail and leads to a parking area below, and a bridge on a side road (milepost 13.2).

Gauge

Currently available via the Internet (Alsea River at Tidewater) or by calling the Portland River Forecast Center (see Appendix A). A reading of 3 feet is adequate to cover most rocks; 5 feet is plenty of water.

Rob Blickensderfer

20 Drift Creek (Alsea River Tributary) Meadow Creek to Lower Bridge

Class: 3	Length: 17 miles
Flow: 500–1000 cfs	Character: wilderness
Gradient: 23 fpm, C	Season: rainy

Drift Creek flows through the Drift Creek Wilderness Area in one of the most remote regions of the Siuslaw National Forest. It is a rare experience to paddle through a magnificent wilderness surrounded by the hush of an old-growth forest and to return home the same day. Farmland is found only along the last 5 miles.

From the put-in below Meadow Creek the gradient is fairly continuous with many class 2 rapids and an occasional more difficult rapids. Lower flows require much rock dodging. About one-third through the run, boaters enter the Wilderness Area, the largest in the coast range. A trail, almost hidden in the forest, drops down 1200 vertical feet and two miles from the ridges on each side of the creek. Around mile 11, a fairly narrow and steep class 3 drop is the last significant rapids and signifies fewer and easier rapids ahead. The gradient decreases for the rest of the trip. In a couple of miles the creek flows under a private bridge where take-outs are not allowed. About 3 miles farther is an impressive high waterfall on the left. It's a flat 2 miles farther to the take-out. An outgoing tide can be helpful.

Hazards

Expect one or more portages around fallen trees or logs in the creek. They seem to move from year to year.

Access

Bring a Siuslaw National Forest map and *Oregon Gazetteer* for both the put-in and take-out vehicles. It is easy to get lost in this area.

Go to the take-out first. From US 101 on the coast go to N. Bayview Road at the northeast end of the Waldport bridge. Drive 6.7 miles east and turn right onto May Road. Continue 2.7 miles to the bridge over Drift Creek, the take-out, on river left downstream of the bridge.

To reach the put-in, return to N. Bayview Road, then continue 5 miles back toward US 101. Turn right (north) onto S. Beaver Creek Road and go 5.2 miles to the intersection with N. Beaver Creek Road. Turn right and continue for 10.4 miles to the intersection with 1000 Line Road. Turn right and continue 4.6 miles to the second turn-off to the right. Go through the gate. After the road crosses Drift Creek, you can put in anywhere along this road. There is a nice put-in just before the road ends, about 2 miles below the gate.

Gauge

None exists. With the Alsea River gauge at 5.5 feet and the Siletz River gauge at 5.3 feet, Drift Creek has adequate flow. For a close estimate of the flow see Pat Welch's Flow Page (Drift Creek, Alsea) (see Appendix A).

Carl Landsness, Rich Brainerd, Rob Blickensderfer, and WKCC Editors

Siuslaw River and Tributaries

21 Siuslaw River
Milepost 3 to Swisshome

Class: 1+(2+)	Length: 8 miles
Flow: 2500 cfs	Character: forested; logging
Gradient: 16 fpm, C	Season: rainy

The Siuslaw River makes a 20-mile loop away from Oregon 126 from Turner Creek to Mapleton. The upstream section of the loop constitutes this run. It is in a narrow valley flanked by a one-lane gravel road, a working railroad, and a few houses. Few of these intrusions of humanity are noticeable from the river, and the run has a pleasant, rural character. The paddling is easy, the current is strong, and small creeks and waterfalls are frequent.

However, be prepared for three class 2+ rapids. Each is conveniently marked by a railroad bridge. The first is a sloping drop under the first railroad bridge at 2.5 miles. A short quiet section is followed by a sweeping left bend and class 2+ rapids under the second railroad bridge at 2.8 miles. The third is at 6.5 miles, about 0.3 mile below the third railroad bridge. A cliff overhanging the road and a large rock on river right mark the rapids. The remainder of the run is relatively easy. Between the fourth trestle and the take-out is an island that cannot be seen from the road. The best route as of this writing is left of the island. The take-out is a boat ramp on river right, 1 mile below the fourth railroad bridge at a left bend in the river marked by cliffs and a high waterfall on the right.

Hazards

Scout the three class 2+ rapids during the shuttle. The second has a broad clear channel on the left. The center bridge piling hides the main drop from view. The third has a hole at the bottom that becomes large at 2500 cfs and takes much of the flow; it can be portaged more easily on the left.

Access

Oregon 126 is near the put-in and Oregon 36 is near the take-out. From Oregon 126, 19 miles west of Noti, drive to an intersection approximately 1 mile below Linslaw County Park. Turn right, go 150 yards, and cross a concrete bridge. Turn left onto Stagecoach Road/Richardson Upriver Road, and go 3 miles downriver to the put-in, a rough boat ramp at milepost 3.

Continue driving downriver to the take-out, which is 1 mile below the fourth railroad bridge and 0.7 mile above the intersection with Oregon 36 at Swisshome.

Gauge

Located at Mapleton. Currently available via the Internet (Siuslaw River near Mapleton) or contact the River Forecast Center in Portland (see Appendix A).

Steve and Sandy Cramer

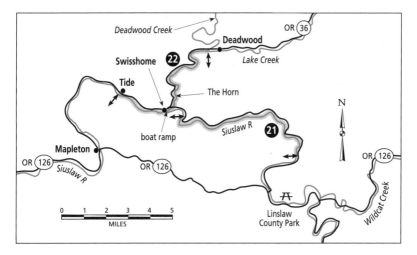

22 Lake Creek
Deadwood Creek to Tide

Class: 2+(3); 3(4)	Length: 8 miles
Flow: 1600–5000 cfs;	Character: rural
10,000–31,000 cfs	
Gradient: 26 fpm, PD	Season: rainy

Lake Creek is named for Triangle Lake in the Oregon Coast Range. Immediately after or during a major storm, it is an excellent big-water run. At lower flows, it is a superb class 2+ river with good action and lots of surfing waves. Emerging from the lake, the creek meanders a few hundred feet, turns a swift corner, and drops over several falls into logjams and difficult rapids. A common put-in is 10 miles downstream at Deadwood Creek, which still provides a chance to warm up for The Horn. Boaters who prefer a less ominously named put-in, or who wish to vary the length of their runs, can put in at any of the unimproved county parks 1 to 3 miles up- or downstream of Deadwood. A popular play run put-in is at Schindler Park about 1 mile below Deadwood.

The first few miles of the run have several small holes, innumerable waves to play on, and wide-eyed anglers who watch boaters go by. After turning a corner, you will be engulfed in a series of drops and big waves at Ledges, the lead-in rapid above The Horn. The Horn is a unique rapids, formed by a hard volcanic formation. The rapids starts with small waves and keeps building up to bigger waves and holes. The last set of gigantic waves forms below a monster rock that bisects the river. When running the rapids, keep far left. Once in the rapids, stay upright. A large wave near the bottom crashes down on boats and can even stand decked double canoes (C-2s) on end. This rapid may also be run to the far right of the huge center rock. At low flows, The Horn is class 3.

The 4-mile run from The Horn to the take-out continues with big waves and holes. Below The Horn, where the river bends right, a significant shelf produces a very wide and unfriendly hole at some levels. It is easy on the right at all flows. Immediately below this, at the bottom of the left bend, is Bus-stop, another significant shelf hole. Safe passage is either on the far left, or one can sneak cautiously between the right side of the hole and the rock wall on the right river bank. Grassy Lawn waves are next, followed by the Grassy Lawn hole on the left. The last few miles are on the Siuslaw River, which continues to provide many surfing waves and holes, including Mill Wave and Red Hill. When boats are dragged out at the small town of Tide, the question is always the same: "Did you run The Horn?"

Hazards

The Horn should be scouted from the road during the shuttle. The Bus-stop hole should be avoided. About 2 miles above the take-out, where a small tributary comes into the Siuslaw River, is a human-made structure on the left bank. It is often submerged at higher flows and should be avoided.

Access

Oregon 36, which connects the Eugene area with Florence on the coast, parallels this section of river. About 7 miles west of Triangle Lake, the upper put-in is found at one of the small county parks on the south side of the road. Other put-ins can be found along the road, including the popular one at the confluence of Deadwood Creek. Five miles downstream from Deadwood Creek, Lake Creek flows into the Siuslaw River.

The take-out is 3 miles farther at the small park in the town of Tide. A boat ramp is accessible about 1 mile below The Horn on the south side of Lake Creek, with access via Stagecoach Road. Most access points, including Deadwood Landing and Tide Landing, require a Lane County Parking Pass which may be purchased in Mapleton or in Eugene.

Gauge

The gauge reading for the Siuslaw River at Mapleton is given in several daily papers or can be obtained from the River Forecast Center in Portland; it is also currently available via the Internet (Siuslaw River at Mapleton gauge) (see Appendix A). The 1996 floods washed away the Mapleton gauge, and it was replaced about 1999. Boaters used to the former gauge will want to add about 2 feet to the new gauge reading for a comparison of the two. A level of 6 feet on the 1999 gauge is the minimum; a level of 10 to 12 feet is optimum for playing, and a level of 16 feet is beginning to be big water. The flow of Lake Creek at Deadwood is approximately one-third that of the Siuslaw at Mapleton.

George Ice and WKCC Editors

South Coast Rivers

Region 2

West Fork Millicoma River

23 West Fork Millicoma River
Henrys Falls to Stonehouse Bridge

Class: 3(4)	Length: 6.2 miles; 9+ miles
Flow: 400–2000 cfs	Character: canyon; forested
Gradient: 44 fpm	Season: rainy

This run is enhanced in its upper end by numerous small play holes and waves, which are derived from the wide, shallow, and ledgy character of its sandstone bedding. At moderate levels, only two significant rapids interrupt the run's class 3 serenity. Both can be scouted by car, although the road does not parallel most of the river. Flowing beneath a canopy of maple, cedar, fir, and aromatic myrtle, the river attracts many new sweepers annually.

Henrys Falls, a class 4 10-foot drop, occurs 1.6 miles into the run. It is scouted left, run in the chute, or easily portaged river right. This encounter is always stimulating. A mile later is a low-water river crossing. At 4.8 miles into the run is Girl Scout Triple Drop, named for the old facility below. It is located 0.5 mile inside the Elliot State Forest boundary; look for sweepers here during the shuttle. Girl Scout Triple Drop begins with a turbulent chute into a small pool, directly above a 5-foot diagonal ledge drop. This is a tough portage on the left. An ender wave is encountered after the S turn below. Drift another 1.1 miles to a 6-foot ledge, which is usually run right. Take out right after another 0.3 mile; higher flows permit continuing about 3 miles through another class 3 rapids, near some cabins, and on to Stonehouse Bridge, or even beyond.

Hazards

The easy portage to the right of Henrys Falls can be difficult to reach after scouting on the left because of the lead-in class 3 rapids. The keeper hole in the center grows at higher flows. At flood, Henrys is a huge, riverwide hole, and the rest of the run is class 4- to 5-.

Access

From south Coos Bay, turn east off US 101 toward Allegany/Coos River; begin counting mileage. Cross the Isthmus Slough bridge and stay left. At Boyd's market, mile 1.1, turn right onto the Coos River Highway. Cross the Ross Slough bridge at 2.1 miles, and continue to the green steel bridge, 3.4 miles from US 101. Cross over the bridge, stay right, and follow the road for 10.4 miles, where it crosses the West Fork bridge into Allegany, 13.8 miles from US 101. From here to the East Fork, continue straight. Restart your mileage at the West Fork bridge and proceed left up the West Fork Millicoma River for 4.8 miles, to Stonehouse Bridge, and park the take-out vehicle there. Check the river flow (see Gauge). (If it is necessary to drive to the lower-flow take-out at mile 8, continue 5.3 miles to the Deans Mountain junction and stay right to where a river access road can be located behind a locked steel gate. There's not much room here, so park off the road opposite the gate.)

To reach the put-in, continue upstream another 1.7 miles to an overlook, 260 feet directly above Henrys Falls. It is about another 1-mile drive downhill to the put-in (10.9 miles from Allegany), next to the river among tall red cedars. The old Vaughn Ranch gate a little farther confirms your location. The turnaround is quite small.

Gauge

None exists. Use the top edge of the concrete abutment on river right under Stonehouse Bridge (see Access). At 2 feet below the abutment, expect an abrasive run. Water near the top edge of the abutment indicates great fun for the advanced boater. Water over the abutment and up on the pillar indicates pushiness and sticky holes. This river requires an amazing amount of rain to come up, and it drops very quickly afterward.

Richard Dierks

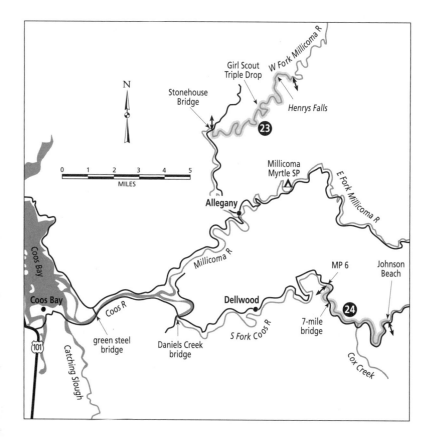

South Fork Coos River

24 South Fork Coos River
Johnson Beach to Milepost 6

Class: 3	Length: 6.1 miles
Flow: 500–3000 cfs	Character: private land; forested; canyon
Gradient: 23 fpm, C	Season: rainy

This is a nice beginning and intermediate run. The sections above and below it can be run, too, but are shallower. The sandstone riverbed is wide and strewn with small to medium-size boulders. It becomes quite muddy and laden with wood during heavy rains, due to logging activity. Regeneration of streamside clear-cutting is beginning to improve the appearance of the corridor. The Coos River can be run only on weekends because the Weyerhaeuser Company restricts access during the week.

From the Johnson Beach put-in, 12.1 miles above Dellwood, it is 1.1 miles to the remnant of the splash dam, which was used to flush logs downstream years ago; while it poses no obstacle to boaters, swimming is discouraged. On January 19, 1989, at milepost 9.5, a boulder slide crushed the car of a passing family of four, killing the mother. At 2.6 miles from the put-in, 40-ton boulders still clog the river below, creating a class 3 pool drop where previously only flat water could be found.

Cox Creek enters left of the halfway point, milepost 9, and is a convenient start and/or end point for shorter runs. Less than 1 mile before the take-out, the 7-mile bridge crosses overhead, followed by a long class 3 rock garden. After 6.1 miles, the road turnout on river right indicates the usual take-out, although some may want to continue into the pool below.

Hazards
The new rapid, easily observed from the road at milepost 9.5, drops about 4 feet through a reversing wave. The large boulder in the rapids moved in 1991 and may move again, so beware.

Access
From Coos Bay on US 101, follow the shuttle directions (as far as the green steel bridge, 3.4 miles east of US 101) for the West Fork Millicoma River: Henrys Falls to Stonehouse Bridge run. Follow the Coos River toward Dellwood by passing under this bridge, and at mile 4.4 cross over the concrete Daniels Creek bridge. At mile 8.7 turn right into the Weyerhaeuser Company's Dellwood log dump/truck shop, and stop at the guard shack. You will not be permitted through on weekdays. Drive 0.5 mile through the facility and proceed upriver to the take-out at milepost 6.

To reach the put-in, continue upstream. At mile 8.4, the junction right leads to the upper end of the North Fork Coquille River; Cox Creek is at mile 9, and the put-in is at the turnout just past milepost 12.

Gauge
None exists.

Richard Dierks

South Fork Coquille River

25 South Fork Coquille River
16-Mile Bridge to Milepost 3.2

Class: 4(5), T; 4+(5)	Length: 12.9 miles
Flow: 400 cfs; 3000 cfs	Character: forested; gorge; canyon
Gradient: 60 fpm, PD; C	Season: rainy

Deeply cut into sedimentary formations of the coastal mountains, the South Fork Coquille River offers some of the finest technical whitewater in Oregon. Historically, this is timber and mining country but, surprisingly, the excellent scenic quality of the corridor has been maintained. Campsites are available at China Flat, Daphne Grove, and Myrtle Grove. The run is divided into four sections in acknowledgment of the varied gradient and character of the river. At medium flows, the three upper sections are usually run together, but a more demanding combination is provided by sections 3 and 4. During low water, only section 3 is enjoyable. High runoff provides a fast, turbulent run from the top to Coal Creek.

SECTION 1: 16-MILE BRIDGE TO KELLY CREEK, 3.6 MILES
Put in at the bridge or 100 yards upstream. Beware of rebar. The whitewater is technically demanding class 3 to 4 with a gradient of 86 fpm involving boulder gardens that are difficult to scout or portage. Most of it is not visible from the road, and sweepers are abundant. About 2 miles below the put-in, 0.5 mile after passing under the concrete bridge at Daphne Grove Campground, an 8-foot vertical drop is followed by a boulder garden. The 8-foot drop can be scouted from the road 0.7 mile up from Kelly Creek at the gravel turnout. The take-out is 0.2 mile below Kelly Creek.

SECTION 2: KELLY CREEK TO MYRTLE GROVE CAMPGROUND, 4 MILES
The action slows down as the gradient decreases to 33 fpm. This class 2 cool-down section is a good place for intermediate boaters to join the run. An easier put-in is at China Flat Campground, 1.5 miles below. The section ends at Myrtle Grove Campground with a class 3 rapids.

SECTION 3: MYRTLE GROVE CAMPGROUND TO COAL CREEK, 3.1 MILES

Deep within vertical canyon walls, beautiful side-stream waterfalls exceed 100 feet, aromatic myrtle trees crowd the channel, and beaver sign is plentiful. The narrow class 4 pool drops are more demanding than the gradient of 45 fpm implies. Immediately below the put-in is a series of blind drops followed by a short flat section. As the river sweeps back to the road, it begins an exciting descent into Roadside Narrows, which should be scouted from the road. Hole-in-the-Wall is next, featuring a dangerous outlet among the boulders on the left of the pool. Note the ender hole below. Nearly continuous whitewater continues to Coal Creek, which enters through two large culverts on the right. Because of its narrowness, this upper section remains runnable at lower flows than the others.

SECTION 4: COAL CREEK TO MILEPOST 3.2, 2.2 MILES

Even more demanding rapids lie a short distance below Coal Creek as the gradient increases to 111 fpm for the first mile. It begins with a steep and narrow portion that narrows into a boulder field that has captured many logs. The canyon then tends left and constricts into a class 5 jumble, which is scouted and run or portaged right. Negotiating the approach through the reversal and around the large boulder can be tricky: No safe route can be found to the left. Rather, the safe route is located at a point even with milepost 5 on the road high above. More rapids and 1 mile of flat water follow. The take-out is at the gully-washed site of an old footbridge, following a nice cliff exposure of shale.

Hazards

Sweepers are always a problem and must be aggressively scouted. Section 1 is quite technical at intermediate flows. At high flows the rapids become easier, except for the 8-foot drop, which forms a class 5 keeper hole. At high flows, most of the drops disappear. In section 3, below Myrtle Grove Campground, Roadside Narrows and Hole-in-the-Wall become class 5 at high water. Hole-in-the-Wall is dangerous because of the person-size outlet among the boulders on the left of the pool. Section 4 below Coal Creek requires increasingly advanced abilities as the water levels rise. At high water the canyon becomes 1 mile of wild froth with major log hazards. To avoid a reversal, the first walk may come after a short distance. A second portage will avoid the riverwide log barricade. About halfway through, the class 5 rapids must be scouted or portaged.

Access

To reach Powers, see the South Fork Coquille River: Powers to Baker Creek run. Several accesses are available along the road upstream from Powers. The lower take-out is at milepost 3.2 at the end of the field on the right. An overgrown trail leads to the river. Parking is available, clear of the gate, a couple of hundred yards before the trail.

Continuing upriver, the road becomes NF 33. Accesses are available at Coal Creek, 5.4 miles above Powers; Myrtle Grove Campground at 8.5 miles; China Flat Campground at 10.8 miles; Kelly Creek at 12.5 miles; and Daphne

Grove Campground at 14.3 miles. The upper put-in is at the bridge 16 miles above Powers, with parking at the Coquille River Falls Research Natural Area.

Gauge

None exists. Use the river-right pillar on 16-Mile Bridge. When the water just touches the pillar, the reading is 0 feet. Low is 1.5 feet, medium is 3 feet, and high is 5 feet. The maximum flow recorded at Powers is 48,000 cfs. When the

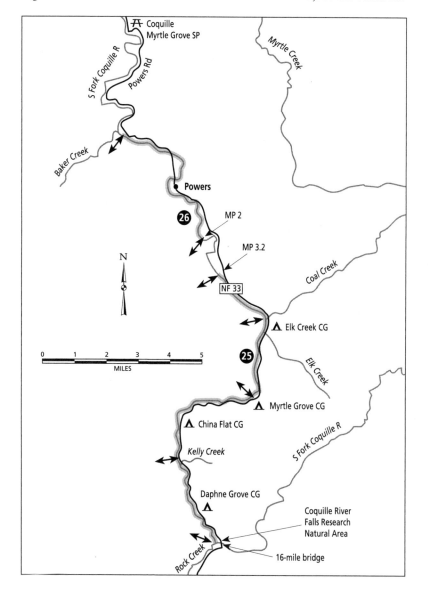

water is up to the pillar (0 feet), section 3, Myrtle Grove Campground to Coal Creek, is the only runnable section. A gauge of 1.5 feet indicates that section 3 is runnable with only some class 4, but section 4 is tight and technical. The premium level for all sections is probably 3 feet.

Richard Dierks

26 South Fork Coquille River
Powers to Baker Creek

Class: 2+(4)	Length: 6.5 miles
Flow: 400–1500 cfs	Character: wooded; rural
Gradient: 12 fpm, C	Season: rainy

The upper 2 miles of this run are wide and shallow, and the scenery is open and pleasant. As the South Fork Coquille River meanders through Powers, high riverbanks hide the town, but the scenery is occasionally contrasted by washed-out bridges and Powers's dual solution to old automobile disposal and riparian erosion. Farther on, the river enters a scenic canyon, flows over a new fisheries weir, and offers some class 3 activity and then a 10-foot class 4 drop. After 1 mile, take out on the right just upstream of the next bridge.

Hazards
Beware of human-made hazards such as rebar. During the shuttle, the class 4 rapids can be seen from the road by driving 0.8 mile up from the Baker Creek junction and looking down into the canyon. Although a pool sits above the drop, beginners should take note of the lead-in class 3- activity. Run the drop right, off the pillow, or portage through the boulders on the right. The new weir can be seen from the Forest Service station, just before Powers.

Access
The Powers Highway joins Oregon 42 at the confluence of the Middle Fork and South Fork Coquille River, 4 miles southeast of Myrtle Point. The community of Powers is 17.5 miles upstream on Powers Road. To reach the take-out, drive 15.5 miles toward Powers, turn right at the Baker Creek turnoff, and proceed 0.3 mile to the boat ramp, river right, just upstream of the bridge across the river.

For the put-in, continue upstream through Powers—following the signs to China Flat, Illahe, and Agness—to the parking area at milepost 2, just past Orchard City Park.

Gauge
None exists. See the South Fork Coquille River: 16-Mile Bridge to Milepost 3.2 run.

Richard Dierks

Elk River

27 Elk River
Butler Creek to Fish Hatchery

Class: 3-4+	Length: 12.5 miles
Flow: 400–3000 cfs	Character: canyon; forested
Gradient: 43 fpm, PD-C	Season: rainy

The Elk River is a beautiful pool drop stream. The green waters carve narrow passages beneath tall timber and large trees bridging the river. Nearly all the run can be scouted from the road. High flows last only as long as the storms producing them.

SECTION 1: BUTLER CREEK TO PURPLE MOUNTAIN CREEK, 5.5 MILES, CLASS 3(4)

The first 0.5 miles of this section are fairly continuous class 2 until a class 3+ slot, which can be easily portaged. After the slot rapid, the river continues with class 2 rapids until the gradient increases and the river drops through a long boulder garden (class 4) created by an immense landslide. Scout this drop from the right at the first sign of large boulders blocking the main channel and the large landslide on the right. Run center to right through several large holes at high water or several fun ledges at low water. Portage on the right. Several more fun class 3 to 3+ rapids separated by flat water follow this boulder garden. Take out on the left at Purple Mountain Creek or continue down through the class 4 gorges of the next section.

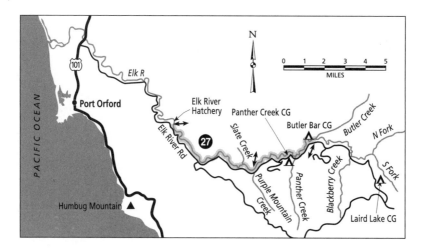

SECTION 2: PURPLE MOUNTAIN CREEK TO ELK RIVER HATCHERY, 7 MILES, CLASS 4

The first 1.5 miles are active class 3 and 4, dropping at 60 fpm. Successive rapids intensify and merge with higher water. Be careful of rocks in the bottom of several drops at low water. This fine upper series ends at mile 1.6 with a drop through a strong reversal into a turbulent pool exiting hard right. The next 3.6 miles are class 2 and 3. Just downstream of a tight S turn around a boulder is a pushy class 4. Near mile 5, begin the 0.3-mile class 4 lower gorge, dropping 150 fpm. Not easily scouted from the water, the final class 4 is a couple hundred yards farther and is usually run right. Paddle another mile, and take out left on the gravel bar past the hatchery gates and trolley cable crossing.

Hazards

Scout all major drops from the road during the shuttle. At high water, the gorges in section 2 become more difficult and continuous. Be careful of sweepers at high water.

Access

Between Langlois and Port Orford, 47 miles south of Coos Bay, turn east onto Elk River Road (US 101, milepost 297.5). Drive upriver 7.5 miles to the Elk River Hatchery, which is the take-out and the gauge location.

The paved road upstream parallels the river for 7 miles to the section 2 put-in at the bridge over Purple Mountain Creek. For the section 1 put-in,

Fun class 4 on the Elk River (Pete Giordano)

continue upstream another 5.5 miles and turn left onto Butler Creek Road. Put in at the bridge over Butler Creek.

Gauge

Located at the end of the parallel concrete fish returnways at the most downstream part of the hatchery. A low-runnable reading is 4.5 feet. Above 7 feet or so, the river begins to pump. When water laps at the steel grating above the gauge, which corresponds to 12 feet, it is well into flood. Call the Elk River Hatchery (541-332-7025) for the level.

Richard Dierks and WKCC Editors

Chetco River

28 Chetco River
Chetco Gorge

Class: 3(4, 5), P	Length: 8.7 miles
Flow: 500-3000 cfs	Character: forested; canyon
Gradient: 27 fpm, C	Season: rainy

The Chetco River is a famous southwestern Oregon stream noted for fine fishing and crystal-clear water. The initial 3 miles of the run consist of long stretches of flat water with a few class 2 rapids. After several fun class 3 and 4 rapids, the river returns to flat water until Chetco Gorge. Candy Cane, the second major rapid in the gorge, can be scouted on the left or right but is most easily portaged on the right. Candy Cane consists of large boulders, which constrict the river from forming swirly currents and large holes. A few hundred yards farther, the river again disappears. This is Conehead, named for the monolithic centerpiece into which the torrent descends. Portage on the right or run right avoiding the undercut rock in the center and the pin rocks on the right. The remaining 2 miles are flat.

Hazards

Candy Cane rapid, 1 mile below the steel bridge, can be scouted or portaged. Conehead should be portaged on the right, although it has been run on the right when clear of logs.

Access

Contact the Rogue River–Siskiyou National Forest office before going (541-618-2200). There are seasonal closures of roads in this area, especially during the wet season, to protect the Port Orford cedar trees from root disease. From US 101 in Brookings, go east on Curry County 784, along the north shore of the Chetco River. After crossing the river, the road enters Siskiyou National Forest and becomes NF 1376. About 16 miles from Brookings, cross the South Fork

Chetco River and go left on NF 1407 for 0.6 mile. Turn left on NF 170 for 0.5 mile to the Chetco Gorge trailhead, a washed-out bridge, and the take-out.

From here, some attention to road numbers is required if you want to reach the put-in before nightfall. Back at NF 1407, head upstream for 0.1 mile, then turn right onto NF 1917. After another 3.1 miles, turn left onto NF 060. Stay right at the unmarked (as of 1992) junction that appears after another 2.8 miles. After another 1.5 miles, turn left onto Primitive Road 067, and go a final 1.5 miles down to the river. The driver who is careless at the bottom may need a four-wheel-drive vehicle to get unstuck.

Gauge

Currently available via the Internet (Chetco near Brookings) (see Appendix A). Once at the take-out, observe the abutment of the former bridge at the take-out. A vertical distance of 5 feet from the river to the top of the wooden cross beam indicates a lower-medium flow. At 3 feet, expect an upper-medium flow.

Richard Dierks and WKCC Editors

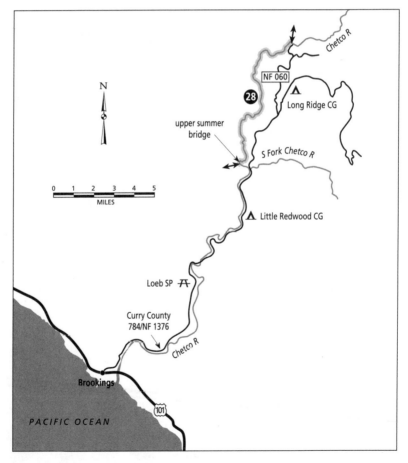

Smith River and Tributaries, California

29 North Fork Smith River
13 Miles above Gasquet to Gasquet

Class: 3; 5	Length: 13 miles
Flow: 800 cfs; 12,000 cfs	Character: wilderness; clear water
Gradient: 45 fpm, PD	Season: rainy/snowmelt

This is a run of rare isolation and beauty. Even at high levels, the water is crystal clear, like a river of bubbling champagne. Although the authors have run this stretch in as little as 1.5 hours at high water, it is best to start early and plan a long day. Hiking out after dark would take out all the fun.

Many distinct drops, as well as a couple of small gorges, are found on this run, but the entire trip is less severe than the Middle and South Fork gorges and ranks between them and the stretches above them in terms of difficulty. Big (but generally friendly) hydraulics develop at high water.

Hazards
This is a long run with a long shuttle, so give yourself plenty of time. The isolation makes walking out or getting help difficult, so plan to be self-sufficient.

Access
The take-out is in Gasquet, California, at the confluence of the North Fork with the Middle Fork Smith River. Gasquet is on US 199 east of Crescent City, which is on US 101. To drive to the take-out, take Gasquet Flat Road from the east end of Gasquet and drive about 0.2 mile to the bridge over the Middle Fork. Just over the bridge, walk left down a dirt road about 200 yards to the North Fork Smith River. From the river, the confluence and large rock outcropping on river left are obvious. An alternate take-out is the put-in for the Middle Fork Smith River: Gasquet to Oregon Hole Gorge run.

To reach the put-in for this run, take US 199 to Left Bank Road. Turn right onto Low Divide Road. Keep straight at all intersections on Low Divide Road. At 14 miles from Left Bank Road, turn on County Road 308. After about 5 miles County Road 308 ends where it joins County Road 305; continue east on County Road 305. This shuttle route climbs several thousand feet and then winds back down, but do not lose heart; County Road 305 crosses the North Fork Smith River about 25 miles from US 199. Put in at the bridge. The area around this bridge is private land. Stay on public land by walking down the steep bank on river left just upstream of the bridge. Although the shuttle from Gasquet takes about 1.5 hours one way, the road is well maintained.

Gauge

Located at Jedediah Smith State Park, which is on US 199 west of Gasquet. The flow is approximately 33 percent of the flow at the gauge.

Bo and Kathy Shelby

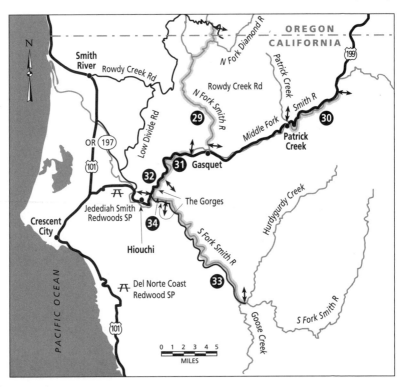

30 Middle Fork Smith River
6 Miles above Patrick Creek to Patrick Creek

Class: 4(5)	Length: 5–6 miles
Flow: 500–2000 cfs	Character: canyon; forested
Gradient: 65 fpm, PD	Season: rainy/snowmelt

This run, which is seldom done, has a spectacular but very tight gorge. The authors ran it when the Jedediah Smith State Park gauge read about 8000 cfs, a good level. The most difficult parts of the gorge can be scouted by walking along US 199 for a mile or so above Patrick Creek. The remainder of the run is not visible from the road. Other drops need careful consideration from the river.

Hazards

The gorge itself, most of which is visible from the road, is the major difficulty. Scout for trees and logs.

Access

Patrick Creek flows alongside US 199. Take out where Patrick Creek enters the Smith River.

To find a put-in, drive approximately 5.7 miles upstream on US 199 and look around for a place to scramble down the bank.

Gauge

Located at Jedediah Smith State Park. The flow is approximately 17 percent of the flow at the gauge.

Bo and Kathy Shelby

31 Middle Fork Smith River
Gasquet to above Oregon Hole Gorge

Class: 2+; 3	Length: 6 miles
Flow: 1000 cfs; 22,000 cfs	Character: clear water
Gradient: 20 fpm, PD	Season: rainy/snowmelt

This delightful run on the Middle Fork Smith River provides a good warm-up for the more demanding runs on the Smith. Several good rapids and play spots can be enjoyed.

Hazards

No particular difficulties are present.

Access

At the downstream end of the town of Gasquet on US 199, put in at the first place where the river is right next to the highway. A laundromat, trailer park, and a wide spot in the road are there. The obvious put-in is on private property, but look for a spot that is not on private land.

The take-out is approximately 5 miles downstream. During the shuttle, look for a highway warning sign, "Slippery When Wet," where a small dirt road angles down to the river (the river is not visible from the road here). Walk down and scout the take-out; it is not obvious from the river.

Gauge

Located at Jedediah Smith State Park. The flow is approximately 55 percent of the flow at the gauge.

Bo and Kathy Shelby

32 Middle Fork Smith River Oregon Hole Gorge

Class: 4; 5	Length: 1.5 miles
Flow: 500 cfs; 22,000 cfs	Character: gorge; clear water
Gradient: 50 fpm, C	Season: rainy/snowmelt

The only thing wrong with this gorge is that it is over too soon. The character of the run changes dramatically with the water level. At low water, the drops are steep but distinct, requiring some tricky moves around big boulders. At high water, the gorge becomes an awesome, turbulent flush in which eddies are hard to find. Oregon Hole Gorge is also known as Middle Fork Gorge.

Hazards

Most of the gorge is visible from US 199, but the road is several hundred vertical feet above the river, luring the unsuspecting paddler into an inappropriate complacency. Be sure to take the time and effort to scramble down to river level and scout carefully; the water is bigger and faster than it appears from above. The last major rapid in the gorge is just barely visible downstream; it can be scouted from river left.

Access

Put in either at Gasquet on US 199 or just above the gorge (both access points are described in the Middle Fork Smith River: Gasquet to Above Oregon Hole Gorge run).

Take out at the bridge where the South Fork Road crosses the river (paddle under the bridge and land on river right at a small gravel beach). A steep trail leads up to a parking area where the South Fork Road takes off from US 199.

Gauge

See the Middle Fork Smith River: Gasquet to Above Oregon Hole Gorge run.

Bo and Kathy Shelby

33 South Fork Smith River Upper Bridge to South Fork Gorge

Class: 3(4)	Length: 10 miles
Flow: 1000–20,000 cfs	Character: forested; canyon
Gradient: 35 fpm, PD	Season: rainy/snowmelt

Most of the drops on this run are gradual and straightforward, with the exception of Pillow Rapids, the sharp drop visible from the road several miles up from the gorge (past the point where the road climbs away from the river and then returns). Surprise Rapids, 0.25 mile above the take-out, can be scouted (or portaged) on river right.

Hazards
Pillow Rapids, mentioned above develops a nasty hole at some water levels; it can usually be avoided by running river left. Surprise Rapids is worthy of a scout.

Access
From US 199, about 1 mile northeast of Hiouchi Hamlet, turn onto South Fork Road. Cross the Middle Fork and the South Fork, then turn left and go up the South Fork. The take-out is about 1 mile above the South Fork bridge (2 miles from US 199), where a large pullout (75 yards long and 40 yards wide) with trails leads down to the river. At this point, the river is not visible from the road. Scout the take-out if you do not want to run the gorge; it is not obvious from the river.

To reach the put-in, proceed upstream, crossing the river twice on bridges high above the river. The put-in is at a bridge about 10 miles upstream. The river is generally visible from the road. It is possible to shorten the run by putting in farther down.

Gauge
Located at Jedediah Smith State Park. The flow is approximately 45 percent of the flow at the gauge.

Bo and Kathy Shelby

34 South Fork Smith River
South Fork Gorge to Bridge

Class: 4; 5	Length: 1.5 miles
Flow: 500 cfs; 9000 cfs	Character: gorge; clear water
Gradient: 60 fpm, PD	Season: rainy/snowmelt

This gorge is a bit longer than the Oregon Hole Gorge, but it still is not nearly long enough. Although the South Fork Road follows the river, the water is generally out of sight. With persistence and scrambling, it is possible to scout most of this stretch from the road; do this before committing yourself to the run. This is one of the most beautiful gorges anywhere, complete with all the classic gorge characteristics: steep blind drops, tough landings for scouting, and powerful turbulent water. This run is particularly difficult and potentially dangerous at high water levels.

Hazards
The run has several distinct drops, which vary markedly with the water level. Be prepared to do your own scouting and make your own decisions.

Access

Put in at any of the access points for the South Fork Smith River: Upper Bridge to South Fork Gorge run or at the take-out for that run.

Take out at the South Fork bridge by paddling under the bridge and landing at the small beach on river right. A trail goes sharply up the bank to the end of the bridge.

Gauge

See the South Fork Smith River: Upper Bridge to South Fork Gorge run.

Bo and Kathy Shelby

Southern
Oregon Rivers

Region 3

Umpqua River and Tributaries

35 Jackson Creek
7 Miles above Cover Camp to Cover Camp

Class: 4(5)	Length: 6.5 miles
Flow: 150–500 cfs	Character: gorge, forested
Gradient: 120 fpm, C	Season: rainy/snowmelt

This run starts out boney and tree-infested with the creek meandering through a beautiful little valley. After a few hundred yards, the creek descends into a very deep gorge, plunging almost 450 feet in elevation over the 3-mile length of the canyon. The creek has a gradient of over 160 fpm for the first mile, lets up a bit for the second mile (120 fpm), and finishes in grand style for the third (160 fpm). This is steep creeking at its absolute best: continuous rapids, blind drops, few eddies, pin spots galore.

The continuous nature of this stretch (solid class 4) means no huge drops will be found. Most are in the 3- to 5-foot range but are so closely spaced that it is difficult to tell where one ends and the next begins. As you come out of the gorge, the gradient lessens to under 100 fpm and the creek takes on more of the character of the lower run. Numerous class 2 to 3 ledges and rapids are interspersed with four class 3 to 4 drops. The first one after the gorge has a large tree in the middle of it. Although the drop itself is not that massive, the tree essentially negates the preferable line. The portage is rather long and cuts through a lot of underbrush.

In a short distance, the next major rapid is a relatively straightforward class 3+ drop into a boiling pool. What adds challenge to this one is that there is a fallen tree 30 feet downstream you can get wedged under if something "unexpected" happens. Starting in the center and moving right drops you into a right-side eddy and avoids the hazard.

The third drop (UV) appears about a mile before Cover Camp. It comes at the end of a long straight stretch. It is actually two 6-foot drops spaced about 25 feet apart. Scout and/or portage right. The first drop takes you through a twisting slide on river left and shoots you out at a 90-degree angle right toward the second slot. The latter is a V-shaped slot that is no more than a couple feet wide at its base. About 95 percent of the flow pours through this narrow space, just begging a boater to jump in and get seriously trashed. At higher flows, boofing on the right and left allows you to completely miss the slots.

The last big drop (Buffy, the Vampire Slayer) occurs soon after the NF 30 bridge. As the stream curves back left, you drop over a 3-foot ledge bisected by a huge fallen tree. Stay left, but take care of the squirrelly water. From above, the creek seems to descend over a ledge and pour under a dagger-shaped rock. Scout and/or portage right. Closer inspection shows that about two-thirds of the water flows under and around the rock. A missed line left and you would likely wedge between the rock and the sheer cliff wall.

Intimate gorge (Jason Rackley)

Hazards

The gorge and the four drops mentioned demand caution. Careful scouting in the gorge is a must as logs could block any channel. Logs can be a problem for the entire run.

Access

From Canyonville, which is about 20 miles south of Roseburg, go east on Oregon 227, following the South Umpqua River upstream. At the town of Tiller, turn left onto NF 28 (South Umpqua Road). Continue on NF 28 for about 5.2 miles and turn right on NF 29. After 12 miles, you will reach Cover Camp, the take-out.

To reach the put-in, continue upstream on NF 29. Parallel the creek for about 7 miles, or until you find a good place to put in.

Gauge

None exists. Jackson Creek is estimated to have about 8 to 10 percent of the flow of the South Umpqua at Tiller. The South Umpqua at Tiller (currently available via the Internet, see Appendix A) should be at least 1200 cfs, while 2000 cfs would be equivalent to a great ride.

Mike Haley

36 Jackson Creek
Cover Camp to NF 31 Bridge

Class: 3(4)	Length: 8.5 miles
Flow: 400–1000cfs	Character: forested
Gradient: 40–50 fpm	Season: rainy/snowmelt

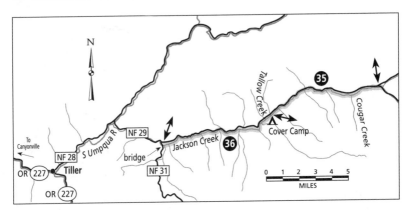

This lower run on Jackson Creek is quite a bit easier than the upper run but still contains numerous ledges and rapids, far too many to remember. Although most rapids are straightforward, three drops are definitely worth mentioning.

After putting in at Cover Camp (below a mandatory portage log), the first mile varies between mini-gorge and something a bit wider. After a mile, Squaw Creek enters on the left over a nice 4- to 5-foot falls, and the volume of the creek increases noticeably. A couple of miles farther, another anchored log spans 95 percent of the streambed. It could be boofed at higher flows but might need to be portaged. After several straightforward class 2 and class 3 ledges and rapids, you come upon a definite horizon line with river mist coming up over it. Scout left. We nicknamed this one "Da Bootie Call" (class 4 to 4+). This more than 8-foot-high riverwide ledge is nastier than it looks. All the water pours over a width of about 10 feet. At higher flows, a ski jump on the left might be an option.

About 0.5 mile farther downriver is Second Thought. Scout left, but portage right. This is a class 3+ to 4- 8-foot slide that runs into the rocks on river left, then does a hard right turn. Another 0.75 mile down is The Gate-Keeper (class 4). This is an easy rapid to run, but the consequences for a missed line are severe. As above, scout left but portage right. The rapid is best described as a ledge shaped like a 30-foot-wide letter J followed by a constriction to about 6 feet at the bottom. At low water, the left 15 to 18 feet may be unrunnable but can be ski-jumped at higher flows. The right side forms a terminal keeper. However, a 4- to 5-foot-wide path of clean water on far river right may permit access around the hole. A strongly recirculating eddy on the right allows enough breathing time before running the gate. This is a 4- to 5-foot-slide into a benign hole that can be very sticky at higher flows. It is imperative not to get sideways here as a boat could easily wedge.

After a relatively quiet mile, you pass under NF 31 bridge. You can run some nice class 3 ledge drops by continuing downstream another 0.5 mile before taking out.

Hazards

The three class 4 drops as well as logs present challenges. Da Bootie Call and The Gate-Keeper can be seen from the road on the drive up, at approximately

6.2 and 4.8 miles, respectively, upstream from the Jackson Creek turnoff. All are easily river scouted.

Access

From Canyonville, which is about 20 miles south of Roseburg, go east on Oregon 227 following the South Umpqua River upstream. Turn left onto NF 28 (South Umpqua Road) at the town of Tiller. Continue on NF 28 for about 5.2 miles and turn right on NF 29. Go 1 mile to the NF 31 bridge over Jackson Creek.

To reach the put-in, continue another 11 miles upstream on NF 29 to Cover Camp.

Gauge

None exists. This section of Jackson Creek is estimated to have 30 to 35 percent of the flow of the South Umpqua at Tiller (currently available via the Internet; see Appendix A).

Mike Haley

37 Cow Creek
Reuben Road to West Fork of Cow Creek

Class: 3 (4)	Length: 10 miles
Flow: 400–1000 cfs	Character: forested, narrow valley
Gradient: 32 fpm, C-PD	Season: rainy

This beautiful creek features steep terrain and reminds one of the adjacent Rogue River drainage. Numerous tunnels for the railroad paralleling the creek suggest the rugged past of this country.

After flowing through the relatively flat land around Glendale, Cow Creek begins cutting down through a narrow valley. The first five miles of the run, to the bridge over Cow Creek, cannot be seen from the road which is high above the creek. Parts of the run below the bridge can be scouted from the road. There are numerous class 3 and 3+ rapids both above and below this bridge, which could be a possible take-out point. Near the end of the run one passes under a railroad bridge and past a highway bridge on river right over Middle Creek. From here it's only 0.5 mile to the take-out at West Fork bridge on the left.

Hazards

Several drops on this run are blind and should be scouted.

Access

From the north take I-5 exit 103, Riddle. Continue west on the Riddle by-pass which curves southward. Go past Cow Creek Wayside on the right. Turn right onto Cow Creek Road. Upon entering the Cow Creek Road area, watch for small mile markers. At MP 26.7 turn right onto West Fork Road. Cross the bridge and park in the large gravel area on the left. The put-in is 10 miles up Cow Creek Road. Look for a side road on the left (signed "Reuben"). Park there any carry boats about 100 yards on a rough lane to the river.

From the south, and alternatively from the north, take I-5 exit 80 and follow Glendale Valley Road toward Glendale. Upon entering Glendale turn right onto Reuben Road, which later becomes Cow Creek Road at the put-in area. About 8 miles from the I-5 exit, find the side road on the right (signed "Reuben"), the put-in as described above. The take-out is 10 miles downstream on the left under the West Fork Bridge.

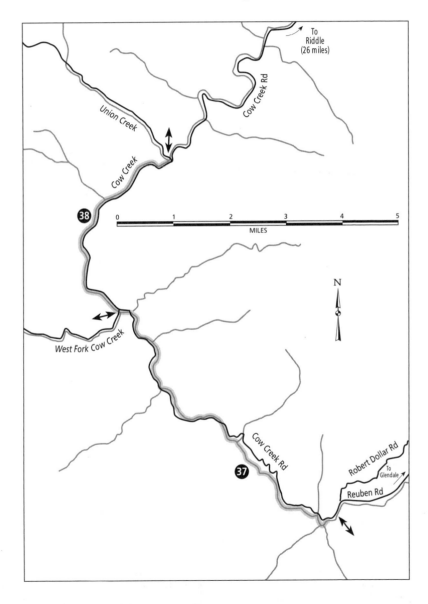

Gauge

Available via the Internet (Cow Creek at Glendale; Cow Creek at Riddle) (see Appendix A). Flow on this section is a little higher than the flow at Glendale and at least half the flow at Riddle. The flood of January 2012 seems to have changed the calibration of the Glendale gauge, making the flow seem significantly higher than the Glendale gauge reading.

Steve Cramer, Rob Blickensderfer, Larry Hodges , and WCKK Editors

38 Cow Creek
West Fork of Cow Creek to Union Creek

Class: 2+ (3)	Length: 6.3 miles
Flow: 700–1400 cfs	Character: forested
Gradient: 16 fpm	Season: rainy

This is a pleasant run through steep terrain thickly wooded with manzanita, madrone, red cedar, and Douglas fir. While plenty of clear-cuts can be seen high on the slopes, lush riverside stands generally contain tall older trees. Cow Creek Road and a working railroad parallel the river but are not obtrusive. The run is a mixture of continuous water and numerous class 2 and 2+ rapids. The only class 3 rapids is the short steep drop about 100 yards below the put-in.

Hazards

None in particular, but always be aware of possible sweepers in a forested river.

Access

Follow the directions for the Reuben Road to West Fork of Cow Creek run. The take-out at the West Fork bridge is the put-in for this run. The take-out for this run is at the Union Creek bridge, river left, at milepost 20.4. Alternatively, paddle another 4 miles to another possible take-out near milepost 16.7 or any other area that is not on private property.

Gauge

See Gauge notes for Cow Creek: Reuben Road to West Fork of Cow Creek. The flow is approximately 1.5 times that of the Glendale gauge and 75% of the flow of the Riddle gauge.

Steve Cramer, Rob Blickensderfer, and Larry Hodges

39 South Umpqua River
Campbell Falls to Three C Rock

Class: 3(4+); 4(5)	Length: 12 miles
Flow: 600 cfs; 4000 cfs	Character: forested
Gradient: 29 fpm, PD	Season: rainy/snowmelt

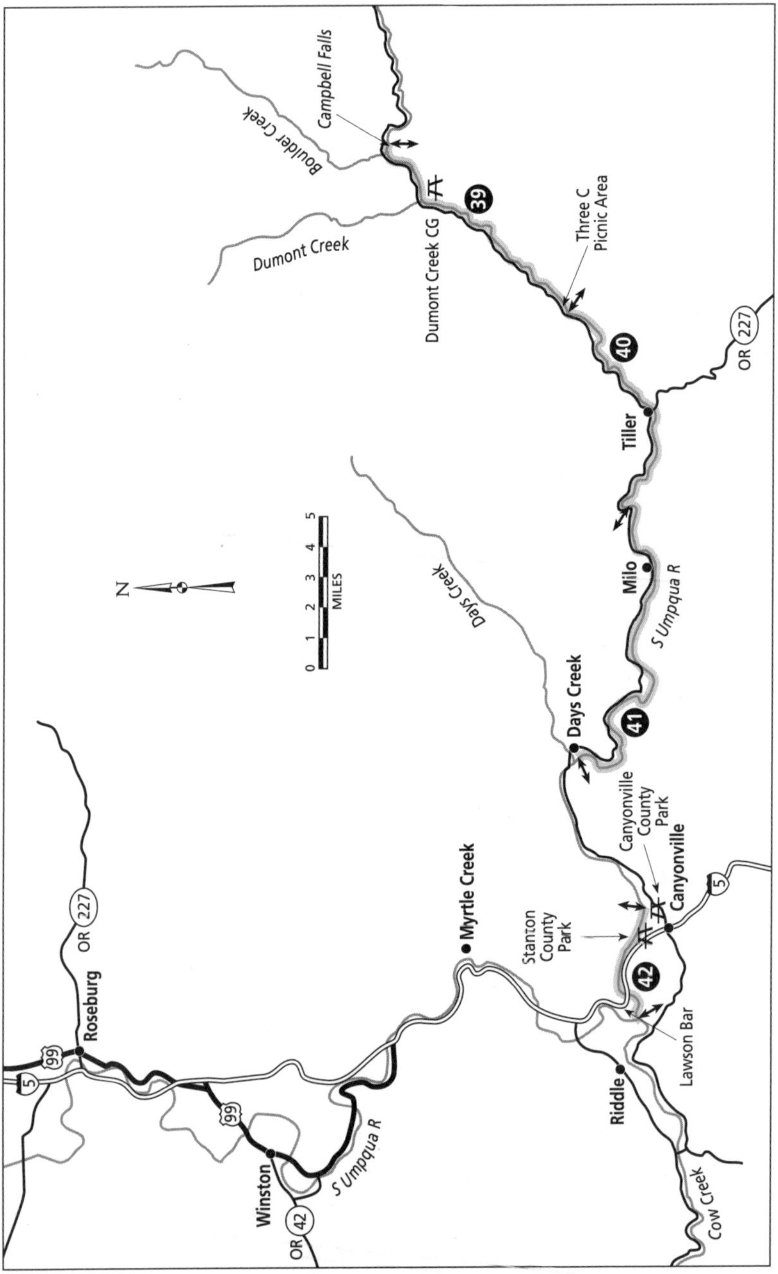
Campbell Falls
Boulder Creek
Dumont Creek
Dumont Creek CG
39
Three C
Picnic Area
40
OR 227
Tiller
N
0 1 2 3 4 5
MILES
Days Creek
Milo
S Umpqua R
Days Creek
41
Canyonville
County
Park
Canyonville
5
Stanton
County
Park
Myrtle Creek
42
Lawson Bar
Riddle
Cow Creek
OR 227
Roseburg
99
5
99
Winston
OR 42
S Umpqua R

The run starts with a bang at Campbell Falls (named in honor of World War II pilot and war hero Robert Campbell) and its 14-foot vertical drop into a pool with a narrow exit. There is a chute along the far left wall, but the falls seems to be the saner route at most water levels. An alternative put-in is 75 yards downstream on river right.

The major rapids downstream change from narrow chutes through rock outcroppings to powerful riverwide ledge drops as the flow increases. The first major rapid, Diversification Drop, is located 1.9 miles down from the put-in. Two distinct chutes appear at low flows. River left is fairly straightforward; however, the right chute requires a quick left turn just as you drop over the 5-foot falls. Just 0.5 mile farther, Boulder Creek enters on the right, and 200 yards below is a drop similar to Diversification Drop. Both of these drops can be scouted from the road. Dumont Creek, with campground and rest rooms, is less than 1 mile downstream.

The third rapid worth mentioning, Triple Drop, is located about 8 miles farther down, just a couple of miles before the take-out. Three distinct drops in this 100-yard-long rapids give a great ride.

Hazards

Campbell Falls and the three other rapids mentioned above present difficulties. Scout or portage.

Access

The run is east of Interstate 5 between Roseburg and Medford. From the north, take Oregon 227 at Canyonville and proceed 23 miles east to Tiller. From the south, take Oregon 62 from Medford to Oregon 227 to Tiller. In Tiller, take County Road 46 upstream for 5.4 miles to the take-out at the Three C Rock.

The put-in is 11.4 miles farther upstream at Campbell Falls. Hike about 200 yards on a fairly good trail down to the river.

Gauge

Located at Tiller. Currently available via the Internet (South Umpqua at Tiller gauge) or call the National Weather Service in Medford or the River Forecast Center in Portland (see Appendix A).

Terry K. Wyatt and Jeff S. Wolfe

40 South Umpqua River
Three C Rock to Milepost 22

Class: 3(4)	Length: 8.5 miles
Flow: 1500–4000 cfs	Character: wooded
Gradient: 23 fpm, C	Season: rainy/snowmelt

Although the nature of most of this run is class 1 and 2, several class 3 and class 4 rapids appear at high flows. From the put-in, the river flows at a nice tempo through a small canyon. After passing a concrete bridge at mile 1.6, it is another mile to a demanding class 3 rapid where most of the river pours against a large boulder. At mile 3.6, a class 4 riverwide ledge can be scouted from the right. The river passes under the Oregon 227 bridge in Tiller at mile 4.7. The last major rapid is at mile 7.2, near the downstream end of a recent major road cut. The river piles up against a huge boulder on the right bank as it makes a tight left bend. Part of the water flows upstream on the right to form a strong boiling eddy feeding through trapped logs and debris that should be avoided. Several hundred yards downstream are the remains of a log bridge and a concrete bridge swept away in past floods. It is about 1 mile to the take-out.

Hazards

The class 3 rapid at mile 2.6 should be run well left of center to avoid a large upstream pour-over hole on the right, followed by a massive rock in midstream with most of the water smashing directly into it. The class 4 rapid at mile 3.6 is a combination of a ledge with a sticky reversal followed by a hole of raft-flipping proportions. The class 3 drop at the road cut is potentially the most dangerous. It can be scouted and portaged on the left.

Access

The put-in for this run is the take-out for the South Umpqua River: Campbell Falls to Three C Rock run.

The take-out for this run is at about milepost 22.5 on Oregon 227, where the river makes a sweeping left bend close to the road through a broad area of low rock outcroppings. Parking can be found on the riverside shoulder of the road.

Gauge

Located at Tiller. See the South Umpqua River: Campbell Falls to Three C Rock run.

Steve Cramer and Rob Blickensderfer

41 South Umpqua River
Milepost 22 to Days Creek

Class: 2+(4)	Length: 13.5 miles
Flow: 1500–4000 cfs	Character: rural
Gradient: 13 fpm, C	Season: rainy/snowmelt

The scenery varies at almost every turn—low rock cliffs, volcanic tuff, extensive gravel bars, and rolling hills. The river has many pleasant riffles over gravel bars that become very fast and turn into big waves at higher flows. It passes under a covered bridge at mile 2.1, and from there it is only about 0.5 mile to the concrete bridge in Milo. At mile 3.6 is a low ledge with a sticky reversal. After several miles of slow water, one hardly suspects the major class 4 rapid at mile 11.2, where the river slices through a low rock outcropping. Below this drop, the river bounces through delightful water with many play spots to the take-out.

Hazards
The class 4 rapid at mile 11.2 consists of a fast chute leading into a riverwide hole with a collapsing upstream wave that takes the full flow of the river. This rapid can be easily portaged on either side.
Access
The put-in for this run is the take-out at milepost 22.5 for the South Umpqua River: Three C Rock run to milepost 22.

The take-out is a boat ramp on river right located 50 yards upstream from the Oregon 227 bridge in Days Creek.

Gauge
See the South Umpqua River: Campbell Falls to Three C Rock run.

Steve Cramer and Rob Blickensderfer

42 South Umpqua River
Canyonville County Park to Lawson Bar

Class: 2(3)	Length: 5 miles
Flow: 600 cfs	Character: rural
Gradient: 12 fpm, PD	Season: rainy

A classic example of a pool drop river can be experienced on this short run. After putting in at the pleasant Canyonville County Park, it is about 0.5 mile to the first drop, a straightforward class 2- rapids just as a bridge comes into view. A little farther along, a park is seen among large fir trees on the left. This is Stanton County Park on the road just north of Canyonville, and it offers an alternate access to the river. About 0.25 mile below the park is the most difficult rapids on this section, consisting of class 3 channels over ledges. It can be scouted or portaged on the left. A mile farther is a class 2 rapids with several channels through willows. The next rumble heard is not a rapids but the traffic on the Interstate 5 bridge overhead. Below the bridge are enjoyable small rapids among scenic rock formations. An extensive gravel bar on the left indicates the approach to the mouth of Cow Creek, on the left, followed by Lawson Bar on the right. One may take out on the right either above or below the class 2 rapids at Lawson Bar.

Hazards
The class 3 rapids mentioned above are quite technical at low flows.

Access
Canyonville is a short distance off Interstate 5. To reach the put-in, go to the center of town and take Oregon 227 eastward toward Tiller for 1.1 miles. Turn left on County Road 215, which leads directly to Canyonville County Park.

The take-out at Lawson Bar can be reached by returning to Interstate 5 and proceeding northward. Take exit 102, turn west, and follow the sign to Lawson Bar (dead end).

Gauge

Located at Winchester. Call the River Forecast Center in Portland (see Appendix A). The flow is about 25 percent less than at Winchester. A flow of 800 cfs at Winchester is adequate.

Rob Blickensderfer and Steve Cramer

43 Copeland Creek
NF 300 Bridge to North Umpqua River

Class: 4+(5) T,P	Length: 5 miles
Flow: 250–600 cfs	Character: canyon, forested
Gradient: 125 fpm, C	Season: rainy/snowmelt

To the unsuspecting, Copeland Creek is just another side tributary on the Boulder Flat run of the North Umpqua; however, this creek offers much more. Adventurous souls will be rewarded by numerous ledges, boulder gardens, slides, and falls on one of the best class 4 creeks in the state.

After 0.3 mile of easy class 2 warm-up, the first drop of consequence occurs on a hard right turn. A boof down the center line is recommended, though dropping through the narrow river right slot can result in a stern squirt or even a mystery move. The next 0.75 mile holds many similar types of drops and several fun slides. When the creek divides around a large island, take the right channel and proceed carefully as Paul Bunyan Falls lurks just downstream. Aptly named, this 18- to 20-foot falls is choked with massive logs wedged in both sides. Portaging, the only sane option, can be accomplished on the right via a rather long, circuitous hike or down the center of the island by scrambling across and down the permanent logjam.

A few hundred yards downstream of the falls is class 5 Sneaky Snake, a 10-foot high, V-shaped ledge. Most of the creek pushes toward the narrowest part of the V, forming a deadly keeper hydraulic. Rescue here would be all but impossible because of the sheer, high walls and slippery, moss-covered rock. Be certain to catch the small eddy on the left and scout from the jumble of boulders. Run center angling left or, better yet, portage left and seal launch below the hydraulic. The remaining mile to the road bridge is class 2 to 3.

Below the bridge, the creek drops into a deep gorge for more than 2 miles of very technical, class 4+ creek boating. Halfway through this section is Fountain of Youth, a 15-foot-plus falls. Scout and/or portage left. Run the falls 8 to 10 feet off the right shore with plenty of momentum or risk grinding to a halt at the lip of the falls. The remainder of the run is nonstop boulder gardens. The last few hundred yards on the North Umpqua seems like huge water compared to the previous 5 miles.

Hazards

The run is very demanding. In many locations, a boat could become pinned, and numerous logs must be avoided. Sneaky Snake should be thoroughly scouted before running the drop.

Access

Copeland Creek is located about 34 miles east of the town of Glide on Oregon 138. Between 32 and 33 miles east of Glide, Oregon 138 crosses the North Umpqua River. The take-out is a turnout 1.1 miles farther upstream on the north side of the highway.

To reach the put-in, drive another 0.1 mile upstream and turn right onto Copeland Creek Road (NF 28). After 2.4 miles, turn right onto NF 2801. Continue upstream another 2.3 miles and then turn left onto NF 300. Cross the creek and turn right into the primitive "Camp Wobegone" site, the put-in.

Gauge

None exists. The North Umpqua River should be between 7 and 9 feet at the Glide gauge. Lower levels are possible, but then the creek requires extremely technical rock dodging. At higher levels, this run becomes pushy class 5 and should be attempted only by expert creekers.

WKCC Editors

Making the move at Sneaky Snake, Copeland Creek (Jason Rackley)

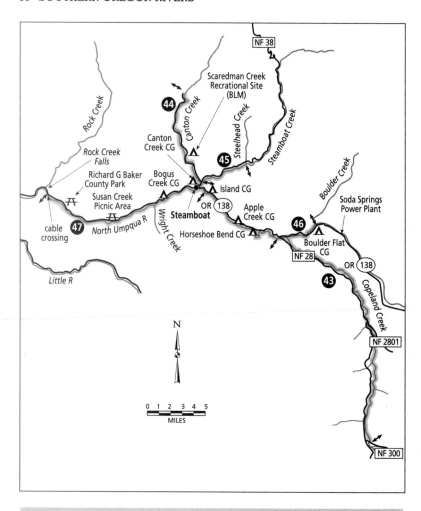

44 Canton Creek
6.5 Miles above Steamboat Creek to Steamboat Creek

Class: 3(5); 4(5)	Length: 6.5 miles
Flow: 300 cfs; 2000 cfs	Character: forested
Gradient: 70 fpm	Season: rainy

This entertaining and scenic tributary of Steamboat Creek is an excellent choice for intermediate paddlers. The road is always close by, but it never intrudes on the run. The ledgy nature of the creek provides many nice surfing holes and waves between rapids, all of which adds up to one of the best all-around runs in the area.

Below the put-in bridge, the creek flows over many small drops and several long class 3 boulder gardens that have generous eddies for boat scouting. The creek is always quite wide, so generous flows are necessary for an enjoyable day.

Once you pass under the third bridge below the put-in, the water accelerates over several smaller ledgy drops before a long moving pool that leads to the lip of a 15-foot waterfall (class 5) with no obvious route except at very high water. The portage around this drop is very easy on the left, and the entire drop is visible (and scoutable) on the shuttle.

Below the falls, two more significant rapids should be scouted. The first is a 5-foot ledge that is visible from the road just below a fun, twisty chute. The second drop is just downstream and contains a significant riverwide hole. More continuous rapids and surfing lead to the confluence with Steamboat Creek, where you can take out or continue down to the North Umpqua.

Hazards
The creek is always very wide, so logs are easily avoidable. The two lower ledges develop formidable holes at high water.

Access
From Oregon 138, turn up Steamboat Creek Road and drive 0.5 mile to the lower Canton Creek bridge. This is the take-out.

To reach the put-in, turn up the one-lane asphalt road that parallels Canton Creek. About 2.1 miles from the take-out is the class 5 waterfall, just before the second bridge over the creek. Continue upstream for a total of 6.4 miles to the fourth bridge, which is the put-in.

Gauge
Visible. Good medium flows occur after heavy rains when the North Umpqua at Glide is between 7 and 9 feet and Steamboat Creek is 3500 to 5000 cfs. Due to the wide nature of the creek, lower flows are not recommended.

Jason Rackley

45 Steamboat Creek
Steamboat Falls to Canton Creek Campground

Class: 4(5)	Length: 6 miles
Flow: 600–2500 cfs	Character: forested
Gradient: 40 fpm	Season: rainy/snowmelt

Steamboat Creek enters the North Umpqua River 1 mile west of Island Campground. Its feeling of isolation and good class 4 action make dipping a paddle into it worthwhile.

The put-in is just below Steamboat Falls where the road is near the river. Steamboat Falls can be run, but it is not recommended because of cement and steel rebar at its base. A line down the center-right has been relatively clean. A mile of easy play water allows a warm-up before a class 4 rapids. After 0.2 mile, a class 5 rapids can be scouted or portaged on the right. The remaining portion of the run is class 2 and 3 with an occasional easy class 4. Little Steamboat Falls lies at the end of the canyon and ranges in difficulty from class 4 at moderate flow to class 5 at high flows. It makes an excellent take-out.

Hazards

At levels above 5 feet, the portage around the class 5 rapids becomes very difficult, as does the rapids. Check for logs.

Access

From Oregon 138 along the North Umpqua River, take Oregon 38 northward up Steamboat Creek. Canton Creek Campground, 0.5 mile upstream, is the take-out.

From the campground, drive 5.5 miles upstream. Put in where the road comes near the river. An alternate put-in is 100 yards up Steelhead Creek, which provides a short class 3 section.

Gauge

Located on Steamboat Creek just downstream from Canton Creek. Currently available via the Internet (Steamboat Creek near Glide gauge) (see Appendix A). A good low flow is 3.7 feet.

Eric Brown

46 North Umpqua River Boulder Flat to Gravel Bin

Class: 2 to 4	Length: 16 miles
Flow: 800 cfs; 2000 cfs	Character: forested
Gradient: 39 fpm, PD	Season: year-round

SECTION 1: BOULDER FLAT TO HORSESHOE BEND, 7 MILES, CLASS 2 TO 3

Most of this run can be scouted from the road. The river is characterized by swiftly moving water and fairly continuous activity in moderate-size waves amid numerous rocks and other obstacles. None of the rapids is difficult, though in several spots large holes and bigger waves are encountered. Snags are a hazard at times, and it is not unusual to encounter a tree spanning all or most of the stream. Just beyond the second bridge, a rocky ledge spans 80 percent of the river, creating a very narrow chute along the right bank. At lower water levels, this chute is virtually the only runnable spot. You may readily get slammed into the wall on the right by the force of the current. It is a potential spot for lodged debris.

SECTION 2: HORSESHOE BEND TO STEAMBOAT, 9 MILES, CLASS 3 TO 4

This run on the North Umpqua River can be described as pool drop. Between Horseshoe Bend and Apple Creek Campgrounds, the river passes through a narrow gorge full of short, steep rapids that vary in difficulty. Most can be scouted from the road. Several of them require meticulous maneuvering between rocks and holes, especially Pin Ball Rapid, class 4. The pool drop pattern of the river continues all the way to Steamboat. Go slowly and get a look at the rapids that remain.

Hazards

Section 1: The rocky ledge just above the take-out should be checked for debris in the right chute. The ledge may need to be portaged. *Section 2:* Pin Ball Rapid is a boulder-choked drop not visible from the road. It is located about 0.3 mile below the bridge below Apple Creek Campground. Scouting is advisable. The rapids occurs on a right bend of the river with a large gravel bar just above it on the left. At water levels that allow for the bar to exist, it is possible to pull in at its base and scout from the left bank.

Access

The put-in at Boulder Flat Campground is approximately 50 miles east of Roseburg on Oregon 138.

The take-out for section 1 is at Horseshoe Bend Campground, also on Oregon 138.

For section 2, put in at any of the wide spots along Oregon 138 near Horseshoe Bend Campground. An alternate put-in is the small turnout 0.2 mile upstream from the Dry Creek Store, which is approximately 1.5 miles above Horseshoe Bend.

The best take-out is 0.2 mile below Island Campground at Gravel Bin.

Gauge

Currently available via the Internet (North Umpqua at Glide gauge) (see Appendix A). The river is dam controlled and runnable all year.

Kent Wickham and WKCC Editors

47 North Umpqua River Steamboat to Cable Crossing

Class: 3(4)		Length: 16 miles
Flow: 1500–3000 cfs		Character: forested
Gradient: 21 fpm, PD		Season: year-round

This stretch, although highlighted by several of the North Umpqua's biggest rapids, is generally less technical than the upstream runs. Rapids are separated by long flat stretches.

The Steamboat Inn marks the site of an exciting rocky rapids in the left channel, and a sometimes-runnable falls in the right channel. Do not trespass on Steamboat Inn property when scouting. Below Steamboat 6 miles is Wright Creek Bridge, which is followed in another 0.2 mile by Bathtub Rapid. At low water, Bathtub deserves a scout.

Small fun drops continue for several more miles. A very large cliff rising from water's edge on the left is seen 200 yards above Island (or Staircase) Rapid, the North Umpqua's best ride. Several miles below Island Rapid, and marked by the Forest Service boundary sign at the side of the road, is Sleeper Rapid, a long sweeping turn ending in a troublesome hole. A notable rapids encountered at Susan Creek State Park is followed by a notoriously flat 4 miles. At Richard G. Baker County Park, a 5-foot falls known as Little Niagara helps to justify paddling the preceding flat stretch. Cable Crossing is the last convenient take-out above Rock Creek Falls. The run may be shortened by taking out at the Susan Creek Picnic Area, although the motor-home traffic may be heavy.

The mouth of Steamboat Creek is a holding area for migrating steelhead. From mid-July through October, numerous anglers fish here. Confrontations have occurred in the past, and relations between boaters and anglers have been somewhat strained. Please be courteous. During fishing season, it is a good idea to plan put-ins after 10:00 a.m. and take-outs before 5:00 p.m. to leave prime fishing time to the anglers. If a lot of anglers are present, it is best to avoid the area altogether and to put in 4 miles down at Bogus Creek; with the exception of the rapids right at Steamboat, very few good rapids will be missed.

Hazards

Below the recommended take-out at Cable Crossing are two very demanding rapids, Rock Creek Falls and The Narrows. These rapids should be considered by experts only. Rafters might find it necessary to portage Bathtub at low flows due to the narrowness of the chutes. At Island Rapid, the river divides into a broad, shallow left channel, which fizzles out to nothing, and a roaring right channel that approaches class 4. Island can be scouted from the road with difficulty. Sleeper is a long but rather innocuous rapids that starts out easy but requires a very tricky cut at the end to avoid a very large hole (a large rock at low flows). It can be scouted from the road.

Access

The best put-in is at the river access just below Island Campground on Oregon 138. Bogus Creek Campground is an alternative.

The take-out is at Cable Crossing, a poorly marked but very good access just up from Rock Creek Falls, or at Susan Creek State Park.

Gauge

Currently available via the Internet (North Umpqua at Glide gauge) (see Appendix A).

Kent Wickham

48 North Umpqua River
Idleyld Park to Winchester

Class: 2+(3)	Length: 25 miles
Flow: 1500 cfs	Character: rolling hills
Gradient: 11 fpm, PD	Season: year-round

This unheralded gem of a run moves through terrain transitioning from forested mountain canyon to hilly pastureland. Near sunset, the hills of scattered oak become a breathtaking masterpiece of shadow and gold. By June, the river is comfortably warm, yet mountain clear with plenty of flow, a rare treat for Oregon boaters. What is more, this run contains a fairly continuous offering of class 2 whitewater. All these factors combine to make this one of the premier whitewater runs of western Oregon for open canoers and a very enjoyable one for novice kayakers.

Immediately after the put-in is Salmon Hole, a class 2+ straightforward drop with some big waves. In the 5 miles from here to Colliding Rivers, there are many class 2 and 2+ pool drop rapids with fairly straight routes through 2- to 3-foot standing waves. At Colliding Rivers, the river is constricted by several large rock formations; it makes a sharp right turn after colliding head-on with Little River. A narrow class 4 drop makes a shortcut turn to the right. Do not be caught by it. The standard route is generally a class 3- with a rather tight right turn midway. This drop changes with the flow.

The river then starts its transition into open hills with a much wider streambed. The rapids take on more of a gravel bar nature with longer rapids (mostly class 2), but also longer flat-water stretches. The waves get smaller, but the drops get more technical, especially at summer flows under 3000 cfs. Play spots are not as plentiful as along the first 5 miles.

About 6 miles below Colliding Rivers, the river makes a bend to the north, announcing Whistler Park Falls, a class 3- drop with several relatively turbulent routes. From here, the river makes a horseshoe bend around Whistler Bend County Park and begins the final 10 miles. About 4 miles down is Dixon Falls, a class 3- drop around the right side of an island. It starts with a slightly technical approach with poor visibility. The drop itself is a turbulent chute with side curlers, but it is a straight shot with a pool finish, so a swim is not too serious. The left channel around the island is a possible alternative, but it is very rocky and technical.

Downriver about 0.5 mile from Dixon Falls are three more class 2 rapids. After another 2 to 3 miles, the river makes a big horseshoe bend to the south, with Umpqua Community College visible high on the right bank. When the water slows to a halt due to the Winchester Dam, start looking for a small boat ramp on river left, the take-out.

Hazards

Colliding Rivers, Whistler Park Falls, and Dixon Falls are rated as class 3-.

Access

Put in just below The Narrows (class 4) at the end of the town of Idleyld Park on Oregon 138. It is a scramble down the bank. Another put-in is at a little park named Lone Rock, about 1 mile east of the town of Glide on Oregon 138. Most drift boaters put in at a boat ramp 0.3 mile below Colliding Rivers; just west of the Oregon 138 bridge, take the first dirt road to the north and put in over the bank. Whistler Bend County Park is a convenient access point about 7 miles west of Glide on County Road 223. Access is also available across the river from the park at Jackson Wayside on North Bank Road.

The take-out is reached from Winchester, located on US 99 a few miles north of Roseburg. Take Page Road east out of Winchester along the south

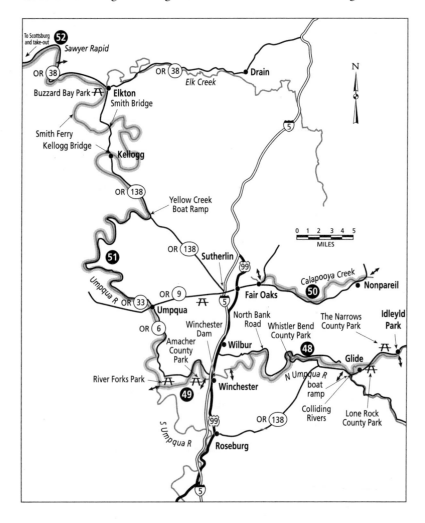

side of the river. A small boat ramp is upstream about 1 mile. An alternate take-out is at the boat ramp 0.3 mile below Colliding Rivers

Gauge
Currently available via the Internet (North Umpqua at Glide gauge) (see Appendix A).

Carl Landsness

49 North Umpqua River
Winchester to River Forks Park

Class: 2	Length: 6.5 miles
Flow: 1000 cfs	Character: valley
Gradient: 9 fpm, PD	Season: year-round

Here the river makes another transition in character as it enters bottomland terrain and vegetation not unlike the Willamette River basin. Surprisingly few houses are visible, considering the proximity of roads. The frequency of rapids decreases, but those that exist have nice standing waves. This section is known as Roseburg's "beer and float" run. A warm summer day finds many Roseburg-area residents leisurely rafting or tubing down to River Forks Park.

The first 4.5 miles to the Garden Valley Road bridge is intermittent class 1 and 2-. The mile following the bridge is locally known as "Sunburn Alley" to commemorate those who fall asleep without their suntan lotion on this notoriously slow and flat stretch.

Afternoon naps are abruptly ended by Burkhardt Rapid, a class 2+ ledge drop that can be a nice jet ferry at higher water levels. Another class 2+ drop with moderate waves quickly follows. A little more whitewater brings you to the confluence of the North Umpqua and the South Umpqua Rivers, with a nice beach on the right at River Forks Park.

Hazards
Burkhardt Rapid and several other class 2+ ledges present the only difficulties.

Access
Put in at Amacher County Park on the south side of the US 99 bridge in Winchester, beneath the Interstate 5 high bridge.

To reach the take-out, follow Winchester Road west 5 miles. It becomes Wilbur–Garden Valley Road. After 2 miles, turn left and go 1 mile south to a sign indicating River Forks Park, the take-out.

Gauge
Currently available via the Internet (North Umpqua at Winchester gauge) (see Appendix A).

Carl Landsness

50 Calapooya Creek
Nonpareil to Driver Valley Road

Class: 3+(4) T	Length: 3.7 miles
Flow: 300–800 cfs	Character: rural, narrow canyon
Gradient: 51 fpm, PD	Season: rainy

The first 1.5 miles are through open valley past the homes and outbuildings of the farming community of Nonpareil. The rapids are primarily broken ledges of increasing height. At about 1.0 mile is a 4-foot ledge that has been run up against the left wall at higher flows. At 1.5 miles, the creek enters a steep, narrow gorge. The first drop entering the gorge is through a narrow slot with the flow smashing into the right wall. At low water, the drop was not undercut, but there is risk of logs wedged below the surface. The drop can be carried on the right along an abandoned road. Below the first drop, the action is nonstop for 1.9 miles. The drops are tight, technical, and abusive to boats at low water. At higher water, the drops are technical and the action is fast. With sufficient eddies for scouting, none of the drops are blind. If one has time to notice, the gorge walls are near vertical, rising 40 to 80 feet above the creek, and the gorge has a wonderful remote feel. Below the gorge is 0.25 mile of relaxing water on which to unwind.

Hazards
The first drop entering the gorge.

Access
From Interstate 5, take Nonpareil Road east through Sutherlin to Nonpareil. Put in on river left under the bridge just upstream of the store and downstream from the water treatment plant and dam. Take out on river right at the first Driver Valley Road bridge out of Sutherlin. (A second Driver Valley Road bridge is 3.5 miles downstream.)

Gauge
None exists.

Steve Cramer and Larry Hodges

51 Umpqua River
River Forks Park to Scottsburg

Class: 1(2)	Length: 84 miles
Flow: 1000–4000 cfs	Character: forested; agricultural; roaded
Gradient: 4 fpm, PD	Season: year-round

From the confluence of the North and South Umpqua Rivers west of Roseburg, the main Umpqua winds leisurely through the Coast Range to the Pacific Ocean near Reedsport. Numerous small farms and houses dot the river's banks, but many stretches show little development and the development one does see is fairly unobtrusive. Roads follow most of the river, but significant traffic is noticeable only on stretches below Elkton and along one short stretch near Kellogg. The predominant scenery is the forested hills of the Coast Range, enjoyable even with the considerable logging that has taken place.

The Umpqua's riverbed is quite wide, capable of holding typical winter storm flows in excess of 50,000 cfs and the occasional 100,000+ cfs flood. Yet summer flows are in the 1000–3000 cfs range. As one can guess from the low gradient, the Umpqua contains long stretches of slow or flat water interspersed with riffles and small rapids. As the river drops, it becomes restricted in places to narrow channels in the bedrock. Some of these develop into short class 2 to 2+ rapids, depending on the river level.

The Umpqua is runnable year-round by experienced boaters able to deal with the hazards of high-volume rivers. Newcomers should wait for summer with its lower flows and warm water. This combination provides a good setting for easygoing canoeists.

The numerous boat ramps along this 84-mile stretch allow boaters to choose any of numerous possible runs. Note the Bicycle Shuttler's Delight: A trip from Kellogg Bridge to Smith Bridge is about 14 river miles, mostly roadless, but the shuttle is just over 2 miles.

Hazards

Although the rapids are few, they vary with water level and can still be tricky. Be prepared to scout. Inexperienced boaters can get into trouble if they do not stay alert. The last rapids above Smith Bridge may be tricky.

Access

The uppermost put-in is the take-out for the North Umpqua River: Winchester to River Forks Park run.

The river offers many access points (river miles differ from highway miles). The bridge on County Road 9 is near the town of Umpqua (rivermile 103); follow Garden Valley Road from River Forks Park; or from Interstate 5, exit 136 (Sutherlin/Oregon 138), head west on County Road 9 to Umpqua. Bullock Bridge is on County Road 57 (rivermile 80); follow County Road 33 from the town of Umpqua, or follow Oregon 138 out of Sutherlin until it reaches the river (around milepost 13), or follow Oregon 138 south from Elkton on Oregon 38; one can cross the bridge and go upriver a couple of miles to a boat ramp or follow Oregon 138 north about 1 mile to the Yellow Creek Boat Ramp. Kellogg Bridge is on Oregon 138 (rivermile 71), near milepost 6. Smith Bridge is on Oregon 138 (rivermile 57), near milepost 4. The bridge on Mehl Creek Road/County Route 67 is at rivermile 49; from the junction of Oregon 38 and Oregon 138 in Elkton, head south about 0.3 mile and turn right to cross the river; the boat ramp at Buzzard Bay Park is on river left 0.3 mile below the bridge. The Oregon 38 bridge is at Scottsburg (rivermile 27).

Gauge

Currently avaaialable via the Internet (Umpqua at Elkton gauge) (see Appendix A). Typical summer flows are in the 3- to 4-foot range (1000–3000 cfs).

Dan Valens

52 Umpqua River Sawyers Rapid

Class: 2+(3)	Length: 2.3 miles
Flow: 800–5000 cfs	Character: broad, wooded valley
Gradient: 13 fpm	Season: year-round

Because of predictable flows, this has long been a popular stretch when coastal streams are too low to run. After putting in, paddle immediately across the broad river to scout the class 3 chute from river left. Although revealed only during low flows, this narrow chute is turbulent and novices often walk or swim it. The other class 3 rapids follows shortly and is run down the middle. It does not flush at high water but does develop a couple of play spots below on far right and left. Take out at the boat ramp on river right.

For a 3-mile flat-water warm-up prior to Sawyers Rapid, put in at Bunch Bar, milepost 30.

Hazards
The first chute at the put-in is a bit rowdy for beginners but is easily portaged. High water means colder water and longer swims.

Access
Oregon 38 follows the river. The put-in is at the turnout at milepost 27, upstream and east of Reedsport between Scottsburg and Elkton.

Take out at Scott Creek County Park, near milepost 24.5.

Gauge
Currently avaialable via the Internet (Umpqua at Elkton gauge) (see Appendix A).

Richard Dierks

Rogue River and Tributaries

53 North Fork Rogue River Natural Bridge to Woodruff Campground

Class: 3+(5)	Length: 3 miles
Flow: 400–1500 cfs	Character: forested
Gradient: 75 fpm	Season: year-round

This fun run has only recently been discovered by boaters around Oregon but more than likely has been run for some time by local boaters. The run contains a lot of fun class 3 to 4 rapids set in a narrow canyon with beautiful forested banks. Be sure to take some time to hike upstream and gape at the natural bridge, where the entire river disappears into a hundred-foot-long lava tube that has to be seen to be believed.

Immediately upstream of the recommended put-in is a tough class 5 rapid with a large cave on the left. Most boaters will opt to put-in just below the pedestrian bridge. Just downstream from the put-in, the action starts immediately with a long, steep drop with some big holes and interesting moves, then the river assumes a pool drop nature. After some smaller rapids, paddlers arrive at Karma, one of the best rapids on the river. Karma is very long and the last part is not visible when scouting because the river takes a sharp left turn at the bottom. It starts with a wide-open boulder garden that narrows into a fast runout with a couple of sticky holes before the river takes an abrupt left turn and drops over an 8-foot sloping ledge with weird crosscurrents.

Below Karma are some easier drops, and then the river slows and takes a sharp turn to the right. Paddlers need to be extra cautious here as there is a 20-foot class 5 waterfall a hundred yards downstream from here. Get out at the sharp right bend (the portage trail is clearly visible up the side of the hill) and portage the falls. You can scout the falls by hiking up the hill to where the river bends back to the left. Knob Falls has been run but was nicknamed "Therapy Falls" by locals after an expert boater took a swim here that can only be described as a near death experience.

Immediately below the falls are three successive rapids. The first is pretty small, and the second has some weird rock formations in the middle that can be avoided on the right. The third drop is just downstream and should be approached with caution as wood has been here in the past. The river narrows here to about 20 feet wide and plunges into a uniform hole that is easier than it looks. At least one member of the party should always scout this rapid for wood.

The river then mellows out, with some long flat-water stretches punctuated by a couple of very narrow slots. Be careful in the slots as a boat or wood could wedge in one of the slots pretty easily. The last drop is right above the Woodruff bridge take-out and can be seen from the bridge beforehand. The river divides here around a rocky island. The left channel drops into a gnarly undercut visible from the take-out bridge, but the right side swings around and plunges over a really nice 6-foot ledge that is a perfect way to finish this run.

Hazards
Use caution around Knob Falls.

Access
To get to the take-out, take Oregon 62 east from Medford toward Lost Creek Lake and Prospect. Continue 6.25 miles past Prospect and turn left

onto NF 68, following the signs to Woodruff Campground. The take-out is at the bridge over the North Fork Rogue 1.8 miles from Oregon 62.

To reach the put-in, return to Oregon 62 and turn left. Travel 3.5 miles and turn left at the signs for Natural Bridge Park. The put-in is down a short trail on river right just downstream of the pedestrian bridge. *Note:* There is no established access at this point, so be discreet. Access could be closed if conflicts arise with other park users or park staff.

Gauge

Currently available via the Internet (Rogue River at Lost Creek Dam [inflow] gauge) (see Appendix A).

Jason Rackley and Pete Giordano

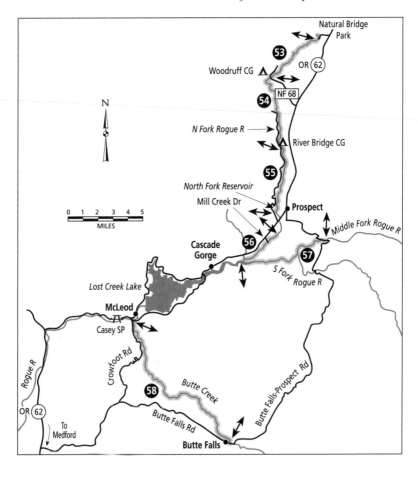

54 North Fork Rogue River Takilma Gorge

Class: 4+	Length: 3.8 miles
Flow: 400—500 cfs	Character: forested
Gradient: 38 fpm	Season: year-round

The Takilma Gorge section of the North Fork of the Rogue River is short but fun, with year-round flows and great rapids. Do not be deceived by the mild gradient. The gorge in the middle of the run has a gradient over 100 fpm with several difficult rapids and sheer walls on both sides. Climbing out of the gorge is next to impossible.

From the put-in, the run is scenic but flat for a mile before boaters enter the gorge. The first rapid, Entrance, is straightforward and marks the last realistic chance to exit the river before running the gorge.

The major rapids in the gorge are named Number One through Number Five. Number One is a steep drop over two riverwide ledges. The ledges produce big holes at high water, while at low water the second ledge has a severe sieve on the right and a narrow slot on the left. Several hundred yards downstream is Number Two: a relatively easy drop that pushes against the right wall a bit. Below Two the river slows a bit above Number Three, which is complicated by a riverwide log just above it. The log can be portaged pretty easily through the huge undercut in the wall on the right. Below the portage, you launch directly at the top of Number Three, which has a few big boulders blocking the main flow and then a riverwide L-shaped ledge. This ledge must be run either far left or right because in the middle is a large pothole/cave that has been explored by a few paddlers. A large log is currently pinned vertically in the pothole, which is exactly where not to go.

Another pool lies above Number Four, which is difficult to scout from the top of the gorge but can be scouted (but not portaged) from river level on the left. This three-part rapid develops a couple of powerful holes at high flows. A swim in Number Four would result in a long swim through the rest of the gorge (and rapid Number Five) as the walls are totally vertical here. Boaters finish the gorge by running through some big hydraulics and twisty moves in Number Five.

Hazards

Vertical walls make escape from the gorge virtually impossible except by running the rapids. For this reason, the entire gorge should be scouted before committing to the run. This is most easily done by hiking downriver from the put-in on a good trail. When you are peering down into the gorge from 30 feet up, it is difficult to estimate the size of the holes. Stuff that looks inconsequential from above certainly does not feel that way when you are in it. Number One can be very dangerous at low water; scout carefully and set safety by having people on the banks to rescue someone if an accident occurs.

Access

The take-out is at River Bridge Campground. See the North Fork Rogue: River Bridge Campground to North Fork Reservoir run.

To reach the put-in, return to Oregon 62 and turn left. Travel 2.2 miles and turn left on NF 68, following the signs to Woodruff Campground. The put-in is at the bridge over the North Fork Rogue 1.8 miles from Oregon 62.

Gauge

Currently available via the Internet (Rogue River at Lost Creek Dam [inflow] gauge) (see Appendix A).

Jason Rackley and Pete Giordano

55 North Fork Rogue River
River Bridge Campground to North Fork Reservoir

Class: 3(4)	Length: 5 miles
Flow: 400–2000 cfs	Character: forested
Gradient: 40 fpm	Season: year-round

This is a beautiful run, with massive fir trees and clear, cold whitewater. The North Fork Rogue is one of the few rivers in Oregon where you can experience a combination of alpine boating and a hot summer sun, usually with enough water all summer. The rapids in this run, though easier than the upper North Fork section, have some of the same characteristics: lots of ledgy mossed-over lava rocks and the constant potential for sweepers. Many of the rapids are fairly technical and require catching an eddy before threading the needle between the rocks. Many of the rocks are the nasty type that lurk just below the surface and grab your boat at unexpected moments. There are plenty of class 3+ drops in this short run. There are two or three class 4 drops in the second and third miles. The routes through the rapids are generally easy to see and, if not, scouting is always possible. After reaching the reservoir, continue paddling 0.3 mile to the take-out.

Hazards

Sweepers are a constant threat. Scout the ledge rapids 1 mile below the put-in. A couple of ledges could form some sizable holes at flows over 1000 cfs. Other rapids may also require scouting to check for sweepers.

Access

To get to the take-out, drive an hour north from Medford on Oregon 62 past Lost Creek Lake until you see signs for the turnoff to Prospect. About 0.5 mile beyond the first turnoff for Prospect, Oregon 62 crosses an aqueduct. The dirt road immediately on the left past the aqueduct and paralleling it is the take-out road. Turn left and drive 0.25 mile to the North Fork Reservoir, the take-out. (If you reach the Prospect Ranger Station on Oregon 62, you've gone too far.)

Eddy-hopping on the North Fork Rogue River (Jason Rackley)

To reach the put-in, return to Oregon 62 and continue 3.8 miles past the Prospect Ranger Station to the sign "River Bridge Campground." Turn left and drive 1 mile to the river.

Gauge

Currently available via the Internet (Rogue at Lost Creek Dam gauge) (see Appendix A). The gauge is the total inflow into Lost Creek Lake, which is predominantly made up of the North Fork and South Fork of the Rogue River. Generally this section of the North Fork is 50 percent of the inflow. It is runnable most of the year.

Hayden Glatte

56 North Fork Rogue River
Mill Creek Falls to Lost Creek Lake

Class: 4+	Length: 3 miles
Flow: 500–1000 cfs	Character: canyon
Gradient: 94 fpm, C-PD	Season: snowmelt

This short but beautiful stretch of river begins and ends with 0.3-mile hikes to the put-in and the take-out. The run is well worth the extra effort. Along the entire length are high canyon walls, waterfalls, and stands of old-growth trees. Allow a full day to do the portaging and scouting and to enjoy the numerous play spots.

The put-in is just below the spectacular 173-foot Mill Creek Falls, which cascades into the middle of the Rogue. The run begins with a bang, with a gradient of 180 fpm. This translates into nonstop class 4+ action for the first 1.5 miles. Considerable scouting and possible portaging are necessary. The irregular basaltic rocks in the riverbed demand tight technical boating, and logjams are quite possible.

After mile 1.5, the discharge from the powerhouse on the right doubles or triples the flow. Below the powerhouse, the river becomes class 3 pool drop in character for the second half of the trip. Once on the reservoir, paddle a few hundred yards down the North Fork arm to Skookum Creek, which enters on the right. A good trail leads uphill to Mill Creek Drive.

Hazards

The first half, especially, requires scouting for routes and logs.

Access

To get to the take-out, drive north from Medford on Oregon 62. Go past Lost Creek Lake to Mill Creek Drive. Go up Mill Creek Drive 1.7 miles, where you will see a narrow turnout on the right with a sign that says "Camping

Prohibited." An old-road-turned-trail leads to the North Fork arm of the lake.

To get to the put-in, continue up Mill Creek Drive another 3.7 miles to Mill Creek Falls Viewpoint parking lot. Walk down the trail 0.3 mile to the actual viewpoint (a large map at the parking lot shows the trails). Near the viewpoint, a steep trail leads to the river.

Gauge

Currently available via the Internet (Rogue at Lost Creek Dam gauge) (see Appendix A). The gauge is the total inflow into Lost Creek Lake, which is predominantly made up of the North Fork and South Fork of the Rogue River. Generally, the North Fork below the powerhouse is 70 percent of the total flow, whereas the North Fork at Mill Creek Falls is 20 percent of the total. It is usually runnable when the total is 2500 to 5000 cfs.

Hayden Glatte

57 Middle Fork Rogue River Butte Falls Road to Lost Creek Lake

Class: 5	Length: 6 miles
Flow: 400–800 cfs	Character: forested; gorge
Gradient: 88 fpm, PD	Season: rainy/snowmelt

This is a steep run with the most difficult rapids in the first 2.5 miles on the Middle Fork and in the narrow gorge where the Middle Fork flows into the South Fork. Some of the gradient is 160 fpm. Brush, logs, and tight maneuvering provide ample opportunity for bridges, pins, and broaches, of which there have been plenty. Scouting and reasonable thinking carry the day.

After 2 miles of technical class 4 and 5 boating with some portages, the gorge appears—there is no mistaking it. The entire gorge should be scouted from the right before entering it. It contains three serious rapids, one class 5. If any of these rapids are jammed with logs, the only options are to hike 0.5 mile around the gorge or to hike up and out to the road on the right slope. The upper half of the rapids leading to the gorge can be portaged on the right, while the lower half is run down into the gorge. The second rapids, class 5, is a longer one, beginning on the Middle Fork, colliding into the South Fork, and continuing another 50 yards. The third rapids is a short class 4. None of these can be portaged due to the vertical gorge walls. Scout carefully before entering the gorge. It is no place for the faint of heart or the claustrophobic. Once out of the 0.5-mile-long gorge, the South Fork is class 3 to the lake.

On completing the run, paddle 0.25 mile out the South Fork arm of the lake and up the North Fork arm a couple hundred yards to where Skookum Creek enters on your left. A trail leads 0.3 mile up to Mill Creek Drive.

Hazards

This is an expert run. Class 4 and 5 rapids lead up to the gorge, and a class 5 in the gorge cannot be portaged. The entire run requires scouting. Before entering it, be sure to scout the 0.5-mile-long gorge. Attempting this run at flows under 400 cfs at the put-in is not recommended because many of the drops become unrunnable. A combination of rain and snowmelt is needed to provide enough water.

Access

To get to the take-out, drive north from Medford on Oregon 62. Go past Lost Creek Lake to Cascade Gorge, which is essentially a store on the right where Mill Creek Drive begins. Go up Mill Creek Drive 1.7 miles, where you will see a narrow turnout on the right with a sign that says "Camping Prohibited." An old-road-turned-trail leads to the North Fork arm of the lake.

To reach the put-in, continue up Mill Creek Drive to the town of Prospect and turn right at the Prospect Hotel onto Butte Falls Road. Go 3.7 miles to where the road parallels the Middle Fork; this is your put-in.

Gauge

Call the Army Corps of Engineers for the total flow into Lost Creek Lake, which is predominantly made up of the North Fork and South Fork of the Rogue River. Generally, the South Fork carries 30 percent of the total flow and the Middle Fork about half of the flow of the South Fork, or about 15 percent of the total inflow. Usually the Middle Fork is runnable when the gauge gives an inflow of 3000 to 4500 cfs.

Hayden Glatte

58 Big Butte Creek
Butte Falls Picnic Area to Crowfoot Road

Class: 3+(4)	Length: 12 miles
Flow: 400–900 cfs	Character: wooded
Gradient: 66 fpm	Season: rainy

Beginning among firs and ending among oaks, this run cuts through some wonderful country. It is creek-type boating with the usual hazards of small riverbeds and heavy vegetation. Expect several portages around logjams. The upper stretch is fast, continuous class 2 and 3 water with a gradient of 120 fpm. At some swift blind corners, very small eddies need to be caught. Butte Falls, a 15-foot runnable waterfall, is located about 1 mile into the run. If waterfalls are not for you, the portage is on the right. Progressing downstream, the character becomes more pool drop, mostly in the class 3 to 3+ range with an occasional class 4. All can be scouted or portaged at river level. Around mile 8, the gradient again becomes 120 fpm.

Hazards

Brush, logs, and the 15-foot runnable Butte Falls are the difficulties on this run.

Access

From Medford, drive north on Oregon 62 for 28 miles. Just past Casey State Park, turn right onto Crowfoot Road and go to any of the obvious take-out spots. The preferred take-out is 2.5 miles up Crowfoot Road to Netherlands Road, which crosses Big Butte Creek.

To get to the put-in, continue up Crowfoot Road to Butte Falls Road. Turn left and go just past the town of Butte Falls to Butte Falls–Prospect Road. After crossing Butte Creek, enter the picnic area, the put-in, about a mile from Butte Falls.

Gauge

None exists. The flow into Lost Creek Lake should be between 2500 and 3500 cfs. When judging the flow at the put-in, consider that about 100 cfs for irrigation is removed below Butte Falls.

Hayden Glatte

59 Grave Creek
6 Miles to Confluence with Rogue River

Class: 3	Length: 6 miles
Flow: 500–1000 cfs	Character: forested
Gradient: 42 fpm, PD	Season: rainy

This is a small technical stream with short, twisting blind drops in the section not visible from the road and very few play spots, just nice scenery. The run continues down to the confluence with the Rogue River and can include Grave Creek Rapid.

Hazards

Possible hazards include low swinging footbridges and brush along the bank.

Access

The take-out is at the boat ramp beneath the Grave Creek Bridge across the Rogue River (see the Rogue River: Grave Creek to Foster Bar run).

To reach the put-in, take the road toward Wolf Creek from the northeast end of the bridge. Follow this for 4 to 6 miles to a point where it returns to Grave Creek after winding up the hill.

Gauge

None exists. Flow is flashy and depends on rainfall. The author made the run when the Rogue was running 4000 cfs at Marial; however, it is unlikely that a dependable correlation can be made between the Rogue and Grave Creek.

Karen Wilt

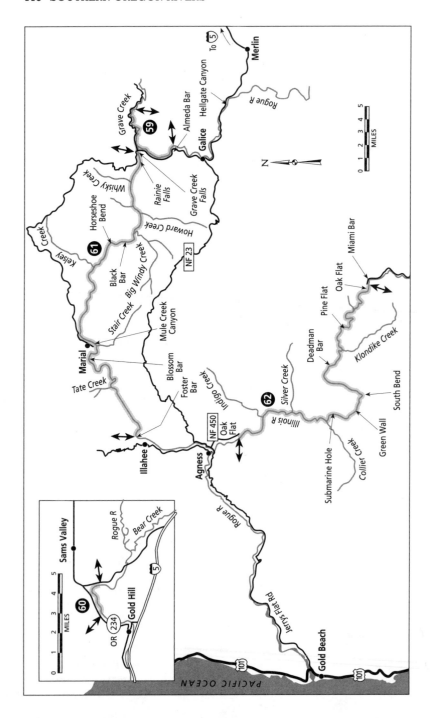

60 Rogue River
Above Nugget Falls to Gold Hill Boat Ramp

Class: 4-	Length: 2 miles
Flow: 800–3000 cfs	Character: forested; residential
Gradient: 20 fpm, PD	Season: year-round

This short run on the Rogue is gaining popularity because it provides enough good play spots and challenging rapids for an afternoon of boating. The put-in is in a short flat stretch, from which it is possible to paddle upstream to a rapids with some small play waves for warm-up. The first play spot downstream is at a broken weir, which has a hole in the right center. An excellent ender hole is located on the downstream edge of the broken weir, but use caution at lower flows since some boats have been folded here.

Nugget Falls immediately follows. This is a class 3+ or 4 drop, which can be run down the middle of the left channel. It is a good idea to scout the falls the first time down. Pull off on the left bank under the trees and take the trail to the rock bar. This is an easy scout, and the trail can also be used to rerun. A big surfing wave follows the drop.

Nugget is followed by a fairly long flat stretch that ends at the dam above Powerhouse Rapid (class 4). Either of two slots can take you through the dam, both of which are right of center near the downstream bend in the dam. The best route from here follows the base of the dam downstream, weaves through some grassy clumps, and follows the channel through the main class 4 drop that is nearest the island on the left. For those wishing to avoid the maneuvers described above, take the route on the far right side of the river where the dam joins the bank. This slot leads to a class 2+ route around the main drop.

Hazards

Nugget Falls and Powerhouse Rapid present some difficulties. Powerhouse cannot be scouted from the river, so must be scouted from Upper River Road on the east side of the river. Upper River Road turns off of Oregon 234 east out of Gold Hill just after the road crosses the river. Go upriver about 1 mile to a pullout on the left. The last drop can be seen from here, but the entrance is hidden by some trees. It may be a good idea to run Powerhouse with someone who has been through before, since the entrance is tricky.

Access

Gold Hill is near Interstate 5 between Medford and Grants Pass. Take Oregon 234 out of Gold Hill toward Sams Valley and Crater Lake. It is less than 1 mile to the take-out, a boat landing on the right.

A little more than 1 mile farther (in a long straight stretch), a gravel road turns off the main road and goes back to the river and the put-in. To make a longer trip, a class 2+ section can be added by driving a few miles farther up Upper River Road, where you can put in at a number of spots along the road.

Gauge

Contact the Grants Pass Filtration Plant or the *Grants Pass Daily Courier* (www.thedailycourier.com, 800-228-0457).

Garvin Hamilton

61 Rogue River
Grave Creek to Foster Bar

Class: 3+	Length: 35 miles
Flow: 1200–6000 cfs	Character: protected; popular
Gradient: 13 fpm, PD	Season: year-round

This run on the Rogue is one of the best-known whitewater runs in the United States. Flowing through the Siskiyou Mountains northwest of Grants Pass, it is classified Wild and Scenic, with the river preserved essentially in its natural condition. The banks vary from steep forested slopes to vertical rock walls. The river provides class 3 rapids connected by slower stretches and deep pools.

Recreational use of the Wild and Scenic section has a long and diverse tradition. Private lodges and cabins are located in several places, and many of these are reached only by boat or trail. Jet boats from Gold Beach originally delivered the U.S. mail but later took passengers on popular excursions; these boats can be seen cruising at water-skiing speed along the lower 12 miles of the Wild and Scenic section. Drift boaters have long floated the river for the fine steelhead fishing. Zane Grey's writings were inspired by the solitude and wild setting of his cabin at Winkle Bar.

The scenery, rapids, easy access, and possibility of 2- to 5-day float trips make this a very popular run. Permits, selected by lottery, are required. Leftover or unclaimed launching dates sometimes become available. Permit information may be obtained from Siskiyou National Forest, River Permits (14335 Galice Road, Merlin, OR 97532, 541-479-3735).

The Wild and Scenic section is a forgiving and enjoyable stretch of water. Dam-controlled flows normally are above 2000 cfs, and the river is runnable throughout the year. Warm summer weather, warm water, rapids ending in pools, and sandy beaches for camping make this a great place for a laid-back trip. One should expect to see lots of other people during the summer season, although the author's first trip was a cold and snowy one in February, when he saw no one else.

The Rogue River Map, published by Frank Amato Publications and available from the Forest Service, contains a handy blow-by-blow description, which to this writer seems unnecessarily replete with dire warnings. Follow it for the first few rapids and make up your own mind. Other accounts are given in *Wildwater Touring Techniques and Tours,* by Scott and Margaret Arighi; *Handbook to the Rogue River Canyon,* by Quinn's Staff; *The Rogue River Guide,* by Kevin Keith Tice; and *West Coast River Touring: The Rogue River and South Including California,* by Dick Schwind (see Bibliography).

Rainie Falls, 2 miles below the Grave Creek put-in, is the first of the two major rapids on the Rogue. It is mandatory to scout or portage Rainie Falls. In the next 20 miles, tributary streams, such as Russian, Howard, Big Windy, and Kelsey Creeks, provide pools for swimming, nice camps, and places to scramble up the streambeds. Numerous play spots can be found for kayaks, including an ender hole at Black Bar Rapid. Take care not to hurry.

At Marial the river takes a sharp bend to the southwest and enters Mule Creek Canyon. The narrow canyon, with vertical walls, is one of the run's few continuous stretches of whitewater (about 0.5 mile). Blossom Bar, about 1 mile below Mule Creek Canyon, is the Rogue's second major rapid. Many rafts have been hung up or destroyed on the boulders there. Tate Creek, about 7 miles below Blossom Bar, is a stop that should not be missed. About 0.2 mile up the creek is a pool with an exciting rock slide. The terrain above the slide is very beautiful and worth a hike.

Try not to be annoyed by the jet boats on the lower part of the river. This section also has lots of wildlife; it is common to see great blue heron, salmon, deer, otter, and bear.

Hazards

At Rainie Falls, a short portage trail is located on the left bank and offers the best place to get a close-up view of the falls, always fun to look at. Although the waterfall is run occasionally, most people run the small fish-ladder channel on the far right bank, while the more adventurous run the steeper channel through the middle of the rock "island" between the fish ladder and the falls.

In Mule Creek Canyon, the major problem is turbulence caused by constriction, rather than large waves or holes. Everything seems to wash out of here eventually, but several places have been known to hold boats, spin them around, or push them into the walls. Swimmers are difficult to pick up until they get out of the narrow part of the canyon, but even they should look around to appreciate the scenery.

At Blossom Bar, stop on the right and clamber up the rocks to scout. The run starts on the left side in a channel that ends in a bunch of boulders, so the next move is to the right into a center channel. At low water, this ends in boulders, so scout carefully and move fast. Dodge a few more rocks, and that is it.

Access

The put-in at Grave Creek is reached by taking the Merlin exit off Interstate 5, just north of Grants Pass, and proceeding west through Merlin and toward Galice. A popular put-in is 3 miles below Galice at Almeda Bar. The Grave Creek put-in is another 3 miles downstream at the bridge.

The shuttle to the take-out goes back along this same road just past the town of Galice, then over the mountains and west toward Agness on NF 23. After joining NF 33 at the Rogue River, follow it downstream 1 mile, cross the river, and go upstream to Foster Bar. NF 23 may be closed by snow early in the season, so check with the Forest Service or inquire locally. If the road is impassable, drive to Grants Pass, take US 199 south to Crescent City, take US 101 north to Gold Beach, and proceed upstream toward Agness. Shuttle services can usually be arranged at the Galice Resort.

Gauge

Currently available via the Internet (Rogue River at Agness) or by calling the River Forecast Center in Portland (see Appendix A). The Galice Ranger District provides the Grants Pass reading.

Bo Shelby

62 Illinois River
Oak Flat to Oak Flat

Class: 4+(5)	Length: 31 miles
Flow: 500–3500 cfs	Character: forested; remote
Gradient: 24 fpm, PD	Season: rainy

The Illinois, a crystal-clear tributary of the Rogue River, is one of the premier whitewater runs on the West Coast. In 1984 it received protection under the National Wild and Scenic Rivers Act. Flowing out of the Siskiyou Mountains south of Cave Junction, the Illinois runs in a northwesterly direction through the north end of the Kalmiopsis Wilderness. The canyons and mountains here are as steep and rugged as any in Oregon. The area is largely devoid of topsoil, but kalmiopsis, a plant in the heather family, grows here. Natural landslides and erosion are evident along the river. Look at the landscape and enjoy it, but treat it kindly. For a detailed description of the river, see *Handbook to the Illinois River Canyon,* by Quinn et al. (see Bibliography).

The Illinois is truly a wilderness river that tests both the skill and strength of boaters. Once a trip on this river is undertaken, boaters are on their own. The only trail is miles from the river and very difficult to reach except at Pine Flat. The whitewater is tough, even for the best boaters. Help is hard to get. Check the weather forecast, because a heavy rain can transform an 1800 cfs trip into an 8000 cfs nightmare.

The river is technical at levels below 800 cfs. Flows of 1000 to 1500 cfs seem to be the easiest, when most of the technical drops are flushed over enough to make them easier to run. Flows over 3000 cfs turn the river into boiling holes and rapids.

The first 10 to 12 miles are characterized either by pools with very steep class 4 boulder–bar drops of up to 10 feet or by long rock gardens. Between miles 4 and 5 are three class 4 rapids, with the third one, York Creek Rapid, being the biggest. Rivermile 7 brings the boater to Pine Flat, where the canyon opens into large meadows on both sides of the river. About midway through Pine Flat, the river swings to the left, offering what appears to be two channels around a large rock in the middle of the river. On the left side is a class 2 route that can be run except at low water. On the right side is a chute with a raft-stopping hole at the bottom. Scout this one carefully from the right. The hole is tougher than it looks. Rafts and kayaks have been flipped end over end in it. Pine Flat makes an excellent campsite for the first night of a 3- to 4-day trip. Backpackers are sometimes seen because this is one of the few places where they have access to the river.

From Pine Flat down to South Bend, the river continues in pool drop fashion through beautiful deep green pools and many nice class 2+ to 3 drops. Klondike Creek, named for the mining done along its banks, enters from the left about 2 miles below the last meadow of Pine Flat. Deadman Bar is a long straight bench on the right about 2 miles farther downstream. It is difficult to spot from the river because it is up a 35-foot rock bank. Several groups can share the grassy area without intruding on each other. Beware of poison oak when scrambling up the rocks, especially in the spring when the plant is not in leaf.

South Bend, at mile 17, should be called "Last Chance" because it is the last chance to camp before Green Wall. South Bend Bar is located on the inside of a tight right turn in the river. A large creek cascades down the left bank; a large pink boulder on the right marks the spot. Sometimes this campsite gets washed away. The next 4 miles are the toughest of the trip. Immediately below South Bend is a good class 3+ drop, followed in 0.5 mile by Fawn Falls, the class 4 rapids before Green Wall. Fawn Falls does not look like much on the approach, but a sweeping rock garden leads to a solid 3+ drop that cannot be seen from above. An eddy on the left next to a boulder at the bottom of the rock garden provides a good spot to scout the remaining portion of Fawn Falls. Two alternatives are available: One is the falls on the left, the other is the tricky S turn on the right.

A short distance below Fawn Falls is Green Wall, class 5. An innocent-looking rock garden, Prelude, leads into the main drop. Land left, well above the class 3+ lead-in rapids, or, if confident, catch the eddy on the left at the end of it. A portage here is a tough 400 yards through a maze of truck-size boulders. Scout Prelude as carefully as the main rapids. Below the lead-in is a very short section of relatively calm water followed by a drop of 7 to 8 feet. Take the middle or left channel; the right side is a keeper for all but the largest of rafts. Below are more rapids with water rushing into the Green Wall itself on the right and a big hole in the middle. Stay off the right wall.

From Green Wall to Collier Creek are three class 4 to 4+ drops and six class 3 to 3+ drops that are quite technical and challenging. Do not hesitate to scout if in doubt. Submarine Hole, class 4+, 3 miles below Green Wall, can cause problems, especially for rafters. It is readily identified by the huge boulder in the middle of the bottom of the rapids. Avoid the right slots. The canyon is steep and rocky through this 3-mile section, and no campsites are available.

The end of the major rapids is signaled by Collier Creek on the left at mile 21.7. About 100 to 200 yards below Collier Creek, a campsite may be found up the left bank. Other campsites are located 2 to 3 miles downstream and less than an hour from the take-out. Most notable is a site high above the river on the right at Silver Creek. Land on the downstream side of the creek, climb 30 feet to the trail, and follow it upstream, across the bridge, and up to the top of the bluff.

From here to the take-out, the river flows placidly through country that is a feast for your eyes. Sit back and enjoy it. You are one of the lucky ones who have run the Illinois.

Hazards

Expect eight class 4 to 4+ rapids. Some of the named rapids are York Creek, Pine Flat, Fawn Falls, and Submarine Hole. Green Wall, class 5, is considerably more difficult and longer than the others. The 3-mile section below Green Wall has the greatest concentration of difficult rapids.

Access

To reach the put-in at Oak Flat, drive west on US 199 from Grants Pass to Selma. In the middle of town, turn west on Illinois River Road. This becomes NF 4103. Drive 17 miles to Oak Flat at a broad gravel bar.

To reach the take-out, return to US 199 and continue to the Pacific Coast, then go north on US 101 to Gold Beach. Drive up Jerrys Flat Road along the south bank of the Rogue River for approximately 34 miles. After crossing the Illinois River, turn right onto Oak Flat Road, NF 450, and continue 4 miles to the broad grassy area of Oak Flat, the take-out.

An alternate take-out is located 4 miles downstream from Oak Flat, past the confluence of the Illinois with the Rogue, at a public boat landing on the right just downstream from Agness. Shuttle service can usually be hired at the Galice Resort in Galice.

River permits are required. They are free of charge at this time (2012) and can be obtained from the self-issue 24-hour kiosk at Ray's Food Place Market in Selma.

Gauge

Currently available via the Internet (Illinois River near Kerby gauge) (see Appendix A).

Ron Mattson

Upper Willamette and McKenzie Drainages

Region 4

Upper Willamette River and Tributaries

63 Brice Creek
Upper NF 22 Bridge to Champion Creek

Class: 4+(5) T,P	Length: 2.6 miles
Flow: 250–600 cfs	Character: forested
Gradient: 221 fpm, C	Season: rainy/snowmelt

Brice Creek, a tributary of the Row River, drains a relatively uncut section of the Umpqua National Forest. Its clear water, beautiful scenery, and great rapids make it a creek worth paddling. Upper Brice Creek is a nearly continuous series of class 4 rapids, with long boulder gardens, big holes, and steep drops. Road scouting is the best way to see what this section offers, but beware: It is harder than it looks.

About 0.75 mile above the road bridge is Parker Falls, a sloping 15- to 18-foot drop that is followed by a tough gorge (be sure to check for logs). The remainder of this upper section is relatively trashy, so a better starting point is the road bridge. Bubble Trouble, an 8-foot ledge at milepost 10, should be scouted because it develops a nasty hydraulic at high flows. Several hundred yards below this ledge is The Snake, a rapids that is usually portaged due to a pin spot (left) and undercut boulders (right). A group of three rapids starting 0.6 mile above the Champion Creek bridge should be noted. Orthodontists' Nightmare is a steep and short boulder drop with tight twisty moves. A hundred yards downstream is Le Mans, a twisty drop with a false right channel. Several hundred yards below this is Hop, Skip, Splat, which has pin spots and a terminal hole. It is normally portaged but has been run on the left. The run can be combined nicely with Lower Brice Creek.

Hazards
The run is very demanding. In many locations a boat could become pinned against a rock.

Access
The take-out is reached by taking exit 174 from Interstate 5 near Cottage Grove and following Row River Road eastward to Disston. At Disston, take Brice Creek Road about 8 miles to Champion Creek Road and a bridge, the take-out.

The put-in is 2.4 miles upstream at the first bridge or another 0.7 mile to a rough trail leading to Parker Falls.

Gauge
None exists. An inflow of 2200 cfs to Dorena Lake is adequate (see the Row River: Wildwood Falls to Dorena Lake run). For a close estimate of the Brice Creek flow see Pat Welch's Flow Page (see Appendix A).

Eric Brown and WKCC Editors

Threading the needle on Upper Brice Creek (Jason Rackley)

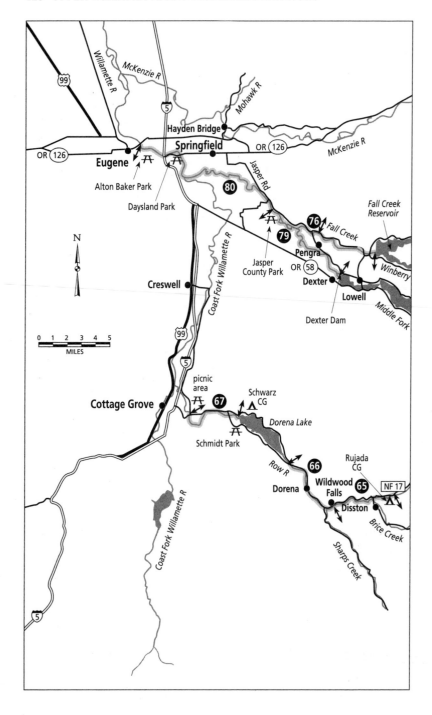

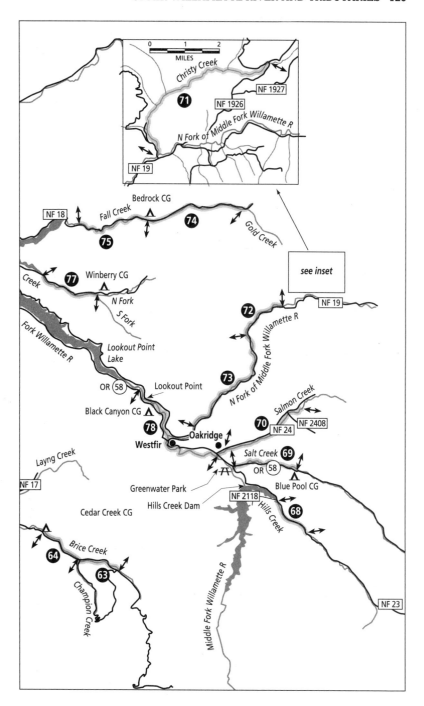

64 Brice Creek
Champion Creek to Cedar Creek Camp

Class: 4(5) T
Flow: 250–750 cfs
Gradient: 118 fpm, PD

Length: 3.6 miles
Character: forested
Season: rainy/snowmelt

This run is characterized by a narrow streambed with class 3 and 4 pool drop rapids spiced up by several larger drops, all of which are easy to portage. Scout carefully.

The first mile is the most difficult. Several small ledges are followed by three big drops. The first is Trestle Rapid. Scout left. The best line is to skid-jump off the end of the L-shaped ledge on river left, although runs down the center have been made. Just downstream is Arthur's Ledge; scout or portage left. At low water, the right route is advised, but at high flow a nasty hydraulic develops. Downstream 50 yards is Pogo, a tricky drop that has been run by dropping through a slot just left of the bedrock island. Scout from this island. About 0.5 mile downstream is Cheese Grater; scout from the left. Runs down the center have been made but take care.

From here, fun class 3 and 4 rapids break up occasional class 2 rapids. Around mile 1.8, logs have been a problem. At mile 2, a large class 3+ rapids named Fun (Gumdrop) splits around a house-size boulder; go left with enough speed to punch a sticky hole. The right is clogged with debris. Just downstream, on a sharp left-hand bend, is Not Fun, which should be checked for logs. Above the take-out 0.2 mile, a class 3+ rapids leads to a small eddy above Laura's Thighs, a class 5 crack. Scout or portage on the right. A side creek enters here. Just downstream is Cedar Creek Campground, the take-out. One can extend this run 1.2 miles with class 2 and 3 rapids by continuing to the road bridge.

Hazards

Large drops occur over step ledges with dangerous holes at the bottom or rocks that can likely pin a boat.

Access

The take-out is reached by taking exit 174 from Interstate 5 near Cottage Grove and following Row River Road east to Disston. At Disston, take Brice Creek Road 4.5 miles to Cedar Creek Campground, the take-out.

For the put-in, follow Brice Creek Road another 3.6 miles to Champion Creek Road. Put in just west of the bridge.

Gauge

None exists. The inflow to Dorena Lake (phone: 541-937-3852) should be 1200 cfs minimum; 2000 cfs is optimum. For a close estimate of the Brice Creek flow see Pat Welch's Flow Page (see Appendix A).

Eric Brown and WKCC Editors

65 Layng Creek
Rujada Campground to above Wildwood Falls

Class: 3(4); 4(5)	Length: 4.5 miles
Flow: 750 cfs; 4000 cfs	Character: forested
Gradient: 42 fpm, PD	Season: rainy

This exciting run is on a tributary of the Row River. It is normally class 3 to 4, but becomes a challenging class 4 to 5 run at flood stage. The entire run can be scouted from the road while running the shuttle. When nearby Brice Creek is too high or too low, Layng Creek can be a fun alternative. As usual, at higher flows the river is unforgiving to the unprepared. Just below the put-in is Rujada Falls, a 4-foot drop. Run left. About 0.5 mile downstream is The Plunger. At high water, it can be quite dangerous and should be scouted from the road. Below the confluence with Brice Creek is some of the most enjoyable whitewater of the trip. At high water, it is a fast, continuous flush, complete with large waves and big holes. Be sure to recognize the take-out just above Wildwood Falls. The falls have been run at high water.

Hazards
The Plunger and log strainers are hazards that should be checked from the road.

Access
Take exit 174 from Interstate 5 at Cottage Grove and drive about 16 miles east on Row River Road, past Dorena Lake. Turn left onto Lower Brice Creek Road at the signs to Wildwood Falls. Follow this road for 0.8 mile to the fabulous 16-foot falls. The take-out is above the falls in Wildwood Park on river right.

To get to the put-in, continue upstream to the intersection with NF 17. Turn left and go another 1.5 miles to Rujada Campground, the put-in.

Gauge
None exists. The inflow to Dorena Lake (phone: 541-937-3852) should be 1000 cfs minimum; optimum flow is 2000 to 4000 cfs.

Jason Bates and WKCC Editors

66 Row River
Wildwood Falls to Dorena Lake

Class: 2+(4); 3(4+)	Length: 6 miles
Flow: 500 cfs; 4000 cfs	Character: rural
Gradient: 33 fpm, PD	Season: rainy

This nice short run drops through little gorges, passes huge boulders, and several houses. The class 4 drop is a falls near the end of the run just above a covered bridge. It is normally run on far right but has been run by experts in the left chute at low flows. It is easily portaged on the left.

Hazards
The class 4 falls near the end presents the only difficulty.

Access
Take exit 174 from Interstate 5 at Cottage Grove and drive east on Row River Road. After about 4.5 miles, continue straight (right) onto Shoreview Drive and proceed to the head of Dorena Lake. After crossing the Row River, turn left onto Row River Road. Go 0.7 mile to a picnic area on the left that leads to the lake and the take-out.

To reach the put-in, return to Row River Road and head east toward Culp Creek and Disston. After 4.5 miles, at the junction with Lower Brice Creek Road, bear right and cross the bridge over the Row River. Go 0.5 mile and turn left into LaSells Stewart Park. The put-in is at the base of Wildwood Falls, river left.

Gauge
Above Dorena. Available via the internet, flow should be 500 cfs minimum. Optimum flow is 600 to 2000 cfs.

Jason Bates and WKCC Editors

67 Row River
Dorena Dam to BMX Park

Class: 3	Length: 4.5 miles
Flow: 300–1500 cfs	Character: rural
Gradient: 35 fpm, PD	Season: dam-controlled, rainy

This run includes four major drops (4 to 6 feet each) and several minor drops, all of which make this a quick, exciting run. The first quarter of the run winds through some narrow channels where riverside brush can be a hazard. Point of information: This Row rhymes with cow.

About 0.5 mile below the first bridge is a major drop that is 50 to 75 feet long. The rapid occurs on a hard right turn and scouting is advisable. At levels higher than 600 cfs, a narrow right channel can be used. About 100 yards below the first drop is a second major drop, which also should be scouted. It is usually run on the left, although at high water an exciting channel exists on the right. Within the next 0.5 mile is the third drop. Start on the right and guide through the slot on the left, coming off the 3-foot drop at the bottom.

The last major drop is 0.8 mile downstream, right next to the road (to the delight of passersby). Scout this rapid on the way up, and plan to hit the narrow slot. The remainder of the trip is less exciting, but it is still fun because of the many ledges that traverse the width of the river and the sneaky rocks that inhabit the streambed.

Hazards

Scout the first two class 3 rapids at the 0.5-mile mark. On the first trip down the river, scout the third major drop, 0.5 mile farther, and the fourth major drop 0.8 mile after that.

Access

Take exit 174 from Interstate 5 at Cottage Grove and drive east on Row River Road. After about 1.5 mile, turn left into the Cottage Grove BMX bike park, which is the take-out.

To reach the put-in, continue east on Row River Road and then straight (right) onto Shoreline Drive for 0.4 mile. Turn left into Schwarz Campground and drive back to the river. The gate to the park may be locked in the winter, necessitating a 0.2-mile carry.

Gauge

Available via the Internet (Dorena Dam discharge) (see Appendix A). Minimum flow is 300 cfs. Optimum flow is 500 to 1000 cfs.

Larry Mooney and WKCC Editors

68 Hills Creek
Upper Reaches to NF 2118 Bridge

Class: 4(5) T; 5 T	Length: 4 miles
Flow: 250 cfs; 700 cfs	Character: forested, canyon
Gradient: 109 fpm, C	Season: rainy/snowmelt

Hills Creek is one of the more demanding creeks in the Eugene area. Slides, falls, boulder gardens, gorges: This run has them all. About 0.2 mile above the bridge are back-to-back 20-foot and 12-foot falls. Unfortunately, these have collected a fair amount of wood in recent years, so running these is not advisable. Put in at either the base of the 12-foot falls or at the road bridge. The first mile is a series of class 4 boulder gardens, ledges, and slides. The creek soon straightens and narrows, which is the signal to eddy out right and scout a long complex series of class 4 and class 5 drops. The class 5 is an unmistakable hard right turn through a jumble of boulders with extreme pinning/broaching potential. Portaging right and seal launching at the base of this drop is the best option. After another 100 yards of rapids, eddy out left and scout The Plunge. Here the creek narrows after a left turn and gives the boater two options: Boof left over the guard rocks and land in a turbulent feeder eddy or hug the right wall and punch the beefy hole at the bottom. At high flows, most of the water slams into a deadly pothole/undercut on the right; portaging is probably a wise choice.

Class 2 to 3 rapids occur for the next 0.4 mile. On a hard left turn, the creek divides around a giant boulder and then descends into a turbulent, vertical walled gorge (class 4). This is a mandatory scout, either on the drive up or before committing to it. In the past, a root wad plugged the gorge at it narrowest point, with most on the creek going under it. The root wad is gone, but current logging in the area could change that. The remainder of the run has several class 3 to 4 rapids that are easily scoutable by boat. If the lake is low, class 2 to 3 rapids continue another 0.5 mile to CT Beach picnic area, an alternative take-out.

Hazards

The long, complex class 5 rapid and the vertical walled gorge should be scouted on the drive up. The latter is at milepost 2, and the former is another 0.4 mile upstream. Debris from logging in the area is also a continuous hazard.

Access

From Eugene, take Oregon 58 to Oakridge. After crossing Salmon Creek just east of town, go 1.2 miles and then turn right on Kitson Springs Road (NF 23) toward Hills Creek Dam. Go 4.2 miles on NF 23 to NF 2118, turn right and cross the bridge, the take-out. Return to NF 23, drive 3.8 miles upstream to the bridge, the put-in.

Gauge

None. The flow can be approximated by taking the inflow to Hills Creek Reservoir and dividing by 5 (winter) or 4 (spring). Phone 541-937-3852 for the flows.

Mike Haley

69 Salt Creek
McCredie Springs to Kitson Springs Road Bridge

Class: 3(4); 4(4+)	Length: 8.5 miles
Flow: 400 cfs; 1200 cfs	Character: forested
Gradient: 99 fpm	Season: rainy/snowmelt

Salt Creek is a small tributary that enters the Middle Fork Willamette River just east of Oakridge. It is fed mainly by snowmelt after warm spells in the spring, but large winter rainstorms occasionally bring the creek to a runnable flow. The continuous nature helps ease what many might call a steep gradient. Though play spots are few, the constant class 3 action creates an enjoyable cruising stream.

At mile 0.2, Luggage Inspector Rapid starts a series of class 3+ and 4 rapids. First-timers may want to scout on the right. At mile 0.3, Unclaimed Baggage Hole warrants a scout or portage on the right. At high flows, the riverwide hydraulic gets gruesome and a portage is recommended. For the next 1.3 miles, the river is an enjoyable 3+ roller coaster at high water and technical class 3 at lower flows. Remember to scout whenever the river drops out of sight. Beyond mile 1.6, the river maintains a steady class 2 to 3 personality, but watch out for blind turns and logs.

Hazards
Logs are a constant problem, especially in the first and last miles. Be especially aware of a potentially dangerous logjam immediately below the put-in.

Access
Take Oregon 58 to Oakridge. Continue past Oakridge for about 1 mile and turn right onto Kitson Springs Road toward Hills Creek Dam. After 0.2 mile, the road crosses Salt Creek at the take-out.

For the put-in, drive back to Oregon 58 and turn right. Proceed 8.1 miles and turn right into the parking area at the put-in.

Gauge
None exists. The flow can be approximated by subtracting the outflow of Hills Creek Reservoir from the inflow to Lookout Point Reservoir and dividing the difference by 5 (winter) or 4 (spring). Phone 541-937-3852 for the flows.

Eric Brown

70 Salmon Creek
1.5 Miles above NF 2408 Bridge to Fish Hatchery Road Bridge

Class: 3+(4+); 4-(5)	Length: 7.5 miles
Flow: 300 cfs; 800 cfs	Character: forested
Gradient: 63 fpm, C	Season: rainy/snowmelt

Salmon Creek is great for intermediate to advanced paddlers wanting to boat smaller volume runs. For less excitement, the mile-long class 4 to 5 gorge can be avoided by putting in at the NF 2408 bridge. The 3 to 4 miles of Salmon Creek above the gorge are a combination of shallow braided channels and more continuous stretches of class 2 to 3 whitewater, both of which contain a substantial amount of wood (logjams, partial blockages, sweepers); thus, running this upper section is not recommended.

After about 150 to 200 yards of warm-up, the run drops into a deep mile-long gorge. The entrance into this section is denoted by a massive moss-covered cliff on river left. Immediately after going far right through the "guard" logjam, the first rapid is a class 3+ slalom that opens into a log-choked gravel bar. After carefully maneuvering, eddy out left and scout the first of two long, complex class 4+ boulder gardens. Runs down the center or far left are recommended. The next 0.5 mile contains numerous smaller class 3 and 4 rapids and ledges, interspersed with copious wood. Scout what you cannot see around. The second class 4+ rapid soon occurs and should be scouted right. Runs down the right side are best, but at higher flows this rapid can be sneaked on the left side. Class 2 rapids remain to the NF 2408 bridge.

Below the bridge, the creek gives paddlers another 1.2 miles of a splashy class 2 until arrival at Salmon Creek Falls Campground. Here the streambed makes a hard right turn and plunges through a class 3 rapid that contains several big boulders. Be certain to inspect the channels before committing because the narrow slots in this drop often collect wood. Below the boulders, boaters negotiate a fun series of waves and crosscurrents. A swim here would be bad, as a few hundred yards downstream is Salmon Creek Falls (class 4). At the falls, the creek divides around a bedrock island with the right channel a nearly vertical 12-foot drop and the left side a long slide into a hole. Both sides are run easiest on the far right.

About 0.5 mile downstream, the creek crosses under the NF 207 bridge and signals the beginning of a class 3 mini-gorge. This several-hundred-yards-long rapid is a series of small slides and ledges that develop into beefy holes at higher flows. The entire gorge can be easily scouted and/or portaged along a hiking trail on the right bank. The next 2 miles are easy class 2 water, but stay alert for logs and fallen alder. As you approach the railroad bridge, eddy out right and scout the fish hatchery diversion dam. This is an easy class 3 slide, but it has collected a large number of logs in recent years. The remainder of the run is uneventful.

Hazards
The mile-long gorge contains quite a lot of wood debris and should be run with extreme caution. Salmon Creek Falls and the lower class 3 mini-gorge can be easily scouted on the drive up. Fallen trees are a problem, especially the last few miles. Be certain to scout the hatchery diversion dam before running it.

Access
From Eugene, take Oregon 58 to Oakridge. After crossing Salmon Creek just east of town, drive about 1 mile and turn left on Fish Hatchery Road. Continue up this road for 1.3 miles and again cross Salmon Creek. The north side of the bridge is the take-out.

To reach the put-in, turn right onto NF 24 and drive 5.2 miles to NF 2408. Less daring souls can put in at the bridge, while the more adventurous can drive 1.5 miles above the bridge and put in by scrambling down to the creek when it is again in sight of the road.

Gauge
None. The flow can be approximated by taking the difference of the inflow to Lookout Point Reservoir minus the outflow from Hills Creek Reservoir and dividing by 5 (winter) or 4 (spring). Phone 541-937-3852 for the flows.

Mike Haley

71 Christy Creek
NF 1926 Bridge to North Fork of the Middle Fork Willamette River

Class: 5 T,P; 5+ T,P	Length: 6.3 miles
Flow: 150 cfs; 400 cfs canyon	Character: old growth, clear-cut,
Gradient: 178 fpm, C,PD	Season: rainy, early snowmelt

This is a run for the adventurous expert boater. Log-choked channels and boulder sieves abound. Allow lots of time for scouting and/or portaging, go with a small, solid group, and bring your headlamp and bivouac gear. Also, be prepared to bounce off a lot of rocks.

After an easy mile, the bottom drops out and the creek descends 210 feet in the next 0.3 mile (that is 700 fpm). You must decide what is runnable and what must be portaged with difficulty along the right bank. The creek tapers off a bit after a log-choked drop around an island (the small left channel is probably the easiest), and soon the flow increases by a third. Very steep boulder gardens are intermittent between easier stretches. Logjams are very frequent. Some can be run; most are usually portaged with difficulty.

About 3.5 miles into the run, the wood finally disappears and better stuff beckons. In the next mile, the creek loses about 460 feet of elevation. First, an extremely steep boulder garden drops for about 150 yards and culminates with a 10-foot falls. Scout your lines from the right bank. In the gorge below, eddy out against the sloping left wall and scout a double waterfall that plunges about 20 feet. The portage around this class 5+ is obvious. A short distance below this falls, the creek cascades over an innocent boulder drop and then plunges 40 to 45 feet through a huge triple drop. The first is a big 20-foot sliding falls, then a retentive 4-foot ledge, and finally a 12-foot affair that splits around a central rock outcropping. Scout from the left. A bit below this huge rapid is another 30-foot sliding falls that splits into 3 pitches; scout it from the right.

The remainder of the run holds some tough class 5 boulder gardens and some fun slides as the creek tapers off. Eventually you will see a camp on the right bank and the creek will taper to class 2 for the last mile. The final hundred yards of class 4 to 5 are on the Miracle Mile of the North Fork of the Middle Fork Willamette. It feels like a large river after being on Christy Creek.

Hazards

Running out of daylight. There are many logjams and boulder sieves. The whole run is one long hazard, but it would be fun if it weren't for all the logjams in the first half of the run.

Access

From Eugene, take Oregon 58 to Westfir. Head up the North Fork of the Middle Fork Willamette (NF 19) to the take-out bridge that crosses the river just below the confluence with Christy Creek (NF 1925). To reach the put-in, continue up NF 19 for 1 mile to the next bridge that crosses the river (NF 1926). Take NF 1926 to the top of Christy Flats. It is about 3 miles to the put-in and hopefully there will not be snow blocking your way.

Gauge

Visual. The North Fork of the Middle Fork should be between 6 and 12 inches on the NF 1925 bridge gauge below Christy Creek. Visually inspect the creek at the put-in for between 100 and 300 cfs. If the shallow riffles below the bridge have 4 to 6 inches of water, you probably have a good flow. If more than 300 cfs are flowing beneath the bridge, you probably will want to go elsewhere.

Steve Stuckmeyer

72 North Fork of the Middle Fork Willamette River
Miracle Mile through The Gorge

Class: 4+(5) T; 5 T	Length: 4 miles
Flow: 300 cfs; 800 cfs	Character: old growth; canyon
Gradient: 106 fpm	Season: rainy/snowmelt
(first mile is 213 fpm)	

The North Fork offers exciting whitewater, superb scenery, and easy access. It flows into the Middle Fork Willamette River just below Westfir, near Oakridge. This section contains the Miracle Mile, a very steep, very tight, very technical section on which numerous professional and other hard-core kayakers have trained. Although many rapids along the Miracle Mile are named, it is best run for the first few times with someone who knows the complex, twisty routes, as well as the location of several dangerous logs. Eddies are small and difficult to catch. All except three drops can be scouted by boat. Whenever the run divides around an island, go left.

After 0.3 mile of easy class 2 to 3 water, the bottom drops out. In the mile between the two bridges, the gradient is 213 fpm. After zigging and zagging down the first few rapids (Initiation, Confusion), go left at the first island. Richochet and Shark's Tooth soon follow. The latter requires careful maneuvering to run an extremely narrow slot. Below the second island is Whoop-de-do, class 5. Scout or portage left. The run is mainly class 4 to 4+ down to the confluence with Christy Creek. Just around the bend below the second bridge is Dragon Slayer (class 5), a jumble of rocks in the river followed in 50 yards by a cliff on the right. The scout requires wading and gives boaters soggy sneakers. The bottom hole can cartwheel boats, suck boaters out of boats, or pin boaters to the bottom. After another long stretch of class 4 water, the river appears to turn right and plow into the canyon wall at Spinal Compression (class 5). Runs down the center or far right are possible, but a portage left might be more advisable.

Below Spinal Compression, the river mellows to class 2 to 3 for 1.5 mile. Another road bridge and high cliff walls on river left signal the start of The Gorge, a 0.5-mile-long section of class 4 rapids ending in a class 5 boulder garden. At high water, the hydraulics in this section are very powerful. The Gorge has three main obstacles: a drop on the right, a very large curling wave/hole that crosses the entire river about halfway through the section, and a tight class 5 boulder garden at the end. The slots in the boulder garden are barely wide enough for boats. Scout carefully from river right. Take out another 0.2 mile at the last bridge

Hazards

The Miracle Mile and The Gorge. The latter can be scouted on the drive up. Logs are ever-present in the very steep sections. Pinning and broaching potential is very high. Several of the holes are also extremely treacherous. Also check for logs and cables in the class 5 rapid in The Gorge.

Access

To reach the take-out, see directions to the put-in for North Fork of the Middle Fork Willamette River: Bottom of the Gorge to Westfir run. To reach the put-in, continue upriver another 4.8 miles to where the road is close to the river. Put in at one of the two muddy turnouts.

Gauge

The flow at the put-in is about half that at Westfir. See the North Fork of the Middle Fork Willamette River: Bottom of the Gorge to Westfir run.

Jason Bates, Jim Reed, and Mike Haley

73 North Fork of the Middle Fork Willamette River
Bottom of The Gorge to Westfir

Class: 3;4	Length: 8 miles
Flow: 750 cfs; 2500 cfs	Character: forested
Gradient: 33 fpm, PD	Season: rainy/snowmelt

The run below The Gorge is rated class 3 and has three noteworthy rapids: Shotgun, Bull's-eye, and Ledges. Shotgun is a twisting left turn with a small 3-foot drop that can be seen from the road. Bull's-eye can be recognized by a large rock that blocks the main channel on the left. Boaters may go either right or left of the rock, but some have been known to go straight over the top, giving it the name Bull's-eye. Typewriter, just below Bull's-eye, demands a right-to-left move to avoid a large hole on river right. Ledges is difficult to scout from either the river or the road. It consists of a narrow channel on the far left that becomes apparent only at the top of the drop. Ledges can be recognized by a wall of rocks on the left at the start of the drop. It is located near the end of the run.

Hazards
Shotgun, Bull's-eye, Typewriter, and Ledges are class 3 rapids that present some difficulties. All can be scouted from the river or from the road.

Access
Take Oregon 58 east from Interstate 5 south of Eugene at Exit 188. Proceed 32 miles and turn left to Westfir. A convenient take-out is the former log weighing station located about 0.75 mile upstream from the covered bridged in Westfir. An alternate take-out, above Ledges, is at a bridge 3 miles upstream of the covered bridge in Westfir.

The normal put-in is 8 miles upstream at the first bridge below The Gorge. Those who wish to run The Gorge as described in the North Fork of the Middle Fork Willamette River: Bottom of The Gorge to Westfir can put in just above the second bridge, allowing for a brief warm-up.

Gauge
For a close estimate of the flow see Pat Welch's Flow Page (North Fork of the Middle Fork Willamette) (see Appendix A). Alternatively, the flow can be estimated from the recording at 541-937-3852. Subtract the Hill Creek outflow from the Lookout Point inflow; divide by 2 to give the flow at Westfir.

Gene Ice and WKCC Editors

---

74 Fall Creek
Gold Creek to Bedrock Campground

Class: 3; 3+	Length: 8 miles
Flow: 500 cfs; 2000 cfs	Character: forested
Gradient: 55 fpm, PD	Season: rainy

This section of upper Fall Creek is paddled less often than the Bedrock run, even though it contains many of the same features as that section and is a bit easier. Class 3 paddlers who want to consider smaller creeks should find this to be a good training run. After 0.2 mile, the creek drops over a narrow 5-foot ledge. Scout and/or portage. The remainder of the run contains numerous play holes, surf waves, and several smaller ledges.

Hazards
In addition to the first ledge, which must be scouted, this run contains a few log-jams and several other near portages. Boaters should always remain alert for wood.

Access

The take-out for this run is the put-in for the Fall Creek: Bedrock Campground to Fall Creek Reservoir run.

To reach the put-in, continue on NF 18 another 7.5 miles to the bridge at Gold Creek.

Gauge

None. The flow is about 60 percent of that in the Fall Creek: Bedrock Campground to Fall Creek Reservoir run.

Mike Haley

75 Fall Creek
Bedrock Campground to Fall Creek Reservoir

Class: 3(4); 4(5)	Length: 9 miles
Flow: 800; 3000 cfs	Character: forested
Gradient: 42 fpm, PD	Season: rainy

The Bedrock section of upper Fall Creek is one of the more exciting and beautiful runs in the Eugene area. The worst drawback of this run is the unpredictable flow. With the exception of two difficult rapids, intermediate paddlers may consider the run. Be certain to put in below the riverwide log just downstream of the campground bridge.

Within 0.5 mile of the put-in is the first class 3 drop. It starts out with a riverwide ledge, then narrows considerably. The water in this slot is turbulent and will flip an unwary boater. This drop is usually run best on the left. Below here is a series of ledges and pools. Several class 2 and 3 rapids are interspersed in this green Eden. The beauty of the stream's banks contrasts with the water, which is usually muddy at high flows.

Beyond the second bridge, begin preparing for Fish Ramp Rapid, which can be very difficult and potentially dangerous with a strong guard hole at the top. Scout this rapids during the shuttle. It can be reached by a short unmarked road leading down to a BLM boat ramp. This is the only road leading to the river above the open rural lower section of the run. Immediately above the turnoff for this road, the main road follows the river for a short distance.

Between the last bridge and the reservoir take-out lurks the second class 4 rapids. It is a 6- to 7-foot steep slide into a diagonal hole. Scout this drop before attempting to run it.

Hazards

Scout Fish Ramp Rapid and the steep slide between the last bridge and the take-out. Intermediate boaters may wish to portage around Fish Ramp Rapid. Be alert for fallen logs such as the longtime log just below the Bedrock Campground bridge. At flows above 2500 cfs, this river is strictly for experts.

Access

From Oregon 126 on the east side of Springfield, turn south on 42nd Avenue, which becomes Jasper Road and passes through the town of Jasper. Continue past Fall Creek Reservoir, on its north side. The put-in is at Bedrock Campground, 7.5 miles upstream from Fall Creek Reservoir on NF 18. The trail just above the campground bridge leads to the river and sometimes looks more like a mudslide than a path. Be careful.

Boaters can take out either at Fish Ramp Rapid just downstream from the second bridge, at the last bridge, or at Fall Creek Reservoir.

Gauge

None. The flow can be approximated by multiplying the inflow to Fall Creek Reservoir (phone: 541-937-3852) times 0.75. Minimum flow is 500 cfs.

Doug Tooley and WKCC Editors

76 Fall Creek
Fall Creek Dam to Jasper County Park

Class: 2(3)	Length: 9 miles
Flow: 1000 cfs	Character: rural
Gradient: 10 fpm, PD	Season: dam-controlled

With the exception of the Willamette River and the McKenzie River at Hayden Bridge, this run on Fall Creek is the closest whitewater to the Eugene–Springfield area. It contains some excellent play spots that are good for beginners to try surfing. Because this portion of Fall Creek is not prone to flooding, fallen trees remain in the river, so watch where you are going.

The first 0.5 mile of the run is the most interesting, with a nice series of short class 2 rapids. Throughout the run are many good play spots with eddies on both sides of the river. The run ends with a class 3 rapids located just downstream from the Pengra covered bridge. The class 3 rapids can be scouted easily from the bridge. Decked boaters should have no problems with this rapids. Open canoes risk swamping in the 3- to 4-foot standing waves. Boaters who do not wish to run the Pengra bridge rapids can take out on river left, at the base of the bridge.

Just around the corner from Pengra covered bridge, where Jasper Road bends near the river, is a possible take-out. It is also possible to paddle down to the confluence with the Middle Fork Willamette River and then continue to Jasper County Park for an additional 4 miles.

Hazards

Some boaters may opt to scout the class 3 rapids just below the Pengra covered bridge.

Access

From Oregon 126 on the east side of Springfield, turn south on 42nd Avenue, which becomes Jasper Road. It passes through the town of Jasper, where the lower take-out on the Middle Fork Willamette is located across the river.

To reach the put-in, continue on Jasper Road to Fall Creek Dam access road and follow signs to the dam. The optional upper take-out at Pengra covered bridge is passed on the way to the put-in.

Gauge

Available via the Internet (USGS gauge: Fall Creek below Winberry Creek) (see Appendix A). Or phone 541-937-3852 for Fall Creek Reservoir outflow.

Doug Tooley

77 Winberry Creek
Winberry Campground to Fall Creek Reservoir

Class: 3+(5) T,P	Length: 4.8 miles
Flow: 300–800 cfs	Character: forested
Gradient: 45 fpm, PD	Season: rainy

Winberry Creek is perfect for an afternoon trip. It is one of the better runs of moderate difficulty that help one become accustomed to creek boating. The run can begin on the South Fork of Winberry Creek, which includes a short class 3 to 4 gorge, or at the confluence of the North and South Forks at Winberry Campground. Take special care on the first 100 yards of Winberry Creek and on the South Fork as the Forest Service has installed fish habitat logs. Immediately below the confluence of the forks, scout the class 3 slide for logs on the right. Downstream 1.7 miles are Bloody Elbow, a class 3 rapids that twists under a small bridge. Another 0.4 mile below is a gorge section that can be scouted from the road. This 0.7-mile gorge section is class 3+, with some class 4 water. Below the gorge 2 miles is Bridge Over Troubled Waters, a class 5 drop that has been run, but which has a very dangerous pin spot. It can be recognized by a 3-foot ledge 50 yards upstream of a definite horizon line. Portage on the left. Take out at the bridge above Fall Creek Reservoir.

Hazards

The pin spot at Bridge Over Troubled Waters is a severe hazard. Fallen alder, fish habitat logs, and logjams are recurring hazards in this narrow, steep creek.

Access

From Interstate 5 south of Eugene, take Oregon 58 east to Lookout Point Lake at Dexter. Turn left at the covered bridge, go through Lowell and north toward Unity. In Unity turn right onto West Boundary Creek Road. Proceed about 0.5 mile, turn right on Winberry Creek Road, and go 5.5 miles to the first bridge over Winberry Creek, the take-out.

The put-in is 5.6 miles farther upstream at Winberry Campground.

Gauge

Currently available via the Internet (Winberry Creek near Lowell gauge) (see Appendix A). Alternately, the flow can be approximated by dividing the inflow to Fall Creek by 4 (phone: 541-937-3852).

Eric Brown and WKCC Editors

78 Middle Fork Willamette River
Oakridge to Lookout Point Lake

Class: 2+	Length: 10 miles
Flow: 1000–3000 cfs	Character: forested hills
Gradient: 18 fpm, PD	Season: year-round

This is a beautiful run for a sunny day in October, when the discharge from Hills Creek Dam is increased and before winter rains have brought up other rivers. The banks are lined with trees, so houses and roads seldom intrude upon the landscape. The current is fast, creating frequent class 1 and 2 rapids of all shapes and sizes. It is a challenging run for the novice, exciting for most open canoers, and nice and splashy for more experienced boaters. You will probably see a number of drift boaters and shore-bound fly anglers; be courteous by giving them a wide berth.

Immediately below the Greenwater Park put-in is a long class 2+ rapids, which has lots of waves and crosscurrents but requires little technical maneuvering. At 3.5 miles, the river crosses under Oregon 58. There is a small Forest Service park, Ferrin Park, on river right just below the bridge. At 4.8 miles, a second bridge on the road leads to Westfir. There is a good eddy and road access on river left, just below the bridge. Immediately below this is Hell's Gate Rapid, a rocky and technical class 2 at low water and class 3 at high flows. The remaining 5 miles to the take-out are similar to the first half of the run, except that the highway is more visible and audible. Depending on the water level in Lookout Point Lake, the last 0.2 mile of the trip may be flat.

Hazards

Novice boaters, beware: There is no warm-up before the long, splashy class 2+ rapids near the put-in. Hell's Gate Rapid, just below the second bridge, is the most technically difficult of this section. It is easily scouted from the bridge on the road to Westfir.

Access

Take Oregon 58 east from Interstate 5, just south of Eugene, and proceed upstream about 28 miles to the take-out at Black Canyon Campground, at the

In the heart of the Miracle Mile, North Fork of the Middle Fork Willamette River
(Jason Rackley)

head of Lookout Point Lake. A boat ramp, which remains open later into the
fall than the rest of the park, sits at the park's downstream end.

To reach the put-in, continue east on Oregon 58 another 4 to 5 miles to
Westfir Junction. To continue road scouting, take a left, cross the bridge,
turn right toward Oakridge, and rejoin Oregon 58 in 1.3 miles, at the east
end of the Oregon 58 bridge over the Middle Fork. The put-in is at
Greenwater Park, at the upstream edge of Oakridge.

An alternate put-in is 2 miles farther upstream near the base of Hills Creek
Dam. This put-in appears to be popular with drift boaters, but this section
has not been run by the authors. It is reputed to be class 2 to 2+.

Gauge

Available via the Internet (Middle Fork Willamette Near Oakridge) (see Appendix A). Or phone 541-937-3852 for Hills Creek Reservoir outflow. In dry years,

enough water may not be released in July and August for a good run. If Hell's Gate Rapid, which can be viewed from the bridge, looks runnable, the whole run will have enough water.

Rob Blickensderfer and Rich Brainerd

79 Middle Fork Willamette River
Dexter Dam to Jasper County Park

Class: 2	Length: 8 miles
Flow: 2000 cfs	Character: rural
Gradient: 14 fpm, C	Season: year-round

The Willamette River makes its transition from the wild water of its upper reaches to the slower water found below Eugene on this and the Jasper County Park to Alton Baker Park run. The trip begins with the fairly turbulent and fast water discharged from Dexter Dam, and it continues at a brisk pace. The rapids are fairly small and straightforward, although at low water several exposed rock shelves require careful maneuvering.

About midway through the run is an area where trees have been deposited by high water and the river subdivides into several channels. The exact configurations of the channels and logjams can vary each year. Beyond this point the river is a little less steep. Take out either on the left at Jasper County Park, where picnic tables can be seen from the river, or at 0.2 mile downstream at the Jasper bridge.

Hazards
A potentially dangerous section is encountered about midway on the run where the river splits into several channels and logjams are present. At some flows, a portage may be required. The casual boater without solid class 2 experience should not attempt this run on the Willamette.

Access
Dexter Reservoir is situated along Oregon 58 about 18 miles southeast of Eugene. It is easiest to drive first to the take-out at Jasper County Park. The park is 0.2 mile upstream from the Jasper bridge on the south side of the river. A more convenient take-out is under the southern end of the bridge.

To get to the put-in, follow the road along the north side of the river through Fall Creek to Lowell and on to the base of Dexter Dam. The put-in is a bit of a scramble down riprap.

Gauge
Currently available via the Internet (Middle Fork Willamette at Jasper gauge) (see Appendix A). Alternately, phone 541-937-3852 for Dexter Reservoir outflow.

Rob Blickensderfer

80 Willamette River
Jasper County Park to Alton Baker Park

Class: 2(3)	Length: 14 miles
Flow: 2000 cfs	Character: residential; industrial
Gradient: 16 fpm, C	Season: year-round

Jasper County Park to Alton Baker Park is a popular summer run for Eugene residents and is the site of the annual Willamette River Race. Although racing boats try to finish this stretch in less than 1.5 hours, the run is more often enjoyed at a leisurely float pace. Do not expect a wilderness run here; rather, enjoy a gathering of happy folks, especially during the summer when hot weather drives rafts, canoes, and crafts of all pedigrees onto the water. Despite its popularity with novice paddlers, the river merits respect. During summer, the water is mild but rocks are plentiful. During spring, winter, and fall, the water can be brutally cold.

The run begins on the Middle Fork Willamette River at Jasper County Park or under the Jasper bridge. The water is fast with a few surfing waves for the first 5 miles to Clearwater Boat Landing on the right. The river then splits around a rocky island, resulting in whitewater on both sides. About 4 miles below, look on the left for the mouth of the Coast Fork Willamette River. The railroad bridge and the two highway bridges at the west end of Springfield are the best watermarks. Below these bridges is Day Island with Day Island Park on the right, a possible take-out. Beaver are often seen near or below the park.

Just below Day Island, the river offers Pizza Rapid, named for a local pizza establishment on the left bank. A flat section extends below this rapids to the weir at the head of the I-5 Rapid. A sign posted on the riverbank warns boaters that the coming stretch is the most dangerous on the river. (Do not expect to see this sign from the river.) The weir is about 100 yards upstream of the Interstate 5 bridge. At this point, you have a choice between two routes for the remaining 2 miles to Alton Baker Park:

1. For an easy paddle to Alton Baker Park, take out at the boat landing on the right above the I-5 Rapid. Portage 200 feet to reach the Canoe Path, a pleasant canal that flows to Alton Baker Park.

2. To continue downstream, scout the weir and the I-5 Rapid. They consist of a low rock wall and a broken weir with various slots, followed by a reasonably long rapids with a large wave at the bottom. The far right slot is the only safe route. Under no circumstances should any of the other slots be run, as debris and reversal action can make them unrunnable. Waves and holes become quite large at high water. Rafts are particularly prone to being trapped in the hydraulics behind the weir.

Below the I-5 Rapid, the river passes under two of Eugene's bike/footbridges. At the second one, about 1 mile below the I-5 Rapid, a large standing wave is encountered in the main channel on the left.

Boaters flock to this spot in the summer to do enders and prolonged surfs. The wave may be avoided by sneaking to the right. A mile downstream, the Ferry Street Bridge signals Alton Baker Park on the right and the end of the run.

A convenient circuit can be made by paddling from Alton Baker Park up the canal and down the Willamette. This loop obviates the need for a shuttle.

Hazards
The weir ahead of the I-5 Rapid is dangerous at all water levels. Do not attempt to run any slot except the far right. The the I-5 Rapid may swamp open boats at high water.

Access
Jasper County Park is on the south side of the Middle Fork Willamette River about 0.2 mile above the Jasper bridge. The town of Jasper is a few miles southeast of Springfield off Oregon 126. Jasper County Park offers good parking, but the carry to the water is about 50 yards. An alternate put-in under the Jasper bridge has less desirable parking but a shorter carry to the water. Another put-in or take-out is about 5 miles downstream at Clearwater Boat Landing, on the road between Jasper County Park and Springfield.

The take-outs are in Springfield and Eugene, respectively, on the north side of the river. The one above the I-5 Rapid is off Centennial Boulevard east of the Interstate 5 underpass. The Alton Baker Park take-out is near the junction of Centennial Boulevard and Coburg Road.

Gauge
The flow is regulated so that the minimum is runnable. Currently flows are available via the Internet (Willamette at Eugene gauge) (see Appendix A).

Gene Ice

McKenzie River and Tributaries

81 South Fork McKenzie River
Above French Pete Campground to Cougar Reservoir

Class: 3(4-); 4(5)	Length: 8.5 miles
Flow: 1500 cfs; 3000–4000 cfs	Character: forested
Gradient: 81 fpm, C	Season: rainy

For most McKenzie River boaters, the South Fork is just another tributary that enters the main river unnoticed somewhere between Rainbow and Blue River.

Above Cougar Reservoir, however, lies the free-flowing South Fork McKenzie River, one of the more interesting rivers of the Upper Willamette system. At flows above 2500 cfs, the South Fork is a superb experts-only run. At flows below 2000 cfs, the long rapids are no longer continuous and the South Fork is suitable for paddlers with a dependable roll.

Although the South Fork McKenzie drainage is adjacent to the North Fork of the Middle Fork Willamette River, it has greater fluctuations in flow. It is usually runnable only during or shortly after a hard rain. The spring snowmelt is undependable. Furthermore, some of the best rapids are exposed only during the fall and early winter when Cougar Reservoir is lowered.

The first half of the run consists of shallow and rocky class 2 rapids. Soon, however, side creeks begin to add volume and the gradient begins to pick up. Watch for logs. Below the confluence with French Pete Creek lies a long major rapids with holes and large waves. After French Pete Rapid the river quiets down for about 1 mile, to the bridge at the top of the reservoir. Below this bridge, the river cuts deep into mud walls of the lowered lake and the second major rapids follows. This rapids has two 90-degree right turns that can be run to the inside. Few eddies can be caught along this 0.8-mile stretch. The rapids finally comes to an end in the lowered reservoir.

The walk to the take-out is a bit muddy, but well worth the trouble. A welcome treat is a soak at the Cougar Reservoir Hot Springs on the way home.

Hazards
The run is very fast. The last rapids should be scouted.

Access
To reach the put-in, take Oregon 126 east from Springfield past Blue River and take the Cougar Reservoir exit on the right. Proceed to the top of Cougar Dam. From the dam, drive along the west bank. Toward the end of the lake on the other side of the reservoir is a boat ramp, which is the take-out. Proceed over the bridge across the South Fork. The take-out is to the left about 1 mile down the gravel road.

The put-in is to the right, toward French Pete Campground, about 8.5 miles upstream from the take-out.

Gauge
Currently available via the Internet (South Fork McKenzie above Cougar Lake gauge) (see Appendix A). Alternately, contact Cougar Dam (phone: 541-822-3344) for the inflow to Cougar Reservoir.

Gene Ice and WKCC Editors

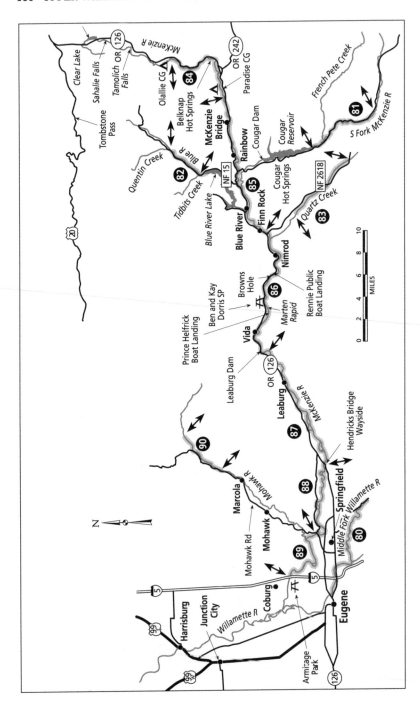

82 Blue River
Quentin Creek to Blue River Lake

Class: 4(5) T	Length: 5 miles
Flow: 250–900 cfs	Character: forested; logging
Gradient: 91 fpm, C,PD	Season: rainy/snowmelt

Blue River is a technically demanding, high-gradient tributary of the McKenzie River located only 39 miles east of Eugene. Approximately 0.5 mile below the Quentin Creek put-in is a class 5 triple drop called Food for Thought. This drop has been run successfully but may require a difficult portage on the right. The remainder of the river is class 3 to 4 and requires extensive scouting both from the road and the river.

Technical drops of 3 to 10 feet are numerous, as are extensive boulder gardens that require precise boat handling. Due to logging activity in the area, boaters should be wary of log debris and sweepers. From Tidbits Creek, located 1 mile from the take-out, the river broadens and flattens, building up for one last long boulder garden just before the take-out.

Hazards

Beware of logs. In recent years, dangerous logs have been obstructing the exit of Food for Thought and also several of the boulder gardens immediately downstream. Avoiding the first mile is often the best option.

Access

Take Oregon 126 east from Springfield toward Blue River. About 2 miles east of the town of Blue River, turn north from Oregon 126 onto NF 15. The take-out is located at a boat ramp at the upper end of Blue River Lake, about 4 miles from the Oregon 126 turnoff.

The put-in is about 5 miles farther, at the confluence of Quentin Creek and Blue River. If you wish to avoid the log-filled first mile, put-in at the bridge over Cook Creek.

Gauge

Currently available via the Internet (Blue River below Tidbits Creek gauge) (see Appendix A).

Ron Mattson

83 Quartz Creek
Milepost 7.5 Bridge to Milepost 2 Bridge

Class: 3+(4) T	Length: 5.5 miles
Flow: 250–750 cfs	Character: forested, logged
Gradient: 115 fpm, C	Season: rainy

If you are an intermediate creek boater looking to hone your skills on harder runs, Quartz Creek is one of the best in the upper Willamette Valley. This continuous little alder-lined creek is technical rock dodging at low water and a nonstop class 3 to 4 slalom at higher flows.

The put-in is a log-choked bedrock ledge a hundred yards downstream of the Mile 7.5 bridge. This class 4- ledge is runnable on the far left but some overhanging branches complicate the line. Warm up in the swirling eddy below the ledge because the continuous nature of the creek keeps paddlers occupied almost immediately. About 0.5 mile downstream, the creek splits around an island. The main right channel has an obvious horizon line with several vertically pinned logs and a large log forming a pour over. Run the drop far left or, better, portage on the island. The next 2.5 miles are mainly class 2+ intermingled with several class 3 drops. After the first bridge, some large boulders signal the beginning of larger, pushier class 3+ rapids that continue for 0.75 mile. After this section, the creek mellows out a bit and the drops get less concentrated. The last mile contains numerous waves and holes to play in, though some can be a bit shallow. The take-out is the fourth bridge over the creek. Below the take-out, the creek flattens out dramatically and becomes braided and log choked before finally flowing into the McKenzie below Finn Rock.

Hazards
The area surrounding the creek has been heavily logged, so wood is an ever-present danger. Though this section had no major logjams blocking the creek channel as of December 2001, that could change at any time. Remain alert for fallen alder and other sweepers, as well as for wood protruding from shore. The general fast pace of the creek could cause problems for swimmers.

Access
From Eugene, drive east on Oregon 126 along the McKenzie. Turn right onto Quartz Creek Road (NF 2618) just before the Finn Rock Store. Cross the McKenzie and continue up Quartz Creek Road for 2 miles to where a small road takes off to the right and crosses Quartz Creek, the take-out. To reach the put-in, continue up Quartz Creek Road 5.5 miles until you reach a bridge over the creek. The road closely parallels the creek all the way up, allowing paddlers to see much of the creek. Put in on the log-choked bedrock ledge a hundred yards downstream of the bridge.

Gauge
None exists, but a minimum flow seems to correlate with the South Fork McKenzie at around 1500 cfs (winter) and 1200 cfs (spring). A couple of days of heavy rain are usually needed.

Mike Haley, Jason Rackley, and Pete Giordano

84 McKenzie River
Olallie Campground to Paradise Campground

Class: 3	Length: 9 miles
Flow: 700–2000 cfs	Character: forested
Gradient: 60 fpm, C	Season: year-round

Within its tree-lined banks, the McKenzie rushes with almost nonstop rapids between Olallie and Paradise Campgrounds. This continuous run has few play spots. The first few miles are a fun, bouncy ride. At the first bridge, a wave on the left can be surfed at some water levels.

A few miles downstream lies Fishladder Rapid, class 3, the most difficult rapids on this run. It starts at a left turn just as you see powerlines ahead across the river. To scout, land on the right. This rapids is usually also scouted from the left during the shuttle. Pull off onto a dirt road at milepost 16, about 5 miles above Paradise Campground, and walk 100 yards to the river.

Below Fishladder, the river continues to offer miles of interesting rapids. Just across from the Belknap Hot Springs resort, look for an eddy and plumes of steam arising on the right. The hot springs add some welcome hot water to warm your cold hands during winter runs.

Paradise Campground is a fitting name for the end of the trip. Take out on the left.

Hazards

Fishladder Rapid should be scouted by those unfamiliar with it.

Access

Drive east from Springfield on Oregon 126 to the take-out at Paradise Campground, located about 4 miles east of McKenzie Bridge. Paradise is partially closed during the winter. Take a close look at the take-out to be able to recognize it from the river.

The put-in is at Olallie Campground, about 9 miles upstream on Oregon 126.

Gauge

Located at Rainbow. Currently available via the Internet (McKenzie River at Above South Fork near Rainbow gauge) or contact the River Forecast Center in Portland (see Appendix A). The minimum flow is runnable.

Gene Ice

85 McKenzie River
Paradise Campground to Finn Rock

Class: 2+	Length: 18 miles
Flow: 700–2000 cfs	Character: wooded; cabins
Gradient: 31 fpm, C	Season: year-round

A short distance below Paradise Campground, the McKenzie loses some of its continuous nature and takes on a pool drop character. A long boulder garden beginning at the town of McKenzie Bridge and ending above the covered Rainbow Bridge is one of the most significant rapids on this stretch. About 0.2 mile below Rainbow Bridge, where the river nears the main highway, is an S curve that ends in a rocky stretch with a strong diagonal wave on the right.

Below this, the river eases into a nice class 2 paddle for experienced open canoers with a good back-ferry. Play spots are few but are highlighted by an excellent ender hole just across from the Redsides log scaling station, about halfway down. Even decked double canoes (C-2s) can do incredible enders on the wave on the right. Paddlers sometimes spend a whole day here seeking the perfect ender. Below Redsides the river becomes flatter.

Hazards
The class 2+ stretches at Paradise and below McKenzie Bridge are the most difficult. Several log hazards have been seen in the section below Blue River in recent years. Look for hazard information posted at the put-in or call the McKenzie River Ranger District office (phone: 541-882-3381).

Access
Take Oregon 126 east from Springfield to the rest area at Finn Rock. Kayakers can take out here, but rafters will find the gentle bank across the river easier. To reach this, cross the river on the concrete bridge and turn left on the gravel road and then left into the boat ramp.

The put-in is at Paradise Campground about 15 miles upstream on Oregon 126 (see the McKenzie River: Olallie Campground to Paradise Campground run). Alternate put-ins are at the McKenzie trailhead 2.5 river miles below Paradise or McKenzie Campground 2.33 miles below Paradise.

Gauge
Located at McKenzie Bridge and Vida. Currently available via the Internet (McKenzie River at Vida gauge) or contact the River Forecast Center in Portland (see Appendix A). The minimum flow is runnable.

Gene Ice

86 McKenzie River Finn Rock to Leaburg Dam

Class: 2(3)	Length: 10 to 15 miles
Flow: 900–3000 cfs	Character: wooded; cabins
Gradient: 21 fpm, C	Season: year-round

When people speak of "The McKenzie," they usually mean the run from Finn Rock to Prince Helfrich Boat Landing. This run is one of the most popular day trips in Oregon. It offers rapids for paddlers of many skill levels, good scenery, and outstanding play spots. The run consists of long quiet stretches interspersed with exciting rapids and play spots. However, cold water is a danger to the unprepared.

Below the put-in 2 miles is one of the best play spots, Clover Point, just above and within sight of the bridge at Nimrod. It is identified by a large flat rock outcrop on the right bank. About 0.8 mile downstream is Eagle Rock Rapid, class 2, identified by the rock cliff on the left. The best ride is down the chute near the left side. A short distance below Eagle Rock is a long series of surfing waves along the left side. Pleasant class 1 and 2 water continues for several miles. Silver Creek Public Boat Landing is on the right at mile 4, followed in 2 miles by Rennie Public Boat Landing.

The most famous hole on the river, Brown's Hole, is next. It can flip a small raft or swamp a drift boat, but it can be easily avoided by staying to the right. Barely visible from upstream, it is located near the end of a straight section. A rock wall on the left about 30 yards upstream of a right jog marks Brown's Hole, about 15 feet from the left wall. For a thrill going downstream, kayakers can try to punch through the hole. If this is not enough, they can return to the hole and enter it from either side.

About 3 miles farther downstream, the river passes Ben and Kay Dorris State Park, with a boat ramp. Ahead is Marten Rapid, class 3, and an excellent hunting ground for scuba divers stalking watches, glasses, wallets, and other items "contributed" by unwary drift boaters, kayakers, and rafters. Marten Rapid can be a fun ride, but many people end up swimming through it. To run Marten Rapid, look for the largest boulder in the center of the river in the middle of the rapids; a good channel is about 10 feet to the right of the boulder at most river levels. Beware of the large hole on the right toward the bottom of the rapids. This is a notorious ender spot but should be approached only by competent paddlers. Most people take out 0.5 mile downstream at Prince Helfrich Boat Landing, marked by a suspension footbridge across the river. Boaters may continue on a few miles to any of several other accesses.

Hazards

Brown's Hole can flip a raft and be very sticky for kayaks at some water levels. It can be totally avoided by going on the right. Marten Rapid can be more violent than Brown's Hole and contains some dangerous rocks. The water temperature, even in the heat of the summer, is always cool. A long swim through Marten Rapid with little on but a swimsuit (quite a common occurrence) can be quite dangerous, especially without a life jacket.

Access
Put in at Finn Rock on Oregon 126 east of Eugene, 2.7 miles beyond Nimrod. Cross the bridge and turn left into the unimproved Finn Rock boat ramp, provided by Rosoboro Lumber Company. Some boaters with limited time choose to put in at boat ramps located 0.5 mile and 1 mile below, or about 4 and 6 miles below at Silver Creek and Rennie Boat Landings, respectively.

The common take-outs are Ben and Kay Dorris State Park and Prince Helfrich Boat Landing, located at the end of Thomson Lane, on the south side of the highway 1 mile below Ben and Kay Dorris State Park. Another take-out downstream is available at the boat ramp at Leaburg Dam.

Gauge
Currently available via the Internet (McKenzie River near Vida gauge) (see Appendix A). The minimum flow is runnable.

Gene Ice

87 McKenzie River
Leaburg Dam to Hendricks Bridge Wayside

Class: 2	Length: 15 miles
Flow: 900–2000 cfs	Character: agricultural
Gradient: 14 fpm, C	Season: year-round

This run is fairly quiet compared to the upper runs, but it is very enjoyable. The scenery is more typical of Oregon's agricultural countryside than the dense forests found upstream. The river meanders in deep pools around large islands and runs swiftly through sharp turns with tricky currents. Although some of the turns require careful attention, no major rapids are present until the very end. About halfway through the trip, the river runs under the only bridge, then past a golf course and some farmland. Most of the channels around islands appear to be open, but close inspection for the best route is required, especially at low water. One of the channels to the right becomes an irrigation ditch.

Hazards
The most significant rapid is about 0.5 mile above the take-out, identified by the high ridge on the left that slopes down to river level. The river drops to the right, forms some high waves, and then runs swiftly out through some large rocks. In general, some of the turns are tight with brush at low water and require controlled back-paddling by open canoeists.

Access

To reach the put-in, take Oregon 126 east from Eugene to Leaburg Dam, cross the dam, and use the drift-boat slide just below the dam. The take-out is at Hendricks Bridge Wayside, at mile 11.5 on Oregon 126.

Gauge

The flow is controlled by the Leaburg Dam. Contact the River Forecast Center in Portland (see Appendix A).

Gene Ice

88 McKenzie River
Hendricks Bridge Wayside to Hayden Bridge

Class: 2	Length: 9 miles
Flow: 900–2000 cfs	Character: agricultural; paper mill
Gradient: 11 fpm, C	Season: year-round

This run at Springfield's doorstep has much to offer and is an ideal run for beginning boaters. During the summer, the banks are lined with juicy blackberries and the cold water provides refreshing relief from the heat. Several surprisingly good rapids, including Hayden Bridge Rapid, are in store for paddlers.

The first few miles are quite calm and provide a good warm-up. In low water, some rapids near the top can be scratchy, but things get better. About halfway down, a tricky right turn has strong eddies on both sides. This is a good place to practice ferrying. Watch the trees and sky; on several trips eagles have been sighted. Do not look skyward too long, however. There is a rapids with large standing waves. This is a fine place for surfing, but the waves can be easily avoided on the left.

The biggest rapid, Hayden Bridge Rapid, class 2, is at the end of the run. The rapids is below Weyerhaeuser Paper Mill with its highly visible smokestacks. Eugene paddlers often come to Hayden Bridge Rapid to practice. The excellent eddies allow a skillful paddler to work to the top of the rapids.

Hazards

Hayden Bridge Rapid is difficult. The best channels are to the left. The rapids climax in a sharp left turn. Statistics say this is one of the most dangerous rapids in Oregon. The power of the water is certainly not the problem; it is the coldness of the water and the people who do not wear life jackets. Downed trees are usually present in the section above the rapids.

Access

From Interstate 5 in Eugene take Interstate 105 east to Mohawk Road. Hayden Bridge is about 0.5 mile north on Mohawk Road. The take-out is a boat landing on the left bank next to a water intake station.

To get to the put-in, return to I-105, travel east to the junction with Oregon 126, and drive east to Hendricks Bridge Wayside, which has a paved parking lot and boat ramp.

Gauge

Located at Vida. Contact the River Forecast Center in Portland (see Appendix A). The minimum flow is runnable.

Gene Ice

89 McKenzie River
Hayden Bridge to Armitage Park

Class: 1	Length: 8 miles
Flow: 900–2000 cfs	Character: agricultural; residential
Gradient: 7 fpm, C	Season: year-round

This run makes an excellent canoe paddle close to Eugene and Springfield. Though it offers very few rapids, it is pleasant. The most difficult rapids are just above Armitage Park but can be avoided if desired. One of the most enjoyable parts of this float is gliding by the Coburg Hills. After finishing the run, Armitage Park makes a fine spot for a picnic.

Hazards

None in particular.

Access

See the McKenzie River: Hendricks Bridge Wayside to Hayden Bridge run for directions to Hayden Bridge, the put-in for this run.

The take-out at Armitage Park is located on Coburg Road. *From the north:* Take the Coburg exit from Interstate 5, and turn south on Coburg Road. *From the south:* Take Interstate 5 to Belt Line Road. Follow Belt Line west to the first exit, Coburg Road, and go north.

The shuttle may be run via Interstate 105 or via the following route along back roads: Cross Hayden Bridge and take an immediate left on Old Mohawk Road. After about 1 mile, turn left on Hill Road and continue for about 0.5 mile. Turn left again on McKenzie View Drive, which intersects Coburg Road just across the river from Armitage Park.

Gauge

Located at Vida. Contact the River Forecast Center in Portland (see Appendix A). The minimum flow is runnable.

Gene Ice

Whitewater as far as the eye can see, North Fork of the Middle Fork Willamette River by Tim Goodfellow

Mohawk River

90 Mohawk River
Gate on Mohawk Road to Hileman Road Bridge

Class: 2(3-) T	Length: 5.8 miles
Flow: 400 cfs	Character: wooded; residential
Gradient: 39 fpm, C	Season: rainy

The Mohawk River, a tributary of the McKenzie River, drains a small valley devoted largely to logging and farming. This run is meandering, shallow, narrow, and continuous in character, and it has strainers. The river cuts through basalt for the first 2 miles and then through alluvial deposits. The first mile has several ledges, including one 4-foot ledge (class 3-) and a sloping 5-foot ledge under a bridge and into a pool. A high waterfall cascades down to the river on the left within this first mile.

Downstream the river flows quickly between easy riffles. In 1991, two large logs and two low wires spanned the river in the section between miles 3.5 and 5. At about mile 5, the river pours over a log that forms a 2-foot drop.

Hazards
The ledges in the first mile provide the most difficult whitewater. Downed trees are common, and logjams may be encountered. Two wires cross the river near mile 3.5 in the vicinity of several geodesic dome homes. The first is only 4 feet above the water; the second is about 10 feet up.

Access
From the mid-Willamette valley: Go to the put-in first. Take the Brownsville exit from Interstate 5 between Albany and Eugene and travel east on Oregon 228 to Crawfordsville. Turn south on Brush Creek Road 0.3 mile east of Crawfordsville. Go 8.2 miles to the intersection with Mohawk Road. Turn left (east) and go 1.6 miles to the put-in at a locked gate.

For the take-out, return to Brush Creek Road (its name changes to Marcola Road roughly 7 miles from Oregon 228) and continue south. The take-out is at the bridge on Hileman Road just east of Marcola Road.

From the Eugene area: From Interstate 5, travel east on Oregon 126 for about 2.5 miles to Marcola Road. Turn left (north). After crossing the McKenzie River at Hayden Bridge, go 15 miles to Hileman Road and the take-out bridge.

To find the put-in, continue north on Marcola Road (its name changes to Brush Creek Road) to its intersection with Mohawk Road. Turn right (east) and go 1.6 miles to the put-in at a locked gate.

Gauge
Currently available via the Internet (Mohawk River near Springfield gauge) (see Appendix A). A flow of 1000 cfs at the gauge is about 400 cfs at the put-in.

Steve and Sandy Cramer

Mid-Willamette Valley

Region 5

Marys River

91 Marys River
Blodgett to Philomath

Class: 1+(2)	Length: 19 miles
Flow: 400–900 cfs	Character: wooded; rural
Gradient: 10 fpm, C	Season: rainy

The Marys River flows east from the Coast Range to its confluence with the Willamette in Corvallis. It is a mild-mannered and isolated stream ideal for canoers and kayakers interested in scenery and mild whitewater. The rapids on the upper section are slightly easier and farther apart than the rapids on the last 5 miles near Philomath. The exception is the class 2 series of shelves about 0.5 mile below the covered bridge in Wren. Several options are available for put-ins and take-outs.

Hazards
The brushy banks and downed trees can present problems for novice boaters on this narrow stream. The class 2 shelves 0.5 mile below the covered bridge must be portaged at low flows.

Access
The uppermost put-in is about 1 mile downstream of the US 20 bridge in Blodgett, east of Corvallis (above here, the river is choked with wood). A popular put-in is at the covered bridge a few miles upstream from Wren; take Marys River Road along the south side of the river.

Other access points are the US 20 bridge in Wren and farther downstream at the Oregon 223 bridge in Wren. The lower take-outs are west of Philomath at the US 20 bridge or the Oregon 34 bridge, which is another mile downstream.

Gauge
Currently available via the Internet (Marys River near Philomath) or call the River Forecast Center in Portland (see Appendix A).

Bill Ostrand and Richard Hand

Calapooia River

92 Calapooia River
22 Miles above Holley to Bridge 13 Miles above Holley

Class: 3(4)	Length: 9 miles
Flow: 600–1000 cfs	Character: Wooded, remote
Gradient: 65 fpm, C/PD	Season: Rainy

This uppermost section of the Calapooia contains the toughest and most technical whitewater the river has to offer. Though the run is class 3 overall, the three most difficult rapids would be very difficult to portage, so come prepared to run at least one class 4 rapid. The road closely follows the river the whole way, making scouting possible on the drive up. The gradient numbers are deceptive: Though the average is 65 fpm, the section containing the short gorge is about 120 fpm for a mile. Always scout the boulder garden in the gorge before committing to it, preferably from the road because wood is almost always present in some of the chutes.

Warm up at the put-in because the river is quite continuous for the first 2 miles. Some class 3 whitewater leads to the gorge, just over a mile downstream from the put-in. Here the walls close in and the river takes a hard left and plunges through the biggest drop on the river. The hole at the bottom of the main chute is not the problem: Getting to it is the trickiest part. This jumble of boulders may be too shallow to run at lower flows. At higher flows, the holes here could become quite challenging, though a sneak route may open on the right.

Below this section, the river opens up again with some more fun, smaller drops. At mile 2.3, the river once again squeezes through another interesting boulder garden. The entrance moves here require care—scout carefully for undercuts. The next 5 miles are easier, but keep an eye out for logs and a few small but sticky ledge holes. At mile 7.5 is a long boulder garden that is considerably easier with many more lines than the first two—this one is clearly visible from the road on the drive up. Class 2 water leads to the take-out at the road bridge.

Hazards

The boulder garden in the gorge should always be scouted—a log in the wrong spot here could be dangerous. This rapid can be scouted from the road 8 miles above the take-out. Look for the obvious steep walled gorge when the road bends to the left. At optimal flows, this rapid is hardy class 4. Because of extensive logging in the area, be alert constantly for wood in the river.

Access

Follow the directions to the Calapooia River: Bridge 13 Miles Above Holley to Bridge 4 Miles Above Holley run. The bridge 13 miles above Holley is the take-out for this run. As of 2007, the road is usually closed by a locked gate at this bridge, eliminating vehicle access to the put-in upstream. However, the gate may occasionally be open during the fall hunting season. Contact the Weyerhaeuser hotline or website for information on these closures, 888-741-5403 or www.weyerhaeuser.com/businesses/recreationalaccess/oregon. The put-in is 9 miles above the take-out, down a bank, and through about 100 yards of mossy alders. A small logjam might be found just above the put-in. It is visible from the road and very easy to portage on the far left if you decide to put in above it for a longer run. The 3.7-mile section above the put-in can be run for a longer day. The river in this upper section is quite narrow and is continuous and scenic class 2 to 3 with a gradient of 95 fpm.

Gauge

None exists. This section is good a day or two after a storm when other rivers

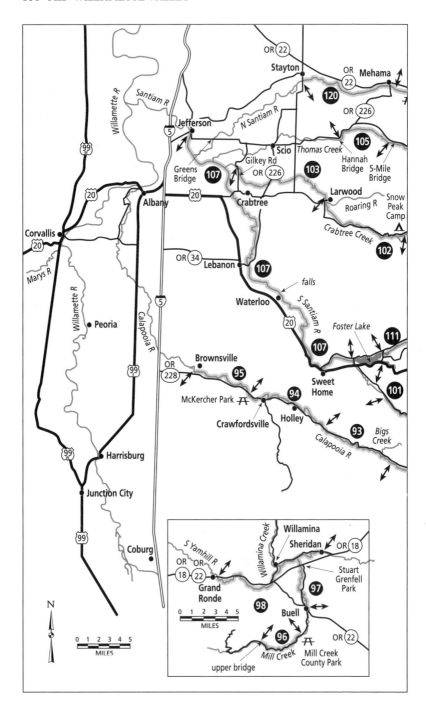

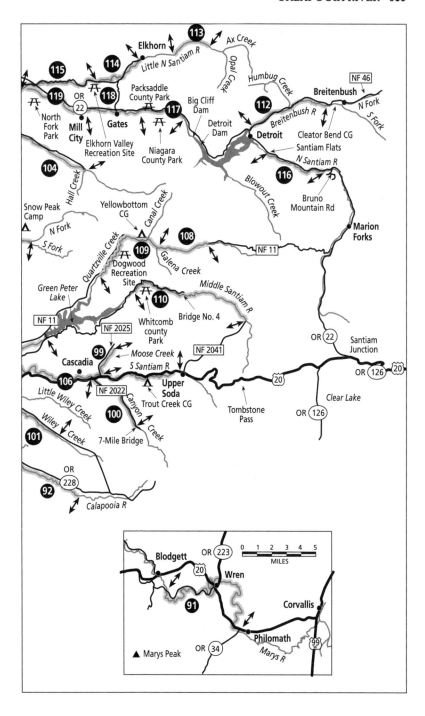

in the area are medium high. For a close estimate of the Calapooia's flow see Pat Welch's Flow Page (Calapooia River at Holley) (see Appendix A).

Jason Rackley, Mike Haley, and WKCC Editors

93 Calapooia River
Bridge 13 Miles above Holley to Bridge 4 Miles above Holley

Class: 3	Length: 10 miles
Flow: 700—2500 cfs	Character: forested; logging; residential
Gradient: 48 fpm, PD	Season: rainy

The beginning of the run is swift, with sufficient gradient and rocks to immediately lead the boater into class 2 to 3 rapids. Spend a few minutes warming up by playing on the easier waves near the put-in. Within several hundred yards, a rock-strewn section sweeps past a point occupied for years by a logjam on the right. At mile 1.5, the river veers to the right with a rocky class 3 drop.

Bigs Creek enters on the right at mile 2, and a single cable marks mile 3.2. Below mile 4, the channel narrows and a ledge develops a tricky curl that can produce a tail stand or dump a too-complacent boater. Below is the rocky rapid of The Narrows. Downstream 1 mile, look for a small brushy gravel bar and a prominent culvert protruding from the road fill on the right. This marks a short class 2 drop and interesting play spot. Dollar Drop, named for the former town of Dollar, is at mile 6.5, 0.2 mile after passing beneath a bridge. Pull out on the right to scout the 4-foot drop over a ledge. From here to the take-out, the water is class 1 and 2.

Hazards
Scout Dollar Drop at mile 6.5. A hazardous reversal forms along the left half of the base. The runout is reasonably good, with a good eddy on the right.

Access
From Interstate 5 between Albany and Eugene, take the Brownsville exit and turn east on Oregon 228. At the village of Holley, 4 miles upstream from McKercher Park, turn right on Upper Calapooia River Road. Three take-outs permit runs of 8 to 10 miles. The take-out for the longer run is at the bridge 3.6 miles above Holley. This take-out requires a difficult carry up a steep embankment. Much easier take-outs are up the road another 1.3 and 1.7 miles at undeveloped parking areas near river level. One is below and the other is above a side-road bridge.

The put-in is where the road forks to the right before crossing the river on a concrete bridge, 12.5 miles above Holley.

Weyerhaeuser Co. has recently (2010) installed a gate on the road 10.5 miles above Holley which may at times block access to the upper 2 miles of the run. Contact the Weyerhaeuser hotline or website for information on possible closures, 888-741-5403 or www.weyerhaeuser.com/businesses/recreationalaccess/oregon.

Gauge

None exists. The flow is unregulated. An estimated flow of 700 cfs at Holley is low but good. Flow fluctuates widely and rapidly in response to rainfall. The flow does not correspond to the Albany gauge. For a close estimate of the Calapooia's flow see Pat Welch's Flow Page (Calapooia River at Holley) (see Appendix A).

T. R. Torgersen and WKCC Editors

94 Calapooia River
Bridge 4 Miles above Holley to McKercher Park

Class: 2	Length: 10 miles
Flow: 400–1200 cfs	Character: rural
Gradient: 18 fpm, PD	Season: rainy

On this run, the gradient slackens considerably compared to the upper run. The relatively easy rapids and numerous riffles make it a good choice for open canoes. Two rather rocky rapids present within the first 0.5 mile. Along miles 2 and 3, the river winds its way through farmland but maintains reasonable speed. The most difficult rapid is over a rocky shelf 0.2 mile below the double bridges at Crawfordsville.

Hazards

Widely fluctuating storm-influenced flows make sweepers and debris jams potential hazards. The class 2 rapids just below Crawfordsville may warrant scouting; land on the left.

Access

From Interstate 5 between Albany and Eugene, take the Brownsville exit and head east on Oregon 228. At the village of Holley, 4 miles upstream from McKercher Park, turn right on Upper Calapooia River Road. The put-in is at the concrete bridge 3.6 miles from Holley on Upper Calapooia River Road. The parking place is good but requires a carry that is a little steep. The bridge at McClun Road, 2 miles above Holley, is an alternate put-in.

The take-out is at McKercher Park, 5.8 miles east of Brownsville. A good landing can be made at the upstream end of the park. Be certain not to overrun the take-out, as a class 4 rapids arises a few hundred yards downstream.

Gauge

None exists. The flow is unregulated. An estimated flow of 400 cfs at Holley is low but good. Flow fluctuates widely and rapidly in response to rainfall. The flow does not correspond to the Albany gauge. For a close estimate of the Calapooia's flow see Pat Welch's Flow Page (Calapooia River at Holley) (see Appendix A).

T. R. Torgersen

95 Calapooia River
McKercher Park to Brownsville

Class: 1 P	Length: 7 miles
Flow: 600-2000 cfs	Character: agricultural
Gradient: 11 fpm, C	Season: rainy

The gradient of this run is much less than that of the two upper runs. Here the river assumes a gentle, meandering course with occasional riffles and flows through pastoral country. This is an ideal stretch for a gentle canoe run. The section from Brownsville to Tangent is unrunnable because of logjams and brush.

Hazards
A former weir has been breached about 4 miles from the put-in. In low water conditions boaters should avoid the remaining rocks and remnants of an old wooden crib dam.

Access
From Interstate 5 between Albany and Eugene, take the Brownsville exit and head east on Oregon 228. McKercher Park is a quaint county park about 6 miles east of Brownsville on Oregon 228. The put-in is immediately below the falls at a small sandy beach. A good unloading point is the turnout at milepost 12, just after a bridge but before the park entrance. A short path leads down to the beach. The park offers picnic tables and rest rooms.

The take-out is on the right in the city park downstream from the bridge at Brownsville.

Gauge
The flow is unregulated. An estimated flow of 600 cfs at Holley is acceptable. Flow fluctuates widely and rapidly in response to rainfall. The flow does not correspond with the Albany gauge. For a close estimate of the Calapooia's flow see Pat Welch's Flow Page (Calapooia River at Holley) (see Appendix A).

T. R. Torgersen

Mill Creek

96 Mill Creek
Upper Bridge to Mill Creek County Park

Class: 3(4) T	Length: 5.5 miles
Flow: 400–1000 cfs	Character: forested; hilly
Gradient: 50 fpm, C	Season: rainy

At least five Mill Creeks are named in Oregon; this one flows from the Coast Range northeastward to the South Fork Yamhill River. The stream is quite narrow and gives one a more intimate feeling with the water than does any other river the authors know. From the put-in at the upper bridge, the water is fairly gentle for about 1 mile. Then comes the class 4 Triple Drop, which should be scouted on the drive to the put-in. This rapid has been run at estimated flows of 500 to 700 cfs; at lower flows, it appears too steep and rocky.

Just below Triple Drop, the river slows on a 90-degree curve to the left, then begins a 0.2-mile accelerating drop through The Gorge, with a dynamic class 4 ending. Once a boater enters this fast water in The Gorge, there is almost no turning back or getting out. Only a few small eddies can be used for stopping, and the rock walls are too steep to allow one to climb. To scout, first look upstream from the road for the whitewater at the lower end of The Gorge. Check for logs. Then go up the road about 300 feet and climb down to the creek. Although difficult, you can get down to creek level at a single place. Walk downstream as far as possible to see if the upper part of The Gorge is obstructed. The two major drops in The Gorge are bigger than they look from here. Below The Gorge, some stretches of the river are relatively quiet. After 0.5 mile, you will pass an island, and later another island.

The next landmark is a bridge, below which the road is on river left. Straight downstream from this bridge is a fast, steep drop. After another mile is the second bridge and the road is back on the right. Just below this second bridge is The Claw, class 3. At low water, The Claw has a large exposed rock area in the middle and the route must be picked. At high water, the rocks are covered. In either case, the bottom hole tends to reach up and claw at the sterns of boats.

The third and last bridge is 1 mile farther downstream and warns that you are near the take-out. The water picks up speed below this last bridge and leads to the final drop, The Twist, a 3- to 4-foot blind drop that is quite fast, with a turbulent runout. Take out immediately on the left, at Mill Creek County Park.

Hazards

Triple Drop is aptly named. It can be seen from the curve in the road at a pullout about 1 mile below the put-in. The Gorge is a mandatory scout, since a log block here could be fatal. The Claw, class 3, is easier than The Gorge. It can be seen from the road just a short distance below the second bridge. The Twist, the last drop, is straightforward and can be observed from the take-out at Mill Creek County Park, just opposite the parking lot.

Caution: Do not continue below Mill Creek County Park. Within 0.1 mile is a steep, twisting, narrow class 5 gorge that is often choked with wood.

Access

Weyerhaeuser owns most of the land on the upper river. The company maintains a gate blocking access to the upper river about 0.5 mile upstream of the take-out. Contact Weyerhaeuser at 888-741-5403 or www.weyerhaeuser.com/businesses /recreationalaccess/oregon to find out the status of the gate. It is occasionally open during hunting season in the fall.

Oregon 22 crosses Mill Creek about 22 miles west of Salem. Just west of the bridge, a crossroad runs along Mill Creek. Drive upstream 2.3 miles to reach the take-out at Mill Creek County Park.

Continue upstream another 5.6 miles to a concrete bridge, the put-in. Alternate put-ins can be found along the road downstream of The Gorge.

Gauge

None exists. The flow is unregulated. The run is best at high water after heavy or sustained rains.

Rob Blickensderfer and Steve Holland

97 Mill Creek
Buell County Park to Sheridan

Class: 2- T	Length: 10 miles
Flow: 500–1500 cfs	Character: forested; agricultural
Gradient: 21 fpm, C	Season: rainy

This run on Mill Creek is quite enjoyable at high water when numerous class 2 surfing waves develop. After 7 miles, Mill Creek empties into the South Fork Yamhill River, but because there is no access nearby, you must travel 3 miles down the Yamhill to the take-out in Sheridan. The 3 miles of the South Fork Yamhill, with its gradient of 5 fpm, are uneventful; but when Mill Creek has adequate water, the Yamhill rolls along, making it only a 15- or 20-minute trip.

Hazards

Trees can block the entire river, but the alert boater will find it possible to land in time.

Access

Oregon 22 crosses Mill Creek about 22 miles west of Salem. Just west of the bridge, an intersecting road runs along Mill Creek. Drive downstream 0.3 mile to Buell County Park, the put-in.

To reach the take-out in Sheridan, return to Oregon 22 and go west 5 miles to Oregon 18. Turn right and proceed 5 miles to the Sheridan exit. The boat ramp is in downtown Sheridan, one block upstream of the highway bridge on river right.

Alternatively, you can take out before the confluence with the South Fork Yamhill at Stuart Grenfell Park, just south of Oregon 18 on Harmony Road.

Gauge

None exists. The flow is unregulated. This run is runnable after long or hard rains.

Rob Blickensderfer

South Fork Yamhill River

98 South Fork Yamhill River
Grand Ronde to Sheridan

Class: 2(3) T	Length: 15 miles
Flow: 700–3000 cfs	Character: wooded; flat
Gradient: 10 fpm, PD	Season: rainy

This run keeps open canoers busy and entertains beginning kayakers with many good surfing waves. Put in at the upstream right side of the bridge on Oregon 18. Only 0.2 mile downstream is a 3-foot ledge, class 2, followed by 1 mile of riffles. At about mile 2 is an old log bridge followed by a highway bridge. About 0.5 mile farther is a small ledge drop. After another 0.5 mile is a second highway bridge. For the next 2 miles, a secondary road runs along river left.

Below the put-in 5 miles is a modern concrete bridge, and 1 mile farther is an old suspension footbridge. About 0.5 mile farther is a 1.5-foot ledge followed in 100 yards by a 2-foot ledge; 0.5 mile farther is another 2-foot ledge with a channel on the right. After another 0.5 mile the river passes under a very high concrete bridge, at Oregon 18, then an older concrete bridge, at Oregon 22, that provides reasonable access.

Just below here (mile 7.5) is another ledge rapid, class 2, with a maze of willows in fast water. After 0.5 mile is a steel bridge (which might be removed in the future; it is presently closed) near the town of Willamina. At mile 9, in the town of Willamina, Willamina Creek enters from the left. A mile downstream is The Ledge, class 3. A sawmill on the left bank is the landmark. Fast water leads to The Ledge. To scout, land on the left. The chute about a third of the way across the river from the right bank has been run at high water.

The river gradually slows as it approaches the town of Sheridan. A mile below The Ledge (at mile 11), Mill Creek enters from the right. A mile below Mill Creek is a maze of willows in medium-fast water. Two miles farther is the railroad bridge near Sheridan and the highway bridge in downtown Sheridan (mile 14). The boat ramp is on the right, one block upstream of the highway bridge.

Hazards

The Ledge, at mile 10, is difficult to scout because the riverbanks are so steep that it is hard to get out of one's boat. A fast riffle leading to The Ledge makes it difficult to get close enough in a boat to pick a safe route. Parts of The Ledge have potentially dangerous reversals. To scout, land on the left bank above the sawmill. The far left chute, and the chute about one-third of the way from the right bank, are feasible. Other ledges can be run by experienced boaters without scouting. Probably the second-greatest difficulty is willow trees growing in the river, especially at mile 7.5.

Access

Several accesses to the river are available and the choice depends upon the section to be run. The upper put-in is on Oregon 18 about 26 miles west of McMinnville (34 miles west of Salem), where a bridge crosses the river just east of the community of Grand Ronde. A parking lane and a good path to the river are on the west side of the river, between the highway and the railroad trestle. Other accesses are available along the road that follows the river from miles 3 to 5, south of Oregon 18 and 22.

Another access, a good take-out for a shorter trip, is at the Oregon 22 bridge on the downstream left bank. The bank is fairly steep, but a good parking area is situated above. In Sheridan, a boat ramp is located on the east side of the river, one block upstream from the highway bridge.

Gauge

Currently available via the Internet (South Yamhill at McMinnville gauge) or call the River Forecast Center in Portland (see Appendix A). The flow is unregulated.

Rob Blickensderfer

South Santiam River and Tributaries

99 Moose Creek
Cub Creek to South Santiam River

Class: 3(4+) T	Length: 4 miles
Flow: 300–800 cfs	Character: forested
Gradient: 105 fpm, PD	Season: rainy

Moose Creek, although short, is a nice intermediate run if you happen to be in the area. The run contains many short, fun boulder gardens and small ledges set in a pretty forested canyon. Most of the harder rapids cannot be seen from the road, but at most flows the rapids are easy to scout at river level. There is a tough rapid (class 4+) just upstream of the road bridge near the take-out that can be scouted by hiking down to the creek from the road.

Hazards

The narrow rapid just upstream of the road bridge should be scouted before the trip. Most boaters will choose to portage on the right. Logs can present problems on this small creek.

Access

US 20, east of Albany and Sweet Home, follows the South Santiam River. Turn left on NF 2025 2.25 miles east of Cascadia State Park. Bear left at the junction after 0.2 mile and continue to the bridge over Moose Creek. This is the take-out.

To reach the put-in continue upstream on Moose Creek Road until the road ends. Scramble down the steep bank to reach the creek.

Gauge

None exists. A flow of 1200 to 2000 cfs on the South Santiam River at Cascadia generally means adequate flow. The South Santiam gauge is currently available via the Internet (South Santiam at Cascadia gauge) (see Appendix A).

Pete Giordano

100 Canyon Creek
7-Mile Bridge to South Santiam River

Class: 5 T	Length: 7.5 miles
Flow: 200–1000 cfs	Character: forested; canyon
Gradient: 100 fpm, C/PD	Season: rainy

Canyon Creek is one of the few true class 5 creeks in Oregon. Steep, continuous drops with undercuts and log hazards make Canyon Creek an excellent run for expert boaters. Unstable geology also makes Canyon Creek one of the more dynamic creeks in Oregon, with rapid configurations changing every few years after big flood events. Only a couple of the big rapids can be scouted beforehand, so consider carefully before committing to the run.

The first 0.5 mile of the run is flat, with several logs, and gives no indication of the intense rapids found farther downstream. The first major rapid, Chocolate Chips, consists of a tricky ledge drop at the top and a narrow slot into a hole at the bottom. Scout/portage on the right. Another 100 yards downstream is the beginning of Chicken Little, a long, complex boulder garden that often contains wood. Several sharp ledges and steep boulder gardens follow Chicken Little all the way to Terminator. Boaters must run the narrow slot on the right to avoid being pushed into a dangerous sieve on the left. Scout/portage on the right. Immediately below Terminator is a very steep boulder garden, Day of Judgment. Most boaters run Day of Judgment by boofing down the middle to avoid sieves on either side of the rapid. Scout/portage on the right. More steep rapids continue for another mile before the gradient decreases and the rapids become smaller and less frequent.

Be on the lookout for a steep drop near the middle of this flatter section. Osprey Rapid can be scouted or portaged on the right. The mile above the take-out contains many fun class 3 to 4 rapids set in a beautiful canyon and is a great way to end the day after the challenging rapids upstream.

Hazards

Unstable geology can change rapids and deposit dangerous wood in many of the rapids. Large hydraulics develop at high water, making several of the harder rapids very dangerous.

Access

US 20, east of Albany and Sweet Home, follows the South Santiam River. East of Cascadia State Park 1.8 miles, US 20 crosses Canyon Creek. Turn north (left) on a short spur road that leads to the confluence of Canyon Creek with the South Santiam River, the take-out.

For the put-in, follow Canyon Creek Road (NF 2022) along Canyon Creek for 5 miles to a landslide that blocks the road. Follow the trail down to the creek. The trail begins next to the bridge over Black Creek. In order to reach the upper put-in, you must drive a long way around on forest roads that are often snowed in when the river is running.

Gauge

None exists. A flow of 1200 to 2000 cfs on the South Santiam River at Cascadia means adequate flow. Also, Canyon Creek generally has more water than Wiley Creek and less water than Blue River. All these gauges are currently

Warming up with a little air-time on Canyon Creek (Josh Knapp)

available via the Internet (South Santiam at Cascadia, Wiley Creek Near Foster, and Blue River below Tidbits Creek) (see Appendix A).

Pete Giordano

101 Wiley Creek Upper Bridge to Middle Bridge

Class: 4(5-) T	Length: 7 miles
Flow: 300–1500 cfs	Character: forested; canyon
Gradient: 102 fpm, C/PD	Season: rainy

Despite logging in the area, Wiley Creek remains one of the most beautiful creeks in the mid-Cascades. The moss-covered canyon has numerous fun class 3 and 4 rapids. The one drawback is a gate that is often locked on the road about 3 miles from the put-in. Still, the long hike makes this stream even more enticing. Once on the water, you soon forget the hike. The upper part is very technical, with a gradient of 160 fpm. The lower mile, below Cascade Falls, is through a wonderful class 3 gorge.

You will have little time to warm up as the run starts very fast in a tight, technical streambed with a gradient of 160 fpm. After 0.75 mile, eddy out and scout left at the first major horizon line. Ricochet, a twisty 8-foot flume, is more difficult at lower flows and can be easily portaged on the left. The next mile is continuous class 3 to 4 rapids with numerous blind corners. Careful scouting is a must as logs are an ever-present danger. At the end of this mile is Taint Natural, a three-tiered drop featuring a human-made fish ladder on river left. At levels higher than 6 feet, the drop is class 5. Scout/portage on river right. After another mile of class 3 water, the gradient lessens significantly for 2 miles until Cascade Falls. A boater can either shoot through another human-made fish ladder on the right or over the unbroken top of the ledge on river left. The mile below Cascade Falls is through a wonderful gorge containing several class 3 ledges.

Hazards

Beware of large holes at flows above 4 feet. Logs are a problem at times. Scout Taint Natural and Cascade Falls on the drive to the put-in.

Access

From Interstate 5 at Albany, follow US 20 east to Sweet Home and cross the bridge over Wiley Creek. Turn right on Wiley Creek Drive and proceed 3.7 miles to a junction. Turn right and cross Little Wiley Creek. Follow the road 0.7 mile to a fork. The bridge immediately on the right fork is the take-out.

To reach the put-in, continue upstream along the east bank for 3 miles. If the gate is locked, park and begin the long hike. If unlocked, continue about 4 miles upstream to a road bridge on the right.

Gauge

Currently available via the Internet (Wiley Creek at Foster gauge) (see Appendix A).

Eric Brown and Arthur Koepsell

102 Crabtree Creek
North Fork Bridge to Larwood Park

Class: 3 T; 4	Length: 10 miles
Flow: 700 cfs; 2000 cfs	Character: forested
Gradient: 91 fpm, C	Season: rainy

Crabtree Creek is located between the South Santiam River and Thomas Creek. It is easy to reach, enjoyable to run, and interesting, as the river makes the transition from mountain to valley. The upper 2 miles are tight and rocky. About 1 mile from the put-in, just past the confluence with the South Fork on the left, is an interesting class 3 plunge, worth a scout. The river sieves its way through large cobble-bar rapids in the middle section of the run, and the lower section has several large bedrock ledges that spice up the end of the run. Some of the rapids are fairly steep, and seeing the bottom of each drop is often quite difficult.

A heavy rain is needed to bring up the river to a runnable level. At bankfull flows, rocks and eddies disappear on the upper section and are replaced by large holes, great waves, brush patches, and trees. Cobble islands create blind channels that could dead-end in alder stands or possibly contain sweepers. Play spots are found everywhere on the lower part.

Hazards

At high flows, the brushy banks and the speed of the water eliminate most eddies. Sweepers could be a problem in this narrow streambed. Heavy logging in the basin and high water have combined to increase the presence of wood throughout the run. Most logs are on the bank but can shift from year to year.

Access

The upper 4 miles of the run are on private property and are usually closed to the public. Contact the Weyerhaeuser hotline or website for information about the closures, 888-741-5403 or www.weyerhaeuser.com/businesses/recreationalaccess/oregon. One can put-in at the concrete bridge at a locked gate for a class 2(3) run with a gradient of above 50 fpm.To reach Crabtree Creek, take US 20 east from Albany, then Oregon 226 east from US 20. A few miles past the Crabtree exit, look for Fish Hatchery Road. Turn east and continue about 7 miles to an intersection near Larwood Park. Go to Larwood Park, the lower take-out. To reach the upper, more common take-out, bear right (south) on Meridian Road just before reaching Larwood Park. After 0.5 mile bear left on East Lacomb Road, proceed another 1.8 miles, and make a left onto

Island Inn Drive. Head upstream following the river for 0.7 mile. The take-out is located at a pullout where the river is next to the road.

To reach the put-in, continue upstream for 1 mile to the first intersection. Turn right, and then immediately turn left onto the private logging road. After 1.2 miles, cross the river and continue up the road another 4.1 miles to a large parking area. Just past there, turn right and head downhill about 1 mile to the North Fork Bridge. The gate on the road may be closed, necessitating a 0.3-mile hike down to the bridge.

Gauge

None exists, but the level can be estimated from the take-out or at several places along the road on the drive up to the put-in. Generally, the areas visible from the road are shallower than the rest of the run. For a close estimate of Crabtree Creek's flow see Pat Welch's Flow Page (see Appendix A).

Lance Stein and WKCC Editors

103 Crabtree Creek
Larwood Park to South Santiam River

Class: 2-	Length: 15.5 miles
Flow: 600 cfs	Character: rural; wooded
Gradient: 14 fpm, C	Season: rainy

The lower river contrasts dramatically with the upper as Crabtree Creek empties into lightly wooded farmland. Larwood Park, where Roaring River meets Crabtree Creek, is an attractive place further enhanced by a covered bridge. This long stretch is divided into two sections.

SECTION 1: LARWOOD PARK TO OREGON 226 BRIDGE, 8.5 MILES

With a gradient of 21 fpm, the first 6 miles provide steady class 1+ and 2- water with a few play spots. The last few miles to Oregon 226 are still swift but with only occasional class 1+ riffles. An alternate put-in (the upper take-out for the Crabtree Creek: North Fork Bridge to Larwood Park run) a few miles upstream from Larwood Park provides a class 3- rapids and additional class 2 action. The take-out is at the Oregon 226 bridge.

SECTION 2: OREGON 226 BRIDGE TO SANTIAM RIVER, 9 MILES

With an average gradient of 7 fpm, the current slows dramatically and the river loses some of its open feeling as the bank vegetation thickens. Herons and beavers call this section home and occasionally add a surprise to an otherwise silent drift. A few miles below the put-in, a barbed-wire fence extends most of the way across the river. At mile 4, under a railroad bridge, a class 2 ledge drop has a clear path down the center. Take out at the bridge. Alternatively, one can continue a few miles down the South Santiam and then the main Santiam to Jefferson, thus adding 8 miles.

Hazards

The barbed-wire fence across the river a few miles below the Oregon 226 bridge is dangerous.

Access

Take US 20 east from Albany to Oregon 226 east. A few miles past the Crabtree exit, look for Fish Hatchery Road. Turn east and continue about 7 miles to an intersection near Larwood Park; go left to the park. The Oregon 226 bridge, the take-out for the first section and the put-in for the second section, is between Crabtree and Scio.

To reach the take-out for the second section, go 1 mile west from Crabtree on Oregon 226, then 2.5 miles north on Gilkey Road toward Jefferson to the bridge across the creek near the South Santiam River.

Gauge

None exists, but this run is generally runnable throughout the winter and spring, especially after a good rainstorm. For a close estimate of Crabtree Creek's flow see Pat Welch's Flow Page (see Appendix A).

Carl Landsness

104 Thomas Creek
Hall Creek to 5-Mile Bridge

Class: 3(4) T	Length: 5 miles
Flow: 800 cfs	Character: forested; logging
Gradient: 68 fpm, PD	Season: rainy

Thomas Creek drainage is situated between the North Santiam River and Crabtree Creek. It is fed by winter rain runoff. The upper section of Thomas Creek descends in pool drop fashion through a steep-sided river valley that has limited access by road. A scenic 40-foot falls is 1 mile upstream of the put-in. A half mile below the Hall Creek put-in is a nasty chute that plunges directly into a wall from a pool trapped by several very large boulders. Scout and, possibly, portage on the left.

The next 2 miles of river provide easy class 2 and 3 rapids. The river then enters a narrow, forested canyon and descends toward the take-out in pool drop, class 3 rapids. The second major drop occurs at mile 3, at a constriction as the river bends right, away from a 20-foot vertical wall on river left. The last of the major drops consists of several ledges that form sticky hydraulics at high flows. The first ledge is the biggest and extends from the left bank to a large midstream boulder. This ledge can be punched with momentum on the left. A narrow sneak route exists on the right side of the boulder, but check for logs before committing.

Hazards

Three ledge drops located at 0.5 mile, 3 miles, and 4.5 miles below the put-in should be scouted and possibly portaged—most easily on the left. Thomas Creek flows through clear-cuts and thickly forested areas, so scout all drops for logs. A hazardous section occurs at mile 2.5, where a debris dam usually blocks part of the river.

Access

The entire run is on private property and is closed to the public by a locked gate at the take-out. From Interstate 5 near Albany, take US 20 east and then Oregon 226 east. Proceed 9.2 miles northeast of Scio. At the intersection of Oregon 226 and Thomas Creek Road, proceed 6.9 miles up Thomas Creek Road to a side-road bridge on the right, the take-out.

To reach the put-in, continue east along the north side of the river. Stay right at all intersections until reaching the ridge-top intersection, 3.9 miles from the take-out, and go straight at this intersection. Make an immediate right at the next intersection, 4.0 miles above the take-out. Descend to the river, pass the first two intersections, and turn right on one of the short access roads 6 to 7 miles above the take-out, or continue until the road ends just below Hall Creek, which enters Thomas Creek from the south.

Gauge

Currently available via the Internet (Thomas Creek at Scio gauge) (see Appendix A).

Curt Peterson and WKCC Editors

Punching through the Ledges on Thomas Creek (Jason Rackley)

105 Thomas Creek
5-Mile Bridge to Hannah Bridge

Class: 2+(P) T	Length: 9.5 miles
Flow: 900–2500 cfs	Character: forested; logging
Gradient: 40 fpm, PD	Season: rainy

From the bridge at the put-in, the river moves right along. Some rather steep rocky drops occur, but no blind drops as in the upper run. The rapids seen from Oregon 226 between Hannah Bridge and Jordan Bridge are typical of the difficulty of this run. The mean river gradient is close to 30 fpm for most of the river run; however, the gradient is much steeper in two sections. Between miles 3 and 4 above Jordan Bridge, the river drops 100 feet, and at the remnants of the Jordan Dam, the drop is about 20 feet.

Hazards
The old Jordan Dam and the chute below should be portaged. The main current sweeps under brush in several places. This run becomes class 3 at higher flows.

Access
For the put-in, see the take-out for the Thomas Creek: Hall Creek to 5-Mile Bridge run.

From Interstate 5 in Albany, take US 20 east and then Oregon 226 east. Proceed 6.5 miles east of Scio, to Camp Morrison Drive. The take-out is at Hannah Bridge, just off Oregon 226 on Camp Morrison Drive. An alternate take-out is the concrete bridge on Oregon 226, 3.5 miles east of Scio. Parking is limited at both areas.

Gauge
Currently available via the Internet (Thomas Creek at Scio gauge) (see Appendix A). Optimal flow is 1600 cfs.

Mark Hower

106 South Santiam River
Mountain House to Foster Lake

Class: 4(5+) P	Length: 3 to 19 miles
Flow: 800–3000 cfs	Character: forested; canyon
Gradient: 45 fpm, PD	Season: rainy/snowmelt

The upper South Santiam is magnificent. This run can be made only after substantial rainfall or snowmelt. The rapids are pool drop, and all the more difficult rapids can be portaged. The upper South Santiam can be divided into four short sections.

SECTION 1: MOUNTAIN HOUSE TO TROUT CREEK CAMPGROUND, 3 MILES

This class 2+ to 3- portion is somewhat of a rock scraper at lower water, but it is much easier than what lies ahead.

SECTION 2: TROUT CREEK CAMPGROUND TO US 20 BRIDGE, 3 MILES

Some flat water and some nice class 2 and class 3 rapids are found on this section. The highlight is Longbow Falls, an abrupt 3-foot drop with a fast entry. The runout from the falls is somewhat turbulent but free of rocks.

SECTION 3: US 20 BRIDGE TO CASCADIA STATE PARK, 5 MILES, CLASS 3 TO 4

This is the most exciting stretch of whitewater on the river. Most of these rapids are peppered with large rocks and require quick judgment and skillful maneuvering or a good roll and a strong boat. As in most high Cascade rivers, logs can be a problem. The Monster, 2 miles after the US 20 bridge, is class 5+ and should be portaged either up the left bank to the road or over the rocks on the right. This conversation piece makes a nice lunch spot. Crawdad Rapid, a small twisty drop only 20 yards below The Monster, looks easy but munches a lot of boaters.

A mile below The Monster is Tomco Falls, adjacent to Tomco Mill. This true waterfall has a 5- to 10-foot double drop. The height of the falls is usually about 8 feet; however, the estimate will vary as you scout it, go over it, and look back up at it. As the flow increases, the height of the drop decreases. The runout is turbulent but free of rocks and other rapids. The easiest portage is on the left, but at low water you may be able to portage over the rocks on the right.

Shortly after Tomco Falls, a series of large haystacks is followed by a small drop with a tricky hole that throws boats against the left wall. Eddies exist on both sides above the hole. Catch the right eddy and sneak the hole on the right. Shortly after this hole, the river narrows to less than 10 feet. The gap can be blocked by a log, hence the name The Plug. Below The Plug is a long gorge. On this most scenic stretch, the river runs for 1 mile between 30- to 50-foot-high rock walls. Notwithstanding the proximity of the road, you will likely feel incredibly isolated. The rapids in the gorge are less violent than those upstream. The gorge section ends at Cascadia Park. A gravel bar on the right, upstream from the bridge, is the take-out. Stairs and a railed path lead to the parking lot. This lovely park is complete with rest rooms, picnic areas, and a soda spring.

SECTION 4: CASCADIA STATE PARK TO FOSTER LAKE, 8 MILES, CLASS 3(4)

After 2 miles of relatively flat water is Tree Farm Rapid, class 4. This maze of rocks and turbulence can be scouted from Tree Farm Park during the shuttle. After Tree Farm Rapid, the river contains long flat stretches between rapids with good surfing waves. Below the recommended take-out, the river flows through a deep canyon with few rapids before reaching Foster Lake.

Hazards

Several rapids should be scouted before running: Longbow Falls, The Monster, Crawdad, Tomco, The Plug, and Tree Farm. The first three can be scouted from the road. The Monster (class 5+) is seen from a right turn in the road (driving upriver) about 1.5 mile downstream of the US 20 bridge. The Monster can be portaged on either side and requires some effort. Tomco Falls can be scouted from just beyond a deserted house in a cow pasture 0.5 mile above Canyon Creek; The Plug is scouted from just upstream of Canyon Creek; Tree Farm is scouted from the riverbank inside Tree Farm Park.

Access

Section 1: US 20 east of Albany follows the South Santiam River. The Mountain House Cafe is located at Upper Soda, about 24 miles east of Sweet Home. The uppermost put-in is along the road above Mountain House, where the river is visible. Above this put-in, the river makes a tumultuous 40-foot drop. Take out at Trout Creek Campground.

Section 2: Put in at Trout Creek Campground. Take out on the right at the US 20 bridge. Scout the take-out eddy, it may be small.

Section 3: Put in at the US 20 bridge on the right side of the river. If you want to warm up, put in farther upstream along US 20. The take-out is located at Cascadia State Park approximately 11 miles east of Sweet Home.

Section 4: Put in at Cascadia State Park or at the covered bridge about 1 mile downstream. Take out at the steep trail located at a small parking area near milepost 36 on US 20. The lowermost take-out is at Foster Lake on Quartzville Drive (just off US 20) just east of Foster.

Gauge

Currently available via the Internet (South Santiam at Cascadia gauge) (see Appendix A).

Chet Koblinsky, Rob Blickensderfer, and WKCC Editors

107 South Santiam River
Foster Dam to Jefferson

Class: 1 P; 2(4) P	Length: 3 to 40 miles
Flow: 900 cfs; 1500–3000 cfs	Character: rural
Gradient: 39 fpm	Season: year-round

Typical of rivers within the Willamette Valley are the tree-lined dirt banks, gravel bars, riffles, and sweepers on this run. The river flow is rather slow in most places, but the scenery is better than one might expect so near population centers. The run is divided into five sections that can each be run separately, each with its own put-in and take-out, or the sections can be combined as desired.

SECTION 1: FOSTER DAM TO SWEET HOME, 3 MILES

This short section has the most action on this run, with small, evenly spaced class 1+ rapids at low flows. At high flows, canoers find an exciting class 2 run. At flood levels, kayakers find many excellent surfing waves. The put-in for this section is a pleasant park at the base of Foster Dam on river left. The most difficult rapid is the S turn about 2 miles below Foster Dam. Just past the water intake for Sweet Home is a fine surfing wave as the river drops into the large pool at the take-out for this section, the boat ramp in Sweet Home on the south side of town near the bridge.

SECTION 2: SWEET HOME TO WATERLOO, 11 MILES

Warning: There is a falls at Waterloo. The put-in is the boat ramp in Sweet Home on the south side of town near the bridge. The only major rapid, US 20 Rapid, occurs 2 miles below Sweet Home as the river bounds off the highway embankment on the left. Large standing waves and strong eddies here provide an excellent spot for practicing surfing and ferrying. Beyond are only a few more small shelves before the river flattens out for the rest of the way to Waterloo Falls. Kayakers have run Waterloo Falls, class 4, at high water, but at low water novices have become stranded on rocks, necessitating rescue by the county sheriff river unit. Unless you are prepared to run Waterloo Falls, take out on the left above the falls, in Waterloo Park. An alternate take-out is about 4 miles above Waterloo at the bridge on McDowell Creek Road. The nearby landowners do not want people on their property; therefore, take out near the bridge within the public right-of-way.

SECTION 3: WATERLOO TO LEBANON, 5 MILES

The put-in is below the falls in Waterloo Park. The river flows nicely for the first 2 miles, then slows as gravel pit workings are seen and a dam is approached. The fairly difficult but mandatory portage of the 10-foot dam is on the right. Never attempt to run the dam in any type of craft because the backwash can hold bodies or rafts for hours or days. The take-out is on the left in the city park north of downtown Lebanon.

SECTION 4: LEBANON TO CRABTREE, 11 MILES

Put in on the left in the city park in Lebanon. The river is class 1 at flows up to 3000 cfs. It is characterized by flat water, gravel bars, and sweepers. A poor take-out with no boat ramp is at the bridge on Oregon 226 about 1 mile west of Crabtree. A good take-out on river left about 0.1 mile downstream of the bridge is available upon purchase of a permit from Linn County.

SECTION 5: CRABTREE TO JEFFERSON, 10 MILES

Put in at either of the take-outs mentioned above for the previous section. This section is similar in character to the previous section. After 8 miles, the North Santiam River enters from the right and the volume increases the last 2 miles on the Santiam River. The take-out in Jefferson is at a boat ramp on the right 100 yards downstream of the US 99E bridge.

Hazards

Rapids to watch for are those 2 miles below Foster Dam and US 20 Rapid. Waterloo Falls is normally portaged. The 10-foot dam below Waterloo *must* be portaged. *Never attempt to run the dam in any type of craft.*

Access

Put-ins and take-outs are given above for each section. The put-in for the entire run is a park at the base of Foster Dam on river left. From Interstate 5 at Albany, take US 20 east to about 1 mile east of Sweet Home and follow the signs to the park, which is about 0.5 mile north of US 20.

The take-out for the entire run is in Jefferson just east of Interstate 5 about 6 miles north of Albany. Take the Jefferson exit and look for US 99E; the take-out is at a boat ramp on the right 100 yards downstream of the US 99E bridge.

Gauge

Currently available via the Internet (South Santiam near Foster gauge) or by calling the River Forecast Center in Portland (see Appendix A). The flow is controlled at Foster Dam. A minimum flow of 900 cfs is maintained during the summer.

Rob Blickensderfer

Middle Santiam River and Tributaries

108 Quartzville Creek
Above Gregg Creek to Galena Creek

Class: 4+(5+); 5(5+)	Length: 6 miles
Flow: 700 cfs; 2000 cfs	Character: forested; mining
Gradient: 120 fpm, PD	Season: rainy/snowmelt

Clear water, old growth trees, and short, thrilling drops make a first trip down this section an unforgettable experience. That said, in a few places a missed line could have serious consequences, so be careful.

The run begins with a 0.5-mile warm-up section and then paddlers arrive at Technical Difficulties (TD), the longest single rapid on the run. TD starts out with a steep boulder garden and ends with an 8-foot ledge that is usually run middle or left. The boulder garden has a pin spot that has caused some problems in the past about halfway down. Look for a 2-foot pour over and boof left here. The rock in the pour over can be spotted from the road far overhead if you look carefully and the flows are right. Even grazing this rock can stall you enough that you slide back into the hole, so be careful here, too. Immediately below Technical Difficulties on a left turn with a small island in the middle of the river is Grocker, a fun ledgy drop that can be run on either side, although most boaters opt for the exciting 6-foot boof on the left side.

More fun drops continue as you work your way down the river. Immediately downstream of the first road bridge is Wrapped Bridge Rapid, a small rapid that contains the remains of the old road bridge on the right. Below Wrapped Bridge is Pick-Up Sticks, a rapid complicated by an enormous logjam blocking most of the flow. Some years it has been possible to run this rapid on the right, but currently the right chute is blocked with wood. Approach this drop carefully as most of the current plows into and under the logs in the middle—if you blunder into this one, they will not find you until summer.

The last major drop on this section is Double Dip, a very dangerous series of ledges that terminates in an evil, narrow pour over backed up by the wall on the left. Double Dip is the kind of drop where you could do everything right and still get the beating of a lifetime (or drown, for that matter). Double Dip should only be run after taking every possible safety precaution.

Hazards
Double Dip is extremely dangerous and should be portaged on the left. Be on the lookout for wood in several of the steep, narrow drops.

Access
From Interstate 5 at Albany, take US 20 east to Sweet Home. Take Quartzville Road (NF 11), which follows the river on its north side past Foster Lake to Green Peter Lake for approximately 25.8 miles to the bridge at Galena Creek. Alternate take-outs are just above Double Dip or at the bridge 27.8 miles from US 20.

The put-in is located about 31 miles from US 20 on the right before the bridge.

Gauge
The flow is unregulated. Currently available via the Internet (Quartzville Creek near Cascadia gauge) (see Appendix A).

Jason Rackley and Pete Giordano

109 Quartzville Creek
Galena Creek to Green Peter Lake

Class: 4; 5	Length: 10 miles
Flow: 800–3000 cfs; 8000 cfs	Character: forested
Gradient: 65 fpm, PD	Season: rainy/snowmelt

Lower Quartzville Creek is a good prelude to the upper run (see the Quartzville Creek: Above Gregg Creek to Galena Creek run). It does not have quite the gradient and is not as intense as the upper run, but its pool drop character still presents a challenge. At 800 cfs, stretches of relatively calm water culminate in 6- to 8-foot vertical or very technical drops; the whole run is quite rocky. At 1500 cfs, the run is at its easiest and play spots abound. Above 2500 cfs, large waves and holes punctuate almost every rapid, but routes are fairly easy to find. At flows of 6000 to 8000 cfs, it is a hardy class 4.

The most serious drops/rapids occur within the first and last 2 miles of the run. The three big ledges upstream of Yellowbottom Campground are definitely worth scouting. The first occurs after a hard left bend and can be scouted on the right. Just downstream a house-size boulder marks the spot of the second drop. At low flows, keep right and punch the hole between the boulder and the side of the cliff. At higher flows, a sneak chute on the far left is recommended. The third ledge is a bit farther downstream and is usually run on river left with momentum. The middle 6 miles are mainly class 2. Do not get too complacent as the few class 3 ledges (Tractor Beam, Bankshot) in this section have sticky holes that have surprised good boaters. Once past Dogwood Recreation Site, the rapids pick up again with several long class 4 boulder gardens that spice up this last section into the lake.

Hazards
Most of the ledges on this run have sticky holes that only get worse at higher flows. On the drive up, scout the first 3 ledges and the class 4 boulder gardens at the end of the run. Most other hazards are seen on the drive up or can be scouted easily once on the river.

Access
From Interstate 5 at Albany, take US 20 east to Sweet Home. Take Quartzville Road (NF 11), which follows the river on its north side past Foster Lake to Green Peter Lake for approximately 25.8 miles to the bridge at Galena Creek. Many people choose to avoid the first several ledges and put in downstream at Yellowbottom Campground at mile 24.8.

The take-out is at the first parking spot along the upper lake, approximately 16.5 miles from US 20. For a shorter run, Dogwood Recreation Site (18 miles from US 20) is a convenient take-out, but some of the best rapids are between there and the lake.

Gauge
The flow is unregulated. Currently available via the Internet (Quartzville Creek near Cascadia gauge) (see Appendix A).

Ron Mattson and Lance Stein

110 Middle Santiam River
NF 2041 to Green Peter Lake

Class: 3(4) T	Length: 20 miles (5 to 6 miles on lake)
Flow: 700–1500 cfs	Character: forested; wilderness
Gradient: 65 fpm, PD	Season: rainy/snowmelt

Because of the length of this trip, the long shuttle, and the paddle across the lake at the end, most boaters will opt to take 2 days to complete the trip. The first half of this run is the most pristine river run in Oregon's Cascades and the only Cascade wilderness run. The trip begins in a broad basin with scenic views of neighboring mountain peaks. Initially, rapids are class 1, providing a chance to take in the scenery. The tempo picks up at mile 3 with class 2 and 3 drops appearing frequently. About two-thirds of the way through the trip, a class 4 rapid is likely to have its main channel blocked with logs. After the class 4 rapid, the water is more consistently class 3.

The end of the wilderness is marked by a huge clear-cut that gives you a real appreciation of the unscarred vistas and huge trees you have just left behind. About a mile below this point, the difficulty of the river increases with a several class 3 to 4 rapids. The rapids are continuous at 900 cfs, featuring technically demanding boulder dodging among steep twisting drops around blind turns. At 2000 cfs, downstream visibility increases and scouting is necessary at only two places. This is not to say that the run becomes easier at higher flows. Boulders become holes, the speed of the river seems to double, eddies disappear, and twisting drops become screaming chutes of water dumping into waves or boat-eating holes. Save some energy for the 5- to 6-mile paddle across Green Peter Reservoir.

Hazards

The remoteness of the first half of the run would make rescue difficult. Scout the harder rapids from the river. Snow and mudslides make getting to the river difficult. Storms big enough to raise the river to a runnable level usually dump snow at Cool Camp, thereby closing roads. The Forest Service Ranger Station in Sweet Home (541-367-5168) usually knows about pass conditions.

Access

To reach the put-in, take US 20 east from Albany. Drive to Upper Soda on US 20, about 22 miles east of Sweet Home. Turn left on NF 2041. Drive over the pass at Cool Camp (3000 feet elevation) and down to the river. The road ends at a trailhead several hundred yards from the river.

The take-out is located at Whitcomb County Park. Follow US 20 east out of Sweet Home and turn left on Quartzville Road (NF 11). The park is located approximately 11 miles from US 20. In the past, it was possible to take out after the first 8 miles or run just the last 7 miles without paddling across the lake. These take-outs and put-ins are on private Weyerhaeuser property, and Weyerhaeuser currently restricts access. Consult a forest map for directions to these access points and call Weyerhaeuser for current access information.

Gauge

Flow can be estimated by subtracting the flow in Quartzville Creek from the total inflow to Green Peter Reservoir. Both these gauges are currently available via the Internet (Quartzville Creek near Cascadia gauge and inflow to Green Peter Reservoir gauge, respectively) (see Appendix A).

Bill Ostrand and WKCC Editors

111   Middle Santiam River
Green Peter Dam to Foster Lake

Class: 4	Length: 2 miles
Flow: 2000–4000 cfs	Character: canyon
Gradient: 36 fpm, PD	Season: dam controlled

Although short, this run offers some of the best whitewater available in the mid-Willamette area during the summer. Green Peter Dam has two generating turbines, each of which requires 2000 cfs. The flow from the dam is determined by electricity demand. When one turbine is in operation (also called one "unit"), the flow is up to 2000 cfs. If both generators are operating, the flow can be up to 4000 cfs. The water released comes from the bottom of the lake and is very cold, even on a very hot day. Abrupt releases change the nature of the run very quickly.

The last three rapids—Swiss Cheese, Scrawley's Wall, and Concussion—are the major rapids on the run. Swiss Cheese consists of several ledge drops that produce nice play waves at a flow of one unit. At two units, the ledges produce many large holes. The right is the usual route. Parties can regroup at the short pool before the second drop, Scrawley's Wall, where the river forms standing waves and can push the boater very close to the left wall. Another short pool provides a second regrouping spot before Concussion, the grand finale. Concussion is formidable and has lived up to its name at both water levels. At all flows, the right chute is recommended. Boaters generally catch the eddy on the right at the top of the rapid and then ferry across the current to the middle of the river to avoid a large hole. Several large holes and waves confront boaters before the rapid ends abruptly in the slack water of Foster Lake. The center chute has been run, but it contains a very dangerous rock sieve. Several good boaters have had close calls, and rescue in the event of problems is very difficult. Once boaters reach the lake, it is a short paddle to the take-out.

Hazards
Swiss Cheese, Scrawley's Wall, and Concussion present difficulties. A dangerous sieve lies in the middle chute of Concussion. Concussion can be scouted by parking at a spot 3.3 miles from US 20 and hiking down the steep bank to the river. Beware of abrupt releases from Green Peter Dam. Even in the middle of summer, the water is extremely cold.

Access
From Interstate 5 at Albany, take US 20 east to Sweet Home. At Sweet Home, take a left onto NF 11, the road to Quartzville at the upper end of Foster Lake. The take-out is 2.6 miles from US 20 on NF 11. A wide turnout on the right near a gate in the fence that parallels the road gives access to the river.

To reach the put-in, continue up the road along the river toward Green Peter Dam. Park at the first road to the right, 0.5 mile before the dam. Because the gate is locked, boats must be carried down the road. At the second gate, climb the fence and continue 50 yards to the river.

Gauge

The schedule for water releases can be obtained from Foster Dam 1 or 2 days in advance (see Appendix A).

Ron Mattson and WKCC Editors

North Santiam River and Tributaries

112 Breitenbush River
Cleator Bend Campground to Detroit Reservoir

Class: 4 T	Length: 8 miles
Flow: 400–2500 cfs	Character: forested; canyon
Gradient: 80 fpm, PD	Season: rainy/snowmelt

The Breitenbush River starts at the crest of the Cascades north of Mount Jefferson and is one of the major tributaries of the North Santiam River. This run is one of the best intermediate runs in the Cascades, with numerous rapids, crystal-clear water, and beautiful scenery.

This run is rated class 4 because the drops are so closely spaced and require technical precision to run, although the individual drops are mostly class 3. It might be said that the whole is greater than the sum of the parts. The pools are short, and the route is often not apparent until you are almost at the brink of a drop, and sometimes it is not visible even then.

SECTION 1: CLEATOR BEND CAMPGROUND TO ROAD BRIDGE, 6 MILES

This upper section has tight and technical rapids, with many class 3 drops. Short pools are found between the rapids and many eddies. Chutes are narrow, twisting, swift, and deep. Several blind corners should be scouted for logs by at least one member of the party. The run starts with one warm-up rapid before you encounter The Slot. This rapid has a deceptively sticky 4-foot ledge. It then races another 25 yards between sheer rock walls. About 0.5 mile below the slot is The Notch, a V-shaped ledge that is best run on the far right. Run the sticky hole just below a narrow gorge with caution on the right. Several larger rapids in the middle of this stretch should be scouted.

SECTION 2: ROAD BRIDGE TO DETROIT RESERVOIR, 2 MILES

This stretch is markedly different from the upper 6 miles. Big, pushy rapids are separated by small boulder gardens. Shortly below the bridge, boaters encounter an island on a sharp left turn. This is the lead-in to Barbell Rapid. Barbell Rapid should be scouted (not without difficulty) on the drive upriver, 2.4 miles above Detroit, since it is even more difficult to scout from the river. The right channel contains a sticky ledge that should be run on the right with momentum. The left side is a steep boulder garden. Much of the current pushes into the right wall at the end of the rapid. Be careful, as this wall is undercut. A half mile below Barbell is Woo-Man-Chew, a 7-foot waterfall that drops into a deep pool. Scout on the left by landing at the low concrete structure. Woo-Man-Chew looks a lot worse than it really is. At low and medium flows, a run down the middle with momentum is pretty forgiving. At high water, this drop can recycle boats and swimmers—particularly boaters using small boats—for extended periods of time. When Detroit Reservoir is full, the lake reaches just above the small, unnamed Forest Service campground just upstream of Detroit. When the reservoir is low, the rapids continue past the town of Detroit.

Hazards
This river requires a class 4 level of concentration and quick reactions. A quick reliable roll is mandatory. Logs are always a threat, especially in the narrower upper section, so be sure to scout all blind drops.

Access
From Interstate 5 near Salem, take Oregon 22 east to the town of Detroit, at the east end of Detroit Reservoir. From Detroit, take NF 46 east toward Breitenbush Hot Springs. The take-out is at the Forest Service campground 0.5 mile upstream.

To reach the put-in, continue up NF 46 about 9 miles to the bridge above Cleator Bend Campground. To avoid The Slot or Notch rapids, carry boats down the steep trail opposite the small quarry about 1 mile below the normal put-in. This begins the trip just below The Notch.

Gauge
Currently available via the Internet (Breitenbush River above French Creek near Detroit gauge) (see Appendix A). Optimal flow for a first-time run is 400 to 800 cfs.

Rich Brainerd and Pete Giordano

113 Little North Santiam River
Old Mine to Three Pools (Opal Creek)

Class: 4(5)	Length: 4 miles
Flow: 700–2500 cfs (at Mehama)	Character: forested; canyon
Gradient: 100 fpm, PD	Season: rainy/snowmelt

Known to the boating community simply as Opal Creek, this section of the Little North Santiam is revered by advanced and intermediate boaters alike. This area has largely been protected from logging by old mining claims and the tireless effort of The Friends of Opal Creek and other local groups. From the beginning, boaters travel through spectacular old-growth forests, beautiful gorges, and an uncountable number of intermediate rapids with crystal clear water. The rapids are classic pool drop with small pools and numerous eddies throughout the run. This is simply one of the best intermediate runs anywhere.

Below the put-in are many fun rapids, mostly consisting of boulder gardens and a few tight chutes. Expect to do a fair amount of scouting your first time down, although all the drops can be boat scouted by experienced boaters. All the hardest drops have good recovery pools at most flows. Be on the lookout for a steep rapid that plows into two large boulders on the left before squeezing through a narrow slot on the right. The boulders create a dangerous sieve that can be avoided by staying right. About 50 yards downstream from another sharp right-hand corner lurks Big Ugly. Catch the small eddy on the right to scout/portage. Boaters tend to get slammed into the left wall at most flows, so be sure to boof right and stay upright. At low flows, a dangerous pin spot in the left chute suggests a portage. Below Big Ugly, another narrow slot should be scouted for wood.

Do not relax below Big Ugly as shortly downstream is Big Fluffy. At the sight of a dramatic cliff wall on the left and of mist rising below an important horizon line that disappears to the right, eddy out on the right to scout this 15-foot waterfall. Although Big Fluffy has been run at a variety of water levels, the hydraulic at the base has a reputation for punishing even the best of boaters. Scout carefully and set safety before deciding to run this one. The best portage route is to seal launch off the 16-foot platform directly below the falls or jump into the pool below the falls and collect your gear at the end of the pool.

Classic whitewater, classic scenery, Opal Creek (Jason Rackley)

Below Big Fluffy, the gradient tapers off and the canyon walls open slightly, although many more fun rapids are ahead. This section provides plenty of time to soak in the great scenery. Just as the scenery lulls you into a fuzzy state of mind, it is time to run Thor's Playroom. Thor's is a long rapid that can be broken into three sections. Several technical slots at the top lead boaters into a pushy middle section with swirly currents. The final drop that can be seen from the take-out has a powerful hole at the base that can easily separate people from their equipment. A big recovery pool lies just below this rapid.

Hazards
Several drops could pin boaters. Always scout for wood before committing to a drop. Approach Big Ugly and Big Fluffy with caution. Scout Thor's Playroom by hiking down to the river at the take-out.

Access
To reach the take-out, follow Oregon 22 east from Interstate 5 near Salem. After about 21.8 miles, turn left on Little North Fork Road. Turn right after 16.5 miles at the sign for 3 Pools Recreation Site. Stay right at the next fork, and follow this road to its end at the parking area.

To reach the put-in, return to the main road and turn right. The road ends at a trailhead after 4.5 miles. Hike along the road beyond the gate for about 0.5 mile to an old road on the right just after the bridge at Gold Creek. Follow it down to the river.

Gauge
Currently available via the Internet (Little North Santiam near Mehama gauge) (see Appendix A). This gauge is far downstream of the take-out, so it only approximates the actual water level of the run. The correlation between the gauge and the actual water in the run fluctuates depending on whether water is coming from snowmelt or rain.

Pete Giordano and Jason Rackley

114 Little North Santiam River
Salmon Falls to Elkhorn Valley Recreation Site

Class: 2(3)	Length: 6.5 miles
Flow: 800 cfs	Character: forested; valley
Gradient: 30 fpm, PD	Season: rainy/snowmelt

Take time at the put-in to enjoy the view as this crystal-clear river pours over 25-foot Salmon Falls. From the put-in below Salmon Falls, the river flows through much of the Elkhorn Valley as class 1 with occasional technical class 2 rapids through rock gardens.

However, at rivermile 2.5, the run enters The Slot, a 15-foot-wide entrance to a narrow basalt canyon. About 200 feet ahead of The Slot, the river divides around a steep gravel bar. The two flows converge at The Slot and roll off the cliffs with pulsating flows. At a low flow of 800 cfs, The Slot is class 3. At higher flows, this rapids could be extremely difficult.

Below the bridge in Elkhorn at mile 3, the river slows as it passes through the broad Elkhorn Valley. The valley narrows at mile 5 as Elkhorn Valley Recreation Site appears on the left. For the next 1.5 miles, the action picks up and includes two class 3 drops in the last 0.5 mile. These last two drops can be avoided by taking out at the campground on the left above the first class 3 drop.

Hazards

Expect The Slot to increase in difficulty substantially at flows of 1000 to 3000 cfs. The Slot is difficult to portage because it requires a carry of about 0.5 mile around private homes and cliffs. The class 3 ledge and boulder drop at the end of the run can be scouted from the take-out, which is about 100 yards upstream from the entrance gate at the lower end of the recreation site.

Access

From Interstate 5 near Salem, take Oregon 22 east to Mehama. Turn left at the flashing light 0.7 mile east of Mehama (21.8 miles east of Interstate 5) onto North Fork Road. The take-out is at the Elkhorn Valley Recreation Site, about 8.5 miles up this road.

Continue upstream to the put-in at Salmon Falls County Park on the right just below Salmon Falls, just over 5.5 miles above the take-out

Gauge

Currently available via the Internet (Little North Santiam near Mehama gauge) (see Appendix A).

Steve Cramer and Arnie Adams

---

115 Little North Santiam River
Elkhorn Valley Recreation Site to Mehama

Class: 3(4) T	Length: 10 miles
Flow: 750–4000 cfs	Character: forested; canyon
Gradient: 39 fpm, PD	Season: rainy/snowmelt

This run offers a variety of rapids in crystal-clear water. The road appears only occasionally, and a feeling of isolation permeates the upper parts of this run, although many cabins stand along the lower section. Many good surfing waves appear at high water.

Before putting in at Elkhorn Valley Recreation Site, look at the two class 3 rapids visible from the campground road. Then decide whether to put in above or below. Class 2 rapids continue downstream for about 3 miles to the concrete bridge, another possible put-in.

Below the bridge 0.5 mile, the river narrows and drops to the right. Just below the drop, a large rock wall extends almost to the left bank, creating a large S turn. This is easy in low water but formidable in flood.

Just downstream is the most difficult rapid on the run, affectionately known as Troll's Teeth, class 4. As the name suggests, this is a boulder garden with no clean route. At lower water levels it is very technical, and at flood it becomes a mass of holes and keepers to eat you. Approach cautiously and stop to scout on the left before the river disappears among several large rocks. At least one tree or log is usually caught in this rapid. Portage if necessary along the left bank and put in about 100 yards downstream in a large pool. The normal route enters on the right and goes far right behind the huge boulder and then to the left. Below Troll's Teeth is a steep, fast class 3 rapids.

The remaining rapids on this run are quite straightforward and can be run by an experienced boater without scouting. A particularly long and enjoyable section of rapids at North Fork Park is preceded by a large curving undercut cliff on the left, followed by a nice play spot with a fast V, green waves, and generous eddies.

Downstream you will pass under a bridge. At the next rapids, the river narrows to the left and drops sharply in an S turn. The large hole at the bottom of the drop is difficult to miss but usually can be punched. The rest of this run bounces along pleasantly until meeting the North Santiam River. Turn right here, please (!), and play on the nice surfing waves. It is only a short distance to the take-out boat ramp under the bridge in Mehama.

Hazards

Everyone, regardless of experience, should scout Troll's Teeth. Logs and debris from floods frequently plug the channels.

Access

The river is about 18 miles northeast of Salem on Oregon 22. To reach the put-in, take Oregon 22 to Mehama and turn left at North Fork Road (the flashing light 0.7 mile east of Mehama). Boaters can put in at Elkhorn Valley Recreation Site or at the bridges over the river at just over 6 and 8 miles from the Oregon 22 turnoff. To miss the more difficult rapids on the upper section, put in at North Fork Park or, better yet, at a bend in the river 1.2 miles above the park.

Take-outs include North Fork Park, 2 miles upstream from Oregon 22 and the boat ramp under the Lyons–Mehama bridge over the North Santiam.

Gauge

Currently available via the Internet (Little North Santiam near Mehama gauge) (see Appendix A).

Mick Evans

116 North Santiam River
Bruno Mountain Road to Detroit Lake

Class: 3(4); 3+(4)	Length: 7 miles
Flow: 800 cfs; 1700–2500 cfs	Character: forested
Gradient: 67 fpm, C	Season: rainy/snowmelt

With its headwaters in the Mount Jefferson Wilderness, this upper stretch of the North Santiam River is usually runnable from the time the snow begins to melt (usually late March or early April) until late spring. It may also be runnable after several days of hard rain during the fall or winter. It is not uncommon to tramp through snow at the put-in. In any season, the water is always very cold.

Boaters find a continuous gradient that offers constant action throughout the run. Play spots are abundant. At 1700 cfs, the river is not very technical, but eddies are small. At 1300 cfs, the drops become more technical but eddies are more numerous. On a clear day, spectacular views of Mount Jefferson reward boaters who turn around and look upstream.

The first 0.5 mile offers a good warm-up of class 2 and 3 water. The first major rapids, Ricochet, the most demanding of the run, is a class 3+ to 4 boulder garden at mile 0.5 and can be scouted from the road during the shuttle. Some boaters prefer to put in below Ricochet Rapid at Whispering Falls Campground, another 0.3 mile downstream. The next 3 miles of river are class 2+ to 3. After the first bridge, which is about halfway through the run, the river becomes class 3+ with some significant drops and pushy water. Some good rapids occur at the lumber mill in Idanha, but the paddling and playing along this stretch are so much fun that one barely notices the mill. All the rapids can be scouted from the river by eddy hopping. The road is always nearby on river right, but it never seems obtrusive. Fun rapids continue to the take-out, where the superb play-wave, Blowout Wave, is located.

Warning: When the lake is low, a steep class 5 rapid between the take-out and the lake becomes exposed.

Hazards
Difficulties include cold water, possible logs, and the class 4 rapids near the beginning.

Access
To reach the take-out, take Oregon 22 east from Salem to Detroit. From the town of Detroit, continue upriver on Oregon 22 for 2.5 miles to Blowout Road on the right. Go 0.2 mile to the bridge for a take-out, or turn right to Santiam Flats USFS Fee Area for a take-out farther downriver. To find the put-in, return to Oregon 22 and drive upstream 7 miles to Bruno Mountain Road, on the right. Put in under the bridge.

Gauge

Currently available via the Internet (North Santiam near Boulder gauge) (see Appendix A). A good level is 4 feet or about 1500 cfs. The river has been run at 800 cfs, but Ricochet Rapid gets very rocky. At flows higher than 2000 cfs, the difficulty increases.

Laurie Pavey

117 North Santiam River
Big Cliff Dam to Packsaddle County Park

Class: 3+(5) P	Length: 5 miles
Flow: 1000–3500 cfs	Character: forested
Gradient: 26 fpm, PD	Season: year-round

The North Santiam River is regulated by the Detroit and Big Cliff Dams above Gates. The numerous class 2, and several class 3 and 4, rapids make this run, known as Niagara, a fun and exciting stretch of whitewater. The two named rapids in this stretch are The Narrows and Niagara.

The Narrows, class 3+ to 4, is about 0.8 mile downstream from the put-in. It is preceded by a class 3 entry rapid with a large eddy at the bottom on the right. The current continues on the left side and funnels into The Narrows, a 100-yard-long constriction with a large drop. The upper section has a large wave across it, followed by a diagonal hole, very turbulent water, and a good pool at the bottom. The exposed rocks are covered at higher water. At low discharges, experts advise portaging this rapid. Scout this one before running it.

At flows over 3000 cfs, Niagara is a twisting class 5 drop at Niagara County Park. The entrance, at which the river squeezes to a width of merely 5 feet, is followed by a swirling pool that leads into a turbulent snake of water and a drop into a huge, potentially dangerous boiling pool. The walls in Niagara are undercut in places, and several potholes create strange hydraulics. Be prepared for a difficult rescue if someone in your party swims. The boiling pool recirculates along a cliff and makes self-rescue almost impossible. At lower flows, Niagara is significantly easier, but wood in any part of the rapid could be very dangerous. Always scout Niagara.

Several other memorable rapids and features characterize this stretch. Below Niagara, ender holes can be found at some discharges. Packsaddle Dam is about 2 miles below Niagara. The 12-foot dam is used to divert salmon and steelhead for capture to supply eggs for fish hatcheries. The reversal at the bottom is dangerous and a portage is mandatory as reinforcing irons are embedded there. Portage on the right. Just a couple hundred yards below the dam on the right is Packsaddle County Park.

Hazards

The Narrows and Niagara are technically demanding rapids that should be scouted. Portage around Packsaddle Dam.

Access

From Interstate 5 near Salem, take Oregon 22 east past Mill City. The take-out at Packsaddle County Park is about 3 miles east of Gates on Oregon 22.
Proceed to the put-in at Big Cliff Dam, about 5 miles east of Gates on Oregon 22. Stop at Niagara County Park to scout Niagara. About 1 mile east of Niagara is an abandoned gas station on the left. The Narrows is down the bank on the opposite side of the road.

Gauge

Currently available via the Internet (North Santiam at Niagara gauge) or by calling the River Forecast Center in Portland (see Appendix A).

George Ice and WKCC Editors

118 North Santiam River
Packsaddle County Park to Mill City

Class: 2+(3); 3; 4	Length: 6.5 miles
Flow: 750 cfs; 1500 cfs; 4500+ cfs	Character: forested; residential
Gradient: 27 fpm, PD	Season: year-round

This run is one of the more popular boating trips in Oregon. Riffles immediately below the put-in can be used to warm up. Turning the corner, the riffles lead into a small rapid. Following a pool is a fun class 2 rapid that leads into a narrow chute. It has narrow eddies on both sides and can be very turbulent.

The next rapid finishes with an excellent play spot, referred to as The Swirlies, which is identified by rock formations on the left and a very large eddy on the right. The waves at this spot make excellent surfing. The runout is extremely turbulent, with small whirlpools and collapsing swirls. These Swirlies offer an excellent and difficult practice site for the ol' river roll.

About 0.5 mile after passing under the bridge at Gates, a series of bigger rapids begin. The last rapid in this series is Spencer's Hole. Boaters generally choose between punching the hole on the right or sneaking on the left. At high flows, you will find several large waves and holes on the left. A pool awaits below this drop, and occasionally boaters take out here. A short, steep trail leads to a road that goes to Gates.

About 0.2 mile below Spencer's Hole is Carnivore, hidden on the left side of an island. Jim Oliver named this small, twisting, frothy beast when it was hungry and "ate" him. Several mild rapids and play spots are found between Carnivore and Mill City. A big eddy on the right about 200 yards above the

Mill City bridge offers an easy take-out for those not wanting to run Mill City Falls. Mill City Falls is usually scouted by walking out on the road bridge before the trip begins. Otherwise, one can back paddle while looking over the drop. The center-left and center-right of the drop usually have clear chutes, and a sneak slot is on the far left. The take-out is at a path on the right below the bridge. Another take-out is at the boat ramp in Fishermans Bend Park, 1.5 miles downstream, but it is closed in winter.

Hazards

Approach Spencer's Hole and Mill City Falls with caution.

Access

Oregon 22 east of Salem follows the North Santiam River. The put-in is at Packsaddle County Park about 3 miles east of Gates.

The normal take-out is at the small park (with changing rooms) in Mill City, at the north end of the bridge. The optional take-out above Mill City Falls is reached by driving through the paved parking lot at the north end of the bridge and continuing along a short dirt road to the turnaround. The third optional take-out is at Fishermans Bend Park, about 1.5 miles downstream from Mill City.

Gauge

Located at Mehama. Currently available via the Internet (North Santiam at Mehama gauge) or by calling the River Forecast Center in Portland (see Appendix A). At 10,000 cfs, the current and rapids on the river require expert paddling. Summer levels of about 1000 cfs are much less demanding. A flow of about 3000 cfs is optimal for playing, although Spencer's Hole is optimal between 900 and 1400 cfs.

George Ice and WKCC Editors

119 North Santiam River
Mill City to Mehama

Class: 2; 3	Length: 8.5 miles
Flow: 1000 cfs; 3000 cfs	Character: wooded; residential
Gradient: 23 fpm, PD	Season: year-round

A pleasant trip is found below Mill City. The rapids are less demanding than those upstream but should still be respected. Several broken dories, canoes, and kayaks have been observed along this stretch. The rapids tend to become rocky at flows below 1500 cfs.

Several rapids have standing waves that can be surfed even at 1000 cfs. A favorite play spot is at North Santiam State Park, 2 miles below Fishermans Bend Park. A small ledge provides boaters with a good place to practice surfing, S turns, and rolls. The ledge may be avoided by running far right. Near the end of the trip, John Neal Memorial Park, with a boat ramp, is seen on the left and the Little North Santiam River enters from the right. Excellent surfing waves develop along here at flows of 2000 cfs or more. Then the river splits. The left channel has a nice wave for one last fling at surfing. The right channel is also runnable, with the current plowing into a low wall to produce a nice quick turn. As the channels rejoin, the Lyons–Mehama bridge at the take-out comes into view.

Hazards
The ledge at North Santiam Park is typical of the maximum difficulty.

Access
Put in below the bridge in Mill City. Alternate put-ins can be found at Fishermans Bend Park or North Santiam State Park, 1.5 and 3 miles downstream of Mill City, respectively.

The take-out is under the bridge on Oregon 226, between Lyons and Mehama. This is about 0.5 mile south of the junction of Oregon 22 and 226. The take-out is reached from the southwest corner of the bridge. An alternate take-out is available at John Neal Memorial Park at 13th Street in east Lyons.

Gauge
Located at Mehama. Currently available via the Internet (North Santiam at Mehama gauge) or by calling the River Forecast Center in Portland (see Appendix A).

George Ice

120 North Santiam River
Mehama to Stayton

Class: 2- P	Length: 10.5 miles
Flow: 1000–2000 cfs	Character: agricultural
Gradient: 20 fpm, C	Season: year-round

The coniferous forests found along the upper reaches of the North Santiam gradually shift to foothill and farmland vegetation along this run. After about 0.2 mile of smooth water below the put-in, the river begins a series of mild rapids. Following these rapids is a nice play spot on the left known as Beginner's Hole. A particularly troublesome chute for beginners occurs just before a group of three powerlines comes into view. The chute flows from left to right directly into the bank and has a strong, swirling eddy on the inside of the turn. Another 0.2 mile below the powerline is the largest rapids on this run, which should be run on the far left. Below this drop is the traditional lunch stop on the right bank. In late summer, wild blackberries can be added to your lunch menu.

Below the lunch stop are a number of class 1 rapids and riffles. Following a mild rapid, farmland fringed by bird boxes can be seen on the left bank. Below the bird boxes, the river splits and a dam sits in the left channel. The right channel looks inviting but should not be taken because it becomes an irrigation canal with very brushy banks and no take-outs. The trip continues in the left channel below the dam, so a portage is required. At 1000 cfs, boaters can paddle to the far right of the dam and carry over it. At higher flows boaters should take out on the levee at the right of the dam. Salmon and steelhead can sometimes be seen jumping in the fish ladder or up the dam.

The rapids below the dam are rocky and swift. Beyond, the river becomes rockier and shallower. A few of the rapids have current moving into brush.

Hazards

Portage around the dam. The class 2 rapid below the powerline crossing is the most difficult.

Access

Take Oregon 22 east from Salem. The put-in is a boat landing located beneath the Lyons–Mehama bridge, just off Oregon 22 on Oregon 226. In summer, this popular boat landing can be very congested with anglers, rafters, and drifters.

To reach the take-out, take Oregon 22 to the Stayton turnoff and go south through Stayton. The take-out is at the boat ramp at the south end of the bridge that crosses the North Santiam in Stayton.

Gauge

Located at Mehama. Currently available via the Internet (North Santiam at Mehama gauge) or by calling the River Forecast Center in Portland (see Appendix A).

George Ice

Lower Willamette Valley and Clackamas River

Silver Creek

121 Silver Creek
Silver Falls State Park to Silverton Reservoir

Class: 4(5)	Length: 10.6 miles
Flow: 300–500 cfs	Character: deep forested canyon
Gradient: 61 fpm, PD	Season: rainy

Silver Creek drains Silver Falls State Park and the Cascade foothills to the east. The many falls in the park drop over 15 million year old (Miocene) flood basalts from eastern Oregon and Washington. Mountain building in the area has since raised the basalt higher than its original elevation. The run is characterized by falls, steep blind ledges, and gorges. It is mostly pool drop with one rapid that is long and continuous. The put-in is a 1.1-mile downhill hike to the foot of Lower North Falls on the North Fork of Silver Creek.

The base of Lower North Falls introduces 0.75 mile of pleasant small ledges and rapids before you reach the confluence with the South Fork. Logs may require portage in this section. The first large drop after the confluence is Crag Falls, a wide diagonal 10-foot ledge drop preceded by a 150-foot-long shallow, ledgy slide on river left. Crag Falls can be scouted on the left from the slack water at its top.

Next comes Dobo Falls, a 15-foot plunge at a sharp right bend in the river. Dobo Falls is preceded by two riverwide ledges, with rollers that can be sneaked on the extreme left. Do not miss the eddy on river left just above the lip of the falls. The best line at Dobo is a boof on the left, but this line is complicated by the fact that most of the current flows perpendicularly to the lip of the falls and down into the ugly fold on the right side. Portage on the left.

Canyon Falls is an 8- to 10-foot slide just downstream from Dobo Falls. It is difficult to scout and would be a difficult portage because of the steep, slippery canyon walls. Run on the right as a double drop, with a 3-foot ledge 50 feet farther downstream. An old clear-cut on the left marks the park boundary 2.2 miles below the confluence of the North and South Forks. Once you leave the park, look for a green steel bridge over the creek. Just below this bridge is a 4-foot ledge that can develop a sticky hole on the right at some flows.

Dirty Falls, a 15-foot ledge with a short class 2 rapid just before the lip, appears in another 0.25 mile. From upstream, the falls appears like a dam. Scout from the left above the lead-in rapids. Below Dirty Falls, the creek gradually slows and the last 4 miles or so are mellow class 2 with one steep drop known as Murrays Slide. This fun drop has several parts and can be boat scouted at medium flows or bank scouted on either side if necessary. Below this ledge, it is 0.25 mile to the flat-water paddle across the reservoir and out.

Hazards

Do not put in above Lower North Falls. Strict rules forbid ascending or descending the creek banks within the park—you may be cited by park staff if you are caught, so do not do it. The creekside ecosystem is very delicate, so scout carefully and do not leave the creek once you are on it.

Access

From Silverton, follow the signs east on OR 214 (Silver Falls Highway) toward Silver Falls State Park. The take-out is a small park just outside the Silverton city limits on the right side of Oregon 214 at the Silverton Reservoir and upstream of the dam. Continue southeast on Oregon 214 to the Winter

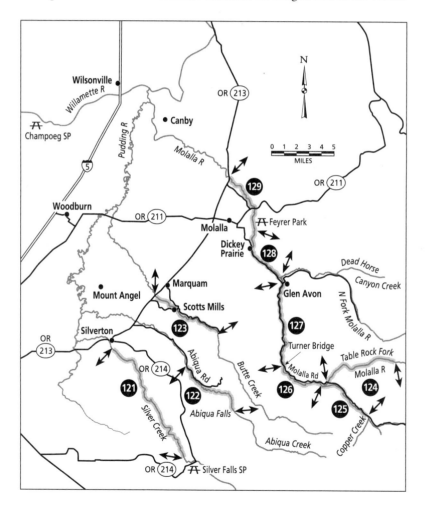

Falls parking lot in Silver Falls State Park. The put-in is a 1.1-mile downhill hike to the base of Lower North Falls. (The hike from North Falls Campground is about the same distance, but the campground may be closed in winter and the trail is not marked.) From the parking lot, it is 0.5 mile down to the bridge over the North Fork, 0.2 mile to Middle North Falls, 0.2 mile to Drake Falls, and 0.2 mile to the base of Lower North Falls.

Gauge
None. Generally has enough water after several days of rain. The Clackamas River (Clackamas River at Three Lynx gauge) should be at least 3500 cfs.

Hank Hays and WKCC Editors

Abiqua Creek

122 Abiqua Creek
Abiqua Falls to Abiqua Road

Class: 2(3)	Length: 7.5 miles
Flow: 400 cfs	Character: forested; residential
Gradient: 80 fpm, C	Season: rainy

Abiqua Creek is in the watershed between Butte Creek on the north and Silver Creek to the south. All are tributaries of the Pudding River, which flows into the Molalla just before the latter reaches the Willamette. Abiqua Creek's gradient and drainage area are similar to both sister streams, but it does not have as much action as either of them. The gradient is fairly constant, with some pool drop. Most rapids are rock gardens.

Above the recommended put-in, Abiqua Falls plunges over a 90-foot sheer drop into a pool. The gradient above the falls is steeper, up to 200 fpm, but there is not a put-in far enough upstream to make the portage around the falls worthwhile.

The first 1.5 miles of this run are class 2, with a few strategically placed sweepers to enliven the experience. The first class 3, Hank's Mistake, has a large padded boulder near the bottom center. At the recommended flows, far right is advised, as the current pushes left all the way from the top. Some nice holes and wave action are found just after the next island.

A mile later comes Pink Bridge Rapid. Pinky is a long boulder garden with a left bend halfway through, where the bridge comes into view. A quick scout for logs is prudent. From here downstream, cabins and homes are occasionally seen, rapids diminish, and in one place the left bank consists of a huge pile of sawdust. About 1.8 miles below the recommended take-out (between miles 8 and 9) is a dam that would be difficult to portage, mainly because of steep banks with barbed-wire fences at the top.

Hazards

Getting to the put-in is probably the hardest part of the run. On the river, Hank's Mistake and Pink Bridge Rapid are the most difficult.

Access

From Oregon 99E in Salem, take Oregon 213 east to Silverton. About 3 miles north of Silverton on Oregon 213 is a blinking yellow light at Abiqua Road Northeast. Take Abiqua Road southeast about 6.25 miles to a concrete bridge over Abiqua Creek. Just upstream is a rocky turnout that makes a good parking spot for the take-out.

To get to the put-in, continue upstream another mile to the end of the pavement at a green steel bridge. Proceed 2 miles from the green bridge, keeping right where the main gravel road swings left. In about another 0.2 mile, several driveways take off in all directions. Go straight on what looks like the main road. This is where the road gets bad. After 3.5 miles of bone-jarring, oil-pan-crunching ride you will come to a grassy pullout on the right. From here a well-defined hiking trail takes off upstream, ending at the base of the falls in less than 0.5 mile. Two short steep sections are part of the 0.25 mile down to the creek. You can continue up the road for a bit to the top of the falls, but the trails to it are not as easy to find.

Gauge

None exists. If you do not mind the rockiness of the boulder garden at the take-out, go ahead and try the run.

Hank Hays

Butte Creek

123 Butte Creek
Fault Line to Oregon 213

Class: 3(4-) T, P	Length: 7.5 miles
Flow: 200–800 cfs	Character: forested
Gradient: 60 fpm, PD	Season: rainy

This run on Butte Creek flows through scenic forested mountain foothills that are an abrupt contrast to the rural countryside found near Mount Angel and Woodburn. It has considerable variety for a small stream: ledge drops, a few slots, S curves, rock gardens, a gorge, one slide, a couple of logs, and two dams. The rapids are separated by long stretches of easier water. An alternate take-out at the park in Scotts Mills shortens the trip by 2 miles.

At a bridge 1 mile below the put-in, there is a 5-foot drop. It is a nose cruncher at low water but less of a problem at higher water. Below the bridge

1 mile is a difficult rapid that should be scouted from the right bank. The rock garden at the top leads into fast water that forms two large riverwide waves, funnels down to 20 feet wide, goes over a 4-foot drop, and bashes onto a rock on the right. The rock garden below is technical at low water. Boaters who choose to portage these two rapids should stay close to the river so as not to disturb property owners.

After another mile, a tight S turn curves first to the left, then right. A rock at the top splits the river. This rapid is difficult to scout from the river, so be sure to check for logs during the shuttle. Several fun rapids and ledges emerge in a scenic gorge just before Scotts Mills Pond, 2 miles farther. Although it is possible to portage the dam and continue downriver, most people opt to take out at the park next to the dam. Adventurous paddlers looking for an exciting finish can run the dam.

Immediately below the dam is a fun rapid with numerous holes and rocks to maneuver around. Midway between the Scotts Mills bridge and Oregon 213 is a second dam with a fish ramp on the left that makes an abrupt right turn. The water smashes head-on into a raised ledge before connecting with the main channel. Portage on the left.

Hazards
The 5-foot drop at the first bridge, the 4-foot drop 1 mile farther down, and the S-turn rapid should be scouted or portaged. The S-turn rapid can be scouted from the road by stopping 2.9 miles after turning onto Butte Creek Road.

Access
From Oregon 99E in Salem, take Oregon 213 east to Silverton. The takeout is on Oregon 213 5.2 miles northwest of Silverton at the Oregon 213 bridge. Alternatively, 4.5 miles from Silverton turn right onto Mount Angel–Scotts Mills Road and proceed 2.5 miles to the park and bridge at Scotts Mills.

From there to the put-in, drive 0.1 mile north of Scotts Mills bridge to Maple Grove Road, which runs east, and turn right. Butte Creek Road angles off to the right 0.1 mile later. Follow it 4.5 miles to a turnoff on the right by some houses. This road crosses a brook and looks down on Butte Creek after 0.5 mile. The road is owned by the Boy Scouts, who prefer boaters use the parking lot at the end of the road rather than park on the shoulder. Put in just below the class 5 rapid adjacent to the parking lot. Local residents prefer that scouting be done from the creek rather than from the road. Please respect their wishes.

Gauge
Visual. Look upstream from the Scotts Mills bridge. If these rocks are wet, the others upstream likely will also be wet. Usually 3 days of rain fill the creek to a fair level.

Andreas Mueller and WKCC Editors

Molalla River and Tributaries

124 Table Rock Fork of the Molalla River
Second Bridge to Gravel Pit

Class: 3 (4) T	Length: 5 miles
Flow: 500–1500 cfs	Character: Continuous, roadside
Gradient: 110 fpm, C	Season: rainy

The upper section of the Table Rock Fork of the Molalla River is a great intermediate run for up-and-coming creekers. Although most of the drops are small, the continuous nature of the rapids keeps boaters on their toes. The road is always close, which allows for easy scouting during the shuttle and an escape route if the rapids are too demanding.

The first major rapid is about a mile below the put-in, immediately after a sharp left-hand turn. It is easily recognized by steep rock walls on either side of the river and boulders that block much of the river. At most water levels, the river drops through a tight, undercut slot on the right and into a hole. The slot can be portaged on the right. Immediately after the slot is a narrow drop that could contain wood.

The remainder of the run is continuous boulder gardens with the occasional larger rapid. Very few pools are present at most water levels, but eddies abound. The last mile before the take-out has a couple of harder rapids than the rest of the run.

Hazards
Scout the drop about a mile below the put-in. Scout the last mile on the shuttle. Potentially dangerous wood could be present anywhere throughout the run.

Access
To reach Turner Bridge, refer to the Molalla River: Turner Bridge to Glen Avon Bridge run. To reach the take-out, follow Molalla Road 4.7 miles past Turner Bridge and turn left just before crossing a bridge over Table Rock Fork. Continue on the Table Rock road another 1.5 miles to a parking area on your right.

To reach the put-in, continue upstream 5 miles to a spur road on the right. Put-in at the bridge over the river on this spur road.

Gauge
Currently available on the Internet (Molalla River at Canby gauge) (see Appendix A), but this gauge is far downstream and does not always correspond well to flows in the upper river. In general, 1500 cfs on the Canby gauge is a good minimum if is raining, but you may need more water if it has not rained for a couple days. Much of the run can be seen from the road, so take a look before you begin.

Pete Giordano

125 Molalla River
Copper Creek to Table Rock Confluence

Class: 3(4) T	Length: 5.1 miles
Flow: 500 cfs	Character: canyon; forested
Gradient: 103 fpm, PD	Season: rainy

This run offers a variety of rapids winding through a deep canyon with pretty views of a moss-laden forest. Being near the upper reaches of the Molalla, this run is runnable only after several days of heavy rain. Immediately below the put-in, where Copper Creek enters the main Molalla, is a small gorge that begins with a sharp, narrow class 3+ drop. This drop can be skipped by starting just downstream. The drops in this beautiful gorge can be scouted from the road or the river. A long boulder garden is situated just before the Copper Creek Bridge, another possible put-in.

The next major rapid, Dungeon, is about 2.75 miles from the put-in. It consists of a boulder garden, several diagonal waves, and a tight S turn with several well-placed holes. Scout this rapid from the road at a point where the road bank drops off several hundred feet. The next major rapid is about 0.5 mile downstream. Lightning Lonnie, named in memory of a firefighter who loved the river, is a 6-foot twisty ledge. The ledge should be negotiated by staying far right or far left, as the middle can cause a vertical pin. The next part of the run consists of several small boulder gardens in another beautiful gorge. All these drops can be boat-scouted by eddy hopping. Boaters who would like a longer day can easily continue another 4.7 miles on the Molalla River: Table Rock Fork Confluence to Turner Bridge run and take out at Turner Bridge.

Hazards

The narrow drop at the put-in can be avoided by starting just downstream. Scout for Dungeon and Lightning Lonnie either from the road or the river.

Access

Two take-outs are possible. To reach both, follow Molalla Road 4.7 miles past Turner Bridge and cross a bridge over the Table Rock Fork. From this bridge, drive another 0.3 mile to a pullout on the right and a short trail to the river. Another small pullout is 0.3 mile farther upstream. Scout both these take-outs before putting on the river, as they are easy to miss if you are not paying attention.

To reach the put-in, continue upstream on the main road until you reach a locked gate blocking a bridge across the river. Park here, but do not block the gate. The lower put-in is at Copper Creek Bridge, approximately 0.75 mile downstream.

Gauge

Currently available on the Internet (Molalla River at Canby gauge) (see Appendix A), but this gauge is far downstream and does not always correspond well to flows in the upper river. In general, 1500 cfs on the Canby gauge is a good minimum if is raining, but you may need more water if it has not rained for a couple days. Another gauge is on the bridge support at Feyrer Park. Minimum recommended flow is 5 feet. An ideal level is 6 feet.

Joe Gymkowski, Rick Kelley, and WKCC Editors

126 Molalla River
Table Rock Fork Confluence to Turner Bridge

Class: 3(3+)	Length: 4.7 to 5.0 miles
Flow: 1000–2500 cfs	Character: forested; canyon
Gradient: 65 fpm, PD	Season: rainy

This scenic and playful run on the Molalla River is mostly class 2, with several class 3 drops near the middle. This portion may be combined with upper portions of the next run to make a longer trip (see the Molalla River: Turner Bridge to Glen Avon Bridge run).

Two put-ins are possible. The first starts on the Table Rock Fork of the Molalla and continues for 0.2 mile before boaters reach the main Molalla. The second put-in is on the main Molalla about 0.3 mile upstream of the confluence with the Table Rock Fork. The next mile past the confluence is mostly class 2 and is a good warm-up. The first class 3 rapid is at the end of this mile and can be seen and scouted from the river by eddy hopping. Shortly below this rapids, boaters pass under Horse Creek bridge. Horse Creek enters the river as a beautiful falls on the left. About 0.2 mile downstream from the falls is Horse Creek Canyon, where the river narrows to a boat length. This class 3+ drop is clean but turbulent. It is a good idea to check for logs before committing to this drop. The flat-water runout gives paddlers a chance to enjoy the beautiful, steep canyon walls. Less than 1 mile downstream, where the river makes a sharp bend to the left and then right, be alert for logs. The final couple of miles are class 2 with some nice play waves and ender spots to enjoy. A common day-trip continues down through the Three Bears run and takes out below Baby Bear (see the Molalla River: Turner Bridge to Glen Avon Bridge run).

Hazards

Horse Creek Canyon is very narrow at the steepest part of the drop. Logs may be a problem, so be sure to scout.

Access

See the Molalla River: Turner Bridge to Glen Avon Bridge run for directions to reach the take-out.

Two put-ins are possible. The first can be reached by continuing 4.7 miles upstream from Turner Bridge, just past the B Ranch residence, to a small turnout on the right and a steep trail that leads down to the river. The second put-in can be reached by continuing across the Table Rock Fork for another 0.3

mile to a small turnout on the right and a trail through the woods to the river.

Gauge

Currently available via the Internet (Molalla River at Canby gauge) (see Appendix A). A good minimum for this run is 1500 cfs on the Canby gauge. This corresponds to a flow of about 1000 cfs in this upper reach.

Laurie Pavey and WKCC Editors

127 Molalla River
Turner Bridge to Glen Avon Bridge

Class: 3 T; 4	Length: 8 miles
Flow: 600–1000 cfs; 2000 cfs	Character: forested; canyon
Gradient: 55 fpm, C	Season: rainy

This run is known as the Three Bears Run. At the minimum flow of about 600 cfs, it is a technical class 3; at higher flows, it is a more enjoyable class 3; and at high water, it becomes big class 4. Several 3- to 4-foot steep drops are visible from the road on the way to the put-in. When running the rapids, some eddy hopping is necessary to pick the correct route. Many of the runouts are riffles leading to the next rapids.

For the first mile or so below the put-in, the water is fast but fairly straightforward. The first major rapids, Papa Bear, about 1 mile downriver, has two distinct parts. Another mile down is the most difficult rapid on the run, Mama Bear. The rapid starts with a boulder garden and some heavy water that leads into a fantastically picturesque gorge with moss-laden columnar basalt twisted into weird and wonderful shapes. The gorge is only 14 feet wide in places, and the water is deep, slow, and eerie. The next major rapids, Baby Bear, is another mile down. It consists of three separate drops.

After the Three Bears come about 4 miles of easier water, but do not forget about Goldilocks, probably the most dangerous rapids. Goldilocks begins with fast water that is split by an island and can be run on either side. The left is easier, especially at low water. At the bottom is a blind turn to the right against an undercut rock that could entrap a boater. The final named rapids, Porridge Bowl, consists of an easier short, fast drop into a wall. A short distance below, Trout Creek enters from the right into a deep pool, followed by a house on the right. Take out on the right where the road is close to the river, about 0.2 mile above the Glen Avon bridge.

Hazards

The Three Bears can be scouted from the road during the shuttle. Mama Bear, leading into the columnar basalt gorge, becomes solid class 4 at high water. Goldilocks cannot be seen from the road. It should be scouted on foot or by careful eddy hopping to check for logs and the undercut.

Access

From Oregon 99E or Oregon 213 between Salem and Oregon City, go
east on Oregon 211 1 mile to the town of Molalla. Continue east on Oregon
211 and take the first right to Feyrer Park. From Feyrer Park, cross the
river and turn right on Dickey Prairie Road. Go upriver and pass through the
community of Dickey Prairie. Continuing upriver, Dickey Prairie Road
crosses the North Fork Molalla, and after 0.2 mile the Glen Avon bridge is

Excitement at Baby Bear, Molalla River (Jason Rackley)

on the right, crossing the Molalla River. Without crossing the river on the Glen Avon bridge, continue 0.2 mile to a wide area near river level, the take-out.

To reach the put-in, backtrack 0.2 mile and cross the Glen Avon bridge. Continue upstream 9 miles to Turner Bridge. Cross the Molalla and continue a little farther up to a roadside pullout on the right.

Gauge

Currently available via the Internet (Molalla River at Canby gauge) (see Appendix A). The recommended minimum flow at Canby is 1000 cfs, which corresponds to about 600 cfs in this upper reach.

Rob Blickensderfer and Joe Gymkowski

128 Molalla River
Glen Avon Bridge to Feyrer Park

Class: 2	Length: 6 miles
Flow: 1000–2000 cfs	Character: agricultural; rural
Gradient: 30 fpm, PD	Season: rainy

On this run, several straightforward class 2 rapids and good play spots alternate with class 1 stretches of fast water. The river is more interesting and not nearly as flat as it appears from the road on the way up to the put-in. Several houses are visible from the river. About 4 miles below the put-in, a private bridge crosses the river. The take-out is at the next bridge at Feyrer Park, on the left. Depending upon the boater's skill and mood, this short run could be combined with the Molalla River: Turner Bridge to Glen Avon Bridge run or the Molalla River: Feyrer Park to Oregon 213 Bridge run.

Hazards

All of the largest rapids, class 2, occur in the upper half of the run. The waves can be relatively large, but the rapids are straightforward.

Access

See the Molalla River: Turner Bridge to Glen Avon Bridge run for directions to both the take-out and the put-in for this run. The take-out is at Feyrer Park east of Molalla.

To reach the put-in from Feyrer Park, continue to Glen Avon and its bridge across the Molalla River. Without crossing the river, continue 0.2 mile to a wide area near river level, the put-in.

Gauge

Currently available via the Internet (Molalla River at Canby gauge) (see Appendix A). The recommended minimum flow at Canby is 1000 cfs.

Rob Blickensderfer

129 Molalla River
Feyrer Park to Oregon 213 Bridge

Class: 1+	Length: 6 miles
Flow: 1000–2000 cfs	Character: rural
Gradient: 21 fpm, C	Season: rainy

This is an excellent run for a beginning kayaker's second river trip. It is relatively free of brush and has numerous riffles and enough small rapids and speed to keep boaters interested. The first bridge, after 2 miles, is the Oregon 211 crossing. The second bridge, after an additional 6 miles, is the Oregon 213 crossing. Take out under the bridge on the left.

Hazards
There are no particular hazards.

Access
To reach the put-in at Feyrer Park, refer to the Molalla River: Turner Bridge to Glen Avon Bridge run.

To reach the take-out, return to Molalla and continue west on Oregon 211 to the intersection with Oregon 213. Go north on Oregon 213 about 4 miles to the bridge over the Molalla River. The take-out is on the south side, river left.

Gauge
Currently available via the Internet (Molalla River at Canby gauge) (see Appendix A). The recommended minimum flow at Canby is 1000 cfs.

Rob Blickensderfer

Clackamas River and Tributaries

130 Nohorn Creek
Nohorn Creek to Peg Leg Falls

Class: 3+ to 4(5) T	Length: 3 miles
Flow: 200–700 cfs	Character: forested
Gradient: 140 fpm, PD	Season: rainy/snowmelt

Nohorn Creek is a small tributary of the Hot Springs Fork of the Collawash River that contains fun class 3 rapids, one great class 4 rapid, and one big class 5 drop. The scenery on this intimate creek is superb throughout the run.

Immediately below the put-in, boaters encounter a sharp ledge drop with a small pool below. Just downstream, boaters enter a small gorge with several fun class 3 rapids separated by small pools. The first drop in the gorge can be scouted only from a small eddy on the right. After the gorge, the creek opens up and contains numerous fun class 3 rapids. There will probably be some wood to avoid, so look downstream before committing to a drop. About halfway through the run, the river curves right and enters Cookie Monster, class 5. Cookie Monster is a long, steep slide into a riverwide hole. Portage/scout from a one-boat eddy on the right before the creek makes the turn. Below Cookie Monster, be on the lookout for a steep ledge drop in a steep walled section of the creek. At most flows, this class 4 drop can be scouted from a small gravel bar on the right or can be portaged with difficulty on the left. The ledge visible from the bridge near the take-out should be run in the center as both the left and the right land on rocks. Peg Leg Falls can be run as a finale.

Hazards

Small eddies above difficult drops and wood are the biggest hazards on this run. Boaters should have class 4 skills to enjoy the run.

Access

From Interstate 205 southeast of Portland, take Oregon 212 east and then Oregon 224 south to Estacada. Continue about 23 miles upstream to Ripplebrook Ranger Station. Turn right on NF 46 and continue to NF 63; turn right on NF 63. After 3.3 miles turn right on NF 70 and continue another 5.8 miles to the parking area at Peg Leg Falls.

To reach the put-in continue upstream on NF 70. Bear right at the junction after 1 mile and turn right onto a small spur road after another 1.7 miles. The put-in is at the bridge just down the hill.

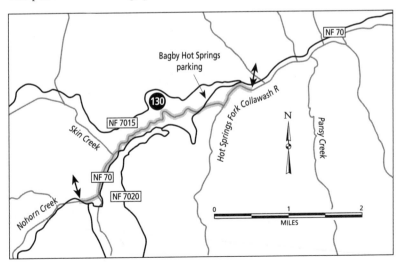

Gauge

Visual. Usually runnable when the Clackamas is 4000 to 6000 cfs. The Clackamas gauge is currently available via the Internet (Clackamas above the Three Lynx gauge) (see Appendix A).

Pete Giordano

131 Collawash River
Elk Lake Creek to Bridge 5.5 Miles from Mouth

Class: 4(5)	Length: 6.2 miles
Flow: 500–1000 cfs	Character: isolated canyon
Gradient: 78 fpm, PD	Season: rainy/snowmelt

This upper section of the Collawash River provides some great scenery and fun class 4 to 5 rapids set in a remote canyon. Unfortunately, much of the first half of the run consists of easy class 2 rapids and several immense logjams. Because of this, the run is seldom done, but it does provide a good challenge for adventurous boaters.

From the crystal-clear pool beneath the bridge at the put-in, the Collawash flows pleasantly through a rugged canyon with occasional class 2 and class 3 rapids. After several miles, you will encounter a huge logjam that blocks the entire river. There is not much current in this section, so getting out of the river is easy. The river remains flat below the logjam until the canyon narrows dramatically and drops over a distinct horizon line. Scout this fun class 4 rapid from the left, and be sure to look downstream as a big class 5 rapid lurks just below. Scout this rapid from the left but portage on the right. The portage is a long climb over and around big boulders and many sharp rocks. After a steep boulder garden and a right turn, the river again drops over several steep ledges that make up The Churn. The first ledge is runnable anywhere, but do not get pushed downstream as the second ledge contains a nasty pin spot. At some flows, a good channel is available on the far left. Scout carefully. Below The Churn, the river has a couple other fun rapids before a second monster logjam that involves some creative climbing to get back down to river level. More good class 4 rapids dot the remaining distance down to the take-out at the highway bridge.

Hazards

The difficult rapids on this run are formed by huge boulders deposited from landslides and can shift from year to year. In addition, there is potential for dangerous wood and pin spots in all the rapids. Scouting and portaging involve scrambling on unstable banks with sharp rocks. The canyon is very isolated, and hiking out is difficult.

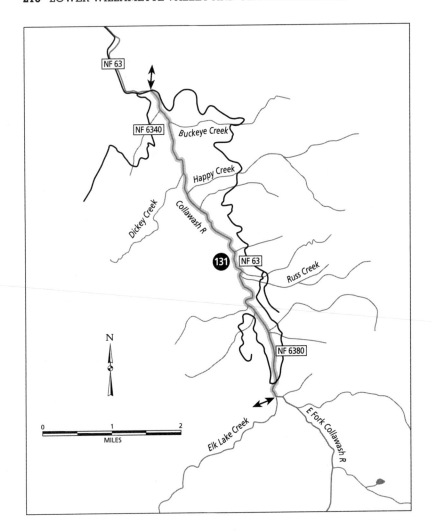

Access

The take-out for this run is the put-in for the Collawash River: Bridge 5.5 Miles from Mouth to Two Rivers Picnic Area run.

To reach the put-in, continue on NF 63 8.6 miles to the bridge over the Collawash, staying right at major intersections after 2.75, 3.6 and 6.3 miles.

Gauge

Visual. The rapids visible from the take-out bridge are a decent indicator of the flow on the upper river. Generally runnable when the Clackamas is over 2500 cfs.

Pete Giordano

132 Collawash River
Bridge 5.5 Miles from Mouth to Two Rivers Picnic Area

Class: 3(4); 3+(5)	Length: 5.5 miles
Flow: 900 cfs; 2500 cfs	Character: wooded canyon
Gradient: 61 fpm, PD	Season: rainy/snowmelt

Enjoyable class 3 rapids and numerous play spots characterize most of this run, except for two difficult class 4 to 5 rapids. Both of these rapids are in the upper 2-mile section and can be avoided by using the lower put-in. From the bridge at the upper put-in, it is only about 0.25 mile to the first major rapid, Boulderdash, class 4, a 0.3-mile-long boulder garden complete with house rocks, narrow chutes, and a serious gradient. Scout the entire rapid from the roadside pullout 5.2 miles above the take-out. This involves some scrambling and peering through trees but is well worth the effort. From the river, scout Boulderdash from either bank. Most of the runnable slots are river left, with the exit near the center.

After 1.5 miles of class 2 rapids, the second class 4 rapid, Chute to Kill, is identified by the cliff on river right. Again, scout Chute to Kill on the way to the put-in from a roadside pullout 3.6 miles above the take-out. The run begins as a steep boulder garden followed by a large hole backed by a guard rock. A solid brace makes life more enjoyable here. A short pool leads into the last drop, a 5-foot plunge down a steep chute into a powerful hole on river left. A right side chute dead-ends in a boulder jam, hence the name.

Below Chute to Kill 0.25 mile, the Hot Springs Fork enters from river left. This optional put-in allows 1 mile of easy warm-up before entering the class 3 section with its many nice play waves and holes. The final class 3, Up Against the Wall, comes at a right bend in the river, just past the only bridge, and marks the end of good whitewater.

Hazards
Boulderdash and Chute to Kill require skillful maneuvering and solid rolls at any flow. Scout both rapids on the way to the put-in; they are likely to become class 5 at higher flows. All the class 3 rapids are visible from the road except Up Against the Wall, but it is an easier rapid than those upstream. Logs and trees create some potential hazards and should be noted on the way to the put-in.

Access
From Interstate 205 southeast of Portland, take Oregon 212 east and then Oregon 224 south to Estacada. Continue about 23 miles upstream to the Ripplebrook Ranger Station. Turn right on NF 46, turn right on NF 63, and continue for 0.1 mile to the confluence of the Collawash and the Clackamas. The take-out is in the Two Rivers Picnic Area, at the confluence.

The lower put-in for the class 3 run is 3.4 miles upstream at the Hot Springs Fork confluence at the Fan Creek Recreation Site. The upper put-in is another 2.1 miles upstream, where a bridge crosses the Collawash.

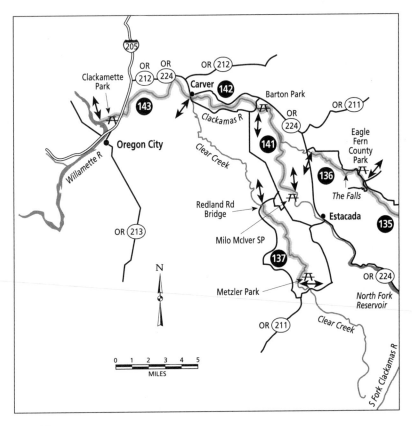

Gauge

None exists. Use the Clackamas Three Lynx gauge. Call the River Forecast Center in Portland (see Appendix A). The flow is about 40 percent of that at the Three Lynx gauge. The authors made the run between 900 and 1800 cfs (2300 to 4500 cfs at Three Lynx).

Jeff Bennett, Tonya Shrives, and WKCC Editors

133 Roaring River
3.2 Miles above Clackamas River to Clackamas River

Class: 4 T	Length: 3.2 miles
Flow: 300–750 cfs	Character: isolated wooded canyon
Gradient: 200 fpm, C	Season: rainy/snowmelt

Roaring River is an interesting, short run for boaters looking for another run in the Clackamas River drainage. Despite its steep gradient, Roaring River is

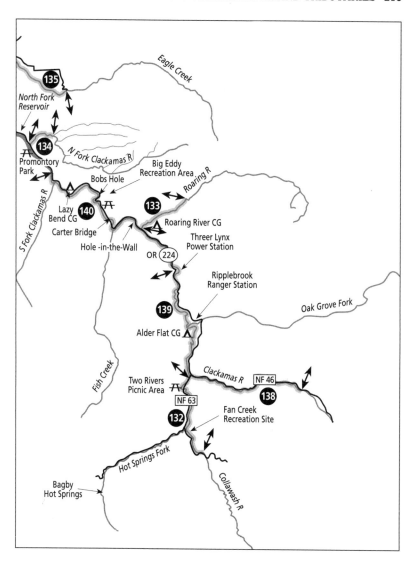

mostly characterized by uniform boulder gardens with the exception of the last mile. Several fun ledges and pushy boulder gardens provide a great end to the run. Be prepared for multiple portages around logs, stumps, and other wood hazards, although most of these are in easier rapids and you will have ample time to get out of the river.

Hazards

The last mile of the run contains several ledges that develop sticky hydraulics at high flows. Wood shifts position every year, so be sure to scout often.

Access

Access to the put-in is blocked by snow much of the winter, creating a small boating window in the fall and spring. The take-out is at the bridge over the Roaring River on Oregon 224 just before the Roaring River campground.

To reach the put-in, follow Oregon 224 downstream 12 miles and turn right across the highway from Promontory Park entrance and then immediately left onto NF 4610. Turn right after approximately 11.5 miles on NF 4611. Follow NF 4611 until it dead-ends. The trail down to the river is about a hundred yards down the road to the left and is well marked. The hike down the trail takes about 20 minutes.

Gauge

Visual. If the rapid at the Oregon 224 bridge looks runnable then the rest of the run should be fine. Generally, if Fish Creek is at least 300 cfs., Roaring River should have enough water. The Fish Creek gauge is currently available via the Internet (Fish Creek gauge) (see Appendix A).

Pete Giordano

134 North Fork Clackamas River
3.75 Miles from North Fork Reservoir to North Fork Reservoir

Class: 4 to 4+(5) P	Length: 3.75 miles
Flow: 250–500 cfs	Character: isolated canyon/gorge
Gradient: 200 fpm, PD, C	Season: rainy/snowmelt

The North Fork of the Clackamas River begins as a tiny stream in the foothills of the Cascades, gradually building in size and plunging through the basalt of the Clackamas River canyon to end in the backwaters of the North Fork Reservoir. The river is at the bottom of a steep and isolated canyon and is dotted with waterfalls, ledge drops, and that ever-present Northwest boater obstacle: wood.

Steep boulder gardens and small ledges characterize the first mile of the run. Most of these rapids can be scouted from a boat, but several are quite steep and should be scouted for wood by at least one member of the group. The first major obstacle is a short gorge with a riverwide ledge near the end. The lead-in to the ledge is swift with very small eddies, and the gorge has contained dangerous wood in the past. Scout early from the right bank.

Once past the gorge, be on the lookout for more fun rapids but also for a small overgrown road on the left bank. The road is just before a left turn with a series of small sliding ledges that end in a runnable 12-foot falls. Although the falls is fun, portaging the unrunnable 50-foot falls below it is much easier if you forgo the falls and hike up the road. Either way, portaging the falls requires hiking up the canyon wall, and lowering boats back down the steep canyon wall several hundred yards downstream. Almost immediately below the unrunnable falls and just downstream of a creek on river right is a steep class 5 waterfall.

The waterfall totals about 20 feet and is a wild ride over two smaller ledges before the final 10-foot drop into a sticky hole. Scout or portage on the left.

The next 0.5 mile contains some class 3 boulder gardens before the river begins to drop through an amazing array of continuous, steep boulder gardens that only relent 0.5 mile from the reservoir. Many of these drops contain wood and numerous pin spots. At high water, eddies can become scarce. Scout often and be safe.

Hazards
The first gorge may become unscoutable at high water. The 50-foot waterfall must be portaged. Many of the hardest rapids contain wood that can shift from year to year. Pin spots abound throughout the whole run.

Access
From Estacada, follow Oregon 224 east about 5.2 miles and park in the small parking area on the left just before crossing the North Fork.

To reach the put-in, return to Oregon 224 and continue east another 1.3 miles. Turn left and then left again. Follow this road another 3.2 miles to a rough road on the left leading down to the river. From here it is an easy 0.5-mile hike down to the river.

Gauge
Visual. The North Fork usually has enough water when Fish Creek is flowing at least 300 cfs or when the Clackamas is over 3000 cfs. Both gauges are currently available via the Internet (Clackamas River above Three Lynx gauge or Fish Creek gauge) (see Appendix A).

Pete Giordano

Steep creek fun! North Fork Clackamas. (Jason Rackley)

135 Eagle Creek
Fish Hatchery to Snuffin Road

Class: 3(4+) T	Length: 6 miles
Flow: 300 cfs	Character: forested; cabins
Gradient: 62 fpm, PD	Season: rainy

Eagle Creek drains the Cascade foothills east of Estacada, and flows generally northwest into the Clackamas River about halfway between Estacada and Barton. It was named for the eagles that used to dip to catch the thousands of spawning salmon. The creek is small and anglers sometimes crowd the banks. Several bridges cross the creek, but paddlers catch only glimpses of the road, and then only in the vicinity of Eagle Fern County Park. The first settler in the area, Philip Foster, was part owner of the Barlow Road, the first real alternative to the dangerous raft route through the Columbia Gorge.

At the put-in, the creek is narrow with overhanging shrubbery. If the water level is high, the current can be intimidating. Sweepers, logs, and blind turns make the upper part of this run quite interesting, although the rapids are usually not too complex. Several logs or logjams are usually available for portaging in this upper section. A little over halfway through the trip is a 15- to 18-foot waterfall. Watch for the 4-foot-high concrete fish ladder bypassing the falls. It is on the right bank past a sharp right-hand bend. Take out on the right in the pool well before the concrete wall. The falls is generally run down a tongue on the right or down the center-right. A large hydraulic can form at the base at high water. Portage on the trail or down the fish ladder.

It is about 1 mile from the base of the falls to Eagle Fern Youth Camp—a large open area on the left. Some of the best action on this run comes in the mile between the camp and the take-out. The creek goes around a right bend and into an interesting boulder garden. It gets worse near the bottom, after a left bend. A short respite precedes some more fun boulder gardens and the bridge at the take-out.

Hazards

The falls, logs, possible logjams, water running into bushes, and boulder gardens between the youth camp and the take-out are the difficulties on this run.

Access

From Interstate 205 southeast of Portland, take Oregon 212 east and Oregon 224 south to the community of Eagle Creek. Oregon 224/211 crosses Eagle Creek about 4.5 miles north of the stoplight in Estacada. Just north of the bridge, turn east onto Wildcat Mountain Drive, which is marked by a sign pointing to Eagle Fern County Park, the fish hatchery, and Dover District. Keep right at an immediate Y and then cross Eagle Creek Road. In less than 2 miles, turn right onto Eagle Fern Road. It is about 2.2 miles from here to the entrance to Eagle Fern County Park. Snuffin Road comes in from the right about 0.8 mile from the park entrance. Either the park or the Snuffin Road bridge can be used as a take-out.

To reach the put-in, return to the junction of Snuffin and Eagle Fern Roads, and find George Road, which starts at this intersection. Follow George Road about 4.5 miles to a right turn onto Rainbow Road. A sign on the left points toward the hatchery, 2 miles away and 600 feet down. A marked parking lot is located next to a private bridge across the creek. Across the bridge is private property, too, so it is better to put in by the parking area.

Gauge

None exists. Generally, Eagle Creek is runnable if the Clackamas is about 3000 cfs, but it drops quickly after rains. Look at the water level from the Oregon 211 bridge or at the put-in.

Hank Hays and WKCC Editors

136 Eagle Creek
Snuffin Road to Eagle Creek Road

Class: 3+(5) P	Length: 5 miles
Flow: 300 cfs	Character: forested; residential
Gradient: 55 fpm, C–PD	Season: rainy

The character of the lower run on Eagle Creek is similar to that of the upper run (see the Eagle Creek: Fish Hatchery to Snuffin Road run). About 0.5 mile below the put-in at the Snuffin Road bridge is a low-head dam (1 to 2 feet). A shallow slide in the center of the dam makes an easy run. A mile below the put-in, the North Fork Eagle Creek emerges underneath a bridge at a left bend in the river. "The Falls," a dangerous class 5 rapid, is 0.5 mile farther. Plenty of action can be had before the falls, and eddies get progressively smaller near the falls. Work toward the right as soon as you see the upstream end of a concrete fish ladder on the right bank, and take out at the upstream end of the fish-ladder retaining wall. If you decide to run the falls, stay far right, boofing off the end of the fish ladder. Most of the current pushes to the left and into a nasty undercut slot on the left bank. The portage trail is up the bank on the right and back down to the river about a hundred yards downstream.

About 1.5 miles of boulder gardens await below The Falls. The first 0.5 mile drops at the rate of 125 fpm. There are usually logs in the biggest rapids, so scout blind corners before attempting a run. The first hard right bend below The Falls quite often has logs. Scout left.

About 0.5 mile below The Falls, a blind left bend around a small island also has several logs wedged between a rock and the left bank. Scout left, from the top of the island. Portaging would not be easy because the banks are sheer on both sides. This is the last really nasty spot, but many more interesting drops and boulder gardens follow along the next mile. A couple of automobiles are also in the creek.

The recommended take-out is the first concrete bridge. Land about 25 feet above it on the right for the easiest hike up to the road. The run could be continued down to the Dowty Road crossing, about 0.5 mile from the creek mouth, or even to Barton Park on the Clackamas.

Hazards

Difficulties include possible logjams, sweepers, The Falls, and the boulder gardens below The Falls. Many anglers are usually present in this section, so courteously avoid them. The Falls can be scouted by looking for a small pullout, yellow gate, and trail on the way to the put-in.

Access

For directions to a put-in at either Snuffin Road or Eagle Fern County Park, see the Eagle Creek: Fish Hatchery to Snuffin Road run.

A vehicle can be dropped off at the take-out on Eagle Creek Road on the way in by taking a right onto Eagle Creek Road (the first crossroad after leaving Oregon 211) and parking in the pullout on the east side of the road before crossing the bridge.

Gauge

None exists. Generally, Eagle Creek is runnable if the Clackamas is about 3000 cfs, but it drops quickly after rains. Look at the water level from the Oregon 211 bridge or at the put-in.

Hank Hays and WKCC Editors

137 Clear Creek
Metzler Park to Redland Road Bridge

Class: 2+(3) T	Length: 7 miles
Flow: 500 cfs	Character: forested; residential
Gradient: 41 fpm, C	Season: rainy

The main stem of Clear Creek drains the north face of Goat Mountain south of Estacada and flows into the Clackamas River at Carver. Because the stream is small and subject to logjams, take a peek around blind bends in the river before committing yourself. Flat water with good current stretches between drops. Most of the land along both banks is private except for two small sections of BLM timber and Metzler Park. Above the put-in, Clear Creek consists of several small feeders with no public access.

From the very beginning the creek is fairly fast and continuous. Keep a sharp lookout for logs or downed trees in the creek. It could be difficult to land before getting into trouble. About 0.5 mile below the park is a good class 2+ rapid. About 4 miles into the run a steel bridge spans the river. This marks the start of a half-mile steeper section consisting of three or four class 3 boulder drops. The last drop has a 3-foot pour over at the bottom. The rest of the run flattens out to class 1 with probably a few logs or trees to portage or pass under. As of 2012 a huge log jam, in slowly moving water, existed in this lower section. The take-out is on the right.

An alternate put-in is down a steep bank where the Oregon 211 bridge crosses Clear Creek. This adds a mile to the trip and will likely include wood.

Hazards
Logjams and logs spanning the river are the main hazards. It can be difficult to stop in the 0.5-mile steep section below the steel bridge. Logs could be very dangerous in this section.

Access
The put-in is about 25 miles southeast of Portland. From Estacada take Oregon 211 south about 4 miles. At the top of the hill, turn right onto Hollman Road. Take the first left onto Metzler Park Road and drive 1.5 miles into the park, the put-in.

To reach the take out, return to Holman Road. After crossing it, the name changes to Springwater Road. About 5 miles farther, take Redland Road, the first left turn after the entrance to Milo McIver State Park. Proceed 1.5 miles to the bridge over Clear Creek, the take-out.

Gauge
None exists. Clear Creek rises and falls abruptly. It has been run when the Clackamas at Three Lynx was at 4400 to 5400 cfs. Check the river level at the bridges described above.

Hank Hays and WKCC Editors

138 Clackamas River
June Creek Bridge to Collawash River

Class: 3+(4); 4	Length: 8 miles
Flow: 800 cfs; 5000 cfs	Character: forested; hot springs
Gradient: 77 fpm, PD	Season: rainy/snowmelt

The Clackamas River above the Collawash confluence contains nearly continuous, intermediate rapids, beautiful scenery, clear water, and a pleasant riverside hot springs. The rocky streambed and consistent gradient provide plenty of action for the first 5.5 miles. Two small, narrow gorges in this first section contain steeper drops and should be scouted from the road during the shuttle to check for wood. Austin Hot Springs, about 5.5 miles from the put-in, make a nice spot to warm hands and feet. About 0.5 mile below the hot springs is a steep drop with a large rock in the middle of the river. The drop is preceded by 50 yards of waves and holes. Boaters generally run just to the right of the center rock; punching through a large wave and avoiding another rock on the right. A sneak route along the right bank is possible at some levels. The left side looks attractive but is dangerously undercut. A long boulder garden (class 3+ to 4) that contains some nice waves and holes as well as large rocks is 2 miles downstream. Scout the entire boulder garden from the road.

Hazards

This run collects a lot of wood in some years. Wood is constantly shifting position so it is important to scout all the more difficult rapids and the rest of the river from the road before starting the run. The significant rapids are 0.5 mile, 2.5 miles, and 4.4 road miles upstream of the take-out. In addition, steel cables left in the river from past stream habitat work could be hazardous.

Access

Oregon 224/NF 46 follows the river for the entire run. June Creek Bridge is about 7 miles upstream of the NF 46–NF 63 junction. Take out on the left immediately before the NF 63 bridge or at several other places around the bridge. See the Collawash River to Sandstone Road Bridge run for directions to the NF 63 bridge. Because the road follows the river for the entire run, any number of alternate put-ins and take-outs are possible.

Gauge

Currently available via the Internet (Clackamas River above Three Lynx gauge) (see Appendix A). The flow on the June Creek section is roughly half to two-thirds that at the Three Lynx gauge.

Pete Giordano

139 Clackamas River
Collawash River to Sandstone Road Bridge

Class: 4(5+) P	Length: 8.5 miles
Flow: 1000–4000 cfs	Character: forested; roadless
Gradient: 43 fpm, PD	Season: rainy/snowmelt

This secluded and scenic run on the Clackamas River can be dangerous and intimidating, particularly at high flows. A reliable roll, reliable equipment, and a competent leader make for a more enjoyable day. Landslides and high water continually shape the rapids and landscape on this run. You should always be wary of logs.

After 1 mile of flat water, the river moves away from the road and boaters begin to encounter some fun class 2 and 3 rapids. The rapids gradually increase in size before reaching Hole in the River rapid. At low flows, this rapid is a maze of rocks, but at high water, when the rocks become covered, several large holes appear in the left and middle of the rapid. Around the next bend is a steep rapid that slams into a huge undercut boulder. Move left immediately below the rapid to avoid being pushed uncomfortably close to the boulder. Below this rapid are many fun class 3 rapids including Rocky's Rapid, where the river bends right after slamming into a wall. About 4.5 miles below the put-in, just below Rocky's Rapid, is Alder Flat Campground. This is the only take-out before the nasty stuff begins downstream. From the trail on the right, it is about 1 mile uphill to the road.

Immediately below Alder Flat Campground is a pushy class 4 rapid called Drop Stopper, named for the large midstream boulder at the bottom. Twice in the next 0.5 mile, the river bends right after slamming into high rock walls. Prelude Rapid, two narrow slots, is just to the right of the second wall. Scouting Prelude from above is recommended because Killer Fang, class 5+, is 150 feet downstream and out of sight. After running Prelude, land on river right for the portage around Killer Fang. At most flows, the majority of water in Killer Fang flows into a dead-end sieve on the right. A small opening is on the left, but the left wall is undercut. Portage over the rocks and slide back into the river in the pool below the sieve. Water can be seen bubbling up from the exit of the sieve deep below the water's surface.

Do not relax after Killer Fang. The next mile has two class 4 rock gardens. The first, Sieve, is around the corner from Killer Fang. After a pushy class 3 entrance rapid, the water slams into the middle of a rock jumble with several undercuts and sieves. The only clear passage is down a chute on the far left. At low water levels, a large tree stump blocks the exit of this chute. Scout and/or portage on the left. Next comes River's Revenge, where some fancy eddy hopping is required to maneuver through the narrow slots between large rocks. Class 2 rapids continue for about a mile to the take-out.

Hazards

This section is very different from the more popular section immediately downstream from the Clackamas River: Three Lynx Power Station to North Fork Reservoir run. Landslides constantly deposit logs into the river and can change rapids from year to year. Logs pose a real threat on any of the rapids and can be difficult to see at river level. As always, scout if the bottom of a rapid is hidden from view. Definitely scout Drop Stopper, Prelude, and Sieve. Although it has been run, Killer Fang is almost always a mandatory portage at any water level.

Access

From the north: From Interstate 205 southeast of Portland, take Oregon 212 east and Oregon 224 south to Estacada. *From the south:* From Oregon 99E northeast of Salem take Oregon 211 east to Estacada. Follow Oregon 224 southeastward from Estacada, past the Three Lynx Power Station 0.25 mile to Sandstone Road. The take-out is on river left just upstream of the bridge where Sandstone Road meets Oregon 224/NF 46.

Continue up Oregon 224/NF 46 toward the put-in. Several put-ins are possible at the NF 46/NF 63 junction, including a nice spot just upstream of the bridge at the junction on the left side of the river. Day use is available on the right just after crossing the bridge. An alternate put-in, located 1 mile downstream at Riverside Campground, skips the beginning flat water.

Gauge

Located at Three Lynx. Currently available via the Internet (Clackamas River above Three Lynx gauge) or contact the River Forecast Center in Portland (see Appendix A).

Roger Van Zandt, Hank Hays, and Pete Giordano

140 Clackamas River
Three Lynx Power Station to North Fork Reservoir

Class: 3(4)	Length: 13 miles
Flow: 750–3000 cfs	Character: forested; popular area
Gradient: 43 fpm, PD	Season: year-round

This section of the Clackamas River is one of the most popular runs in Oregon. The beautiful canyon scenery, quality beginner–intermediate whitewater, and proximity to Portland entice boaters throughout the year. At high water levels, several of the rapids develop large waves and holes, while low water creates rocky, technical rapids followed by beautiful pools. All the major rapids can be scouted from the road.

About 0.25 mile below the put-in is Powerhouse rapid. This rapid can be quite challenging at some flows as the main current slams into the bank and splits. Aim for the large pool on the left as you crash through the waves in the center. For the next several miles, the river moves through many fun class 2 to 3 rapids, including The Narrows, where the river is squeezed between beautiful basalt walls. Around the corner from Sunstrip Campground is Roaring River rapid, a steep, rocky rapid that is generally run on the left. At low flows, the left wall at the bottom should be avoided because it is undercut and has sharp exposed rocks. The next major rapid is Hole-in-the-Wall. At high water, this rapid develops a very dangerous recirculating pocket along the left wall. Avoid it by staying far right. Immediately past the next bridge is the Fish Creek boat ramp, which provides good access for a shorter run.

About 0.5 mile below this bridge and past another bridge is one of the biggest rapids on the run, Carter Bridge. Scout on the left when a third bridge comes into view. The line is generally down the left, avoiding a ledge that extends across most of the river from the right bank. After a short section of easier water, the river plunges through Big Swirly or Slingshot. Run down the middle through the large waves and swirly water, or aim for the large eddy on the left. A boiling eddy forms along the wall on the right at the bottom of the rapid. Just below the large pool at Big Eddy is Rock 'n Roll, a short plunge through some rocks on the right. At some flows, a great play hole develops in the wave train below the rapid. Toilet Bowl, class 3+ to 4, is just around the corner from Rock 'n Roll and contains some huge waves at high water. Scout from the gravel bar on the right. Toilet Bowl is most easily portaged along the left. This is the last big rapid on the run, although several fun class 2 rapids lie ahead in the 2 miles between Toilet Bowl and the reservoir. Bob's Hole, a popular play hole, is also just below Toilet Bowl. This play hole is the site of the nationally famous Bob's Hole Whitewater Rodeo, held every spring. Bob's Hole was named after Bob Breitenstein, who, in his early kayaking years, always insisted on trying to run through the hole but always got knocked over.

The remaining 4 miles to North Fork Reservoir are class 2 and generally easier than the rapids above. Inexperienced boaters may tend to get pushed into the bank in several places. All of this lower section can be seen from the road. Slack water begins just after the South Fork Clackamas enters from the left.

Hazards

All the major rapids can be scouted from the road. Be sure to scout Hole-in-the-Wall, as this rapid is very dangerous at medium and high water. A metal ladder is attached to the upstream rock wall of the pocket that can be used in rescue situations.

Access

Oregon 224 follows the Clackamas very closely on this run and allows for many possible put-ins and take-outs. To reach Oregon 224, go to Estacada and take Oregon 224 southeast upriver. (To reach Estacada, see the Clackamas River: Collawash River to Sandstone Road Bridge run.) The two most common put-ins are at the bridges immediately above and below the Three Lynx Power Station.

Other accesses include Carter's Bridge, Big Eddy Recreation Site, a road pullout just below Toilet Bowl, along the road at Bob's Hole, Memaloose log-scaling station, Lazy Bend Campground, and, finally, North Fork Reservoir.

Gauge

Located at Three Lynx. Currently available via the Internet (Clackamas River above Three Lynx gauge) or contact the River Forecast Center in Portland (see Appendix A).

Bill Ostrand, Hank Hays, and Pete Giordano

141 Clackamas River
Milo McIver State Park to Barton Park

Class: 2+	Length: 8 miles
Flow: 800–3000 cfs	Character: park, lowlands
Gradient: 17 fpm, PD	Season: year-round

This beautiful stretch of the Clackamas River may be run all year. The first 2.5 miles are located entirely within Milo McIver State Park; for a short trip, take out at the lower end of the park. If continuing downstream, it is another 5.5 miles to the take-out at Barton Park.

The put-in at the Milo McIver State Park boat ramp offers a view of the first and largest drop. A ledge across the river provides several good standing waves for surfing. The river twists through the park with more small rapids and goes into a rock garden. The rock garden is followed by a nice play spot

Gearing up (Jason Rackley)

with more standing waves and eddies on both sides. More bends and small rapids are encountered on the way to the optional take-out at Milo McIver State Park's lowest picnic area. From here to Barton Park are several more small rapids and play spots, mostly flat water with occasional class 1 to 2 rapids. Barton Park also has both a boat ramp and picnic area.

Hazards
In high water, the first drop should be checked for the boat-eating hole that develops. A headwall below the play spot mentioned above can circulate a swimmer at high water.

Access
Be prepared to pay an entrance fee at both parks. To reach the Barton Park take-out, from the Portland area take Oregon 212 east and then Oregon 224 southeast. The park, about 7 miles from Oregon 212, closes at dusk.

The put-in is reached by driving upstream on Oregon 224 to Milo McIver State Park. Once in the park, follow the road down the hill. The put-in is at the boat ramp.

The optional take-out for the short 2.5-mile run is reached by driving to the lowest parking lot (and picnic area) within Milo McIver State Park.

Gauge
Located at Estacada. Currently available via the Internet (Clackamas River at Estacada gauge) (see Appendix A). This run is runnable most of the year. Rocky runs have been made at levels as low as 750 cfs.

Bob Collmer

142 Clackamas River
Barton Park to Carver

Class: 2	Length: 5.5 miles
Flow: 800–3000 cfs	Character: residential
Gradient: 14 fpm	Season: year-round

This stretch of the Clackamas River is an excellent training area for beginners. There are many small class 2 drops, usually with eddies close by. The rapids are clean and have good runouts. The scenery is uncluttered, even though some areas have housing on the river's edge. The river class rises to the 2+ level in the spring and drops to the 2- level in the summer. It is runnable all year and is often run in the evening, when daylight permits.

Hazards
The run presents no major problem areas, although several rapids pick up speed and provide some bouncy places.

Access

To reach the put-in at the boat ramp in Barton Park, which requires an entrance fee and closes at dusk, see the Clackamas River: Milo McIver State Park to Barton Park run.

To reach the take-out, return north on Oregon 224 to Carver. The take-out is located at the boat ramp just upstream from the bridge in Carver.

Gauge

Located at Clackamas. Contact the River Forecast Center in Portland (see Appendix A).

Bob Collmer

143 Clackamas River
Carver to Clackamette Park

Class: 2	Length: 8 miles
Flow: 800–3000 cfs	Character: residential
Gradient: 9 fpm, C	Season: year-round

This stretch of river is a fine run for intermediate canoers and beginner kayakers. The rapids are characterized by turns with standing waves on the outside or the middle of the channel, with a nice soft eddy on the inside. The most difficult rapids are a pair of right bends followed by a pair of left bends. The second pair has a central rock to avoid. High rocks and a trestle bridge are next. There is an easy riffle here, but several 17-foot aluminum canoes have wrapped around the bridge piers. The run finishes with a nice long but not too tight S turn. The waves here are irregular and can be fun. Clackamette Park is 0.8 mile farther down on the left. The Clackamas River then flows into the Willamette River.

Hazards

Canoers should know how to handle S turns with high standing waves.

Access

The put-in is at the bridge that crosses the Clackamas at Carver. Carver is located on Oregon 224, 4 miles east of Clackamas, which can be reached from Interstate 205 southeast of Portland.

To reach the take-out at Clackamette Park, go to the south end of the bridge in Carver and turn right on Clackamas River Road, which follows the south side of the river. At the intersection with Washington Street/Oregon 213, turn left. After 1 mile, turn right, cross the railroad tracks, and turn right again immediately after the tracks onto McLoughlin Boulevard. Continue north 0.5 mile to Clackamette Park.

Gauge

Located at Clackamas. Contact the River Forecast Center in Portland (see Appendix A).

Kurt Renner

Columbia Gorge

Sandy River and Tributaries

144 Salmon River Wilderness Trailhead to Arrah-Wanna Road

Class: 2+(3)	Length: 5.3 miles
Flow: 500–2000	Character: forested; cabins
Gradient: 64 fpm, C	Season: rainy

This stretch of the Salmon begins several miles below the Salmon–Huckleberry Wilderness where the river plunges through a beautiful gorge with several large waterfalls. In contrast, this section provides an enjoyable afternoon of fairly continuous class 2 rapids with great wilderness scenery. If you have some extra time, some wonderful old-growth forests can be seen along the first mile of the trail into the wilderness upstream of the put-in.

Rapids begin right from the beginning as the river tumbles through small boulder gardens in a lush forested canyon. About 2 miles into the run is a long boulder garden that ends in a 3-foot ledge. This is the most difficult rapid on the run. After another mile, the canyon opens up and cabins, which detract somewhat from the experience, begin to appear.

Hazards
Logs in places along the bank could be a problem at higher flows.

Access
To reach the take-out, turn right on Arrah-Wanna Road 15.5 miles east of Sandy on US 26. The take-out is at the bridge over the river 1 mile from the highway.

To reach the put-in, return to US 26, turn right, and travel 1.5 miles to Salmon River Road. Turn right and travel 5.2 miles to the bridge over the river.

Gauge
Visual. The Sandy (Sandy River at Bull Run gauge on the Internet) can be used to estimate the flow on the Salmon (see Appendix A). The flow on the Sandy should be a minimum of 3000 cfs.

Pete Giordano

Tsunami Falls, Stebbins Creek (Jason Rackley)

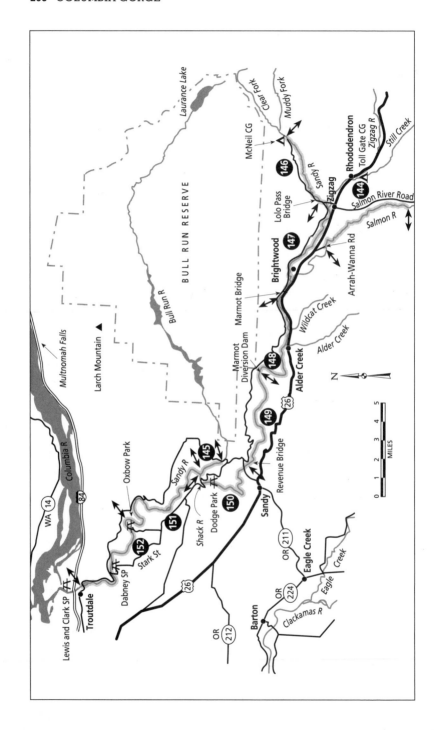

145 Bull Run River
Bull Run Road Bridge to Dodge Park

Class: 3	Length: 2.5 miles
Flow: 700 cfs	Character: canyon
Gradient: 30 fpm, PD	Season: year-round

Portland's municipal water supply is drawn from the Bull Run River about 6 miles above the bridge at Bull Run Road. Consequently, the entire watershed is closed to public access. Only a 2.5-mile section from the Bull Run Road bridge to the confluence with the Sandy River can be run.

This brief run offers six class 3 drops beginning just below the bridge. The last of these drops is Swing-set, named for the cable and basket arrangement strung across the river just below the drop. The river mellows to class 2 for the final 0.5 mile or so to the confluence with the Sandy and the inviting take-out beach in Dodge Park. The run also has a permanent slalom course near the put-in just below the powerhouse.

Hazards

None in particular, with the possible exception of the very steep put-in. The passages are narrow at lower flows, increasing the difficulty slightly. At higher flows, the whole run is filled with large holes and waves and continuous whitewater.

Access

The take-out is at Dodge Park, east of Portland. Follow US 26 to the eastern city limits of Gresham. Turn left onto Palmquist Road. Turn right at the next stop sign, which is SE Orient Drive. Bear left after 2 miles onto SE Dodge Park Boulevard. Turn right after 4.8 miles onto SE Lusted Road and continue down the hill to the bridge over the Sandy River. Dodge Park is across the bridge on the left.

To get to the put-in, go to the east end of the bridge at Dodge Park, head east, and bear left on Lusted Road. Proceed 1.8 miles, then turn left again on Southeast Ten Eyck Road toward Aims. Turn left on Bull Run Road and descend to the bridge over the Bull Run River. Basically, take every paved road to the left after leaving the east end of Dodge Park bridge; the put-in bridge is within 3 miles.

Gauge

Bull Run River at Bull Run gauge (which is located on the Bull Run River upstream of where the Little Sandy River enters the Bull Run River). Available via the Internet (see Appendix A). Currently, the flow is augmented just below the put-in by the PGE powerhouse (when it is generating) with water diverted from the Little Sandy River to Roselyn Lake and then to the powerhouse. Consequently, this section may have more water than the gauge indicates. In approximately 2009, the diversion dam on the Little Sandy is scheduled for removal, and then Bull Run flow will be augmented by the Little Sandy River directly and no longer will be augmented by the diversion of this flow through the powerhouse.

Thom Powell and WKCC Editors

146 Sandy River
McNeil Campground to Lolo Pass Road Bridge

Class: 4+ T	Length: 5.5 miles
Flow: 600–800 cfs	Character: wooded
Gradient: 200 fpm, C	Season: rainy/snowmelt

This run on the Sandy takes you through only one rapid. It begins at the put-in at the McNeil Campground bridge and ends 5.5 miles later at the take-out at the next bridge. It begins as class 4, gets tougher around the middle (4+), and lets up a little toward the end. The run takes about 50 adrenaline-filled minutes to complete (barring unforeseen problems). The rather continuous gradient makes the drops fairly uniform in difficulty, but occasionally a steeper or narrower passage is encountered. The first trip down this run is an unforgettable experience.

This run has a remote feeling to it, but Lolo Pass Road is usually less than 0.3 mile through the woods on river right. The alders and underbrush are quite thick, but anyone who is experiencing early difficulty should quickly opt for the nature walk, for the river gets tougher before it gets easier.

Near the bottom of the run are a couple of houses on river right. This is the start of a development called Zigzag Village. It is imperative that you use the left channels in the vicinity of these houses, for one of the right channels is completely blocked by a logjam.

Hazards

This run usually has many, many logs. At high flows, it may not be possible to stop. The continuous nature of the river—that is, lack of pools between rapids—makes rescue difficult.

Access

To reach the take-out, take US 26 east from Portland and turn left (north) off US 26 at the Zigzag Store onto Lolo Pass Road. The take-out is about 1 mile down this road at the second bridge. (The first bridge crosses the Zigzag River.)

To get to the put-in, continue up Lolo Pass Road. After 3.5 miles, look for a sign that marks entry into Mount Hood National Forest. Just past this sign, turn right on NF 1825, which leads to Ramona Falls. Continue up this road for 1 mile to reach the put-in at the bridge just before the McNeil Campground.

Gauge

Located at Bull Run. Currently available via the Internet (Sandy River at Bull Run gauge) (see Appendix A). Three days of heavy rain are needed, even in winter, to bring this run up to a runnable level. The only way to gauge the flow accurately is to check the water level against some logs that are built into the river-left bank just below the McNeil Campground bridge. When the water is halfway up the lowest log, it is a runnable flow, and if this same log is covered, it is too much. The river level drops rapidly as soon as rains subside, providing about a 3-day period to run the river before it gets too low.

Thom Powell and WKCC Editors

147 Sandy River Zigzag to Marmot Bridge

Class: 2 T; 3	Length: 7 miles
Flow: 700–2000 cfs; 2000+ cfs	Character: forested; residential
Gradient: 70 fpm, C	Season: rainy/snowmelt

The river flows through a broad valley with an almost constant gradient. The sandy bottom gives the river its name, and the boulders give the river its rapids. Areas without boulders form fast-moving pools. The dynamic nature of this type of riverbed makes describing individual rapids pointless. Each minor flood changes the rapids somewhat and may change the locations of deep channels and the best paddling routes. A major flood may completely change the river.

The most difficult rapids are at the top of the run where the river is steepest. Farther downstream are more pools but still plenty of whitewater. After the confluence with the Salmon River (about 0.5 mile above Marmot Bridge), the volume increases greatly and the water takes on more "big-water" characteristics. Many stationary, smoothly shaped waves characterize the lower rapids during medium and high flow levels.

At all levels, even at the highest runnable flows just short of flood, the river does not form dangerous features such as riverwide holes or exploding waves. The most difficult level is at medium-high flows when the river is high enough to form holes behind the large boulders. When the river is so high that rocks and boulders can be heard crashing together on the bottom, consider another form of recreation for the day.

Hazards

No rapids stand out as significantly more difficult or dangerous than the general pace of the river. Occasionally brush extending from the banks and logjams may cause problems.

Access

From the Portland area, take US 26 east to Zigzag. Turn left (north) onto Lolo Pass Road, just east of the Zigzag Store. Continue to the second river crossing, the put-in.

To reach the take-out, return to US 26 and turn right (west). After 6 miles, turn right (north) on Sleepy Hollow Road and proceed 0.3 mile to a road on the right that crosses the Sandy River on Marmot Bridge, the take-out.

Gauge

Located at Bull Run. Currently available via the Internet (Sandy River at Bull Run gauge) (see Appendix A). This run is runnable most of the late fall, winter, and spring. Warm spring days during years of good snowpack may yield excellent runoff when many other rain-dependent rivers are low. If the river appears too low at the put-in, consider putting in farther downstream.

Bill Ostrand

148 Sandy River
Marmot Bridge to Marmot Diversion Dam

Class: 2+(4)	Length: 6 miles
Flow: 700+ cfs	Character: forested; residential
Gradient: 33 fpm, C-PD	Season: rainy/snowmelt

This run on the Sandy River provides a warm-up for boating the class 4 Sandy Gorge, which begins just below the Marmot Diversion Dam.

The first 3 miles of this section begin with a series of class 2 rapids. After another mile and immediately after a long series of waves and holes is Alder Creek Rapid, class 4. Look for an A-frame house and several other houses overlooking the rapids on the left bank. Below Alder Creek, the rapids become progressively easier until the takeout. The Marmot Diversion Dam was removed in 2007. The climb out to the accessible part of the road may be steep at this take-out. Some paddlers continue boating 6.5 miles further onto the next run.

Hazards

Alder Creek Rapid can present a real challenge. The drop appears as a horizon line from upstream. An easy scout or portage is on the right.

Access

From Portland, take US 26 east to the town of Sandy. The lower put-in is about 11 miles east of Sandy. Turn left (north) on Sleepy Hollow Road. Continue about 1 mile to a road on the left that crosses the Sandy River on the Marmot Bridge, the put-in.

To reach the take-out, see the Sandy River: Marmot Diversion Dam to Revenue Bridge run.

Gauge

Currently available via the Internet (Sandy River at Bull Run gauge) (see Appendix A).

Bill Ostrand and WKCC Editors

149 Sandy River
Marmot Diversion Dam to Revenue Bridge

Class: 4	Length: 6.5 miles
Flow: 800–3000 cfs	Character: forested; roadless
Gradient: 40 fpm, PD	Season: rainy/snowmelt

This run is also known as the Sandy Gorge. For almost the entire length of the gorge, the Sandy cuts a winding and often quite narrow canyon through a formation of compacted volcanic ash conglomerate. The walls of the canyon are deeply sculpted and sometimes overhanging, and they rise 150 feet. A multitude of small waterfalls cascading down from both sides, plus lush vegetation consisting of both deciduous and evergreen trees and mosses and maidenhair ferns that cling to the ceilings of caves and overhangs, make this stretch of river among the most picturesque in Oregon.

Most people will choose to put in about 400 yards above the '64 Logjam Rapid. Portage the remnants of this logjam on the right.

For the next 3.5 miles, the river drops with many short enjoyable rapids and one longer class 3 rapids at about mile 2.5. In the last 2 miles are four rapids that should be scouted: Boulder Rapid, Rasp Rock, Drain Hole, and Revenue Bridge. At Boulder Rapid, the canyon narrows dramatically, with a tremendous overhang and free-falling waterfall on the left and large boulders in the middle. It is possible to portage Boulder Rapid along the wall on the far left. The left chute can be scouted from the boulders on the left while the right chute can only be boat scouted. At low flows, most people run the right chute; punching a breaking wave and threading through a boatwide slot on the far right. Boaters can then work their way back to the middle to complete the rapid. Be cautious of wood in and below the slot. At higher water, the left chute becomes more attractive, but be careful to stay left to avoid the undercut rock in the middle.

The difficulty of the next two rapids, Rasp Rock and Drain Hole, varies dramatically with water level. Rasp Rock is a furious 50-yard drop over conglomerate boulders with some big holes interspersed throughout. It is shaped like a funnel with a huge hole at the beginning of the neck and two big boulders at the end. This hole tends to surf boaters into the left wall. Scout or portage from either bank. Check for logs in the narrow chutes at the bottom before committing yourself. Any of the three possible chutes are narrow enough for a boat to wedge crosswise, so if you flip anywhere near the bottom, a wet exit might be preferred to a delayed roll.

Drain Hole looks like the end of the river. A rock jumble forces the water left, and it appears to be dammed by a line of three megaboulders. The water slams into the left boulder, which is dangerously undercut. Logs are present in some of the other narrow chutes. The chute between the right-most rock and the canyon wall is usually open. Scout on the right.

Revenue Bridge Rapid is recognized by glimpses of the bridge through

Boulder Rapid in the Sandy Gorge (Jason Rackley)

the trees when rounding the bend. It is easiest to scout from the left as long as you eddy out high enough to ferry back to the middle of the rapid when you decide to run. It is possible to scout the right side line from the gravel bar on the right, but it is difficult to see the whole rapid from here. The beginning of the drop is steep and tends to push boaters into the right wall. Take out almost under Revenue Bridge on the left. A steep trail winds up to the road.

Hazards

The five major rapids—'64 Logjam, Boulder, Rasp Rock, Drain Hole, and Revenue Bridge—may contain wood and/or undercut rocks and should be scouted or portaged.

Access

From Portland, head east on US 26 to Sandy. From the junction of US 26 and Oregon 211 in Sandy, head east for several blocks and turn left toward Bull Run and Oral Hull Park on Ten Eyck Road. This road switches back down into the Sandy River Canyon (take a hard left at the first Y) and goes across Revenue Bridge, the take-out.

To go to the put-in, continue north on Ten Eyck (which becomes SE Marmot Rd as you climb up the hill). Continue on SE Marmot Road for about 4 miles and take a right on Big Sandy Dam Road—a private but open-to-the-public gravel road that goes down to where the dam used to be. (Marmot Diversion Dam was removed in 2007.) After dropping down the hill about 1.5 miles, the road levels out. Turn into the second pull-out on the right where there are some concrete blocks that fence the abandoned road there. Carry boats about 1/8 mile down the abandoned road. Look for a trail to the river on the right. Take the trail about 50 yards down to the river. An alternate put-in may be found at Wild Cat Creek, about one mile above Alder Creek.

Gauge

Currently available via the Internet (Sandy River at Bull Run gauge) (see Appendix A). The flow can be estimated visually by looking upstream from Revenue Bridge: One sees a rock halfway between the bridge and the bottom of Revenue Bridge Rapid; the flow is ideal when enough water splashes over this rock to create a good visible pour over. The gorge has been run at minimum summer flows and at flood.

Hank Hays, Rod Kiel, and WKCC Editors

150 Sandy River
Revenue Bridge to Dodge Park

Class: 2+ to 3	Length: 5 miles
Flow: 1200–4000 cfs	Character: residential
Gradient: 40 fpm, C	Season: rainy/snowmelt

This is a great run for boaters making the transition from beginner to intermediate. The run starts at Revenue Bridge with a crawl down the hill to the river. The upper part of the run is class 2 with many small rapids. The ride picks up where a long slide area is visible on the left. Below here drops are steeper, more frequent, and sometimes rocky. This is a pretty run, but a little more open and populated than the next runs.

Hazards
Run the lower drops with caution. Follow the main current and be careful of rocks in the drops. At very high water, the water goes into snaggy banks and eddies disappear. Logs may be present in the river at high water.

Access
From Portland, drive east on US 26 to Sandy and turn north on Ten Eyck Road. Follow the road downhill, across Cedar Creek, and over the ridge until it crosses the Sandy River at Revenue Bridge, the put-in.

The take-out is at Dodge Park (see the Bull Run River: Bull Run Road Bridge to Dodge Park run).

Gauge
Currently available via the Internet (Sandy River at Bull Run gauge) (see Appendix A).

Bob Collmer

151 Sandy River
Dodge Park to Oxbow Park

Class: 2+(3)	Length: 8 miles
Flow: 1200–4000 cfs	Character: forested; roadless
Gradient: 23 fpm, PD	Season: rainy/snowmelt

The Sandy River is very beautiful in this area. The forested canyon contains several stands of old-growth trees, and beautiful calm pools separate the fun rapids.

The river is quite isolated for most of this section, which only adds to its appeal. It is a very popular stretch, with people fishing both from the bank and from drift boats. It is a pool drop run, with most of the drops clean and many surfing waves scattered along the entire stretch. Pipeline Rapid, class 3, is 0.5 mile from the put-in and should be scouted for rocks. Pull off in the eddy on the left above the visible pipe across the river. Just around the corner is High Cliff rapid. After the next calm stretch, you will encounter a long boulder garden, Blue Hole, which ends with several large waves. At medium water, a large hole develops at the end of the waves. Work right to avoid the hole. After Blue Hole are several more fun rapids separated by moving flat water.

This run can be boated at extremely high water levels without too many dangerous features developing.

Hazards
Scout Pipeline. Be careful of wood in the river at higher flows.

Access
The put-in is reached by driving to Dodge Park (see the Bull Run River: Bull Run Road Bridge to Dodge Park run).

The take-out is the boat ramp at Oxbow Park, which has an entrance fee. After leaving Dodge Park on Dodge Park Boulevard, go 4.4 miles to Hosner Road. Turn right (north) and proceed about 2 miles to the Oxbow Park entrance. After entering the park, continue to the boat launch farthest upstream.

Gauge
Currently available via the Internet (Sandy River at Bull Run gauge) or call the River Forecast Center in Portland (see Appendix A).

Bob Collmer and Pete Giordano

152 Sandy River
Oxbow Park to Lewis and Clark State Park

Class: 1	Length: 7.5 miles
Flow: 700+ cfs	Character: wooded canyon; roadless; residential
Gradient: 8 fpm	Season: year-round

The Sandy River from Oxbow Park to Lewis and Clark State Park is popular with beginning kayakers, family rafters, sports fishers, and others looking for a scenic float close to Portland. Some small rapids are sprinkled throughout this section, and plenty of eddy lines are available for practicing boating skills. Opportunities abound to view wildlife, including osprey, bald eagle, great blue heron, and various species of waterfowl. The gentleness of the river and the beautiful scenery beckon many boaters to the river.

Hazards

Wood on the banks or on the outside of turns could be hazardous to the unprepared.

Access

Take-outs are available at Dabney State Park and Lewis and Clark State Park, both located along Crown Point Highway. From Interstate 84, take exit 18 and follow the signs to Lewis and Clark State Park. To reach Dabney State Park, continue upstream on Crown Point Highway another 2.7 miles.

The put-in is at Oxbow Park. From Lewis and Clark State Park, cross the Stark Street bridge approximately 2.4 miles south of the park on Crown Point Highway. The bridge is 0.25 mile north of Dabney State Park. Continue on Stark Street for 2 miles and turn left on Troutdale Road. Turn left on Division Street after 1.7 miles and follow Division about 3.5 miles; bearing right as it turns into SE Oxbow Park Road. Turn left at the intersection with Hosner Road and follow the signs to the park at the bottom of the hill. Several put-ins in the park include one good boat launch at the park's far end. An entrance fee is assessed during summer.

You may also put in on the north side of the river. To reach this put-in, continue east on the Crown Point Highway from Lewis and Clark State Park or Dabney State Park and turn right onto Hurlburt Road. Follow Hurlburt Road and turn right onto Gordon Creek Road after about 2.2 miles. Put in at a small pullout where the river is close to the road.

Gauge

Currently available via the Internet (Sandy River at Bull Run gauge) or call the River Forecast Center in Portland (see Appendix A).

Sarah Ostrand and Pete Giordano

Hood River and Tributaries

153 Lake Branch Fork Hood River
Divers Creek to West Fork Hood River

Class: 4+ T	Length: 2.2 miles
Flow: 300-600	Character: gorge
Gradient: 117 fpm, PD	Season: rainy

This run, although short, contains some great rapids set in an intimate gorge. The run is usually done as an addition to a run down the West Fork Hood River for boaters wanting a little more kick than the rapids on the West Fork. After the small boulder gardens, at the beginning of the run, the river drops over a ledge and rips through a narrow slot, Helmet Peeler. Scout on the right. Just downstream is Boat Beater, which has an exciting boof on the right or narrow slide on the left. Next is another fun drop,

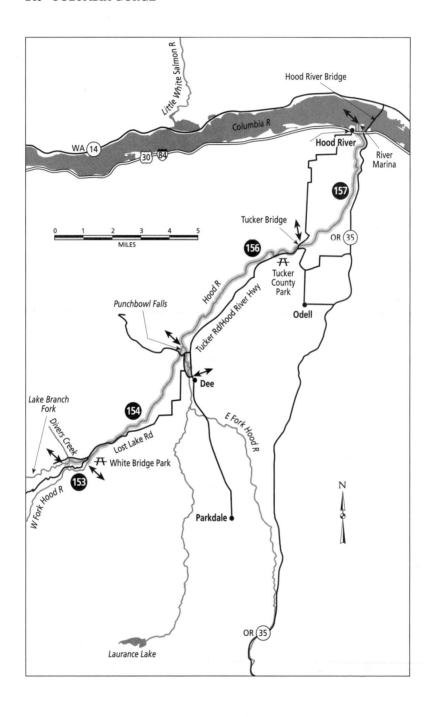

Left or Right. Scout this one carefully as wood tends to accumulate in the narrow channels and underneath the surface. This rapid would be very difficult to portage. Left or Right is followed by several more fun rapids before the West Fork. Take out on the right or continue down the West Fork.

Hazards

The three major drops should be scouted from the right, and first-time boaters will probably end up scouting several other drops. The creek is very narrow in places, so wood could be very dangerous.

Access

The take-out is at the confluence with the West Fork (see the West Fork Hood River: Lake Branch Fork to East Fork Hood River run).

To reach the put-in, backtrack 0.5 mile and turn left. Just after crossing Divers Creek (about 2.6 miles), turn left onto a small spur road. Follow this road about 0.6 mile down to the river.

Gauge

Visual. Generally at least 5 to 6 feet on the Hood River gauge (currently available via the Internet; Hood River at Tucker Bridge gauge) (see Appendix A) means sufficient water for the Lake Branch Fork.

Pete Giordano

154 West Fork Hood River
Lake Branch Fork to East Fork Hood River

Class: 4(5) P	Length: 6.5 miles
Flow: 800+ cfs	Character: forested
Gradient: 100 fpm, PD	Season: rainy/snowmelt

The West Fork of Hood River is one of the best intermediate runs in Oregon. Beautiful basalt gorges, nearly continuous rapids, and an isolated canyon make this a run a classic. The run is a solid class 4 at normal flows, but as flows increase above 3000 cfs, the pools below rapids become small or nonexistent and some of the rapids deserve class 5 attention. The first 2 miles of the run contain many fun class 3 to 3+ rapids and two scenic basalt gorges. About 2 miles downriver from the put-in is a riverwide fish ladder where once there was a beautiful 13-foot waterfall. Portage on the left.

Below the fish ladder, the difficulty of the rapids increases with some steep drops, boulder gardens and large holes. The long boulder garden on a right turn below the fish ladder is one of the more difficult rapids on the run. Boaters generally begin center and work to the right through waves and holes to avoid a large hole that forms in the middle of the river at the bottom of the rapid. Scout the whole rapid from the right bank. Class 4 rapids continue nearly continuously. An extremely sticky hole on the left is found shortly after a large creek enters from the left. The final gorge has some powerful drops with small pools between the drops. Take out on the right before the current picks up speed and plunges over Punchbowl Falls. Some good boaters get eaten by Punchbowl, so run the drop with plenty of momentum or end your day by hiking up the trail on the right bank. If you choose to run Punchbowl, boof hard left into the boiling eddy at the base of the falls. It is another 0.25 mile to the confluence with the East Fork of Hood River and a trail on the right back up to the parking area.

Hazards
Portage the fish ladder on the left. Punchbowl Falls is a large powerful drop and can be scouted from the rocks on the right. Scout the falls and the take-out eddy before you put in.

Access
From Interstate 84 in the city of Hood River, take exit 62 (West Hood River–West Cliff Drive). Follow the signs to Odell and Parkdale, then follow the road toward Dee and Parkdale. Turn right at the sign for Dee–Lost Lake Road. After crossing the East Fork Hood River at Dee, turn right onto Punchbowl Road. Continue on Punchbowl Road, and park on the right near an old gated road just before the bridge over the West Fork Hood River. This is the take-out. The river is about 500 feet down the old road at the confluence of the East and West Forks of Hood River or follow the steep trail down to the river above Punchbowl Falls. Punchbowl Falls can be scouted from this trail.

To get to the put-in, backtrack to the three-way intersection near the bridge over the East Fork Hood River at Dee; keep right at the intersection and follow signs to Lost Lake. Continue upriver on Lost Lake Road. After crossing the second bridge, continue upstream another 1.5 miles, then turn left immediately after crossing the Lake Branch Fork. Carry boats down the road to the river confluence, the put-in, for a total of 6.9 miles from the take-out.

Gauge
Located at Tucker Bridge. Currently available via the Internet (Hood River at Tucker Bridge gauge) or call the River Forecast Center in Portland (see Appendix A). Two-thirds of the flow at Tucker is a good estimate of the flow on the West Fork. A reading of about 5 feet at Tucker is optimum.

John Karafotias and WKCC Editors

155 East Fork Hood River
Sherwood Campground to Oregon 35 Bridge

Class: 4+ to 5	Length: 6 miles
Flow: 200–800 cfs	Character: roadside
Gradient: 155 fpm, C	Season: rainy/snowmelt

There is not much warm-up time on this run. Although the river has some smaller boulder gardens near the put-in, the river shortly takes off downhill like a freight train. The narrowness of the riverbed combined with a relentless gradient and very few eddies along the shore make this run seem a lot tougher than it looks when scouting from the road. Several sections are steeper than others, and several blind corners can contain wood. This is arguably the best continuous class 4 whitewater around, whether it's snowing in February or for those few days each June when the temperatures peg 90 degrees.

At medium and high water, the whole run is essentially one long rapid. Most of the run is visible from the road, especially the steeper sections. If the rapids look big from the road, do not get on the run. The proximity of the road and the unstable geology allow the run to change with each flood event, something entirely unique to this drainage.

Hazards

No eddies, steep continuous rapids, and potential wood combine to make the entire run hazardous. Be sure to scout before committing to the run.

Access

From Hood River, go south on Oregon 35 for 18.5 miles, where the take-out

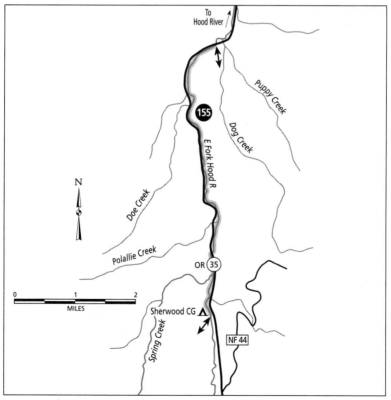

is at the bridge over the river.

To reach the put-in, continue to drive south on Oregon 35 to a pullout on the right just below Sherwood Campground. If wood is obvious as one scouts from the highway curves, use the bridge below or the Polallie trailhead.

Gauge

Currently available via the Internet (Hood River at Tucker Bridge gauge) (see Appendix A). The level at Tucker Bridge should be at least 5.5 feet in the winter, but 4.5 feet is the equivalent in June when it hits 85 degrees in Hood River.

Pete Giordano and Ron Reynier

156 East Fork Hood River
Dee to Tucker Bridge

Class: 3(4); 4	Length: 7.5 miles
Flow: 700 cfs; 2500 cfs	Character: forested; residential
Gradient: 66 fpm, PD–C	Season: rainy/snowmelt

This run is a very popular intermediate run with beautiful scenery, challenging rapids, and good play spots. The first mile is on the East Fork, which is pool drop and runs through a beautiful narrow canyon punctuated by several technical class 3 rapids and one class 4 rapid, Cyclops. Just before the confluence with the West Fork, the river splits around a small island. The right side drops over a uniform 6-foot ledge that can develop a sticky hydraulic at high water. The left side is not as steep but contains more rocks. The water volume doubles after the East Fork joins the West Fork, and the gradient drops off and becomes more uniform. The main stem Hood River is wider but no less challenging than the upper section. At lower flows, the upper section is class 3, with a couple of technical class 4 ledge drops. At higher flows, it becomes continuous class 4.

Hazards

Two rapids should be noted. Approximately 0.5 mile from the put-in is Cyclops, a technical class 4 drop. Another class 4 drop occurs just above Tucker County Park and is identified by an island with most of the river on the right.

Access

From Interstate 84 in the city of Hood River, take the first or second exit and follow the signs to Parkdale and Odell on Tucker Road. After several turns, cross the Hood River, where the take-out is on river right, under the bridge.

To reach the put-in, follow the signs up the river past Tucker County Park toward Parkdale. Stay right on the paved road until the mill at Dee. Cross the bridge and enter a large parking lot on river left. The put-in is about 50 yards downriver, down a steep bank. An alternate put-in is found to the right of the guardrail and down the steep bank at the end of Iowa Drive just before Dee. This avoids Cyclops if it has wood.

Gauge

Located at Tucker Bridge. A reading of 4.5 to 6 feet is ideal but is runnable as low as 3.5 feet. Gauge information is also currently available via the Internet (Hood River at Tucker Bridge gauge) or from the River Forecast Center in Portland (see Appendix A).

Stan Jacobs, Jay Nigra, Ron Reynier, and WKCC Editors

157 Hood River
Tucker Bridge to Hood River Marina

Class: 3; 4-	Length: 5 miles
Flow: 750–3000 cfs; 3500 cfs	Character: forested
Gradient: 60 fpm, C	Season: rainy/snowmelt

Powerdale Dam was removed in 2011, and the Hood River restoration project is brilliant. The first part of the run has bouncy class 2+ rapids but after a mile the river steepens with solid class 3 paddling as one goes right of an island and then through a long sweeping S-turn. More steep whitewater drops away toward the old dam site, now just a beautiful long rapid. The action continues with class 2+ boulder gardens and occasional islands until one sees a slatted retaining wall on the left. The next rapid forms some pushy water at the bottom, especially at high water. A railroad bridge follows and most paddlers stay right, although other options vary year to year. The remainder of the run winds into downtown. The best take-out is at the footbridge located at the west end of the Hood River Marina near the museum.

Hazards

The rapids just after mile 1 become class 3+ to 4- at higher water.

Access

From Interstate 84 in the city of Hood River, take the Hood River/White Salmon exit and proceed north 150 yards and turn left into the Hood River Marina. Drive west on the main road to the footbridge, the take-out.

To reach the put-in, turn right as you exit the marina and follow Oregon 35 south. At mile 6.5, turn right toward Odell. Proceed straight through Odell to Tucker Road. Turn right onto Tucker Road and proceed 1.5 miles farther to Tucker Bridge, the put-in. Alternatively, head south through the Heights in Hood River which turns into Tucker Road.

Gauge

Located beneath Tucker Bridge or on the Internet (Hood River at Tucker Bridge gauge) or from the River Forecast Center in Portland (see Appendix A). Levels of 4–6.5 ft (750–2900 cfs) are ideal, but higher runs are common.

Jeff Bennett and Ron Reynier

Klickitat River, Washington

158 Little Klickitat River
Esteb Road to Klickitat River

Class: 4+	Length: 10.6 miles
Flow: 400–1000 cfs	Character: desert canyon
Gradient: 83 fpm, PD	Season: rainy/snowmelt

The Little Klickitat is a wonderful little creek that runs only during flood events. You are lucky if you can get on this creek once a year; in low water years, this stream never runs at all. All that aside, when the rains fall heavily, this creek is a pleasure. It winds through a remote high desert canyon populated by a variety of wildlife.

Below the put-in, the Little Klickitat is narrow, fast, and brushy as you approach the canyon. No major rapids arise in the first quarter mile or so, but soon enough the creek bends sharply to the right and drops out of sight, signaling the first major drop, which is also the only recommended portage. This first drop contains a dangerous, hidden crack somewhere in the center of the rapid that has trapped a couple of paddlers in the past. At some flows, it may be filled in and is runnable down the far left or right. Scout/portage on the left.

Immediately downstream the gradient kicks off and the creek starts to roll though one steep boulder garden after another. The drops start fairly easy and gradually build in intensity. The creek never really gorges up, but you can definitely get stuck if you boat scout too aggressively, particularly at medium and high flows.

About a quarter of the way into the run is a long rapid with a 5-foot ledge at the bottom. The right side drops onto some rocks, so running the far left side is preferred. Just downstream is a sloping ledge that has a big hole at the bottom. Portage on the left or run the center with momentum. Downstream are more fun rapids as boaters approach Little Klickitat Falls. A rapid leads pretty much right to the lip of the falls, so first-timers should exercise caution above this drop. Several good lines lead over this 17-foot falls on the left and center, but be careful of shallow spots toward the center of the falls. The portage route involves a little scrambling on loose scree, but it is not too difficult.

Below the falls, the rapids mellow out for about three miles of class 2 to 3 before the take-out. At medium and high flows, this stretch has many enjoyable waves to surf and holes to play in.

Hazards
The first ledge has a dangerous pin spot in the center. Scout what you cannot see and watch out for wood.

Access
From Oregon, cross the Columbia River at Portland or Hood River and take Washington 14 east along the Columbia River to Lyle. Here take Washington

142 north to the town of Klickitat. Continue about 5.5 miles to a bridge over the Little Klickitat. This is the take-out.

To reach the put-in, continue on Washington 142 for just over 11 miles and turn onto Esteb Road. Esteb Road is 1.9 miles east of Olson Road and about 0.5 mile after a sharp turn to the right. Follow Esteb Road to a small bridge over the river.

Gauge

Visual. The Little Klickitat needs a lot of water on other rivers to be runnable. The main Klickitat should be at least 3500 cfs but is probably better at 7000 cfs. The flow can be judged by looking at the river above the bridge at the take-out. If the whole width of the river is shallow but runnable, adequate water is probably present upstream.

Jason Rackley

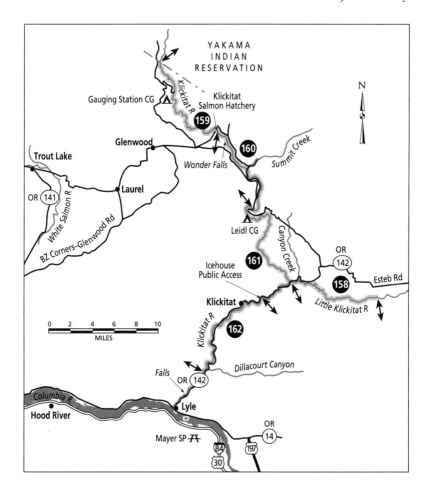

159 Klickitat River
Yakama Indian Reservation to Klickitat Salmon Hatchery

Class: 3; 4	Length: 13 miles
Flow: 800 cfs; 1,800+ cfs	Character: canyon; forested
Gradient: 35 fpm, C	Season: snowmelt

The remote upper run begins near Mount Adams, which was called "Klickitat" by Native Americans. The highest put-in is by the Yakama Indian Reservation boundary. Nonnatives are prohibited beyond here. The put-in is east of the road, down the slope, and through the woods. The long, steep slope with loose soil and many fallen logs requires use of a short line to lower a boat because a runaway boat may not stop until reaching the bottom or crushing a companion. An alternate put-in, preferred by rafters, is located 3 miles downriver at Gauging Station Campground. Once on the river, you will not want to take out because the canyon is remote and mostly inaccessible.

The upper 3 miles are continuous class 3 boating at moderate levels. As flows approach 1,800 to 2000 cfs during peak runoff, the river gets a big-water class 4 push to it. It is not technical, but the continuous nature makes swims dangerous.

After this, the gradient decreases and the lower 10 miles are primarily class 2 with some class 3 headwall drops. At low water, it is technical class 3. At high water, it tends to wash out but is fast. The middle third of the river is highlighted by immense vertical walls of columnar basalt that bend the river in long S turns. The river crashes into these walls, then runs alongside the gray cliffs, drawing dwarfed boaters' wide-eyed gazes upward. The bottom third of the river is mellow but punctuated by a nice class 3 drop near the take-out at the Klickitat Salmon Hatchery. The weir at the hatchery should be scouted or portaged.

Hazards

The upper put-in is tough. The upper river becomes continuous class 4 at high water when the push and continuous nature make swims dangerous. Watch for big holes at high water. The weir at the fish hatchery is potentially dangerous.

Access

From Oregon, cross the Columbia River at Portland or Hood River and take Washington 14 to Washington 141 near the town of White Salmon. Go north for 23 miles on Washington 141 to the town of Trout Lake. Then take the road east to Glenwood. Continue east 3 miles beyond Glenwood to the sign for "Klickitat Salmon Hatchery." Follow the gravel road down to the hatchery. Park at the bottom of the hill, before the buildings. Follow the trail at far left to the river, the take-out.

To reach the put-in, return to the pavement and go back toward Glenwood a few feet. At the Y take the next gravel road to the right to the hatchery. The lower put-in is reached by going about 7 miles up this gravel road to road K1400, which goes to the right; take this road, then turn off onto K1410. (These road signs are small and almost concealed.) Proceed to Gauging Station Campground, the lower put-in. The upper put-in is another 4 miles up to the Yakama Indian Reservation sign on the right. Parking or driving beyond this sign is illegal.

Gauge

Currently available via the Internet (Klickitat River at Pitt gauge) or call the River Forecast Center in Seattle (see Appendix A).

Frank Furlong, Bill Ostrand, and Jon Ferguson

160 Klickitat River
Klickitat Salmon Hatchery to Leidl Campground

Class: 3	Length: 10 miles
Flow: 700+ cfs	Character: forested
Gradient: 36 fpm, C	Season: snowmelt

The first 5 miles below the fish hatchery consist of challenging technical rapids. At flows around 3000 cfs, the rapids wash out and the run involves missing a few big holes and riding big waves. The first class 3 rapids can be seen from the fish hatchery dam. Downstream 2 miles is Wonder Falls, a spring-fed falls on the right and an alternate put-in. Other rapids along the upper section can be scouted from the road. However, about 1 mile below Wonder Falls is a difficult rapids that cannot be seen from the road. Scout or portage left. A long rocky class 2 rapids occurs 1.5 miles below Summit Creek bridge. This is followed by some big boulders and two headwalls with a deceptively vicious eddy on the right of the second wall. The lower 5 miles are relatively easier.

Hazards

The fast water gives the boater very little time to react to riverwide logjams. The dam just below the hatchery has reinforcing rods in the water that must be avoided; portage on left.

Access

For the put-in, go to the take-out for the Klickitat River: Yakama Indian Reservation to Klickitat Salmon Hatchery run. To reach the alternative put-in, go north from Leidl Campground 1 mile toward Glenwood. Turn right on a dirt road near the logging station. Go 3 miles to Summit Creek Bridge. Cross the bridge, proceed upstream until the 30-foot Wonder Falls can be seen on the opposite bank. Put in here or continue upstream another 0.5 mile to a fork; cross the flats to a sandy beach put-in.

To reach the take-out from the fish hatchery, go south from the river to Leidl Campground. At Leidl Campground, turn right for the boat ramp take-out or left and go to the end of the road to a sandy beach.

Gauge

Currently available via the Internet (Klickitat River at Pitt gauge) (see Appendix A). For information on shuttles and logjams, call or visit the Shade Tree Inn in Glenwood (509-364-3471).

Ernie Carpenter

161 Klickitat River
Leidl Campground to Icehouse Public Access

Class: 2	Length: 17 miles
Flow: 500–3500 cfs	Character: wooded canyon
Gradient: 24 fpm	Season: year-round

This is a run for those who want to see beautiful basalt cliffs and ponderosa pines, not for those who want wild whitewater. The 40 class 1 rapids and a few class 2 rapids offer plenty of action for open canoers and beginning kayakers. The canyon is nearly 2 miles wide and 1500 feet deep. The first 12 miles are on Washington State land, but from 1 mile above the Little Klickitat on down is private land. Because plenty of logs are on this river, practice log recognition and log dodging elsewhere before attempting this run.

The put-in is at Leidl Campground, rivermile 33, at the boat ramp below the bridge or at a sandy beach 0.3 mile upstream. The river is braided with many channels for the first 7 miles. The first class 2 rapids is 2.5 miles below the Leidl bridge along a low rock wall on the left. Sneak, scout, or portage right. Stimpson Flats Campground, an alternate river access point, is 0.5 mile farther. A good shaded campground is on the right at rivermile 28, and an abandoned homestead is on a bench to the west. At rivermile 24.5, a four-wheel-drive road comes down to the river. About 5 miles downstream is a series of waves and holes that can be avoided by staying left.

Next, the Little Klickitat River enters from the left, at rivermile 19.5. A class 2 rapids, identified by a cliff on the left and boulders on the right, is 0.5 mile farther. At rivermile 17, 2 miles farther, is the most difficult rapids on this section, the second rapids below the second bridge, class 2. It has a pointed rock in the middle. Scout or portage right. It is normally run left of the pointed rock. The take-out at rivermile 16 is preceded by an old 1880s icehouse on the right that was used to store dry ice made from carbon dioxide produced from local wells. Take out on the right at the concrete boat ramp.

Hazards

Ever-present logs and possible logjams are the greatest danger. Scout if in doubt. At rivermile 29, below Stimpson Flats Campground, the right channel is blocked with logs (1991) and the left channel flows through many sweepers. The class 2 rapids at rivermiles 30.5 and 17 are the most difficult.

Access

From Oregon, cross the Columbia at Portland or Hood River and take Washington 14 east along the Columbia River to Lyle and then Washington 142 north to the town of Klickitat. Continue 2 miles on Washington 142, cross the abandoned railroad tracks, turn right, pass the old icehouse, and go to the public boat ramp, the take-out.

To reach the put-in, return to Washington 142 and continue north along the Little Klickitat River toward Goldendale. After the road leaves the river and reaches a flat summit, turn left on the road to Glenwood. Before reaching Glenwood, cross the Klickitat at Leidl Campground and turn left to the boat ramp or, alternatively, turn right to a sandy put-in at the end of the road.

Gauge

Located at Pitt. Currently available via the Internet (Klickitat River at Pitt gauge) or call the River Forecast Center in Seattle (see Appendix A).

Ernie Carpenter

162 Klickitat River
Icehouse Public Access to Rivermile 5

Class: 2+; 3	Length: 11 miles
Flow: 500–1000 cfs; 1500+ cfs	Character: forested; roaded; residential
Gradient: 20 fpm, PD	Season: year-round

Fun rapids and good surfing waves are found on this run. The river is pool drop with some long rock gardens that can be seen from the road. The last 5.5 miles of the run are in the Columbia Gorge National Scenic Area. Some of the land is private and posted. Do not land or stop for lunch on private land. Some of the rapids can be scouted during the shuttle.

The rapids 0.3 mile above the take-out is the most difficult; scout or portage river left. At low water (1000 cfs), scout by walking up from the take-out but prepare to get soggy sneakers. It is a difficult scout from river right at high water. Scout or portage the dam at the Klickitat Mill on the right. Another difficult drop is about 1 mile below the Pitt Bridge; scout or portage left. If you continue beyond the take-out, beware: You will run into a class 6 waterfall in 2.5 miles.

Hazards

Logs are not as common as upstream, but keep an eye out for the possibility. The rapids in this run get more difficult at higher water. Beware of the class 6 waterfall 2.5 miles below the take-out.

Access

From Oregon, cross the Columbia River at Portland or Hood River and take Washington 14 east to Lyle; at Lyle turn north on Washington 142 and proceed 4 miles upstream along the river to the take-out, a public access on the left with no boat ramp.

To reach the put-in, continue upstream about 8 miles to the town of Klickitat. The Icehouse Public Access put-in is on the right, about 2 miles past Klickitat (see the Klickitat River: Leidl Campground to Icehouse Public Access run). An alternate put-in is another 2 miles upstream, 0.5 mile past the bridge across the river (4 miles above Klickitat) on the left side of the road. An alternate take-out (or put-in) is the dirt road about 0.25 mile downstream from the Pitt Bridge.

Gauge

Currently available via the Internet (Klickitat River at Pitt gauge) or call the River Forecast Center in Seattle (see Appendix A).

Ernie Carpenter

White Salmon River and Tributaries, Washington

163 Trout Lake Creek
Guler Road Bridge to River Road Bridge

Class: 3(4)	Length: 2.8 miles
Flow: 400+ cfs	Character: wooded; agricultural
Gradient: 60 fpm, C	Season: snowmelt

This short but enjoyable run is a nice change if you happen to be in the area. The first 0.5 mile contains many brushy class 2 rapids that culminate in an exciting series of class 3+ to 4 ledges. The ledges can be scouted ahead of time and avoided by using a lower put-in.

After the ledges the river winds through farms and class 2 rapids for about a mile. The next rapid appears above the Old Creamery Road bridge, where the river drops over a few small ledges in a tight channel. After 0.6 mile, the river passes beneath a covered bridge and enters a mini-gorge. By this point, Trout Lake Creek has entered the White Salmon River and the flow has doubled. The gorge contains fast water and many small waves. The trip ends where River Road crosses the river. Just below the take-out, the river drops over a 2- to 3-foot weir. The 1-mile section from the take-out down to the next run is unexplored territory for this author.

Hazards

Scout the ledges in the upper section and portage them, if desired. Brush and trees are potential hazards.

Access

For directions to Trout Lake, see the Klickitat River: Yakama Indian Reservation to Klickitat Salmon Hatchery run. At Trout Lake turn right on Guler Road and put in next to the bridge at the end of this road. To find the optional lower put-in, take the right fork of the road at the south end of the town of Trout Lake. Go 0.2 mile to the put-in beneath the bridge.

To find the take-out, return to Washington 141 and follow Little Mountain Road southeast out of the south end of town. The take-out is 1.6 miles down this road at the River Road bridge.

Gauge

Located at Northwestern Park. Currently available via the Internet (White Salmon River near Underwood, Washington, gauge). The run is good during heavy snowmelt from April to June, or when the gauge at Northwestern Park is above 1200 cfs.

Jeff Bennett

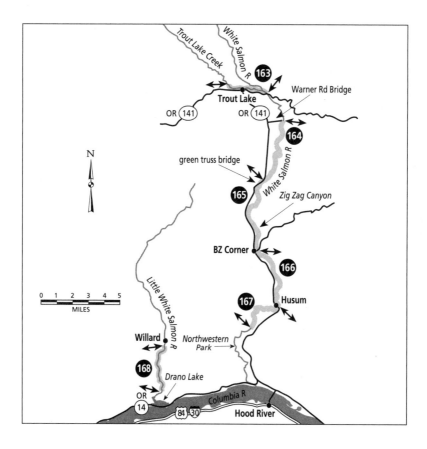

164 White Salmon River
Warner Road Bridge to Green Truss Bridge

Class: 4(5)	Length: 5.1 miles
Flow: 800–1500 cfs	Character: forested canyon
Gradient: 60 fpm, PD	Season: snowmelt

Nicknamed Farmlands, this run can be much more intense than the 60 fpm gradient indicates. It contains numerous class 3 and 4 rapids and some sharp ledge drops of 5 to 15 feet. Since the river is so narrow, a small change in flow creates big changes in difficulty. When flows exceed 1400 cfs, the run contains continuous whitewater and powerful hydraulics; below 1000 cfs, the run becomes enjoyable pool drop with large recovery pools. It is best during spring runoff. By late summer most consider this too low and shift to the Truss which has more water due to underground springs.

After 0.5 mile of warm-up, the river descends into a steep-walled canyon and drops 200 feet in the next 2 miles. It first drops over two 4-foot ledges and enters a narrow 100-yard-long chute with turbulent hydraulics. The second ledge, Sidewinder, can force kayakers uncomfortably close to an undercut ledge on river left at medium flows. A short pool occurs 0.9 mile later before dropping over—or through—Lava Dam. This 15-foot waterfall has a runnable tongue in the center, but be sure to get a good boof as the hydraulic at the bottom tends to stuff boaters behind the falls. Numerous stories are told of boats lost every year at Lava Dam.

Lava Dam is followed by 0.5 mile of pool drop rapids that become pushy at high water, then the canyon opens up and the gradient tapers off considerably. The next 2 miles are mostly class 2 rapids with an occasional class 3. At low flows, this section is very shallow and rocky.

Around mile 4 the river picks up again, then disappears over Off Ramp. Run the marginally runnable 12-foot ledge or the far right side of the ledge. The lead-in is trickier than it looks, so be careful. Portage along the left bank. The last narrow canyon has a bad pin slot on river left. The run ends below the Green Truss Bridge. Save some energy for the strenuous takeout, or put in early and continue all the way to BZ Corner.

Hazards
Wood. The first 2.5 miles become very powerful and nearly continuous above 1400 cfs. At low flows, the middle section is shallow and rocky. The take-out requires a throw rope for hoisting kayaks up the cliff.

Access
The put-in is at the Warner Road bridge, past BZ Corner. For directions to BZ Corner, see the White Salmon River, Washington: BZ Corner to Husum run.

From BZ Corner, drive 8 miles north to Warner Road and turn right. Follow Warner Road about 1 mile to the first bridge. The put-in is on the northeast side of the bridge.

For directions to the take-out at the Green Truss Bridge, see the White Salmon River: Green Truss Bridge to BZ Corner run.

An alternate route allows boaters to scout two major drops during the shuttle: North of BZ Corner 6.6 miles, turn right off Washington 141 onto Sunnyside Road. Lava Dam is beneath an alder stand 0.6 mile up this road (find a small ledge to peer into the canyon), and Sidewinder is found at a wide spot 0.9 mile upstream.

Gauge

Located at Northwestern Park. Flow information is available from the River Forecast Center in Seattle (White Salmon–Near Underwood) (see Appendix A). Flows on the river may be 40 percent lower than at the gauge.

Jeff Bennett, Doc Loomis, Curt Knight, Ron Reynier, and WKCC Editors

165 White Salmon River
Green Truss Bridge to BZ Corner

Class: 4+ T; 5	Length: 5 miles
Flow: 400 cfs; 1000 cfs	Character: forested canyon
Gradient: 119 fpm, PD	Season: rainy/snowmelt

The Green Truss section of the White Salmon is a Northwest classic. This run almost always has enough water to run, making this stretch a world-class destination for expert paddlers in the late spring and early summer. The spectacular basalt gorges on this section are unforgettable, but you probably will not notice the scenery your first time down.

The run starts with a marginal climb down into the canyon, which gets worse every year as erosion takes its toll on the cliff face. (If it is snowing, you will have to rappel to reach the river.) This run is pool drop with a capital D, and the action begins immediately below the put-in with a fun series of class 3 and 4 drops that gradually get bigger as you head downstream.

The first major rapid is The Meatball. Here the river drops to the left over an eight-foot diagonal ledge into a small, turbulent pool. A large boulder (The Meatball) blocks the exit of the pool. This drop requires a leap of faith through the right side slot, but if you haven't run the drop recently, be sure to scout on the left for wood.

Just below the Meatball is Bob's Falls, a sloping 10-foot riverwide ledge that contains the first of the many menacing holes for which this run is known. At higher flows, Bob's begins to resemble a low-head dam and has sent many paddlers swimming; run left with momentum or portage on the left.

Below Bob's a couple of class 3 drops lead to a pool above 25-foot tall Big Brother. This drop is deceptively difficult as the current flows strongly parallel to the lip of the falls, which makes hitting the crucial 3-foot-wide boof flake difficult. A missed line here always has severe consequences because of the dangerous cave under the right wall and the shallow spots in the pool below. Scout and portage on the left side.

Just below Big Brother is Little Brother, a forgiving 15-foot falls that is often run on the left. A short distance below Little Brother is Double Drop, an 18-foot double falls that is rarely run with style. This falls has a rapid leading right to the lip of the drop, so stay alert. Get out to scout and/or portage on the river left side. Paddlers often get pounded by the bottom hole, so be ready to chase some gear if someone rolls the dice and comes up short.

Below Double Drop the difficulty eases and paddlers are treated to the spectacular scenery for which the White Salmon is famous. Springs cascade in from the base of the canyon walls, adding to both the scenery and the flow downstream.

The next major rapid is signaled by a funky basalt outcropping on river left. This is the Cheese Grater, which is generally run center, moving away from the nearly invisible undercut in the river-right wall. Scout or portage on the right.

The walls begin to close in again near Zig Zag Canyon. The two major rapids in this section are long and difficult with serious consequences. Scout Upper Zig-Zag on the right side, and pick your lines carefully. One short pool separates Upper from Lower Zig-Zag, which is scouted on the left side. Lower Zig-Zag is powerful and challenging. Much of the water piles into a boulder in the middle of the river. Getting past the boulder is known as "The Move." This drop always gets the adrenaline pumping as much of the flow funnels into a cave in the river left wall. A mistake here would be regrettable.

Below Lower Zig-Zag are more small, fun drops and play spots until The Flume, a steep drop signaled by a set of pumps on river left.

Just below The Flume is the final pool above 14-foot BZ Falls. Be very careful here as the next rapid leads into the falls, with only a few small eddies on the river-right side just above the lip.

BZ Falls is one of the most dangerous drops on the White Salmon, but lots of paddlers run it anyway. If this drop is not to your liking, you can hike down on the river-right side and climb down to the water a hundred yards downstream. The take-out at BZ Corner is a short float downstream.

Hazards

This run contains many steep, powerful drops that can develop extremely powerful hydraulics. If boaters get into trouble in several of the large rapids, opportunities for other boaters to help are limited.

Access

To reach the take-out from the Portland area, take Interstate 84 east to Hood River. Cross the Columbia River at the Hood River Bridge, turn left onto Washington 14, then turn right onto Washington 141 just before crossing the mouth of the White Salmon River. Follow Washington 141 north, following the signs to Husum. Continue north on Washington 141 past Husum to BZ Corner. Go past the town about 0.2 mile, and turn right at the sign indicating the take-out.

To reach the put-in, continue north on Washington 141 4.7 miles to a dirt road on the right. The put-in is down the steep cliff below the bridge on river right. Parking is available along the main highway or a little way up the highway to a road on the left.

Gauge

Located at Northwestern Park. Flow information is available from the River Forecast Center in Seattle (White Salmon–Near Underwood) (see Appendix A).

Jason Rackley

166 White Salmon River
BZ Corner to Husum

Class: 3+(4)	Length: 5 miles
Flow: 900–2000 cfs	Character: forested canyon
Gradient: 90 fpm, C	Season: year-round

On a hot afternoon, the cold, clear water, nice lunch spots, and good play spots draw rafters and kayakers to this river canyon. The rapids are fairly continuous, especially during the first few miles. The river is very narrow, and one must move from one side of the river to the other and back again.

This exciting class 3+ run has two class 4 drops that can be portaged. If boaters choose to run Maytag, take the short trail upstream and put in in the pool immediately above the rapid. The right trail leads to a put-in on the rock shelf below Maytag. Below Maytag the river immediately begins dropping through continuous class 2 to 3 rapids. Be careful of the undercut cave on the right about 0.5 mile from the put-in. Several bigger rapids appear in the first half of the run. At most flows, they are fairly straightforward. At low flows, they get quite rocky. The last drop, Husum Falls, is a 10-foot vertical drop generally run right of center. Currently (2012) it is more retentive than in past years. Scout Husum Falls from the take-out in Husum. Take out about 150 feet before the falls on river right to avoid the plunge.

Hazards

The first and last drops are by far the most intense. If you cannot see through an entire drop, scout it first.

Access

To reach the take-out from the Portland area, take Interstate 84 east to Hood River. Cross the Columbia River at the Hood River Bridge, turn left onto Washington 14, then turn right onto Washington 141 just before crossing the mouth of the White Salmon River. Follow Washington 141 north, following the signs to Husum. The take-out is on Washington 141 at Husum, either 500 feet below the falls on river left or 150 feet above the falls on river right.

To get to the put-in, continue north on Washington 141 to BZ Corner, go past the town about 0.2 mile, and turn right at the sign indicating the put-in.

Gauge

Currently available via the Internet (White Salmon at Underwood gauge) (see Appendix A) and on the stick gauge at Husum.

John Karafotias and Ron Reynier

167 White Salmon River
Husum to Northwestern Park

Class: 2+	Length: 3 miles
Flow: 900–2000 cfs	Character: shallow canyon
Gradient: 25 fpm, PD	Season: year-round

The scenic lower run on the White Salmon winds its way through a shallow, wooded canyon. It is short, but beginning boaters enjoy the class 2 rapids and play spots. The entire run has opportunities for practicing eddy turns and surfing small waves. The lower end of the run is in transition after the removal of Condit Dam in 2012 and now maintains great class 2 character to the take-out.

Hazards

Rattlesnake, the first drop, is harder than the rest and can be walked on the left. At high water expect class 3 character. The water is always very cold.

Access

For directions to the put-in at Husum, see the White Salmon River: BZ Corner to Husum run.

The take-out is about 2 miles south of Husum, off of Hwy 141. Follow the signs to Northwestern Park. Go over the bridge and turn left into the park.

Gauge

See the White Salmon River: BZ Corner to Husum run.

Bob Collmer and Ron Reynier

Little White Salmon River, Washington

168 Little White Salmon River
Fish Hatchery to Columbia River

Class: 5 T	Length: 4 miles
Flow: 200-700 cfs	Character: steep canyon, gorges
Gradient: 212 fpm, PD/C	Season: rainy/snowmelt

The Little White Salmon has achieved legendary status in steep creeking circles, and its reputation is well deserved. Few runs anywhere have as many high quality rapids combined with such a long season. This creek almost always has enough water to run, which is very unusual for a stream that is so small and so steep. For those who have the skills, the Little White really should not be missed.

Below the put-in you will find some playful class 2 to 3 drops in a very narrow creekbed with small eddies. Soon the creek tilts on edge and careens down through Gettin' Busy, a 0.5-mile-long rapid that will keep even the best boaters entertained. This long boulder garden requires full-on, nonstop reactionary boating and can either be great fun or pure terror, depending on your ability level and flow. At lower flows (below 3 feet), plenty of small eddies appear, and at high flows (3.5 feet and above), the water becomes a massive gauntlet of beefy holes and wild hydraulics.

Gettin' Busy ends abruptly in a blind right corner at Boulder Sluice, a 10-foot ledge that is run far left. Scout or portage on the left. Below Boulder Sluice is one last complex boulder garden before Island Drop, a towering pile of boulders that can be scouted or portaged on the right where the channel divides at the island.

Downstream of Island Drop, many additional classic rapids lead up to Sacriledge, an 8-foot ledge with a powerful hole in the middle and a cave (Dave's Cave) under the left wall. Sacriledge is usually run far left, boofing to the right away from the cave at the bottom, although at low flows a boof in the middle appears. The next significant rapid below Sacriledge is Double Drop, a pair of ledges with a significant hole at the top combined with a powerful hydraulic on bottom left. Scout and set safety on the right. Below Double Drop 0.5 mile is S-Turn Falls, a 12-foot falls followed by a twisty drop downstream.

Below S-Turn, the river mellows briefly and then roars over a second double set of ledges dropping about 10 feet total. Below these ledges, the river gradually builds until it reaches the Bowey Hotel, a long series of diagonal holes and waves that end abruptly with a sharp left turn over a 6-foot pour-over ledge. The hole gets more powerful the farther left you go, so be ready.

Just around the corner from Bowey is Wishbone Falls, a superb 20-foot drop. Flows above 3 feet allow a boof on the left, but at lower flows paddlers are forced to run down the middle and feel the full power of the Little White.

Wishbone empties into a spectacular cobalt pool for a calm moment before the river squeezes itself into a short, tough gorge. The second rapid in the gorge is a sticky U-shaped ledge known as Horseshoe, which should be approached with caution. The middle of the hole at Horseshoe is backed up by a large submerged boulder, so a swim here will not soon be forgotten. (It is possible to set safety at Horseshoe on the right, but someone has to run it first to do so.) Just downstream from Horseshoe is Stovepipe, a nasty 15-foot drop that is almost always portaged on the right.

Below Stovepipe 0.25 mile is Spirit Falls, a spectacular 33-foot drop that defies description. Spirit is often run, but most paddlers opt for the portage on the left utilizing a fixed line. Paddlers running Spirit should examine the ledge blocking the exit of the punchbowl carefully. This drop (known as Chaos) has several near drownings to its credit and should be approached with caution.

Downstream of Chaos are a few smaller drops with some sneaky logs leading to the last significant boulder garden, Master Blaster. Scout and set safety on the right, then go with the flow down the left though the powerful hydraulic at the bottom. Below Master Blaster are a couple of small runnable weirs and then a brief paddle out across the lake, which is a small price to pay for the world-class ride you have just taken.

Hazards
The entire run contains large drops with dangerous features. Scout often if you are not familiar with the run. The run becomes especially dangerous at high flows.

Access
The take-out is at the north end of Drano Lake just before the fish hatchery. On Washington 14, it is 8.1 miles west of the bridge at Hood River or 12.4 miles east of Stevenson, Washington.

To reach the put-in, return to Washington 14 and turn right, travel 0.5 mile and turn right again onto Cook/Underwood Road. After another 6 miles, the road crosses the Little White Salmon at the fish hatchery in Willard.

Spirit Falls, Little White Salmon River, Washington (Jason Rackley)

Gauge

Visual. There is a stick gauge beneath the bridge at the put-in.

Jason Rackley

Wind River and Tributaries, Washington

169 Trout Creek
NF 43 Bridge to Pacific Crest Trail Bridge

Class: 5 T	Length: 3.7 miles
Flow: 150–600 cfs	Character: gorge
Gradient: 180 fpm, C	Season: rainy/snowmelt

Trout Creek is a great run if you are looking for something a little more diffi-cult in the Wind drainage. This run is similar to the hardest drops on the Wind River but is much steeper and more constricted. Oftentimes, only one channel is runnable, so be sure to scout before committing to a drop.

The creek at the put-in is shallow and placid. As boaters travel farther down the creek, the rapids and gradient gradually build into some fun class 3 to 3+ drops. After about a mile of these easier rapids, the floor drops out as the creek begins to descend at over 300 fpm through a dizzying array of boulder gardens and small ledges. Many of these drops are extremely con-gested at low water, which increases the potential of pinning. At high water, eddies are virtually nonexistent and boaters risk careening downriver out of control. The gradient eases off after about a mile, which allows boaters to catch their breath before the take-out.

Hazards

Logs, undercuts, and continuous rapids can be dangerous in the steepest part of the run. Pinning or broaching boats is quite possible.

Access

To reach the take-out, turn onto Wind River Road 5.6 miles east of Stevenson, Washington, and drive 7.2 miles to Hemlock Road. Turn left and go 1.3 miles to NF 43. Turn right and go 1.45 miles to a small footbridge across the river. The put-in is at the bridge over Trout Creek 4 miles farther upstream on NF 43.

Gauge

Visual. Check the bowl-shaped rock below the hiking bridge at the take-out. Water 6 inches below the bottom edge of the bowl is considered a minimum flow. The difficulty of the run increases dramatically with higher flows.

Pete Giordano

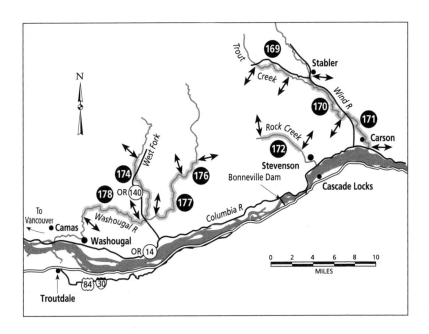

170 Wind River
Stabler to High Bridge

Class: 4+; 5	Length: 6 miles
Flow: 300–1500 cfs; 2500 cfs	Character: forested gorge
Gradient: 90 fpm, PD	Season: rainy/snowmelt

This river has an extremely long season, from the start of the rainy season until late May or June. The river flows through beautiful scenery approaching that of a rain forest. One has the feeling of being deep in an isolated gorge. However, the road is always relatively close on river left and is accessible from almost anywhere along the run. At medium level, the river is calm at the take-out; at the put-in, the river appears to have minimum water.

Put in at Stabler and enjoy the 0.8 mile of technical class 3- warm-up. An optional put-in is on Trout Creek for 0.6 mile of very technical water before reaching the Wind River. The biggest rapids on the Wind are in the first third of the trip and are close together. The first big rapid is Initiation, identified by a house on a cliff on the left and the confluence of Trout Creek on the right. This is most often scouted from river right, but it is difficult to see the second half of the rapid. Boaters must boof a tricky ledge at the top of the rapid and avoid a large hole below a ledge in the middle of the rapid. Four tightly spaced rapids, which become a single mile-long rapids in medium-high water, follow Initation. The final drop in this steep section is Ram's Horn. A large eddy is on the left at the lip of the drop, but unsure boaters might want to catch an eddy higher up on the right to avoid getting swept into Ram's Horn.

Looking downstream from the pool below Ram's Horn, boaters can see a 30-foot waterfall entering the Wind River on the right. Several drops of moderate difficulty follow until boaters reach Climax. At low water levels, Climax is an easy run down the center. However, at water levels above medium-high, careless paddlers have been uncomfortably recirculated for extended periods of time. Fortunately, at these levels Climax can be sneaked on the far right, which is also the side on which to scout or portage. After Climax, the rapids ease up. Take a breather on the second half of the run and enjoy the scenery.

Hazards

Initiation, Ram's Horn, and Climax are the most difficult and are all within the first third of the trip.

Access

The Wind River is near the town of Carson, Washington, which is off Washington 14 about 5.6 miles east of Stevenson. From Carson, drive north on Wind River Road. To get to the take-out, turn left onto High Bridge Road about 1.9 miles outside of Carson. From High Bridge Road, make the first right onto Old Detour Road and follow this dirt road down to the river and the take-out.

To reach the put-in, return to Wind River Road, turn left, and continue north another 5.3 miles to Hemlock Road. Make a left onto Hemlock Road and immediately cross the Wind River. Put in at this bridge or make the first right and then bear right for an alternate put-in.

To get to the Trout Creek put-in, continue west on Hemlock Road from Stabler and turn at the first left, which is Trout Creek Road. Follow this road south until it crosses Trout Creek, the put-in. (Alternately, continue on Hemlock Road and put in about 1 mile higher on Trout Creek. No significant rapids are found along this mile.)

Gauge

Located below Shipherd Falls. The river is usually runnable when the Three Lynx gauge on the Clackamas reads 1900 cfs or more. Water level can also be estimated at the take-out by looking at the pointed rock in the middle of the river. The river has been run when the water level was a foot below the upstream edge of this rock. If the rock is covered, be ready for some continuous class 5 rapids.

Harvey Lee Shapiro and WKCC Editors

171 Wind River
High Bridge to Columbia River

Class: 4(5)	Length: 5 miles
Flow: 800 cfs	Character: forested gorge
Gradient: 50 fpm, PD	Season: rainy/snowmelt

The first 0.5 mile of this run is class 1 and 2 water for warm-up. In the more difficult water below, the pool drop nature allows easy scouting. The excitement begins as High Bridge comes into view. High Bridge Rapid is a long, complex, class 4 boulder garden that becomes quite pushy at higher flows. Another 0.5 mile downstream, the river backs up before crashing through The Flume. This class 5 rapid creates an obvious horizon line and can be scouted or portaged on river right.

Beyond The Flume, the Wind River continues to demand concentration and sound judgment. The next big rapid, Beyond Limits, a steep falls that slams onto a rocky keeper, is usually portaged along the fish ladder on the left. Next, Shipherd Falls creates an unrunnable obstacle that demands a strenuous portage on the left. Eddy out far enough upstream to allow a safe hike along the fish ladder, then portage over and down the cliff on the left bank or throw your boat off the cliff and jump in after. A throw rope comes in handy here. The final mile to the Columbia River is normally class 2. The take-out is on the Columbia River at a boat ramp near the Washington 14 bridge.

Hazards

The Flume, at mile 1, should be scouted or portaged on the right. Beyond Limits (class 5), about another 0.5 mile down, is usually portaged. Shipherd Falls is a mandatory portage. Although the lead-in to the falls is only class 2, use the utmost caution and catch an eddy. Never cross a horizon line before scouting.

Access

In Oregon, take Interstate 84 to Bridge of the Gods at Cascade Locks and cross the Columbia River to Washington 14. Follow Washington 14 east for 7.8 miles. Shortly after crossing Senator Al Henry Bridge, turn left on Old Hatchery Road and proceed 0.4 mile to a developed boat ramp, the take-out.

To get to the put-in, return to Washington 14 and head west. Immediately after crossing Senator Al Henry Bridge, turn right onto Hot Springs Avenue. At mile 1.9, turn right at the four-way stop onto Wind River Road. In 1.9 miles reach High Bridge Road and turn left. Proceed 0.1 mile farther and turn right onto Old Detour Road. Follow this road to the river. The take-out before the last mile of class 2 water is up a long, steep trail to the Carson Hot Springs Hotel, which is 1 mile up Hot Springs Avenue from the take-out.

Gauge

See the Wind River: Stabler to High Bridge run.

Jeff Bennett

Rock Creek, Washington

172 Rock Creek
1.5 Miles above Steep Creek to 3.5 Miles below Steep Creek

Class: 4–4+(5) P	Length: 5 miles
Flow: 300–800	Character: forested
Gradient: 134 fpm, PD	Season: rainy

Rock Creek is a great run located conveniently close to Portland. Much smaller than the Wind River just to the east, Rock Creek offers a great intermediate run with several tougher rapids and a couple of big waterfalls. At low flows, eddies are ample and most of the rapids are rocky. Hold onto your helmet at high flows as eddies disappear and the rapids develop quite some push. Great fun—but be careful.

Immediately below the put-in at the road bridge, the river contains some small boulder gardens and usually some logs to portage. Shortly, though, the river consolidates into some fun ledge slides and small drops. About 1 mile from the bridge, the river drops around a sharp right turn and enters a small gorge with an 8-foot ledge at the head of the gorge. This ledge is very difficult to scout from the river. The ledge is usually run by boofing down the middle. Shortly after this scenic gorge, boaters reach a nasty 10-foot drop that is followed immediately by Heaven and Hell, a sloping 25-foot waterfall. Scout/portage both these drops on the left. There are several fun seal launches back to the river if you decide to portage these drops.

After some fun boulder gardens below the next road bridge the river slows for a mile or so before picking up again. Be careful here as just below a fun boulder garden with a riverwide hole at the bottom is Three Swim Falls, a very difficult 15-foot waterfall that drops into a narrow crack with undercuts. The eddy on the left above the falls is small and can be difficult to catch at higher flows, so be cautious. Put in above or below the next boulder garden, class 5, depending on your mood. More fun rapids continue all the way to the take-out, including a great series of sliding ledges about 0.25 mile from the end of the run. There is a fun play hole just below the take-out bridge.

Hazards

Heaven and Hell and Three Swim Falls are commonly portaged on the left. Portage the nasty 10-foot ledge above Heaven and Hell. The eddy above Three Swim Falls is small, particularly at higher flows.

Access

From the west end of Stevenson, take Rock Creek Drive east 0.6 mile to Ryan Allen Drive. Turn right and follow Ryan Allen Drive 0.5 mile to Red Bluff. Turn left and travel about 2.3 miles to a road on the right that leads down to the river. This is the take-out.

To reach the put-in, return to the main road and turn right. The put-in is at the second road bridge. An alternate put-in is at the first road bridge.

Gauge

Visual. Much of the first 1.5 miles can be seen from the road. The level can also be estimated from the bridge over the river in Stevenson on Rock Creek Drive. If water is flowing through the bushes on the gravel bar in the center of the river, there is plenty of water upstream.

Pete Giordano

Washougal River and Tributaries, Washington

173 Stebbins Creek
South Fork and North Fork Confluence to Washougal River

Class: 5(5+)	Length: 2.9 miles
Flow: 250–750 cfs	Character: canyon/forested
Gradient: 190 fpm	Season: rainy/snowmelt

Stebbins Creek roars through the bottom of Washington's Brice Canyon over a series of waterfalls and powerful, technical drops. At low flows, this run is tight and technical. At high water, it is downright dangerous. If you are smart, you will do it at low flows the first time so you can figure out where to portage and scout.

The first 0.5 mile or so is playful class 2, but soon the creek bends to the right and the fun begins with the first falls, a 10-footer that drops into a 100-foot-long slide that ends at 12-foot Jetboat Falls. Downstream the creek mellows temporarily and then paddlers encounter Get in My Belly, an 8-foot ledge that funnels into a small, recirculating punchbowl with a narrow outlet on the left.

Just downstream is a large, powerful boulder garden, and then Lethal Injection Falls. On the first descent at low water, this drop was run on the low water, but that is not recommended. Eddy out on the left (hard to do at higher water) and carry your boats across the big log that spans the falls. Downstream 50 feet from Lethal is Tsunami Falls, a spectacular 45-foot cascade dropping over four tiers. Tsunami can be scouted or portaged on the left, but this side of the creek is not accessible at high water.

Below Tsunami are more large, technical drops, including one fascinating rapid known as The Zoom Tube, which funnels paddlers into and under an overhanging wall on the left. Below Zoom is one more narrow, foaming crack-ledge with a jagged boulder on the left that the water piles into, so boof left or find out why it is called Bongo Fury. The last drop is known as Mad Dog Falls and can be scouted from the take-out bridge. Mad Dog gets more exciting the farther right you go, so plan on spending a long time under the foam if you go with the flow on that side.

Hazards

Lethal Injection Falls is difficult to identify from above. The only current portage route is across a log that forms part of the sieve blocking the exit of this falls. Portaging this drop may not be possible at high water or during snowy/icy conditions.

Access

To get to the take-out, follow the directions to Doc's Drop on the Washougal River in Washington: Doc's Drop to Dougan Falls run. Just downstream from Docs is a bridge over Stebbins where you get a very nice view of Mad Dog Falls. This is the take-out.

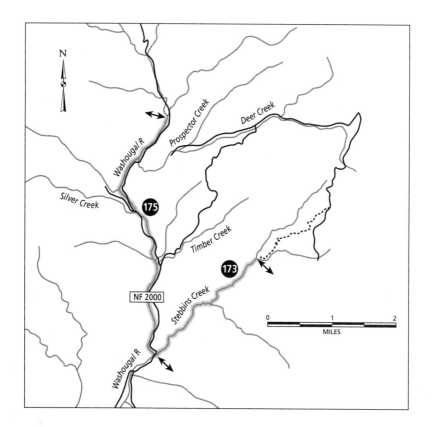

To get to the put-in, head up the gravel road (known as W2000) for about 1.8 miles above Docs Drop and stay right. About 2.3 miles later, you come to the top of Deer Creek divide. Once you cross the first wooden bridge across Deer Creek, turn right and drive about 2.25 miles to a four-way intersection. (About 2.5 miles farther, just before milepost 12, the road crosses the diminutive North Fork of Stebbins Creek.) Turn right again here (following the signs to Beacon Rock and NF 1440). On the far side of the creek, on the right-hand side of the road, follow the signs down to the confluence, which is about a 2-mile hike, mostly downhill, on a good trail. These roads may be blocked by snow in the winter, and they are infamous for causing flat tires; bring a spare.

Gauge

Stebbins has a tiny drainage, so it only runs after a few days of rain in the spring or early summer and all during the winter season. If the creek contains enough water, the rocks on the right-hand side of the channel downstream from the put-in bridge will be covered.

Jason Rackley

174 West Fork Washougal River
West Fork Bridge to Washougal River

Class: 4(5) P	Length: 7 miles
Flow: 400 cfs	Character: wooded canyon
Gradient: 100 fpm, PD	Season: rainy

The West Fork Washougal River is an exciting, steep, and technically demanding run for advanced boaters. In addition to countless class 3 to 4 rapids, the run boasts a gradient often in excess of 100 fpm, as well as five narrow falls that require precise boat handling or portages.

At the put-in, the West Fork appears to be a shallow rock-strewn stream, but constant feeder streams quickly increase the flow. Within 1 mile of the put-in, the river begins to display its true character as it disappears over a horizon line at Teakettle Falls. This 16-foot double drop is generally run left at the bottom due to a rock and shallow landing in the middle. Scout/portage on the right. Numerous small ledges continue until boaters reach a large, narrow waterfall with a constricted exit. Scout on the left, and most will choose to seal launch below the rapid off the rock cliff on the left. Be careful after passing under the road bridge farther downstream as a nasty, narrow waterfall lies just around the next corner. Catch the small eddy on the left and walk down the rock shelf to a fun seal launch platform at the bottom of the falls. A small gorge with several sticky hydraulics is just downstream of a large basalt cliff on the left.

After this gorge, the river is mostly class 3 with an occasional class 3+ rapid until a second basalt cliff is visible on the left. Catch the small eddy on the left to scout the small but difficult ledge that lies at the base of the cliff. The last significant rapids is near a fish hatchery toward the end of the run. This section begins with an 8-foot weir that should be run on the right. Another smaller weir at the bottom of the hatchery can be run anywhere with momentum. Immediately below the second weir is a dangerous falls that should be run far left to avoid the main drop that leads into a powerful hydraulic with undercut rock walls on either side. The main Washougal is about 0.5 mile farther. Save some energy for the near-perfect play hole that forms at some flows on the main Washougal shortly below the confluence with the West Fork. The take-out is on river left about 0.75 mile below the confluence.

Hazards

The steep gradient, falls, and potential for sweepers produce a difficult run that mandates constant scouting. Some portages may require steep scrambles through thick brush.

Access

Cross the Columbia River in Portland and take Washington 14 east to the town of Washougal. From the town of Washougal, follow Washougal River Road 8.4 miles upstream. When Washougal River Road and Canyon Creek Road split, turn right across the bridge. After 75 yards, turn right again onto Sportsman Road and follow it 300 yards to the Washington Game Department Public Access Area, the take-out.

To reach the put-in, return back across the bridge to Washougal River Road and go 0.5 mile farther upstream. Turn left on Skye Road and proceed 3.7 miles. Turn right on Northeast 412th Avenue/Skamania Mines Road and go 2.6 miles to the stop sign. Turn left on 1200 Road and stay left at the first fork. The put-in is 0.7 mile from the stop sign at a turnoff just before the bridge over the West Fork Washougal River. An alternate put-in is at a bridge about 1 mile down Skamania Mines Road.

Gauge

None exists but generally 1500 to 2500 cfs on the East Fork of the Lewis is a good range for this run. Also, the main Washougal has two visual indicators beneath the bridge near the take-out where Washington 140 and Washougal River Road split. First, look at the fence posts on river left. Counting up from the river, the river should be between the fifth and sixth post. Second, look at the steel base plate for the bridge support girder on upstream river right. Water should be lapping on the steel portion of this support. Either cue indicates adequate flow on the North Fork.

Jeff Bennett and WKCC Editors

175 Washougal River
Prospector Creek to Stebbins Creek

Class: 4+(5)	Length: 4.5
Flow: 300–700 cfs	Character: isolated, forested, gorge
Gradient: 102 fpm, PD	Season: rainy, snowmelt

The Upper Washougal is a great run for advanced boaters looking for some challenging boulder gardens and fun waterfalls. Just upstream of Prospector Creek is a narrow plunge that tends to push boaters against the right wall and a fun 10-foot waterfall. The waterfall should be run down the center to avoid the shallow landing on the right and left sides. The crux of the run is the steep, congested gorge immediately below Prospector Creek. The gorge starts out with a fun, ledgy class 4 rapid and builds into solid class 5. Scout each drop carefully as several have dangerous undercuts. These drops get extremely pushy and difficult to portage at high water. Once through the gorge, the river continues to drop through some fun boulder gardens before the next major horizon line. This drop can only be run on the far left as the right side drops onto and through a nasty boulder pile.

The river is class 2 to 3 below this ledge, although several more fun ledge drops, including a riverwide 10-foot falls, spice up the remainder of the run until boaters arrive at Doc's Drop. Scout this 20-foot broken falls before the run as the lines are difficult to see at river level. The far right can be rocky at very low water. The far left side is also runnable.

Hazards
Undercuts and pin spots abound in the gorge section below Prospector Creek. Wood in any of the rapids in the gorge would be extremely dangerous and difficult to avoid.

Access
Cross the Columbia River in Portland and take Washington 14 east to Washougal. Follow Washougal River Road through town. After crossing the Washougal River, continue upstream another 13.4 miles to Dougan Falls. Turn right immediately after the bridge at Dougan Falls and continue another 2.5 miles to the bridge over Stebbins Creek.

To reach the put-in, continue another 1.8 miles upstream and stay right at an intersection. Travel another 3.9 miles and turn left immediately after crossing Deer Creek. Follow this road along Deer Creek until it ends. Depending on road conditions, you might have to hike a short distance to the river.

Gauge
Visual. Look at Doc's Drop near the take-out. If Doc's is runnable, probably a minimum amount of water will be upstream, but a better level will be there if

water is flowing across the entire face of the falls. You can also see some of the lower river on the shuttle to get a feel for the level.

Pete Giordano

176 Washougal River
Doc's Drop to Dougan Falls

Class: 5	Length: 2.6 miles
Flow: 1500 cfs	Character: forested
Gradient: 55 fpm, PD	Season: rainy

This run is a favorite for thrill seekers who like to run waterfalls in catarafts, self-bailing rafts, and kayaks. Most of the waterfalls have shallow landings that discourage a lot of kayakers from making the run. Because the run is short and quick, it can be added to the Washougal River: Dougan Falls to Salmon Falls run.

From the put-in, the action begins immediately with Doc's Drop, a 10-foot drop on a boulder ledge. Downstream 0.5 mile is Reeder Falls, a 4-foot drop just above the bridge. Just below the bridge is Naked Falls, a 15-foot drop over a few ledges, which should be run center because the left is suicidal. The 1.8 miles of class 1 and 2 water that follow allow time to think about Dougan Falls, the grand finale, a 15-foot drop over two ledges. Dougan Falls is normally run close to the right bank.

Teakettle Falls, West Fork Washougal River (Bill Jankovich)

Hazards

The four named falls are rated class 5. Each can be scouted during the drive to the put-in. Scout Dougan Falls at the take-out. Drive 1.9 miles upriver to scout Naked Falls. Upriver 0.1 mile, Reeder Falls can be scouted from the bridge. Scout Doc's Drop at the put-in. If in doubt, stay river right.

Access

Cross the Columbia River in Portland and take Washington 14 east to Washougal. From Washougal, follow Washougal River Road upstream; when Washougal River Road splits, continue straight on Washougal River Road 7.2 miles to the take-out at the bridge below Dougan Falls.

The put-in at Doc's Drop is 2.6 miles upstream.

Gauge

None exists. The flow is unregulated. Several days of hard rain are required. If the flow looks too low to run Dougan Falls, do not run the rest.

Val Shaull and Jeff Bennett

177 Washougal River
Dougan Falls to Salmon Falls

Class: 3-(4) P; 5 P	Length: 6 miles
Flow: 700 cfs; 2000 cfs	Character: wooded; fishing
Gradient: 42 fpm, PD	Season: rainy

Although it is less than an hour from the Portland–Vancouver area, this section of the upper Washougal is not often run. This apparent lack of popularity may be due to the dramatic changes in character of the river over this 6-mile stretch. In the upper section, long stretches of flat water, with occasional class 2 or 3 rapids, appeal to intermediate boaters; but the gorge presents class 4 to 5 water and is difficult to portage. Remember that the banks are private property above the high-water line. Be respectful of private property.

A concrete weir is 1.5 miles from the put-in and just downstream from a short class 3 drop. It is marked by a wire across the river. Portage right. A wooden dam lies just beyond the highway bridge. From December 1 through September 15, sections of the dam are removed for migrating salmon, and it can be run on the left. Otherwise, portage on the right. Both portages can be scouted on the way to the put-in.

The beginning of the difficult water at rivermile 4.5 is marked by a small island and a sharp left turn as the right bank climbs away from the river dramatically. Just downstream of the drop around the island is a sharp riverwide ledge. Scout from the left above the island. A short stretch of easier water follows until the river narrows dramatically and drops over and around some large boulders and through a constriction formed by the sheer rock wall on the right.

Boaters generally start right, then move center and immediately back to the right. The left side drops into a rock sieve at most flows. Scout or portage this section with difficulty on the left. At high water, this rapid is class 5 with huge holes and little room for error. After one more boulder garden, the river broadens again for the last mile before the take-out above Salmon Falls. Be sure to scout the landmarks here because the falls comes up fast around a blind curve. Although Salmon Falls has been run at some levels, it has dangerous rocks and a keeper at the bottom.

Hazards

Two dangerous but easily portaged obstacles appear in the first 3 miles: the concrete weir and the wooden dam. The gorge section is difficult to portage and becomes class 5 at high flows.

Access

For directions to where Washougal River Road splits, see the Washougal River: Doc's Drop to Dougan Falls run. At the split, take Washougal River Road straight; continue 1.5 miles to the Salmon Falls Fish Hatchery. Pull off on the right side of the road near a dirt road that leads down to the river. This is the take-out.

To get to the put-in, follow the road upstream 5.7 miles to the second bridge. Dougan Falls is on the right. The put-in is on either side of the bridge or upstream from the falls.

Gauge

Available via the Internet (Washougal at Washougal) on Pat Welch's Flow Page. Alternatively use the Washington State Department of Ecology site (Washougal at Hathaway Park) (see Appendix A).

Maryann McCormick, Susan Seyl, and WKCC Editors

178 Washougal River
10-Mile Bridge to above Washougal

Class: 3(4); 4	Length: 7.3 miles
Flow: 200–800 cfs; 1000–5000 cfs	Character: forested; residential; agricultural
Gradient: 33 fpm, C	Season: rainy

This delightful run is close to Portland. It has several types of rapids. A class 4 boulder garden, called Big Eddy, is about 2.5 miles below the put-in. A short distance downstream is a steep class 3 rapids with a large hole midstream. Many of the rapids are wide and clean. At high flows, there are numerous surf waves and play holes.

Hazards

Big Eddy, the class 4 boulder garden, can be scouted from the road 4.7 miles above the take-out.

Access

Cross the Columbia River in Portland and take Washington 14 east to the town of Washougal. At the town of Washougal, take Washougal River Road north and go upstream approximately 2.5 miles to the take-out at an unimproved boat ramp.

The put-in is 7.3 miles farther upstream. Cross at the bridge, turn right, and proceed down a gravel road to a public access across the river from the store. There is an access point at a public area 1 mile above Big Eddy.

Gauge

Available via the Internet (Washougal at Washougal) on Pat Welch's Flow Page. Alternatively use the Washington State Department of Ecology site (Washougal at Hathaway Park) (see Appendix A). A flow of 1500 cfs is excellent and occurs when the Twin Rocks in Big Eddy are barely exposed.

Stan Jacobs and Jay Nigra

Central Oregon Rivers

Deschutes River and Tributaries

179 Metolius River
Source to Lake Billy Chinook

Class: 3(4)	Length: 30 miles
Flow: 1300–2000 cfs	Character: forested; fishing
Gradient: 24 fpm, C	Season: year-round

This very unusual river originates in the Cascades beneath Black Butte. Within several hundred feet, the river wells up from the ground and becomes 30 feet wide. Within 0.5 mile, the river swells to an average flow of 1500 cfs, from which it deviates little throughout the year. Because the water comes from underground, it is always frigid. The river level fluctuates so little that the banks are overgrown with heavy vegetation. At the first bridge in the community of Camp Sherman, visitors pause to look for the huge trout waiting to be fed. Throwing a few salmon eggs into the water attracts the fish. The character of the Metolius can be divided into two sections.

SECTION 1: SOURCE TO LOWER BRIDGE CAMPGROUND, 13 MILES
This section has a resort atmosphere with private camps, forest campgrounds, and picnic areas. The source is on private land, fenced to keep the public out. The river flows through meadowlands for the first few miles, and put-ins are along the road. The bridge at the resort community of Camp Sherman, about 3 miles downstream, provides access, as do the improved campgrounds farther downstream. From the source to several miles below Camp Sherman, the river is swift and replete with snags but has no significant whitewater.

The tempo increases below Gorge Campground, which is 3 miles below Camp Sherman and 6 miles below the source. The Gorge is a fast class 3 rapids about 1 mile below Gorge Campground. Along the right bank of The Gorge, a group of springs gush forth into the river. Because of the gorge's inaccessibility, very few people other than boaters have seen these lovely springs. Immediately downstream, the land on both sides of the river is privately owned, so stay off it. One or more of the very low bridges may require a portage. Kayakers sometimes run low bridges bottoms us and roll up once the passage is completed. Wizard Falls, just above a low bridge to Wizard Falls Fish Hatchery, is not a true falls but a turbulent region with narrow channels through lava bedrock. The 3 miles from Wizard Falls to Lower Bridge Campground are class 1. Because this section has been designated for fly fishing only, it is a favorite area for anglers, so respect their space.

SECTION 2: LOWER BRIDGE CAMPGROUND TO LAKE BILLY CHINOOK, 17 MILES
This section contains premier crystal-clear whitewater in a primitive setting. The swiftness and uniform gradient of the water and the thick vegetation make eddies and landing spots hard to find. A swimming boater may float a long way before finding a landing spot. Because of the river's swiftness, these 17 miles

can be run in a day easily. The left bank, below Candle Creek Campground, is private property owned by the Confederated Tribes of Warm Springs; please respect the no-trespassing rule.

Starting at Lower Bridge Campground, the tempo increases for 1 mile, then a long class 3 rapids begins. The lower end of this rapids cannot be seen from the top. Therefore, check before proceeding for possible tree blockage. Numerous long class 2 and 3 rapids with truly beautiful whitewater continue. Wilderness with no access stretches from Lower Bridge to a gravel road extending several miles upstream from Lake Billy Chinook. The most difficult rapid on the river is an easy class 4 located about 3 miles into the run. It is along a straight section of river identified by boulders and large holes at the top, the most difficult part. The river continues at a fast pace to Lake Billy Chinook, where the change to flat water is like a gentle awakening from a pleasant dream. Take out on the right at Monty Campground along the river above the lake or paddle down the lake 2 miles to the first public campground.

Hazards

The greatest danger is the potential, at low water, of a large ponderosa pine completely blocking the river. The potential for large buildups of wood in the river is real, due to the lack of high water. The Forest Service no longer removes dangerous wood from the river, so be cautious. Forest Service fish habitat restoration work is planned for 2008. Numerous logs will be added to the river channel between Riverside Campground and Bridge 99. Be sure to read the signs posted at put-ins and take-outs describing the changes in wood management and be very careful. The Gorge is relatively fast and requires rock dodging. Be prepared for very cold water year-round, about 43 degrees Fahrenheit.

Access

From the west, take US 20 or Oregon 22 east across Santiam Pass, or from the east, take Oregon 22 west from Sisters toward Santiam Pass. The turnoff to the Metolius is 5.5 miles east of Suttle Lake. Follow the signs to "Head of the Metolius." This unusual sight is well worth seeing. The paved road from the Head of the Metolius essentially parallels the river on the east side to Lower Bridge Campground.

Put-ins are available at any of the campgrounds along the road to Lower Bridge Campground. If you put in at Gorge Campground or Wizard Falls, for example, the take-out can be at any of the unimproved camps below Lower Bridge Campground or at the end of the dirt road. If the take-out is at one of the unimproved camps, be sure to find a good landmark because this region all looks the same from the river.

The shuttle to the Lake Billy Chinook take-out is about 35 miles, mostly over gravel roads. From Lower Bridge Campground, go upstream about 0.5 mile on Oregon 14. Turn left onto NF 1490 and climb Green Ridge. At the junction with NF 1140 (Prairie Farm Road), head east on 1140. Farther east, Prairie Farm Road continues as NF 1180 and then 1170 to its end at a blacktop road, Oregon 64, near the lake. Turn left, pass Perry South Campground, and continue another 5 miles to Monty Campground on the lower Metolius, about 0.5 mile above lake water.

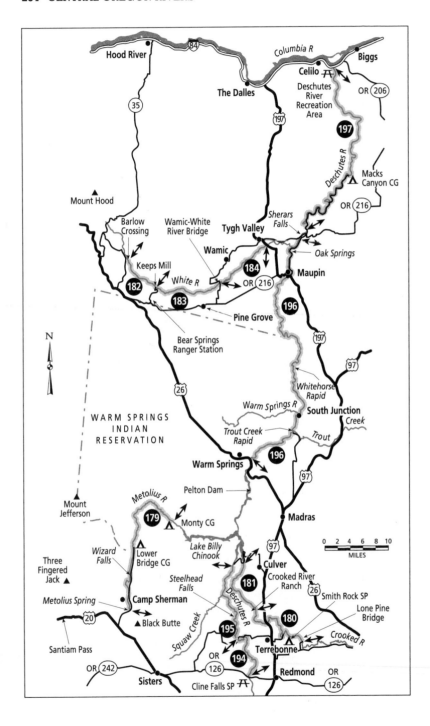

Hood River

Columbia R

Biggs

84

Celilo

The Dalles

Deschutes River Recreation Area

OR 206

35

197

197

Mount Hood

Deschutes R

Macks Canyon CG

OR 216

Barlow Crossing

Wamic-White River Bridge

Tygh Valley

Sherars Falls

Keeps Mill

Wamic

184

Oak Springs

White R

OR 216

Maupin

182

183

196

Pine Grove

Bear Springs Ranger Station

N

26

197

97

Whitehorse Rapid

WARM SPRINGS INDIAN RESERVATION

Warm Springs R

South Junction

Creek

Trout Creek Rapid

Trout

196

Warm Springs

97

Pelton Dam

Mount Jefferson

Metolius R

179

Monty CG

Madras

Wizard Falls

Lower Bridge CG

Lake Billy Chinook

97

Three Fingered Jack ▲

Steelhead Falls

Crooked River Ranch

Culver

26

Smith Rock SP

Metolius Spring

Camp Sherman

181

Lone Pine Bridge

20

▲ Black Butte

Deschutes R

180

Santiam Pass

195

Crooked R

Squaw Creek

Terrebonne

OR 242

OR 126

194

Redmond

OR 126

Sisters

Cline Falls SP

0 2 4 6 8 10
MILES

Gauge

Flow information is unnecessary because discharges range from 1,250 to 2500 cfs with a 58-year mean of 1500 cfs.

T. R. Torgersen and Rob Blickensderfer

180 Crooked River
Lone Pine Bridge to Crooked River Ranch

Class: 3(4); 4(5)	Length: 18 miles
Flow: 800 cfs; 4000 cfs	Character: inaccessible desert gorge
Gradient: 40 fpm, PD	Season: dam-controlled

The Crooked River has many big rapids and runs through a spectacular gorge. Few good put-ins or take-outs are available on this hair-raising run for advanced to expert boaters. Much equipment has been lost in the Crooked River gorge. If you decide to run this river, the next lost paddle or boat could be yours. For rafters, the run requires quality river rafts and expert rowers able to run technical drops of 10 to 25 feet.

Two put-ins are possible for this run, one 4 miles above Smith Rock State Park and the other 1.5 miles above the park. The put-in 1.5 miles above the park begins immediately with 1.5 miles of continuous class 4 rapids followed by a long loop of very slow water around the park. Rock climbers flock to this area year-round for some of the best climbing in Oregon. Boaters who paddle around Smith Rock hear cries of "Crazy!" from above, which may well apply to the small speck hundreds of feet above the river.

About 1 mile downstream of the park is Number One, the first rapid in a series. Number One is a very steep, short drop with a boulder in the center and more boulders and big holes in the left channel. Scout right. About 1 mile farther is Number Two, which may be run on the left or right side of Lava Island. This drop has a difficult approach and should be scouted from the left.

The next rapid is a series of waves called The Bumps, located about 0.2 mile beyond Number Two. The Bumps are a prelude to Wap-te-doodle, a very long drop with powerful hydraulics and a very large hole at bottom center. It can be scouted from the left; note the log on the left. A couple of lesser rapids lie between here and the US 97 bridge that crosses high above.

From the bridge to the next major rapid, No Name, the river is very busy class 3 to 4. No Name is very long and rough, with many boulders and a large hole at the bottom. Scout on the right. Several shorter and easier rapids follow. The next major rapids is Chinese Dam, located at the end of a stretch of flat water along sheer cliffs. The dam was built for mining operations years ago. The river broke through the dam, leaving the center and the left of the riverbed very shallow and with sharp rocks. Scout. Chinese Dam can be quite difficult at lower levels.

Portaging a tough rapid (Jason Rackley)

It is possible to take out just above Chinese Dam Rapid on the left at the access road from the Crooked River Ranch. This take-out requires a very steep climb to the public access road. An easier take-out is about 200 yards below the dam. Public camping facilities are available at the ranch.

Hazards
This stretch is runnable for only a short time each year, usually in late April. This run presents many difficulties that demand special attention. Retreat from the river due to equipment loss or injury is very difficult in most of the canyon.

Access
The put-in is 6 miles east of US 97 between Redmond and Madras. From US 97 at Terrebonne, go east 3 miles to Smith Rock State Park and continue another 3 miles east to the Lone Pine Bridge, the put-in. An alternate put-in is 1 mile east of Smith Rock State Park at the aqueduct.

The take-out is at the resort community of Crooked River Ranch. The roads are public. From US 97 north of Terrebonne, follow the signs to Crooked River Ranch and the clubhouse. Drive past the clubhouse and turn right just before the little white church. Continue on the gravel road to a graveled lot. Hollywood Road—a very rough, steep, four-wheel-drive road that leads down 1.3 miles to Chinese Dam—may be gated, forcing boaters to hike up from the river. A small mining road that provides an alternate take-out is just downstream.

Gauge
In years of low snowfall, no water may be released. For information on planned releases, contact the Oregon Department of Water Resources Watermaster in Bend (541-388-6669) or the Ochoco Irrigation District in Prineville (541-447-6449).

Ron Mattson and Scott Russell

Gauge

None exists. For a close estimate of the White River's flow farther downstream see Pat Welch's Flow Page (White River–Below Tygh Valley) (see Appendix A).

Harvey Lee Shapiro

183 White River
Keeps Mill to Wamic–White River Bridge

Class: 3+(4); 4-(4+)	Length: 12 miles
Flow: 400 cfs; 1400 cfs	Character: forested
Gradient: 46 fpm, C	Season: snowmelt

The water here is always cold, but from January to March the air temperature is also cold within the deep canyon. Winter runs are, therefore, uncomfortably cold and not recommended. In May and June, the air temperature is warmer and the steep canyon rocks radiate heat, resulting in very warm or hot air, especially in the lower half of this run. The character of the run is very similar to what you see at the put-in: continuous fast-moving whitewater over rocks, a few boulders, and an occasional logjam. The river is a continuous class 3+ with a beautiful rhythm of its own. There is one class 4 rapids. At medium levels, eddies and play spots are abundant. All drops are runnable and can be scouted by eddy hopping, except for the inevitable occasional logjam.

The most difficult rapids on the river is about 1.5 miles below Keeps Mill. It can be recognized by the high cliffs on river left one or two drops above the rapid. It should be scouted by first-time paddlers. Problems in this rapid are unpleasant and result in an extremely long and difficult day in this wild canyon. Scout on the right from above before starting the easy lead-in because you fill find no easy eddy immediately above the drop. Normally, this rapid is approached on river left and run right of center. About 8 miles below the put-in, a wire crosses the river, with hanging metal gates on each shore and several others in the river. These mark the Mount Hood National Forest boundary. A short distance below here, the river gains more volume and, at higher water levels, becomes pushy and more memorable.

Hazards

Logjams that require portaging are likely. Most paddlers underestimate the speed of the current, which results in dangerous encounters with logjams on almost every trip. Scout the class 4 rapids 1.5 miles below Keeps Mill.

Access

From the Portland area, take US 26 east; from central and eastern Oregon, take US 26 west from Madras. At Oregon 216, turn east toward Maupin. After 3 miles, look for a small green sign to Keeps Mill/White River on the right side just as the road takes a long curve to the right. (If you see a sign for Bear Springs Ranger Station, you have gone 0.3 mile too far.) Turn left and continue on the main road down to the river. Follow signs to Keeps Mill. The road for the last 1.5 miles is dirt with rock slides. It is slow but passable and arrives at a primitive campground.

To reach the take-out, go back to Oregon 216, turn left onto Oregon 216, and head east toward Maupin, and continue past Bear Springs Ranger Station to Pine Grove. About 3.5 miles past Pine Grove is a small green sign on the right that reads "Victor Road, Wamic, White River." Turn left onto this dirt road and follow it as it jogs right and then left. Shortly after it turns right again, take the first road to the left (a sign to Wamic is on the right side, if someone has not knocked it over). After turning left, note the sign about the road being extremely hazardous, especially in winter. Have faith and continue to the river and the take-out at Wamic–White River Bridge on river left.

Gauge

None exists. For a close estimate of the White River's flow farther downstream see Pat Welch's Flow Page (White River–Below Tygh Valley) (see Appendix A).

Harvey Lee Shapiro

184 White River
Wamic–White River Bridge to Tygh Valley

Class: 3(4)	Length: 11 miles
Flow: 400–2000 cfs	Character: forested canyon
Gradient: 40 fpm, PD	Season: snowmelt

This is a beautiful run through some of the most delightful canyons in Oregon. Do not do this run just for the whitewater. Do it for the scenery and the possibility of seeing hawks, eagles, lynx, ouzels, vultures, mergansers, grouse, deer, deer flies, and butterflies. The river passes springs, caves, beaches, and creeks but, most of all, has a wonderful sense of isolation. The first half of this remote run has the easiest whitewater and the best scenery, where rock walls rise right out of the river. In the run's second half, the steep canyon walls are farther from the river and the difficulty of the rapids increases. At low levels, the run is very technical, especially the last two rapids. At higher flows, the first 9 miles provide fast-moving class 2+ rapids with the last two rapids being more open with greater choices but significantly pushier with bigger waves.

The run starts with a rocky or bouncy rapid just below the put-in. If you have trouble here, return to your vehicle because the rapids on the lower part are significantly more difficult. About halfway through the run, an eroding multihued ash-and-dirt bank on river right signals the start of the more challenging whitewater. Logs frequently complicate this rapid, and all the others as well, so be prepared to dodge, duck, or portage at any time. The two long rapids above Tygh Valley are the most difficult. They start quickly, so pay careful attention and eddy out before entering these rapids.

The first of these is a long, winding class 3+ log-choked rapid. The final rapid is rated as class 4- because it is very long and continuous class 3+ water in the wilderness.

Warning: Below Tygh Valley 3 miles is a 90-foot unrunnable waterfall. It can be viewed from White River State Park.

Hazards

Throughout this run, watch constantly for logjams and use extreme care when approaching them. Be sure to leave room to stop for logjams. Do not underestimate the speed of the current. Consider scouting the last two rapids.

Access

To reach the put-in, follow directions to the take-out for the White River: Keeps Mill to Wamic–White River Bridge run.

From the put-in, continue on the north-side dirt road toward Wamic. Once you progress from dirt to paved road, stay on paved road. (As of 1991, a sign incorrectly points to Wamic via a dirt road.) Follow the paved road to the stop sign; turn right and continue through Wamic toward Tygh Valley. At the stop sign, turn right and follow this road to the Tygh Valley White River bridge. Take out on river right, above or below the bridge.

If you do not have to pick up a shuttle vehicle at Keeps Mill, return to Portland on the north side of the White River. Follow signs to Wamic. (Be careful to make the correct right turn in Tygh Valley toward Wamic. At the right turn, there are two roads; take the left one.) Follow this road through Wamic. About 1 mile beyond Wamic, turn right and follow signs to Sportsman Park and Rock Creek Reservoir. Continue straight on this road, which becomes NF 48 and goes all the way to Oregon 35. Make a left on Oregon 35, which merges into US 26.

Gauge

None exists. A warm day on Mount Hood will raise the river. If the first rapid below the put-in is runnable, probably the entire run is runnable. For a close estimate of the flow see Pat Welch's Flow Page (White River–Below Tygh Valley) (see Appendix A).

Harvey Lee Shapiro and Linda Starr

185 Deschutes River
Wickiup Dam to Pringle Falls

Class: 1(4)	Length: 9 miles
Flow: 500–1000 cfs	Character: forested; osprey sanctuary
Gradient: 4 fpm, C	Season: dam-controlled

This is one of the authors' favorite class 1 runs in Oregon. Many features combine to create a stimulating and often exhilarating experience: high mountain air, clear blue water, ponderosa pines, abundant camping sites, and great fishing are but a few. Perhaps the strongest asset of this region is the dense population of osprey. The sound of an osprey calling and the sight of a vertical dive to pull a 12-inch trout from the water near your canoe are experiences not soon forgotten.

The majority of boaters on this stretch take out at Wyeth Campground on river left. There are signs warning of upcoming Pringle Falls, class 4, which lies just below here. Only expert kayakers should consider this drop, and only after scouting. It is definitely not a rapids for open canoes.

To continue downstream without running the falls, a 1.5-mile but easy portage around Pringle Falls is possible. (Unfortunately, the land on both sides of the falls is private, thus necessitating the long portage.) From Wyeth Campground, follow the entry road to NF 43; turn right and cross the river. Continue about 0.3 mile to the second road on the left and follow it to Pringle Falls Campground.

The falls starts with 200 yards of class 2- whitewater above the NF 204 bridge. Experienced class 2 boaters could eddy out on river right just above the bridge and save almost half the portage distance. The next 100 yards of class 3+ water lead into a class 4 drop with a potential keeper just above a footbridge. The remaining 200 yards are a bouncy class 3.

Hazards

Do not accidentally go over Pringle Falls. The portage around the falls is difficult.

Access

Most people reach this river section from US 97 between La Pine and Bend. About 2 miles north of La Pine, or about 4.5 miles south of the entrance to the La Pine Recreation Area, turn west onto NF 43 at a sign to Wickiup Reservoir. In 9 miles, NF 43 crosses the Deschutes River just above Pringle Falls. The first left after the bridge, NF 4370, leads to Wyeth Campground, the take-out, with a boat ramp.

Reach the put-in at Wickiup Dam by continuing west on NF 43 another 2.5 miles. Take a left onto NF 4380, which runs to the reservoir levee. Turn left again to follow the levee to the put-in on the north (river left) side of the dam. There is a 200-yard carry from a locked gate to the water. The access is public; the gate is intended to keep vehicles out.

Gauge

Flow is regulated at Wickiup Dam. From late spring until early fall, the flow is generally consistent at 1200 to 1600 cfs. At other times, the flow can be severely and abruptly reduced. For information on water release from Wickiup Dam, contact the Oregon Department of Water Resources Watermaster for the Bend region (541-388-6669).

Carl Landsness

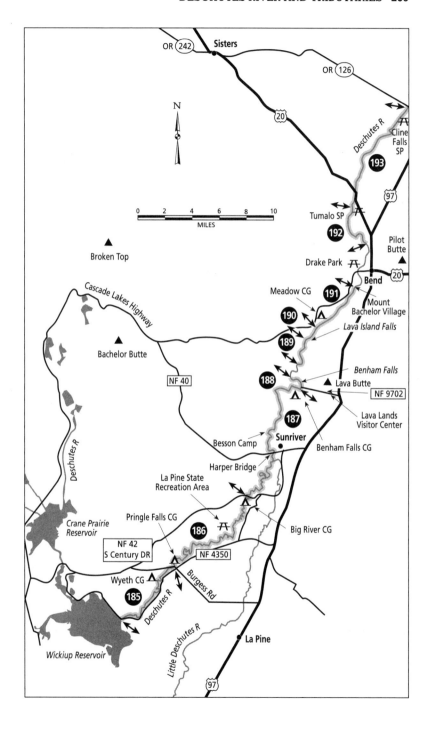

186 Deschutes River
Pringle Falls to Big River Campground

Class: 1(2)	Length: 16 miles
Flow: 500–1000 cfs	Character: forested; marsh grass; waterfowl haven
Gradient: 2.5 fpm, C	Season: dam-controlled

The first 7 miles of this run are similar to the pine-forested run upstream. Near the La Pine Recreation Area, the river begins to slow and meander through wide-open areas of marsh grass. The river is serene, disturbed occasionally by the sounds of fish and waterfowl. Views of the nearby hills and distant mountains further enhance this enchanting run.

Hazards
The Tethrow Logjam blocks the river 4 miles below Pringle Falls. Several signs warn of its presence. The portage is an easy 200-yard walk along the right bank. It is often possible to sneak the logs along the right bank and then run 100 yards of class 2 waves.

Access
Put in at Pringle Falls Campground, below Pringle Falls on river right (see the Deschutes River: Wickiup Dam to Pringle Falls run).

Reach the take-out by driving west on NF 43 for 0.5 mile, and then going right onto NF 4350 for 2 miles. Turn right onto NF 42 and follow it 8 miles to Big River Campground.

To reach the take-out from US 97, drive 2 miles south of Sunriver, turn west onto NF 9724 to NF 42, and continue on NF 42 to Big River Campground. An alternate take-out is at La Pine State Recreation Area. Check the Deschutes National Forest map for details on this alternate access.

Gauge
See the Deschutes River: Wickiup Dam to Pringle Falls run.

Carl Landsness

187 Deschutes River
Big River Campground to Benham Falls

Class: 1(5+)	Length: 18 miles
Flow: 1000–3000 cfs	Character: forested; residential; resort country
Gradient: 1 fpm, PD	Season: dam-controlled

The first 7 miles to Harper Bridge wander very slowly, with houses lining the banks for most of the length. The next 6-mile section passes Sunriver with a noticeably stronger current and a large contingent of leisurely drifters. Below Sunriver, the Deschutes makes a rather dramatic geological transition as it passes around and over the many lava flows of this region. After miles of mirrorlike water, the river is suddenly and violently churned into a frenzy at Benham Falls, a spectacular series of class 5+ ledges, holes, and froth, cascading more than a hundred feet in 0.5 mile (see the Deschutes River: Upper Benham Falls run). The normal take-out is on river right at the Benham Falls boat ramp, just above a footbridge over an impassable logjam.

Experienced boaters might save 0.2 mile of walking above the falls by attempting a quick but tricky portage around the upstream logjam and paddling the 0.2 mile to the falls. However, the take-outs above the falls on river left are small and tricky to catch. Do not miss them.

Boaters who wish to continue downstream to the next run must portage the logjam and the falls. To portage, take out at the boat ramp, cross the footbridge, and follow a small jeep road 0.3 mile to the start of the falls. The portage leaves sight of the river and continues another 0.8 mile or so. Several paths lead down to the river. The exact put-in depends on the skill of the boater. About 200 yards from the base of the steepest part of the falls, the river becomes a series of class 3+ ledges and waves, flowing through several channels and continuing for about 0.5 mile. The final few hundred yards are class 2. Scout it, enjoy the view, and make your choice.

Hazards

Do not get into the logjam just below the take-out ramp. The optional portage around Benham Falls to the next run is 1.5 miles.

Access

Put in at Big River Campground, on river right, by the NF 42 bridge (see the Deschutes River: Pringle Falls to Big River Campground run).

Reach the take-out at Benham Falls from US 97 just south of the Lava Lands Visitor Center. Take NF 9702 west 5 miles to Benham Falls Campground. Alternate accesses are at Harper Bridge and Besson boat ramp, near the middle of the run. Refer to the Deschutes National Forest map for roads and campgrounds.

Gauge

Currently available via the Internet (Deschutes at Benham Falls gauge) (see Appendix A).

Carl Landsness

188 Deschutes River
Upper Benham Falls

Class: 5+	Length: 1 mile
Flow: 700–2000 cfs;	Character: forested canyon
Gradient: 100–200 fpm, C–PD	Season: year-round

At low water, Upper Benham Falls is a series of class 4 drops to an eddy just above Lower Benham Falls, which is a class 5+ cascade. At high water, Upper Benham Falls is a series of class 5 drops to an elusive eddy just above Lower Benham Falls. Scout the entire run before getting on the water. It is a lot bigger and pushier than it looks.

Boaters can portage from the Deschutes River: Big River Campground to Benham Falls run. The put-in is in the calm water 0.5 mile above the parking lot at Benham Falls Campground. The first drop is over a small tongue into a large hole on river left. The current moves to the right, to the second drop, a sharp lava pour over. Stay right, then center, and move right through the next few drops; in the last series of drops, it is crucial to stay on line. Boaters must be to the extreme left side of the river to eddy out above Lower Benham Falls.

Hazards

This run is very dangerous; a swim from upstream makes it a life-threatening situation. This is a serious class 5+ descent. At high water, the entire run is difficult; at low water, the upper part of the falls is the most difficult.

Access

Reach the put-in at Benham Falls from US 97 just south of Lava Lands Visitor Center. Take NF 9702 west 5 miles to Benham Falls Campground. One can also portage from the Deschutes River: Big River Campground to Benham Falls run.

The take-out below Upper Benham Falls is at the Benham Falls parking lot.

Gauge

Currently available via the Internet (Deschutes at Benham Falls gauge) (see Appendix A).

Morgan William Smith

189 Deschutes River
Aspen Campground to Lava Island Falls

Class: 2(3)	Length: 1.5 miles
Flow: 1000–3000 cfs	Character: forested; rafting freeway
Gradient: 16 fpm, PD	Season: dam-controlled

This is the famous "Big Eddy" run. The nearby resorts run an incredible number of visitors down this whitewater mini-run in the summer. One curler here has undoubtedly captured more rafts on film than any other in Oregon.

The first mile offers a few class 2 rapids before the river makes a sharp right turn through a quiet pool above Big Eddy. Big Eddy consists of several curlers. These can be great play spots or potential keepers, depending on the flow. Scouting is advised (left bank). A hundred yards farther downstream is a class 2+ drop with a nice play wave at the top. To play here, catch the small eddy on river right. For the ambitious, it is an easy 300-yard carry back upstream to do Big Eddy again.

The take-out is on river left above Lava Island Falls. It is clearly marked with warning signs. Lava Island Falls is 0.5 mile of class 4 to 6 rapids where several drownings have occurred.

Hazards

Scout Big Eddy Rapid. Take out above Lava Island Falls; do not run Lava Island Falls unless you are a class 5 boater.

Access

To reach the take-out from US 97 in Bend, drive west on Century Drive toward Mount Bachelor; turn south on NF 41. Turn left at the sign to Lava Island Falls. Refer to the Deschutes National Forest map for details.

To reach the put-in, return to NF 41, turn left, and travel just over a mile. Turn left, following the signs to Aspen Campground.

Gauge

Currently available via the Internet (Deschutes at Benham Falls gauge) (see Appendix A).

Carl Landsness

190 Deschutes River
Lava Island Falls to Meadow Camp
Picnic Area

Class: 4 to 6; 6	Length: 1 mile
Flow: 700–2000 cfs;	Character: forested; lava canyon
Gradient: 125 fpm, C	Season: year-round

Lava Island Falls cannot be run in kayaks. The dangerous hydraulic below a ledge on the left side of the island is difficult to see when scouting. Be sure to run the right side of the island. Lava Island Falls is normally portaged at high water. For those not running the falls, paddle across the calm pool at the top of the falls. Portage on river right down the irrigation canal walkway and put in at the bottom of the falls. The action starts immediately, with no real warm-up. This first class 4 section, Cut Up, abounds with sharp rocks, holes, and waves, depending on water level. The current is very swift. Eddy hop down, watching for new logs at all times. Some good play can be had in this section, but look downstream first.

A long calm pool precedes the next difficult section. The river constricts to a small, narrow chute with canyon walls rising from the river. Scout here. A hundred feet downriver on the left is a big eddy and a mandatory scout. Directly below on both sides are small eddies from which boaters may scout.

Do not try to run this drop without scouting. A portage here is an ugly undertaking, but a swim is much worse. Climb up above the river to scout this class 5 ledge drop. Logs are found on both sides of this drop. At high water, you will not be able to see the logs between the large rock in the center and the right shore. Do not run right of the rock. If you do the run, stay left into the 5-foot pour-over; you will understand the name "Barry's Back Ender." Start left, then thread the needle in the center and ski jump the rocks. If you go too far right, you will end up in "Loren's Lunch Stop" under some wood.

High Five is a great play hole just below this drop. At high water, it is big. Beware of the riverwide tree a hundred yards downstream. It is also visible from the scout. One drop past a dangerous logjam on the right, and it is smooth sailing to the take-out on the left at the picnic area.

Hazards
The higher the water level, the more dangerous this run becomes. At high water, it is a serious class 5+ with logjams. The dangerous hydraulic below a ledge on the left side of Lava Island is difficult to see when scouting; be sure to run the right side of the island. The second part has a class 5 ledge drop with logs and a difficult-to-impossible portage. A swim here would be hazardous because of a riverwide log 100 yards downstream, followed by a logjam. The rocks are extremely sharp in this run. A swim could result in injury, loss of equipment or worse.

Access
To reach the take-out from US 97 in Bend, drive west toward Mount Bachelor on Century Drive; turn left at the Meadow Camp Picnic Area sign. Go to the end of the road, then upriver, and park.

To reach the put-in, return to Century Drive; turn left on NF 41, past the Inn of the Seventh Mountain. Take the first left. Follow NF 4120 to the Lava Island Falls shelter sign. Turn left and go to the end of the road. Put in at Lava Island Falls.

Gauge
Currently available via the Internet (Deshutes River at Benham Falls gauge) (see Appendix A).

Morgan William Smith

191 Deshutes River
Meadow Camp Picnic Area to Mount Bachelor Village

Class: 4; 5	Length: 5 miles
Flow: 700; 2,200 cfs	Character: forested canyon
Gradient: 125 fpm, C	Season: year-round

On this run, most of the riverbank is private property with no public access, so once you are on the river, stay on it. The run starts with 1 mile of flat water. After passing a house on the left next to the river, the action begins. Just past two log houses is a great play hole and another smaller but good play spot. Around the corner is the first class 4 rapids, Play Time: continuous eddy hopping with some great play spots. In the middle of this section, Rollodex Hole provides rodeo side surfing. Other ender and play spots abound for the next 0.25 mile.

In the calm water above the diversion dam, get out and scout Darn It on river right. Scout down past the first drop; the lateral wave below is a flipper. At most water levels, this drop is run center; at higher flows it can be run left, then center. Looking back upstream from the river below gives an impressive view.

The next major rapids is called Amazing. It is amazing at high water and amazing if you can make it through the maze of rocks at low water. It is located at the river gauge on the right. Scout all the way around the next corner because there is not a good eddy before the next big drop, which has a log at the bottom. Below here is one of the best play spots on the run, Frank's Fun Hole. Continuing downstream, boaters come to a logjam that looks like it completely blocks the river. Scout on the right. At the bottom is a rompin', stompin' rodeo-riding hole called Ride 'Em Roy. Hang onto your helmet.

The river continues through fallen trees used for fish habitat. Scout the last big drop of the run, where the river drops out of sight. Do not try to play in the big hole at the bottom. It is called 100 Percent because boaters are 100 percent guaranteed to hit a gnarly rock if they flip over. Continue down to the pump house on river left, the take-out.

Hazards

Logs are the biggest problem on this run. A couple of continuous class 4+ drops need scouting. A swim in this stretch could result in injury and loss of equipment.

Access

From Bend on US 97, follow Century Drive to the southwest and go toward Mount Bachelor Village. To reach the take-out, turn left at the Mount Bachelor Village sign and go 100 yards; then turn left onto a dirt road. Park at the blocked-off road leading down to the pump house on the river.

To reach the put-in, return to Century Drive and turn left. Go 3 to 4 miles and turn left at the sign to the Meadow Camp Picnic Area. Follow the road to the end and park.

Gauge

Currently available via the Internet (Deschutes River at Benham Falls gauge) (see Appendix A).

Morgan William Smith

192   Deschutes River
Bend to Tumalo State Park

Class: 3+(4); 4(4+)	Length: 5.2 miles
Flow: 500 cfs; 1700 cfs	Character: canyon; residential
Gradient: 60 fpm, PD	Season: rainy

This run, known as the Lava Canyon run, starts in the heart of town, but most of the run is in a canyon. The one drawback is that the Deschutes is managed here as an irrigation ditch with all but a trickle of water removed through a canal system, except during winter. Boaters feel conspicuous in Bend with a kayak on the rig while others are laden with skis. Still, occasional warm days November through March provide better boating than skiing.

The put-in at the Riverhouse Motel allows boaters to do some paddle twirls in the class 2 rapids there for the gawkers in the restaurant. The next 0.5 mile is fairly flat waterfowl habitat encroached upon by motels and houses adjacent to Sawyer Park. A mansion ahead on river left signals the beginning of the action. Two long class 3+ drops wind past the houses of Rimrock West. The third closely spaced drop, the Wright Stuff, is a tricky shallow ledge at low levels. It is run just right of the large midstream boulder. Downstream 50 yards, an island splits the river into the Flumes of Doom, class 4. Both channels are runnable but are narrow, long, and complex. Because pins have occurred, scouting is required. Near the bottom after the confluence of the channels is an ender spot; however, it can deposit a boat on the boulders.

The river stays very active with class 3 and 4 drops for the next 3 miles with a gradient of 80 fpm. Following a class 3 rapids with a narrow slot entrance, the river bends right and enters a rapids known as T-Rex. The lower end of this long rapids is guarded by a boulder fence best run on the far right. At high flows, this becomes an ugly riverwide hole. The next 0.8 mile is a succession of twisting drops leading blindly into The Ogre. To scout, pull out right by the big log on shore. A house-size boulder at the bottom just as you plunge over the main drop makes things interesting. Swimmers should be aware of the ledges below. Many fun drops and several deceiving small side surf holes continue. The take-out is on the grassy lawn of Tumalo State Park.

Hazards
The named rapids should all be scouted. The narrow technical nature of the run always makes logs a threat. During rare high flows of 1500 cfs and up, it is one continuous rapids from Rimrock West to below The Ogre. Because of the 3500-foot elevation, be prepared for cold conditions.

Access
The put-in is in the north end of Bend on US 97 by the bridge on the south end of the Riverhouse Motel.

The 5-mile shuttle to the take-out at Tumalo State Park is along O. B.

Riley Road, which enters US 97 on the north side of the Riverhouse Motel. A bicycle shuttle is quite easy.

Gauge

Currently available via the Internet (Deschutes River below Bend gauge) (see Appendix A). Optimum flow is 800 to 1200 cfs.

Carl Landsness and Jon Ferguson

193 Deschutes River Tumalo State Park to Cline Falls State Park

Class: 3 (P)	Length: 14.5 miles
Flow: 400 to 1500 cfs	Character: rural; canyon
Gradient: 21 fpm	Season: rainy

This run offers the intermediate paddler one long trip that includes a very scenic canyon or several short sections. Since most of the river is diverted for irrigation in the summer, this run is usually only available from mid-October through mid-April. Because of the length of the run and the short days of winter, an early start is recommended to avoid taking out in the dark. The sun rarely penetrates the lower canyon in midwinter, so be prepared for cold temperatures. Still, on nice fall, winter, and spring days, this can be a wonderful run. If the weather is not favorable for paddling the entire trip, the easier upper sections can provide a fix for die-hard winter boaters.

From the put-in to just beyond the community of Tumalo, the river is class 1 with one class 2 rapid at the lower end of Tumalo State Park, with some nice, small surf waves to play on. Below this section, the river slows as it goes under the US 20 bridge and through the community of Tumalo. Beware of wire fences in some of the side channels. Access at this point (2 miles below Tumalo State Park) is on river left, on the downstream side of the Tumalo Road Bridge.

Below the bridge, the river meanders for about a mile before coming to a class 2+ rapid as the river enters a small canyon. The character of this canyon is only a preview of the much deeper canyon yet to come. Below this rapid, the river again mellows as it passes though typical Central Oregon ranch land. Below the bridge 3 miles (below Tumalo State Park 5 miles) is Twin Bridges. Take the main channel on the right as the left channel takes you into a wire fence and culvert. This is the last public access before entering the lower canyon, so if you had any difficulties with the upper canyon, consider taking out at Twin Bridges. The best access is on river right, just upstream of the bridge.

About 0.5 mile below Twin Bridges, you will pass under a cable tram at the resort of Deschutes River Ranch, followed by a short rapid, Pot Holes, class 2+, which is a low ledge dropping into some swirly water below. Over the next mile, the river gradually picks up speed, as it approaches Awbrey

Falls (2 miles below Twin Bridges). The portage is on the right, and boaters should move toward the right when the river opens up with a horizon line ahead, as it becomes increasingly more difficult to get out of the channelized main current the closer you get to the falls. (Do not get too close on your first trip.) The portage involves boating (or walking, depending upon the level) through a maze of small channels, constantly moving toward the right shore, before carrying the boats a short distance around the falls. This is approximately the halfway point and makes a great lunch spot. The river enters a beautiful canyon for the remainder of the trip.

Immediately below Awbrey Falls is the White Mile, a long class 3 to 3+ rapid that tends to become more difficult (technical) with lower flows. This rapid is typical of, though longer than, most of the rapids yet to come. Below here, the river alternates between long mellow sections, along which you can gaze up at the canyon walls with houses perched on top, and class 2+ to 3 rapids.

The condominiums at Eagle Crest resort, on the top of the river left cliffs, and the lowering of the canyon walls, signal that you are approaching the take-out at Cline Falls State Park on river right. Over the last several years, the Oregon Parks and Recreation Department has been attempting to keep the road into Cline Falls State Park open year-round. If it is closed, you will need to make a long carry up the access road to Oregon 126.

Hazards

Awbrey Falls is a mandatory portage on the right. Beware of wire and wood fences, willows and other streamside brush. A long trip, in often cold weather, makes having proper equipment and clothing mandatory. Emergency exit below Awbrey Falls is difficult.

Access

The put-in is at Tumalo State Park is the take-out for the Deschutes River: Bend to Tumalo State Park run. To get there, drive west from Bend on US 20 toward Tumalo. Shortly after crossing the river, turn left on O. B. Riley Road and follow it to the park. A fee is charged to park here.

To get to the lower access points and the Cline Falls take-out, turn left out of the park and drive downstream on O. B. Riley Road. Cross US 20 and continue north through Tumalo on Cook Avenue. The Tumalo Road bridge access will be at the junction of Cook Avenue, Tumalo Road, and Cline Falls Highway. For the Cline Falls take-out, continue north on the Cline Falls Highway about 10 miles to Oregon 126. Turn east (toward Redmond), cross the river, and turn right into Cline Falls State Park. Should you wish to access the river at Twin Bridges, continue north on the Cline Falls Highway from the Tumalo Road Bridge for 2.8 miles to the White Rock Loop. Turn right and go 0.5 mile to Twin Bridges Road. Turn right again and follow this road, 1 mile, down to the river. The best access is on the upstream side of the second bridge, on river right.

Gauge

Currently available via the Internet (Deschutes River below Bend gauge) (see Appendix A). The level can also be obtained from the Watermasters office in

Bend (541-388-6669). A nice flow is between 600 and 1200 cfs. Tumalo Creek, which enters the Deschutes just upstream of the put-in, adds an additional 50 to 150 cfs to the gauge reading.

Steve and Holly Engquist

194 Deschutes River
Cline Falls State Park to Lower Bridge

Class: 3 (P)	Length: 11.5 miles
Flow: 400 to 1500 cfs	Character: rural; canyon
Gradient: 27 fpm	Season: rainy

This Central Oregon run offers the intermediate paddler a nice trip though two very scenic canyons with the option of a midway access point. Since most of the river is diverted for irrigation in the summer, this run is usually only available from mid-October through mid-April. Unlike the preceding section upstream, these canyons seem to get more sun exposure, making cool temperatures a bit more tolerable.

Starting at Cline Falls State Park, the river flows though a shallow area as it approaches Cline Falls, about 0.5 mile below the park. If the flue gates of the Pacific Power generating station, located at the falls, are closed (check before getting on the river), eddy out on river left at the top of the inlet flue. From this eddy, it is an easy portage around the falls and power station. Alternately, boaters can put in at the base of the falls just downstream of the power station.

Immediately below the power station is a straightforward class 3 rapid as the river enters the first canyon. Another short drop, class 2+, soon follows. Below this rapid, the river mellows to a playful class 1+ for about 3 miles. The scenery is beautiful, with only occasional houses on the rimrock high above.

As the canyon opens up, the river slows, allowing for a maze of brush "islands" that need to be negotiated with care. More homes become visible, and soon the river passes under the low bridge at Tethrow Crossing (3.75 miles below Cline Falls State Park). Tethrow Crossing has been used for centuries, first by local Indians and then later by early Oregon settlers headed for the Willamette Valley, as a place to cross the Deschutes River. An old stage stop and ferry building remain, on river right, just a short walk up the road.

Below Tethrow Crossing the brush islands continue for another mile until Odin Falls. This class 4+ falls can be identified, not only by the sound, but by a large home, river left, on the very edge of the canyon rim. If you choose to run this drop, beware of the remnants of a broken irrigation dam at the top of the falls. An easy portage can be made on river right. After the falls, the river enters its second canyon here.

A few hundred feet downstream of Odin Falls is a simple class 2+ plunge before the river slows considerably to a leisurely pace, allowing lots of time to gaze at the spectacular canyon walls. This slow area lasts for about 0.5 mile before the pace picks up with several pool drop class 2 to 3 rapids over the next 3 miles.

The final 3 miles are once again punctuated by numerous brush islands as the river winds past interesting rock outcroppings. The westerly trend of the river in this area allows for frequent views of Mount Jefferson. The take-out is on river left, at Lower Bridge (the put-in for the Deschutes River: Lower Bridge to Lake Billy Chinook run).

Hazards
Cline Falls is a mandatory portage on the left. Scout and possibly portage Odin Falls on the right. Beware of in-stream and side-stream vegetation.

Access
Put in either at Cline Falls State Park or 0.5 mile downstream on river left. Cline Falls State Park is located about 4.5 miles west of Redmond, along Oregon 126, on the south side of the road. To get to the alternate put-in at the powerhouse, go west a short distance from the park, cross the river, and turn right (north) on 78th Street. Travel about 0.5 mile downstream to a gated access road leading down to the power station. Park along the main road and hike down to the river.

To reach the take-out, travel west from Cline Falls State Park on Oregon 126 for 3.8 miles. Turn right (north) on Buckhorn Road and continue for 4.1 miles to Lower Bridge Road. Turn right (east) and drive 1.5 miles to Lower Bridge. Good parking is on river left.

To reach the alternate access point at Tethrow Crossing, follow the directions above to the alternate put-in at the power station. Continue north on 78th Street, which will eventually become Tethrow Road as it winds down into the canyon before crossing the river.

Gauge
Currently available via the Internet (Deschutes River below Bend gauge) (see Appendix A). Tumalo Creek (about 16 miles upstream) adds an additional 50 to 150 cfs to the gauge reading. The level can also be obtained from the Watermaster's office in Bend (503-388-6669).

Steve and Holly Engquist

195 Deschutes River
Lower Bridge to Lake Billy Chinook

Class: 4 to 4+ (P)	Length: 15 miles
Flow: 500–1000 cfs	Character: inaccessible desert gorge
Gradient: 39 fpm, PD	Season: dam-controlled

This extraordinary run has been overlooked because of its short season, inaccessible gorge, and long paddle out. Magnificent canyon scenery, bountiful wildlife, and challenging whitewater await those who do attempt it.

The river is essentially class 3 for the first 4 miles as it winds through brushy shallows and braided channels. However, at mile 1.5 an obvious horizon line marks Big Falls, an unrunnable 18-foot drop. It may be portaged either side. At mile 4 is Steelhead Falls, a riverwide 15-foot waterfall. Portage on the left or run the falls on the left to avoid a nasty horseshoe-shaped pocket in the middle. The falls is marked by a class 3 entrance rapids, a steepening of the canyon, and a stone wall at the brink of the falls on river right. For 2 miles below Steelhead Falls, the river meanders through class 1 to 2 rapids as the canyon walls steepen. Gradually, the gradient increases and some long class 4 boulder gardens present the first real challenges. After Squaw Creek enters from a huge canyon on river left, the flow increases and class 4 rapids line up in quick succession. Great whitewater and breathtaking scenery combine for the last few miles to Lake Billy Chinook. The final 2 miles are on the lake.

Steelhead Falls, Deschutes River (Jason Rackley)

Hazards

Big Falls at mile 1.5 must be portaged. Steelhead Falls at mile 4 can be scouted from the right or left. A rope could come in handy on either portage. Thick brush along the river can make scouting and rescue difficult in several places. Other difficulties include the shallows and brush in the first few miles.

Access

To find the put-in, drive to Terrebonne, on US 97 15 miles north of Redmond or 17.3 miles south of Madras. Just north of Terrebonne, turn west on Lower Bridge Road (marked by a Crooked River Ranch sign) and proceed 6 miles to the river. Put in at Lower Bridge. Kayakers can shorten the run by following dirt roads behind Crooked River Ranch to Steelhead Falls and carrying to the river.

The take-out is reached by turning west from US 97 toward Cove Palisades State Park, 24 miles north of Redmond or 7.2 miles south of Madras; follow signs to the park. Once at the park, continue south and west to the Upper Deschutes day-use area. Take out on the bridge upstream of the boat ramps.

Gauge

Currently available via the Internet (Deschutes River below Bend gauge) (see Appendix A). Generally, more water is present in this section than the flow indicated at the gauge. In very-high-water years, greater releases from Wickiup Reservoir provide flows that result in some solid class 4 and class 5 rapids.

Jeff Bennett and WKCC Editors

196 Deschutes River
US 26 Bridge to Sherar's Falls

Class: 3	Length: 53 miles
Flow: 3000–8000 cfs	Character: popular desert canyon
Gradient: 12 fpm, PD	Season: year-round

The lower Deschutes runs through a large desert canyon with an active railroad along the river. Rattlesnakes, chukars, and deer live here. The bottom of the canyon can become oppressively hot in the summer. Stiff upcanyon winds are normal in the afternoon. This stretch is a designated scenic waterway. The river has numerous class 2 play spots, good sharp eddies, and several class 3 rapids. The water is clear, fishing is usually good, and campsites are plentiful—but watch out for poison oak. The Confederated Tribes of Warm Springs own the land along the left. The run from Upper Wapinitia, just above Maupin, to Sherar's Falls is a popular day-trip. The tempo is faster on the section from Maupin to Sherar's Falls, one of the most popular summer rafting runs in Oregon.

The first 20 miles below the US 26 bridge (rivermile 98) are fairly flat with only one significant rapid, Trout Creek Rapid. For this reason, most boaters put in at South Junction, 13 miles downstream. At rivermile 94 is a gorge of dark basalt. At rivermile 89 is a large island and the whitewater begins. A mile later, Trout Creek Rapid, class 2, begins on a right turn. The next 8 miles are open valley with dirt access roads on both sides. South Junction is on the right at rivermile 85; the Warm Springs River enters on left.

Whitehorse Rapid (rivermile 76), class 3+, identified by a sharp pinnacle on the right and a steep bank leading up to the railroad on the right, is at the end of a stretch of slack water that ends in a short plunge. Land below here on the right to scout Whitehorse. The rapid begins on a sweeping right bend. A mile later, take the left channel because the right channel runs onto rocks. The water is enjoyable through here. From Davidson or North Junction, where the railroad crosses to the left bank (rivermile 73), little whitewater appears for the next 10 miles. The river passes through the very scenic Mutton Mountains, with windows in colored stone, eroded by wind.

At rivermile 64, Buckskin Mary Falls is run straight down the middle for a fine roller-coaster ride. The next 3 miles produce good whitewater. Upper Wapinitia Rapid (rivermile 55) can be spotted after a left bend where a steel railroad bridge on the left crosses Wapinitia Creek. The rapid begins there on a right turn. Run right. A mile later, Boxcar or Lower Wapinitia Rapid, class 3, begins with an abrupt left turn, then curves right with a very fast current over a ledge across the entire river, with a big hole on the left and a 4-foot drop on the right. Scout the first time through from either bank.

At Maupin, a possible take-out is at the bridge at the city park on the right (rivermile 52). Fine whitewater follows from here to Sherar's Falls. The big waves of Surf City (rivermile 48) provide popular surfing for many boaters. Oak Spring Rapid (rivermile 47.5), class 3+, can cause problems. Look for green growth on the left side of the canyon and the mossy tanks of the Oak Springs fish hatchery. Whitewater begins 200 yards above the hatchery. The lower rapid is made difficult by the two ribs of basalt that divide the river into three channels. At high water, the left channel can be run easily; at low water, the middle channel should be run. The big hole next to the rock, on the right, flips many boaters. The runout is shallow and rocky.

In 0.5 mile, the White River enters on the left with nice waves, followed in 0.3 mile by Upper Elevator. The Elevator (rivermile 46) provides a great wave train with good surfing. A long narrow eddy elevates boaters back up to the top. In 0.5 mile, Sandy Beach on the right marks the take-out. Below Sandy Beach is Osborne Rapid (rivermile 45), a 4-foot drop in a short distance. Although Osborne is fun, the BLM has closed the take-out immediately above Sherar's Falls, so boaters should use the Sandy Beach take-out.

Hazards

Watch for overheating in hot weather, and beware of poison oak. Several rapids present difficulties. Whitehorse Rapid, class 3, drops 25 feet in 300 yards. Upper Wapinitia Rapid has probably the fastest chute on this run. Lower Wapinitia Rapid, also called Boxcar (where a boxcar fell into the river in the late 1940s), class 3, requires going over a 2- to 4-foot ledge and maneuvering around some large boulders. Oak Springs Rapid, a class 3 that becomes more difficult as the water drops and rocks become exposed, is considered the most difficult on this run.

Access

From US 97 in Madras, take US 26 northwest 11 miles. The upper put-in is at the east end of the bridge where US 26 crosses the Deschutes. An alternate put-in is at the end of the road from South Junction. From Madras take US 197 north 22 miles—a fairly slow 12-mile drive over a dirt road to the river— to the turnoff to South Junction. Many put-ins and take-outs sit upstream of Maupin and can be reached by following the road out of Maupin on the east side of the river. A common day run is from Harpham Flats to Sandy Beach.

The take-out farthest downstream is at Sandy Beach, downstream of Maupin and about a mile above Sherar's Falls. From US 197 in Tygh Valley, take Oregon 216 east; from US 97 in Grass Valley, take Oregon 216 west. An alternate shuttle route is a paved road that follows the east bank from Maupin to Sherar's Falls.

Note: A Boater's Pass is required to float on the Deschutes River anywhere between the US 26 Bridge and the Columbia River. Contact the BLM office in Prineville (541-416-6700) for more information or purchase a pass online at www.boaterpass.com.

Gauge

Currently available via the Internet (Deschutes River at Sherar's Falls gauge) (see Appendix A).

Rob Blickensderfer

197 Deschutes River
Sherar's Falls to Columbia River

Class: 3	Length: 44 miles
Flow: 3000–8000 cfs	Character: popular desert canyon
Gradient: 12 fpm, PD	Season: year-round

This run has more horseshoe bends and fewer rapids than the Deschutes River: US 26 Bridge to Sherar's Falls run, but the current is brisk. Allow 3 to 4 days to run this portion of the Deschutes River. From early times, the Native Americans had a bridge across the narrow gorge below the falls. Today they have treaty rights to fish for salmon at the base of Sherar's Falls. During the spring and fall, they stand on scaffolding to dip salmon from the maelstrom below.

A possible put-in is just above the bridge on Oregon 216 at Sherar's Falls (rivermile 44) on the right bank. Bridge Rapid, class 3, is just below this put-in; it is more difficult in low water. A better put-in is 1 mile down the access road along river right past Buck Hollow (this road continues to rivermile 23). At Wreck Rapid (rivermile 39), class 3+, the extreme right is clean; the center is runnable but has some concealed rocks. No major rapids appear for the next 30 miles, but the river moves at 5 miles per hour. Many small rapids are present.

At rivermile 31 at Cedar Island, a dramatic basalt cliff is seen near the end of a large horseshoe bend; a campground sits on the right. Sinamox Island and the abandoned buildings of Hill's Ranch on both sides of the river occur at rivermile 26. A mile later Ferry Canyon, with a railroad bridge over it, emerges on the left. At rivermile 20 are two islands after a right bend in the river. Harris Canyon (rivermile 12) and an old water tank are seen on the right near tall overhanging reddish basalt cliffs. At rivermile 8.5, just below the powerline at Stecker Canyon, is Washout Rapid, class 3, formed in 1995; the run is clean on the right. Freebridge, with old piers remaining, and Kloan, a railroad shed, are seen on the left at rivermile 8.

At rivermile 6, Gordon Ridge Rapid, class 3, occurs after the river makes an abrupt right turn and drops over a 3-foot shelf, followed by heavy whitewater for 0.5 mile. Colorado Rapid, class 3, is on the right 2 miles later and is identified by the old wooden trestle across the mouth. Colorado Rapid is a long series of large standing and breaking waves. Small rafts sometimes capsize here. In another mile, the rapids of Green Narrows rapids is a maze of rock ridges covered with grass that divides the river into numerous channels; the right side is deepest. This leads directly to Rattlesnake Rapid (rivermile 3), class 3. This is the most powerful rapids on this run. The rapids can be scouted from either bank. Most of the river flows over a very narrow upper ledge. The fierce hole below must be avoided. It is normally run on the left. In 2 more miles, Moody Rapid, class 2, consists of standing waves where the fast Deschutes encounters the pool caused by The Dalles Dam. Take out in 0.5 mile on the right at Deschutes River State Recreation Area.

Hazards

Six class 3 rapids are hazards. Bridge Rapid, just below the upper put-in, is difficult to see as it is approached; it can be avoided by using the put-in 1 mile downstream. Wreck Rapid is 4 miles farther. Four other major rapids—Washout, Gordon Ridge, Colorado, and Rattlesnake—come within the last 8.5 miles.

Access

Two possible put-ins are near Sherar's Falls, where Oregon 216 crosses the Deschutes. The first is just above Sherar's Bridge on the right bank. The other is downstream along the right bank on a secondary road about 1 mile, then turn left to get to the boat ramp. See directions to the take-out for the Deschutes River: US 26 Bridge to Sherar's Falls run.

The take-out on the right is at Deschutes River State Recreation Area, just off Interstate 84 between The Dalles and Biggs. The park is visible from the interstate. You can also take out at the boat ramp on the left.

Note: A Boater's Pass is required. (See the Note in the previous run: Deschutes River: US 26 Bridge to Sherar's Falls.)

Gauge

See the Deschutes River: US 26 Bridge to Sherar's Falls run.

Rob Blickensderfer

Klamath River

198 Klamath River
Keno Dam to John C. Boyle Reservoir

Class: 3+	Length: 6 to 7 miles
Flow: 2000 cfs	Character: forested; agricultural
Gradient: 50 fpm, PD	Season: rainy

The best points of this run are the large number of rapids within a few miles, relatively few flat spots, and accessibility to Ashland and Klamath Falls paddlers. Most of the rapids are wide open and can be run by eddy hopping behind boulders. Unfortunately, the water is very dirty from pasture runoff. This is not the river for making many practice rolls.

This seldom-run section of the Klamath is difficult to scout from the banks. The river leaves the road at the put-in and is hardly accessible until the take-out. A few logging roads go to the edge of the river's south side, and a dirt road from Keno is used by anglers on the north bank. None of these roads is easy to find.

The river flows below the dam for about 2 miles of short, busy rapids. Some of the best play spots are in the rapids immediately below the dam. Then an easier section culminates in a rapids with a sharp drop at the bottom. The next notable rapids has waves that pile up on a wall at the bottom and could become more of a face wash in higher water. Next is a section of rocky, pebbly, wide river. The water gathers together again for one last rapids, a good play spot, before the reservoir. This last drop may require scouting, depending on the water level and the skills of the party.

Hazards
The last rapids before the reservoir may require scouting.

Access
From US 97 in Klamath Falls, take Oregon 66 west to Keno, cross the river, make an angled left turn before an overpass, and take the very next left to parallel the logging right-of-way. Continue to a stop sign where a road crosses the right-of-way, bear left (instead of crossing the right-of-way), and drive to a point below the dam where it is convenient to put in.

The take-out is a few miles west on John C. Boyle Reservoir, where Oregon 66 crosses the Klamath at a roadside rest area.

Gauge
Currently available via the Internet (Klamath River at Keno gauge) (see Appendix A).

Karen Lewis

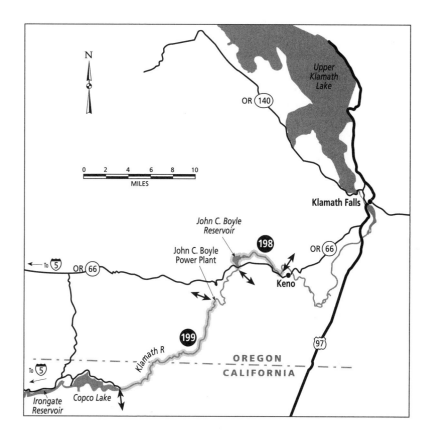

199 Klamath River
John C. Boyle Power Plant to
Copco Lake

Class: 4(5)	Length: 15 miles
Flow: 1500 cfs	Character: roadless
Gradient: 51 fpm, PD	Season: year-round

This dam-release run provides paddlers with some of the most exciting "brownwater" in the Northwest. Brownwater? The Klamath drains warm and shallow Upper Klamath Lake, which supports an abundant growth of algae during the summer. The results are beautiful brownwater rapids and suds-filled slack water. Do not let that deter you from wetting your blades in this challenging river. The thick foam is only decaying algae from the lake. At the normal release of 1500 cfs, this run boasts two class 5, five class 4, thirteen class 3, and twenty-five class 2 rapids.

The length of the trip depends upon which of the six designated access points is chosen for the take-out. Access 6, the farthest upriver, provides a 10.5-mile trip. Access 1 adds about 4.5 miles of class 2 water. The take-outs are provided by the power company and farmers along the river. Respect their property rights and use only the designated access points. The access points are clearly marked from the road and river.

No camping areas are available at the take-outs on Copco Lake, but camping is allowed at Mallard Cove on Copco Lake about 2 miles west of Access 1 on the Copco–Ager Road. Camping areas are found between 3 and 5.5 miles from the put-in. The most popular of these is Frain Ranch, where several century-old log houses still stand. Only a few marginal campgrounds are in the canyon below. Camping is available at the BLM–State Line access. Campsites are available at the Topsy Grade USFS campground 1 mile south of milepost 44 on Oregon 66, between Keno and the power plant turnoff. Potable water is unavailable at Topsy and along the river.

The run starts just below the John C. Boyle Power Plant, where the release from the turbines augments the minimum flow of 400 cfs. One unit (1200 cfs) provides this pool drop river with plenty of action for the expert paddler and a bombproof roll for the intermediate. An occasional release of two units makes it a respectable class 5 challenge. When the flow exceeds 3400 cfs, it is too dangerous to run.

The action begins immediately with 1.5 miles of class 2 to 3 warm-up rapids. The brownwater adds another aspect to reading the river because waves and holes that look safe may conceal rocks just below the surface. After the warm-up stretch, the river flattens out for the next 3 miles, presenting an opportunity to enjoy the abundant wildlife: bald eagles, red-tailed hawks, cormorants, and herons.

Immediately below Frain Ranch, the river is squeezed into a tight canyon, which begins the major excitement. Caldera, a 200-yard class 5 cooker, begins the nearly nonstop 6-mile series of class 3, 4, and 5 rapids. Scout Caldera from either side. If you feel you may be in over your head, take the jeep road on river right that leads back to the put-in. With a gradient of 76 fpm, many of the rapids drop out of sight. Eddy hopping is very difficult and not recommended for first-time boaters. A mile farther is Satan's Gate, a class 4 rapids that drops on a right turn that leads directly into Hell's Corner, a 350-yard class 5 rapids. It can be scouted from the left. The last 50 yards of Hell's Corner is known as the Ego Bruiser and is best run far right to catch the eddy at the bottom before you are thrust into The Dragon, a fun class 4 with some big holes, waves, and obstacles.

A couple of rapids later, enter Dance Hall, a long, shallow rock garden that sweeps right and then left. This leads directly into a 90-degree right-dropping turn known as Ambush, which has wrapped many a boat and embarrassed even those familiar with the river. In 0.5 mile, pass Salt Caves on the left. The action continues for another 3 miles to the Oregon–California border, identified by bridge abutments on both sides of the river and followed immediately by a 4-foot drop known as State Line Falls. An optional take-out is available on the left just above the falls, and another (better) is 0.25 mile downstream. Both are on BLM land with lots of room for camping. This is Access 6.

The trip continues another 5 miles to Copco Lake. The canyon widens as you float along in class 1 and 2 rapids interspersed with some calm stretches. The river passes some working cattle ranches and the historic ghost town of Beswick. The take-out is at Access 1, on the left after 0.5 mile of lake paddling. An alternate take-out is another 0.5 mile along the lakeshore at Copco Store, which charges a small fee.

Hazards

The Caldera, Satan's Gate, Hell's Corner, and The Dragon are long, difficult rapids. The length of the rapids, the proliferation of holes and rocks, and the brownwater all add to the difficulty. The water moves fast enough to flush boats out of most holes, but the rocks are still hard.

Access

From US 97 in Klamath Falls, take Oregon 66 west to between mileposts 42 and 43. The road to the put-in heads south from Oregon 66 between these mileposts; it is marked with a sign to John C. Boyle Power Plant. Follow the road 4.5 miles to the power plant; continue another 0.5 mile to a steep switchback road that leads to the river's edge and the put-in.

Two shuttle routes lead to the take-out; both require returning to Oregon 66. The shorter route should be considered only in good weather and take about 2 hours. Drive west on Oregon 66; between mileposts 25 and 24, look for a row of mailboxes, a dirt road, and a defunct signpost, all on the left. Turn left onto this road. At mile 2.5, take the right fork. Just beyond a group of houses and a farm at mile 8.5, take a right fork again. About 1.5 miles of very steep class 4 road start near mile 10.7. At the junction with a better road near the bottom of the hill, take a left. From here, take every major left fork (Copco Lake should be on your right) until you reach the bridge across the head of the lake at mile 18.5. Cross the bridge and take another left. Access 1 is 0.5 mile upriver from the bridge. Follow the poor dirt road 0.25 mile to the river's edge, the lower take-out. For the upper take-out, cross the irrigation ditch, turn left, and follow the road. Access 6, the BLM–State Line Access, is another 5.5 miles upstream. Total mileage from the put-in to Access 6 is 49 miles.

The other shuttle route, although longer, is more commonly used because it is not so harsh on vehicles and drivers. Drive west on Oregon 66 to Interstate 5, then south on Interstate 5 to the Henley Hornbrook exit, 1 mile south of the California fruit inspection station. Go east 3 miles to the Klamathon Bridge, then right (south) 5 miles to Copco–Ager Road. Turn left and go east 16 miles to the bridge on the east end of Copco Lake. Continue 0.5 mile to Access 1 or 5.5 miles to the BLM–State Line Access. For shuttle service, call the Copco Store.

Gauge

Available from Pacific Power and Light Company by phone (800-547-1501) or Internet (Klamath River below John C. Boyle Power Plant gauge) (see Appendix A). Releases of 1 to 9 hours in duration occur daily, except for a 2- to 3-week shutdown for maintenance that usually starts the first Monday after July 4.

Lance Stein, Dan Valens, Mike Hale, and Noah Hague

Eastern Oregon Rivers

John Day River and Tributaries

200 North Fork John Day River
Route 52 Bridge to Dale

Class: 3+(5)	Length: 41 miles
Flow: 800–1500 cfs	Character: wilderness; placer mining
Gradient: 70 fpm, C	Season: snowmelt

This run high in the Blue Mountains passes through roadless terrain for 23 miles. Open canoes have run everything in this stretch except the short class 5 below Granite Creek and the logjams. The initial gradient is more than 100 fpm and completely free of pools and eddies. Fallen lodgepole pines block the narrow, shallow upper 7 miles about every 0.5 mile, requiring frequent portages. This water is class 1, 2, and 3 in roughly equal proportions. A hiking trail parallels the river the entire roadless section of the river.

Downstream the river becomes a real delight with mile-long stretches of exhilarating class 3 water in the next 20 miles. After 30 miles, the canyon opens up and the gradient drops. Evidence of mining is seen along the entire river, with occasional miners' cabins, camps, and old placer mining operations. However, below Oriental Creek, the river is less interesting because the 10 miles to Dale have been heavily mined and the scenery consists largely of tailings.

Hazards
Granite Creek is easily identified because it flows in immediately following a pack bridge. A short class 5 rapids that requires a moderately difficult portage on the right occurs just below Granite Creek. About 2 miles below Granite Creek is a class 3+ rapids where the river drops 50 feet in 300 yards. Because this rapids would be very difficult to portage or line, it sets the standard for boating ability. Wood in the river presents a serious obstacle in the first 7 to 10 miles. Plan to spend significant time and energy scouting and portaging these hazards.

Access
Take US 395 either south from Interstate 84 in Pendleton or north from US 26 between Redmond and John Day to reach the take-out at Dale, on US 395 between Ukiah and Mount Vernon. The put-in is reached by taking NF 55 east out of Dale, which follows the north side of the North Fork for roughly 6 miles and then goes overland an additional 12 miles to Route 52. Follow Route 52 east about 30 miles to the put-in at the bridge crossing the North Fork at the North Fork John Day Campground. The float can be shortened by taking out upstream of Dale, anywhere between Dale and the Wilderness

Boundary. Follow Route 52 and NF 5506 to reach the upstream access points. Depending on your vehicle clearance, this could shorten the run by 18 miles.

Gauge
Located at Monument. Currently available via the Internet (North Fork John Day at Monument gauge) (see Appendix A).

Paul Norman and Alex McNeily and WKCC Editors

Waterfall magic (Jason Rackley)

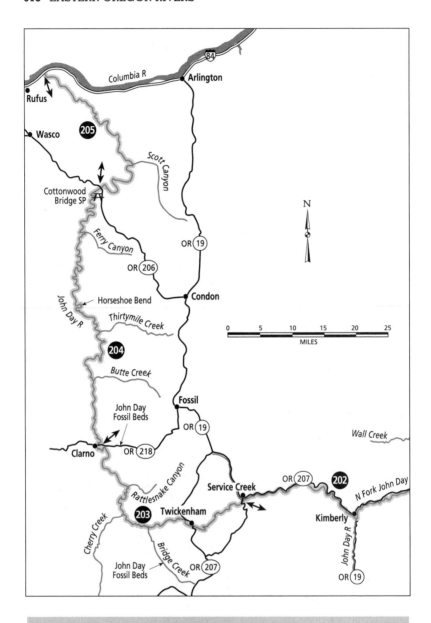

201
North Fork John Day River
Dale to Monument

Class: 2+; 3
Flow: 800–2500 cfs; 4000 cfs
Gradient: 21 fpm, C

Length: 44 miles
Character: forested canyon
Season: snowmelt

This run marks the transition between the foothills of the Blue Mountains and the high desert country typical of eastern Oregon. The terrain is mountainous but not steep, with open forest of ponderosa pine and little evidence of civilization. Wildflowers are abundant in the spring, and walks into the hills above camp are quite worthwhile. The open vegetation makes walking easy and enjoyable. Good campsites are common. The trip is usually done with two nights of camping.

From the put-in at Tollgate Campground to Camas Creek, the river is quite fast and has some holes. If problems arise in these first 3.5 miles, boaters should consider aborting their trip; three major rapids occur in the next 10 miles. The river gradually flattens out over the next 30 miles, but several long class 2- rock gardens and some large standing waves make it interesting all the way. At higher water, the river takes on a class 3- character. At any water level, the North Fork is definitely more difficult and much faster than the lower John Day.

About 6.5 miles below the put-in, the first of the three largest rapids occurs. Grandstand Rapid, class 2+, can be rocky and requires some maneuvering. The rapids begins with a wide curve to left. To scout, land on the right at the curve and walk down the road. The straight, fast drop ends with a curve to the right as a wave rolls off a cliff on the left. A small pool below the rapids is followed by a fast class 1+ rapids.

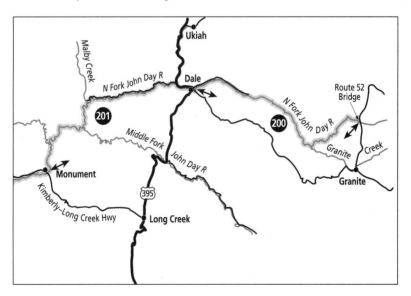

About 0.5 mile after this is a class 2 rapids (mile 8), followed by a cabin on the right (mile 8.5). Surprise Rapid, class 2+ (mile 9), follows in 0.5 mile. The approach is not obvious. Large waves are at the bottom of this relatively short rapids. A hole on river left near the small cliff or the big boil in the middle may surprise boaters.

Chainsaw Rapid, class 2 (mile 11), is 2 miles downstream from Surprise Rapid. A good eddy on river right, ahead of the rapids, provides a landing. The upper section of this rapids has large standing waves between relatively narrow, steep banks. A pool with an eddy and a cabin on the right precede the lower section, a straightforward 500-foot-long rapids. Shortly after Chainsaw is a small white house on the right (mile 10).

Below Chainsaw 1.5 miles is Zipper Rapid, class 2+ (mile 12.5). The approach is an S curve. The main rapids, at the end of the S, is quite similar to Grandstand Rapid but more demanding and can be scouted from either side. Stony Creek enters on the right at mile 15.5. In a little less than 2 miles, Upper Bridge Rapid, class 2- (mile 17.3), a 1000-foot-long fast boulder garden, begins just as the bridge becomes visible. Next is Lower Bridge Rapid, class 2- (mile 18), another 1000-foot-long boulder garden 0.5 mile below the bridge.

At mile 20, an old homestead with a log house sits in a clearing on the right near a creek. Potomas Creek enters 1.5 miles later on the right at mile 21.5, followed by a concrete bridge in 0.5 mile (mile 22). Mallory Creek enters on the right in 0.5 mile (mile 22.5), and 2 miles later Ditch Creek enters on the right (mile 24.5). In another 2 miles, a class 2- rapids (mile 26.5) follows a gentle curve to the left. In 1.5 miles, the Middle Fork John Day River enters from the left (mile 28); several campsites are located below here.

In 4 miles, Cabin Creek enters on the right (mile 32). In 2.5 miles, a class 2- rapid (mile 34.5) forms in a narrow basaltic channel. A mile later, Two Cabin Creek enters on the left at mile 35.5, followed by a class 2- rapids. Shortly after, a barn, cabins, and a house are seen on the right at mile 37.5. Soon after, Wall Creek, a major tributary, is seen straight ahead before the river makes a sharp 180-degree turn to the left. Wall Creek enters from the right at mile 37.7. Pass the bridge in Monument (mile 43.5) and take out at the county park about 0.5 mile downstream on the right.

Hazards

This run is in a remote location. The water is quite cold from the snowmelt, and the weather can turn cold unexpectedly, with frosty nights or snow flurries possible into June. Thus, a smashed boat, lost gear, and cold weather could combine to threaten one's survival.

Access

Several put-ins are in the vicinity of Dale. To reach Dale, take US 395 either south from Interstate 84 at Pendleton or north from US 26 at Mount Vernon, between Redmond and John Day. Several campgrounds are within a few miles of Dale. US 395 follows the north shore of the North Fork for 3 miles, from the bridge over the North Fork on the east, just north of Dale, and the bridge over Camas Creek on the west. The upper put-in is at Tollgate Forest Service Campground, reached from the US 395 bridge just north of Dale by driving upriver 0.5 mile on NF 55 and turning right across another bridge over the North Fork. Several other river accesses can be found downstream along US 395. Lower put-ins can be reached from the west end of the Camas Creek bridge, where an unimproved road follows the north shore of the North Fork and provides a choice of put-ins on BLM land. Some of the land is private, so use only BLM areas.

The unimproved road goes all the way to Monument but is often impassable.

To reach the take-out, follow US 395 south from Dale for 26 miles to the town of Long Creek, then turn west onto the Kimberly–Long Creek Highway and proceed 21 miles to Monument. After crossing the river, drive downstream about 0.5 mile to the county park and boat ramp, the take-out. Shuttles are available from the Service Creek Trading Post (www.servicecreekstagestop.com) and from The Shamrock (in Fossil).

Gauge

Located at Monument and Service Creek. Currently available via the Internet (North Fork John Day at Monument gauge) (see Appendix A). The gauge at Monument includes the flow of the Middle Fork, which usually carries less than half as much water as the North Fork. The flow at Monument is normally 60 to 70 percent of the flow at Service Creek.

Rob Blickensderfer

202 North Fork John Day River/John Day River
Monument to Service Creek

Class: 1+; 2-	Length: 43 miles
Flow: 1000–3000 cfs	Character: farmland; desert canyon
Gradient: 7.4 fpm	Season: Snowmelt

This trip follows the North Fork of the John Day River downstream for 16.5 miles from Monument to the fork's confluence with the main John Day River near Kimberly. The river then continues as the main John Day to Spray and Service Creek. Oregon 19 and the Kimberly–Long Creek Highway follow the river closely for the entire distance. The river valley alternates between broad farmland terraces and steep canyons. Campsites are rare, with little public land along the river. Numerous launch points and class 1+ rapids make this an ideal stretch for beginning boaters looking for a day-trip.

Cross the river in Monument and drive downstream about 0.5 mile to the county park and boat ramp, the put-in. Immediately below the put-in, the river flows into a short, isolated, and beautiful canyon. At about mile 2, watch for a low concrete dam spanning the river around a left-side bend. It can be scouted and portaged on either side, with the least effort on river right. Because the dam face is angled, it can be run, except possibly at low flows. Immediately below the dam is a class 2- rapid that leads into class 1+ riffles and rocks for another 0.25 mile. The river then opens into farmland. At 6.5 miles is a broken concrete weir immediately upstream of a bright blue bridge. Keep far left to avoid turbulence near the weir. Two small BLM campgrounds, Big Bend and Lone Pine, are located on river right at miles 13.5 and 14.5. Both are accessible from the road and could be alternate launch points.

Another launch point is 3 miles downstream at the Oregon 19 bridge near Kimberly. Below this bridge, the main John Day enters from the left, increasing the total flow by about one-half. About 1.5 miles downstream from the confluence is an island on a left bend with a rapid (class 2-) on both sides that is the most difficult of the run. The left side is easiest to scout. The Shady Grove rest area on Oregon 19 is on river right 6.5 miles below the confluence. It has toilets and picnic tables but no camping and is another place for launching. Spray is 14 miles below the confluence and has a park with a boat ramp on river right. The 13-mile segment between Spray and Service Creek offers the most enjoyable canyon scenery and a nice sequence of class 1+ rapids. Alternate launch points found in this segment are just upstream of a small bridge at 8.5 miles below Spray and at Mule Shoe Campground (10.5 miles below Spray).

Hazards
The concrete dam 2 miles below the county park put-in near Monument should be scouted. The broken concrete weir at 6.5 miles below the put-in should be approached with caution and avoided.

Access
Numerous access points are described above. Boats could access the river at Monument, Kimberly, Spray, the bridge 8.5 miles below Spray, and at Mule Shoe Campground. For directions to Monument see the North Fork John Day River: Dale to Monument run. For directions to Service Creek, see the John Day River: Service Creek to Clarno run.

Gauge
Flows are currently available via the Internet (see Appendix A): The gauge at Monument gives flows on the North Fork. The Service Creek gauge gives flows below the confluence at Kimberly. The listed flows are for the Service Creek gauge.

John Van Sickle

203 John Day River
Service Creek to Clarno

Class: 1+(2)	Length: 47 miles
Flow: 1200–6000 cfs	Character: desert canyon
Gradient: 8 fpm, PD	Season: snowmelt

This stretch of the John Day is a favorite for open canoers, drift boaters, and beginning kayakers who want a fine desert wilderness experience. Although a number of ranches and cultivated fields are located at several places along the river, other sections are uninhabited and cut off from civilization by the towering walls of the canyon. Below the put-in at Service Creek, boaters have several easy class 1 rapids and riffles as they feel themselves slipping away from civilization. The sculpture of nature in the twisted basalt canyons presents forms never before imagined. The most beautiful stretch has been designated a scenic river. The other stretches have seen ever-increasing pressures of humanity's relentless efforts to cultivate any land that has water available. Thus the many irrigation pumps flooding alfalfa fields leave boaters with the uneasy feeling that the river may be pumped dry before they reach the take-out.

Campsites are quite plentiful, often with sandy beaches at water level and juniper trees higher up. No campsites are found near the ranching area of Twickenham or along the last 8 miles to Clarno. The trip is normally done with two or three nights of camping on the river.

Six miles after the put-in at Service Creek, the boater encounters Russo Rapid, class 2. The approach is at a curve to the left. The rapids is straight, with a cliff at bottom left. A few miles farther, the land is private all the way to Twickenham. Do not camp along that stretch. The Twickenham Bridge is at mile 12. In 4 more miles is Wreck Rapid, class 2, with a side-breaking wave off the cliff on the right at the lower end. The approach is a slight curve to the right. Boaters can land on river left to scout or portage. Schuss Rapid, or Burnt Ranch Rapid, occurs in another 8 miles (mile 24). At levels below 3000 cfs, a large rock sits in the center at the head of the rapids. Boaters can scout from left or right.

In 3 miles, Cherry Creek enters on the left at mile 27. Some boaters take out here. In another 2 miles, the Big Bend region begins at mile 29.5; the river makes several sweeping bends in a beautiful deep canyon with fine beaches and campsites and numerous class 1 rapids. Toward the end of the Big Bend Region, Rattlesnake Canyon can be seen on the right (mile 34.5); a back road comes in here. In 4 miles, a secondary road on the right at mile 38.5 connects to the highway near Clarno. In 8.5 miles is the Clarno bridge (mile 47). Take out on the right.

Hazards

Open canoers should scout the three class 2 rapids in this run; kayakers with class 2 experience will not have difficulty. In places, the river drives headlong into cliff walls. At high water, the waves rolling off the cliff, as well as the eddy on the inside of the bend, can give the unwary boater problems. Afternoon upcanyon winds are normal and occasionally strong with erratic side gusts. Rattlesnakes and scorpions are present but seldom seen.

Access

The take-out is at Clarno where Oregon 218 crosses the river. Parking and a boat landing are located at the east end of the bridge. Oregon 218 is located between US 97 at Shaniko and Oregon 19 at Fossil (Oregon 19 can be reached from the north from Interstate 84 at Arlington or from the south from US 26 near Dayville).

The put-in near Service Creek is about an hour's drive from Clarno via Oregon 218 east to the town of Fossil. From Fossil, take Oregon 19 south to

Service Creek, which consists of a general store on Oregon 19. The Service Creek Trading Post (www.servicecreekstagestop.com) will shuttle cars to Clarno. Service Creek is the junction of Oregon 207 and Oregon 19; Oregon 207 comes from the south from Mitchell, on US 26. At this junction, go south on Oregon 207 0.2 mile downstream toward Mitchell. The put-in is on river right 100 yards upstream from the bridge on Oregon 207.

Note: Currently (2012) permits are required to float this stretch of river. They are readily available during the off-season but are first-come first-served during the popular late spring and early summer season. Visit www.john dayboaterpermit.com for more information and to obtain a permit.

Gauge
Currently available via the Internet (John Day at Service Creek) (see Appendix A).

Rob Blickensderfer

204 John Day River
Clarno to Cottonwood

Class: 2(3)	Length: 69 miles
Flow: 1200–6000 cfs	Character: desert canyon
Gradient: 11 fpm, C	Season: snowmelt

This run on the John Day is another favorite for many, including open canoers, drift boaters, and kayakers. Because the gradient here is steeper than in the preceding run, the river moves faster and has more wave action. Fewer ranches make boaters feel more isolated along this stretch. It has been designated a Wild River under the Oregon Scenic Waterways System. Many magnificent canyon walls exist, unseen by all but river runners. Allow at least four nights of camping on the river. A very relaxed trip with swimming and side-canyon hiking may last 6 to 7 days.

Put in on the right at the Clarno bridge. In 3.5 miles, boaters encounter a large riffle with big holes in the middle at high water and rocks at low water. In less than 1 mile, Clarno Rapid (mile 4.4) is marked by an island ahead of the rapids; take the left channel. Clarno Rapid is a long, complicated class 3 rapid. It is class 4 above 6000 cfs, and a capsize can have significant consequences. Trees on the left bank are followed by an eddy on the left with a small landing spot just above the main chute. Heavy, fast water, class 2, leads around a left curve and into the main drop about 300 feet downstream. The rapids can be scouted from the left by landing above the class 2 drop. The portage for Clarno Rapid is on the left and is about 150 yards over the rise. The rapid can also be lined with difficulty on the left. Lower Clarno, class 2, continues for 0.3 mile. It is rocky at low water.

On the right below Clarno Rapid is Mulberry Camp (mile 5.3), the last camp and beach not on private land for 6.5 miles. At about 6 miles downstream, powerlines cross the river, followed by old ranch buildings at mile 11.3 that signal 0.3 mile of class 1+ to 2- rapids. About 0.33 mile later, Butte Creek enters on the right at mile 11.9. In 1.6 miles, buildings on the right at mile 13.5, visible straight ahead from far upstream, are the watermark for nearing Basalt Rapid.

Basalt Rapid, class 2 (mile 15.9), is another long rapid. It is class 3 above 6000 cfs and has some meaty pour overs and holes at this level. It is replete with basalt boulders. The approach is not obvious but can be identified by fast water leading around a slight curve to the right, with juniper trees on the right. Land right to scout. Below 3000 cfs, the rounded black basalt rocks are exposed in the rapids and some maneuvering is required. The main rapids is fairly short and curves to the left. Lower Basalt Rapid, with large black basalt boulders in the river, continues for 0.5 mile, with some hole dodging and rock dodging. Good campgrounds are located here and in Great Basalt Canyon for the next 4 miles. Arch Rocks (mile 20) has a large camp on the right.

Thirtymile Creek enters on the right 5.3 miles later (mile 25.3), with an access road to civilization. In 8.2 miles, the river begins a sweep to the right (The Saddle, ahead, is only 300 feet wide), followed by Horseshoe Bend, a 320-degree, 2-mile turn to the left. Within another 3 miles, two springs emerge from the vegetation on the hillside on the left (mile 38.1), identified by a dirt bank on river left and distorted columnar basalt near the river on river right.

In 7.7 miles, Southbound Rapid (mile 45), straightforward class 1+, is headed due south, with a large gravel bar on the left. Landmarks are visible in 4.3 miles at mile 49.3: Hoot Owl Rock, a 6-foot-high "owl," is seen against the skyline about 200 feet above the river; a gravel bar is on the left; and Citadel Rock, a fairy-tale fortress of a rock formation, dominates the view downstream. The river makes a sharp 180-degree turn to the right around Hoot Owl Rock.

In 0.7 mile, Doomsday Wall is on the left at mile 50; the river seems to disappear under the wall. A good ferry is required here. Campsites are less numerous and less desirable from here on. In 3.8 miles, Little Ferry Canyon comes in on the left at mile 53.8; two flat islands can be seen just downstream, and the red bluffs ahead on the left are The Gooseneck. The river first curves sharply right, then makes a long 200-degree curve left around The Gooseneck (mile 54.5).

In little less than 1 mile, Ferry Canyon (mile 55.5) comes in on the right, with Ferry Canyon Rapid, straightforward class 1+. In 4.5 miles, powerlines first become visible on a distant ridge (mile 60). Almost no campsites can be found below here. It is another 9 miles to the take-out at the Cottonwood bridge (mile 69). Take out on the right, just below the bridge.

Hazards

In addition to the rapids described above, the terrain provides difficulties. Spring weather can range from snow flurries to sunny with temperatures above 100 degrees Fahrenheit within a few days. Beware of rattlesnakes, strong upcanyon winds in the afternoons, and the lack of potable water. Scouting Clarno and Basalt Rapid can easily involve long hikes because of the length of the rapids.

Access

The put-in is at the bridge in Clarno where Oregon 218 crosses the river. Parking and a boat landing are located at the east end of the bridge. Oregon 218 is located between US 97 at Shaniko and Oregon 19 at Fossil (Oregon 19 can be reached from the north from Interstate 84 at Arlington or from the south from US 26 near Dayville).

The take-out is at Cottonwood Bridge where Oregon 206 crosses the river. To get from Clarno to Cottonwood, follow Oregon 218 east to Fossil, then take Oregon 19 north to Condon, and then take Oregon 206 north to Cottonwood.

Note: Currently (2012) permits are required to float this stretch of river. See previous run (John Day: Service Creek to Clarno) for more information about the permits.

Gauge

Currently available via the Internet (John Day at Service Creek) (see Appendix A).

Rob Blickensderfer

205 John Day River
Cottonwood Bridge to Columbia River

Class: 2 (5+), P	Length: 39.7 mi
Flow: 700–6000 cfs	Character: desert canyon
Gradient: 7 fpm	Season: snowmelt

This stretch of the John Day can be divided into three sections of very different character: the float from Cottonwood Bridge to Tumwater Falls, Tumwater Falls followed by the 0.4 mi Narrows, and Lake Umatilla as part of the Columbia River/John Day reservoir. This description is based on a late-season run at 700 cfs in an inflatable kayak.

Put in river right at Cottonwood Bridge. The first 25 miles are comparable to the last few miles of the John Day River: Clarno to Cottonwood run. The float goes through relatively open desert canyons, occasionally passing basalt cliffs, and past a few ranches. Stretches with jeep trail access alternate with stretches that have no road access. None of the few rapids in the first 25 miles exceed class 1+. At low water, gravel bars near islands may be a problem; take the narrower channel that drops just before the island; the other channel often ends in shallow gravel bars. Despite a few fences and "No Trespassing" signs, opportunities to camp are plentiful. The McDonald Ford of the Barlow Cutoff of the Oregon Trail crosses the river at about 19 miles. An Oregon Trail monument can be visited a quarter mile up the dirt road on river left. Although the falls are more than 10 miles away, this is the last option to take out before Tumwater Falls. Fishermen and boaters with larger craft often use this take-out.

The river picks up speed at about 23 miles, and in 2 miles numerous boulder gardens provide a welcome change of pace. All the action is well within class 2 at low water, but narrow passages and the more technical character may create challenges for some.

The river makes a 90-degree turn from north to west at about 28.8 miles, continuing west for another 0.5 mile before it turns northwest. This northwest turn indicates the upcoming Tumwater Falls. In addition to the noise, a continuous cliff river right, a black basalt island in the middle (at low to medium water levels), and a series of cliffs on river left provide a clear warning of Tumwater Falls. Take out river right, climb up a 50-foot slope to a trail that parallels the Narrows. The trail is fairly level and an easy walk for several people, but not for larger groups carrying boats. Use this trail for the 0.5-mile portage leading to the beginning of Lake Umatilla, the John Day arm of the Columbia River reservoir. The lower half of the Narrows is a popular smallmouth bass fishing area.

Competent class 5 boaters interested in running parts of the Narrows need the following information. Tumwater Falls is the beginning of the Narrows, a series of cascading falls. The Narrows extends over 0.4 mile for a total drop of about 30 feet. A 30- to 50-foot vertical cliff river right makes access to the river impossible. On river left, a 20- to 30-foot cliff is broken at several places and allows for scrambles down to the river. At low water level, several 5-foot drops are located down deep between the cliffs and are separated by pools.

Below Tumwater Falls to the confluence with the Columbia River, the run is flat water and shared with fishermen in powerboats. Camping is available at Albert Philippi Park, at about 36 miles. Otherwise, undeveloped campsites are on both shores, but very few trees provide shade.

Hazards

In addition to Tumwater Falls and the Narrows, the remoteness of the terrain, heat, and wind pose challenges. Upriver winds on this stretch can be very strong. Rattlesnakes, scorpions, and poison ivy share the riverbank with boaters.

Access

To reach the take-out, take exit 114 on Interstate 84 and go to Le Page Park at the mouth of the John Day. Check with camp host for fees and parking. To reach the put-in, go west on Interstate 84, take exit 109, and go through Rufus and south on Scott Canyon Road to Oregon 206. Go southeast on Oregon 206 to Cottonwood Bridge. Boaters who take out before Tumwater Falls take Klondike Road off Oregon 206 to reach the Barlow Cutoff crossing of the John Day. The gas station in Rufus can be consulted for shuttle service.

Note: Currently (2012) permits are required to float this stretch of river. They are readily available at the launch site. For more information visit www.johndayboaterpermit.com.

Gauge

Currently available via the Internet (John Day at McDonald Ferry gauge and John Day at Service Creek gauge) (see Appendix A).

Horst Lueck

Snake River and Tributaries

206 Donner und Blitzen River
Blitzen Crossing to Page Springs

Class: 3(3+)	Length: 17.3 miles
Flow: 500–800 cfs	Character: remote high desert canyon
Gradient: 49 fpm	Season: Spring snowmelt

The Donner und Blitzen is a National Wild and Scenic River, a superb fly fishing stream, a mountain river in a parched southeast Oregon desert setting with no outlet beyond Malheur Lake, and it is located in a region of exceptional wildlife and biological diversity. It drains the magnificent Steens Mountain, an uplift fault block in the Basin and Range Province. The river flows 17.3 miles and drops more than 800 feet from Blitzen Crossing to Page Springs through a deep, remote basalt canyon. Major tributaries are Indian Creek, Little Blitzen, and Fish Creek, all flowing out of high glacially carved gorges on the west side of Steens Mountain. It is one of the finest whitewater runs in Oregon. The river is demanding, the action is continuous, the scenery and setting are spectacular, and the river is remote, yet it can be run as a (long) day-trip.

The river has three distinct sections: from the South Fork at Blitzen Crossing to Little Blitzen, from Little Blitzen to Fish Creek, and from Fish Creek to Page Springs. Because of the limited access, you paddle all three. The Little Blitzen increases the flow of the South Fork by about 60 percent; Fish Creek adds about the same amount.

The paddling is technical and the action is nonstop class 2+ and 3 for 11.6 miles, then it tapers off to 1+ and 2- for the last 5.7 miles. The river demands excellent boat control and respect for the remote nature of the run. The banks on the South Fork are choked with alder and dogwood. These trees and their roots create continuous obstacles for hundreds of feet along the bank. The South Fork starts out 10 to 20 feet wide; the Donner und Blitzen at Page Springs is 50 to 70 feet wide. Near the end of the run is a 4-foot-high dam that separates the lower river from the upper river and its native population of redband trout. Total paddling and scouting time is about 6 hours.

SECTION 1: SOUTH FORK AT BLITZEN CROSSING TO LITTLE BLITZEN, 3.7 MILES, CLASS 3

This is a narrow, technical stream crowded by brush from both banks, particularly in the first mile. At mile 2.3, in a sharpleft bend, is a class 3+ drop beginning a 1-mile section at 75 fpm. The confluence on the right with the Little Blitzen has a broad grassy delta with a very old jeep trail coming down from the Riddle Brothers Ranch. The canyon walls rise from 75 feet near the put-in to more than 150 feet at the confluence.

SECTION 2: LITTLE BLITZEN TO FISH CREEK, 7.9 MILES, CLASS 3
The river widens substantially at the Little Blitzen. Two 70 to 75 fpm sections are each roughly 1 mile long. They begin about 2 miles and 4 miles downstream from the Little Blitzen. The canyon walls rise more than 400 feet above the river. Very steep side canyons offer some interesting hikes to the rim; in particular, Tombstone Canyon is on the left 2 miles below the Little Blitzen.

SECTION 3: FISH CREEK TO PAGE SPRINGS, 5.7 MILES, CLASS 2-
This section actually starts about 1.8 miles above Fish Creek. Bottomland begins here and gradually expands downstream toward Page Spring. The canyon walls are lower but still 200 feet above the river. Beware of the low dam at the gauging station 1 mile above Page Springs and of the fence across the river at Page Springs.

Hazards
The 3+ drop at 2.3 miles down the South Fork will catch you by surprise on a sharp left bend. The canyon is remote, so prepare for emergencies, injuries, and any need for a layover in the canyon. Cell phones do not count (and will not work).

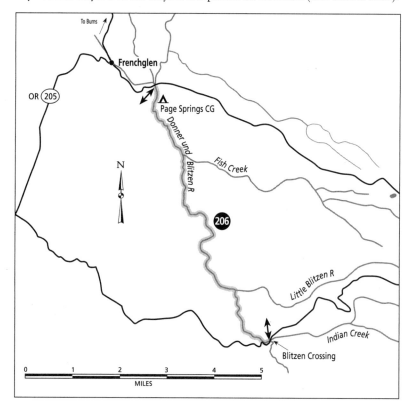

Access
From the west, take US 20 east to Burns. Proceed southeast on Oregon 78 for about 1.5 miles, then go south on Oregon 205 for about 55 miles to Frenchglen and Steens Mountain. Follow the Steens Mountain Loop to the BLM Page Springs Campground, the take-out.

The put-in is reached by continuing south from Frenchglen on Oregon 205 for 10 miles to the south entrance to the Steens Mountain Loop. Turn left onto the loop road and continue 16 miles to Blitzen Crossing. This is the steel bridge where the loop road crosses the South Fork Donner und Blitzen, the put-in. The loop road has four gates. Gate 4, the South Gate, is opened by the BLM in May and provides access to Blitzen Crossing. Gate 3, east of Blitzen Crossing, is opened later, depending upon the snowpack on Steens Mountain. It is possible to arrange some form of shuttle to Blitzen Crossing at the Steens Mountain Resort near Frenchglen.

Gauge
Currently available via the Internet (Donner und Blitzen River near Frenchglen gauge) (see Appendix A).

Steve Cramer and Larry Hodges

207 Powder River Milepost 20.5 to Cable Tram (Milepost 34)

Class: 3(4)T	Length: 13 miles
Flow: 450–900 cfs	Character: desert canyon
Gradient: 30 fpm, PD	Season: snowmelt

The Powder River starts in the Elkhorn Range above the mining town of Sumpter, and flows east through Baker City and into the Snake River at the town of Richland. This run is 20 miles downstream of Baker City, beginning at the eastern end of the Lower Powder Valley and ending just before Eagle Valley. The run is described in two sections separated by the backup, Slide Lake, created by a major landslide in the early 1980s. Adequate flows occur March into June as the result of snowmelt. The average river width is less than 20 feet.

SECTION 1: MILEPOST 20.5 TO SLIDE LAKE, 9.5 MILES, CLASS 2 TO 3
The first 2.5 miles are an easy warm-up with intermittently spaced class 1 and 2 rapids before the more difficult and technically demanding Powder River Canyon. The canyon begins 2 miles downstream from the bridge put-in. The next 4 miles are mostly class 2 with rocky drops rarely over 3 feet high. At 6

miles downstream of the bridge, continuous rocky class 3 rapids begin with numerous narrow chutes. This section ends abruptly at Slide Lake.

SECTION 2: SLIDE LAKE TO MILEPOST 34, 4.5 MILES, CLASS 3

The more adventurous boater might consider boating the outflow of the lake, a 30-foot drop over a distance of 100 feet. Section 2 is similar to the continuous class 3 portion of section 1.

Hazards

Just above and below Slide Lake, the rapids are class 4. Numerous barbed-wire fences cross the river below the take-out at milepost 34.

Access

From Interstate 84 near Baker City, take exit 302 onto Oregon 86 east to milepost 20.5. The take-out is at milepost 34 near the cable tram. Put in at the Oregon 86 bridge crossing.

Gauge

Currently available via the Internet (Powder River near Richland gauge) (see Appendix A). Irrigation diversions occur upstream of the gauge.

Alan Jones

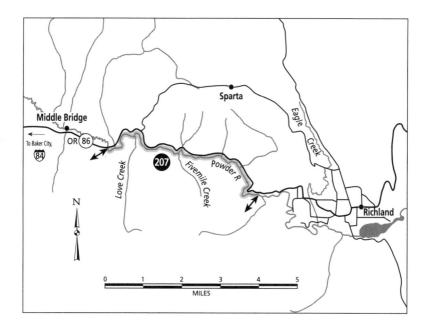

208 Jarbidge River/Bruneau River
Murphy Hot Springs to Bruneau

Class 4(6) P	Length: 69 miles
Flow: 600–2000 cfs	Character: desert canyon
Gradient: 35 fpm, PD	Season: spring runoff

The Jarbidge and the Bruneau carry you through a remote wilderness, on a whitewater extravaganza, in the scenic desert canyons where Idaho meets Nevada. Like the nearby Owyhee, some stretches are characterized by sheer vertical walls adorned with hoodoos dropping to the river. Some hiking is possible. Because of the whitewater challenges and remoteness, the trip requires solid class 4 paddling skills, good judgment, and thorough preparation. Given the portages, five nights out is a comfortable time to allocate. While there is little competition for campsites, some stretches have few suitable sites. From the put-in, the Jarbidge starts as continuous class 2 to 2+, with a few class 3 rapids to keep you alert. This pace continues for 10 miles. While the river lets up a little, Sevy Falls, class 4, appears after about 15 miles. It can be portaged on the right or very carefully on the left over the logjam itself. Similarly, Wally's Wallow, class 4, appears after about 20 miles and can be portaged on the right or carefully on the left over a boulder jumble. After 22 miles, the river difficulty picks up with a series of challenging rapids. First comes The Maze, a good place to practice eddy hopping. Right around the corner is John's Jollies, a long class 4. Jarbidge Falls, class 6, about 29 miles into the trip, is a mandatory portage. Portage left over large boulders. The portage is long and, for rafts, extremely difficult. Below Jarbidge Falls, the river lets up and soon joins the West Fork to form the main Bruneau River. A very hot hot springs is near the confluence.

Easy water continues for miles on the Bruneau, with an occasional class 3 drop, until Five Mile Rapid, which begins at about mile 50. This rapid, truly 5 miles in length, comprises nearly continuous intermixed class 3 and class 4 rapids. The first 3 miles are most difficult, making them a good place to put those eddy hopping skills to the test.

Contact the BLM office in Boise, Idaho (208-384-3300) for maps (the BLM publishes an excellent one) and information about access, river conditions, and regulations on river use. The BLM Web site (www.or.blm.gov/Vale/Recreation/rec-rivers.htm) is very useful.

Hazards

The mandatory portage at Jarbidge Falls, the likely portages at Sevy Falls and Wally's Wallow, and the section known as Five Mile Rapid present difficulties. This canyon is one of the most remote areas in the lower 48 states. Overland rescue would be difficult but could be made easier with a map of the primitive roads in the area. Watch out for poison ivy, particularly at the Jarbidge Falls portage. Purify water, and watch for rattlesnakes. The river is dangerous above 2000 cfs.

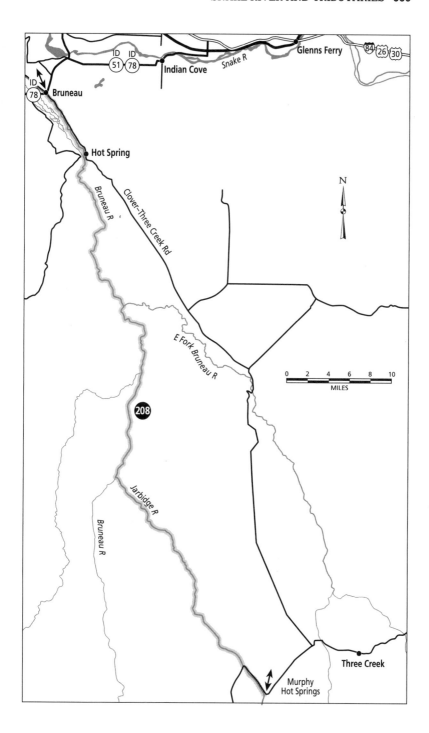

Access

The put-in is at Murphy Hot Springs, near the southwest corner of Idaho. Take Interstate 84 east to Mountain Home, Idaho, turn south onto US 51, and continue 30 miles to Bruneau. Bruneau Dunes State Park offers a nice campground. After arranging the shuttle, drive south on Clover–Three Creek Road. An intermediate access can be found at the confluence of the Jarbidge and the West Fork Bruneau. Access at this point is a long, steep, bad road requiring a rugged, highly capable four-wheel-drive rig. Several take-outs near the town of Bruneau are possible. The one most commonly used is on river right on private property just above Harris Dam. It is off a spur from Clover–Three Creek Road about 10 miles south of the town of Bruneau.

The best trip is doing the Jarbidge and Bruneau together, although rafts would do better on the Bruneau only. Shuttle service can be obtained through Jumbo's Sinclair Station (208-845-2150).

Gauge

Located at Bruneau, Idaho. Currently available via the Internet (Bruneau River near Hot Spring gauge) (see Appendix A). For an enjoyable run, catch the river as it drops through about 1200 cfs. This may occur as early as the last week in May or as late as the last week in June. It will run at about 1200 cfs for as long as 2 weeks. As the flow drops below 800 cfs, kayaks and rafts will be suitable but open canoes will do better. The river is dangerous above 2000 cfs. Care should be exercised in scheduling a trip. Patience must be exercised if the river rises during a trip. The best thing to do is to wait for the water to drop.

Dick Sisson

209 Grande Ronde River
Tony Vey Meadows to Red Bridge State Park

Class: 3(4+) T	Length: 17 miles
Flow: 250–800 cfs	Character: forested
Gradient: 54 fpm	Season: snowmelt

The put-in is near an old dam at the edge of Tony Vey Meadows, though the 8 miles above Tony Vey Meadows also provide an easy and attractive float for boaters and anglers. The river meanders through meadowlands in cattle country, with a potential hazard of barbed-wire fences across the river.

The river changes character abruptly after Tony Vey Meadows and quickly becomes narrow, rocky, and swift. Fairly steep, well-timbered slopes and generally dense streamside vegetation border this section. Several campgrounds and picnic sites afford comfortable rest stops. The Stygian Steps are a series of drops that require scouting from the road during the shuttle, about 3.5 miles upstream from Utopia Campground. On the river, they are about 0.3 mile below the River Picnic Site.

Hazards

The generally narrow channel and rapid descent of this stretch create a run that is potentially hazardous; newly fallen trees may block the channel. Barbed-wire fences and collections of debris can form obstructions on the lower part of this run.

Access

Four miles west of La Grande, take exit 252 on Interstate 84 to Oregon 244 to Ukiah. Proceed 7.5 miles west on Oregon 244 to Red Bridge State Park, the take-out.

To reach the put-in, continue 5 miles southwest on Oregon 244 to Starkey Trading Post on Oregon 51. Go about a dozen miles to the junction with NF 200. This junction is the put-in.

Gauge

Located at Hilgard, near Hilgard Junction State Park. A flow of 900 to 1100 cfs on the gauge gives a boatable level.

T. R. Torgersen

210 Grande Ronde River
Red Bridge State Park to Hilgard Junction State Park

Class: 2; 2+	Length: 8 miles
Flow: 850 cfs; 5000 cfs	Character: forested
Gradient: 22 fpm	Season: snowmelt

The river canyon broadens considerably on this run and is bounded by open forest and some rangeland. A modest gradient and easy riffles make this a fine float for beginners in almost any craft.

Hazards

Rapids constitute little hazard on this run, but beware of barbed-wire fences across the river. A rifle club shooting range is situated on the river about 4.2 miles below Red Bridge State Park. A sign indicating "Danger—Rifle Range, Entering Impact Area," hanging on a wire crossing the river, warns boaters of the potential hazard. Make your presence known to any shooters who may be at this spot.

Access

To reach the put-in at Red Bridge State Park, see the take-out information for the Grande Ronde River: Tony Vey Meadows to Red Bridge State Park run.

To reach the take-out, return to Oregon 244 and proceed 7.5 miles east to Hilgard Junction State Park, 4 miles west of La Grande on Interstate 84. The take-out is on river left at Hilgard Junction State Park, either above or below the bridge.

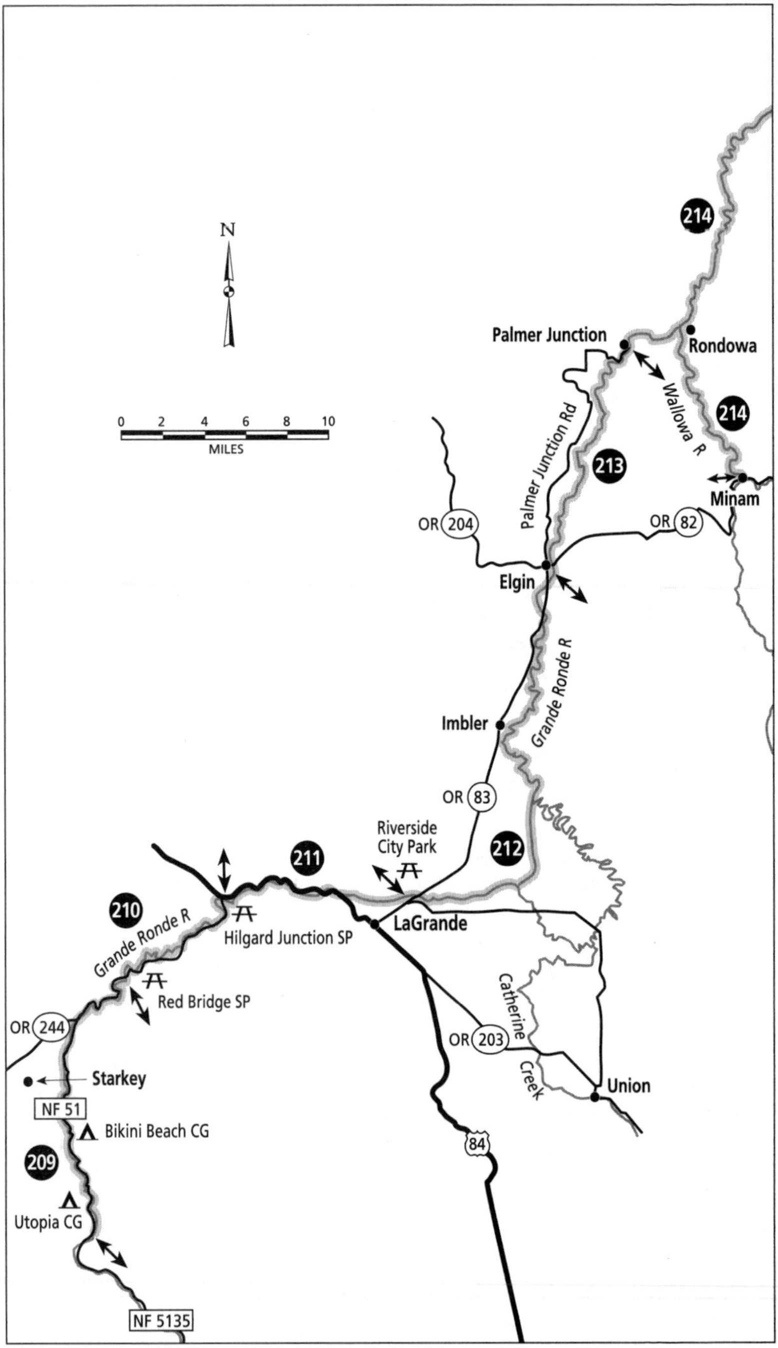

N

0 2 4 6 8 10
MILES

214

Palmer Junction
Rondowa

Palmer Junction Rd

Wallowa R

214

213

Minam

OR 204

OR 82

Elgin

Grande Ronde R

Imbler

OR 83

Riverside
City Park

212

211

LaGrande

210

Grande Ronde R

Hilgard Junction SP

Catherine Creek

Red Bridge SP

OR 244

OR 203

Union

Starkey

NF 51

Bikini Beach CG

84

209

Utopia CG

NF 5135

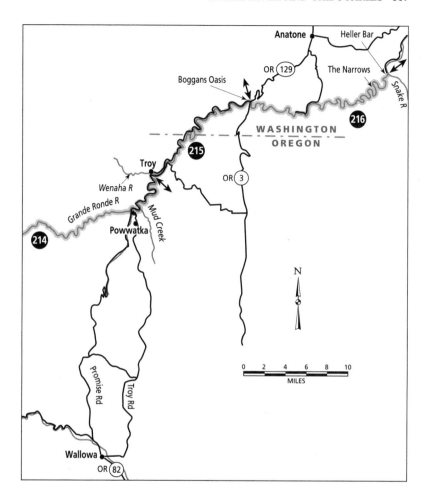

Gauge

At Hilgard, near the put-in.

T. R. Torgersen

211 Grande Ronde River
Hilgard Junction State Park to Riverside City Park

Class: 2(3+); 3(4)	Length: 9 miles
Flow: 1500–6000 cfs; 7,000 cfs	Character: road
Gradient: 26 fpm	Season: rainy/snowmelt

This is a favorite conditioning and play run for local boaters. Raft races on this stretch attract a flurry of floaters in every imaginable type of craft.

The river is wide and gentle at first. After a few miles of warm-up, a ledge called Snoose Falls nearly spans the river to form a good surfing wave. It also marks the beginning of intermittent rapids. The first significant rapids begin when the tall Interstate 84 bridge comes into view. Below the bridge is a series of splendid standing waves as the river veers to the right. Two bridges beyond is Vortex Rapid, a fine play spot and well known spectator vantage for watching rafters and others get "eaten" in the curl. The last rapids, Riverside Rapid, is the most difficult on this run. Take out on the left immediately below the rapids. To avoid Riverside Rapid, take out just before the Spruce Street bridge.

Hazards
Vortex, below the third bridge, can flip a raft. Riverside Rapid, known by kayakers as Baum's Swimmin' Hole, should be scouted when parking the shuttle vehicle before the run. On the river, the sound of the rapids and the presence of the Spruce Street bridge forewarn of the two closely spaced drops and the large curl at the bottom on river right.

Access
The put-in is at Hilgard Junction State Park, Interstate 84, exit 252, west of La Grande.

The take-out is in La Grande at Riverside City Park. Take Interstate 84 to exit 261 in La Grande. Proceed toward town. Turn right before the railroad underpass at the five-way intersection regulated by a traffic signal. Travel one block and take another right onto Spruce Street. Continue for about 1 mile to Riverside City Park.

Gauge
At Hilgard, near Hilgard Junction State Park.

T. R. Torgersen

212 Grande Ronde River
Riverside City Park to Elgin

Class: 1	Length: 32 miles
Flow: 600-5000 cfs	Character: agricultural
Gradient: 4 fpm	Season: rainy/snowmelt

This gentle, slowly flowing stretch has appeal for leisurely day outings. The borders of the river abound with wildlife, including small mammals, waterfowl, and songbirds. In its meandering course through the broad, fertile Grande Ronde floodplain, the river is crossed intermittently by numerous county roads and lanes that grid the valley. This abundance of crossings permits an almost limitless variety of trip lengths.

Hazards

Be on the lookout for obstructing debris and barbed wire.

Access

To reach the put-in at Riverside City Park from Interstate 84, take exit 261 and proceed toward town. Turn right at a five-way intersection, go one block, and turn right on Spruce Street. Riverside City Park is about 1 mile farther on Spruce Street. The put-in is also accessible from Oregon 82 via either of the Interstate 84 exits in La Grande.

To reach the take-out in Elgin, take Oregon 82 north from Interstate 84 in La Grande. In Elgin, take Clarks Creek Road east to Hunaha City Park. The Wallowa–Whitman National Forest map shows road details for alternate put-ins and take-outs along this run in the Grande Ronde Valley.

Gauge

Located at Hilgard. Flows for this run may be difficult to estimate because of water diversions for agriculture.

T. R. Torgersen

213 Grande Ronde River
Elgin to Palmer Junction

Class: 2(3); 2(4)	Length: 13 miles
Flow: 2000–5000 cfs; 8000 cfs	Character: agricultural; hilly
Gradient: 21 fpm	Season: year-round

This run initially retains the agricultural and rangeland character of the Grand Ronde River: Riverside City Park to Elgin run. Within 5 miles of Elgin, the river descends into a deeper, narrower V-shaped valley that characterizes the river's course for much of its remaining length to the Snake River. For a much longer trip, boaters may continue 3 miles to the confluence with the Wallowa River at Rondowa and from there another 36 miles to Troy (see the Wallowa and Grande Ronde Rivers: Minam to Troy run). The former access at Rondowa is on private property and is not available.

Hazards

Andy's Rapids occurs 4 miles from Elgin; scout it. Portage or line on the left, or run the normal route on the right.

Access

To reach the put-in from Interstate 84 in La Grande, take Oregon 82 north to exit 261 Elgin. Take Clarks Creek Road east at the south end of town to get to Hunaha City Park.

The take-out is reached by taking Oregon 82 to Elgin, then west a few streets on Oregon 204 to Palmer Junction Road. The take-out is about 0.5 mile below Palmer Junction at the campsite on river left.

Gauge

Use the Hilgard gauge to estimate flows.

T. R. Torgersen

214 Wallowa River/Grande Ronde River Minam to Troy

Class: 2; 3	Length: 46 miles
Flow: 1200–3800 cfs; 5000–12,000 cfs	Character: forested canyon
Gradient: 22 fpm, C	Season: year-round

This is the popular wilderness run of the Wallowa–Grande Ronde. Boaters may spend two or three nights camping on the river. This section is a designated Wild and Scenic River and is administered jointly by the BLM, Oregon State Parks and Recreation Department, and U.S. Forest Service. Information is available from the BLM office in Baker City (541-523-1256) or at www.or.blm.gov/vale. The BLM patrols the river from Minam to the Snake. A self-issue permit station is located at Minam.

Campsites are pleasant and abundant, except on Memorial Day and Fourth of July weekends when hundreds of boaters appear. This description is dedicated to Tuk-eka-kas and Hin-mah-too-yah-lat-kekt, who, along with other Nez Percé tribal members, respected the land and had the wisdom never to abuse a river or to wish that they could stop it from flowing. They called the Wallowa–Grande Ronde Rivers Welleweah—"River that Flows into the Far Beyond."

A rolling plateau makes up the canyon rim. The canyon walls present tiers of horizontal lava flows that occurred during the Miocene epoch. These stratified formations are the oldest exposed rocks in the canyon and contain pillars, spires, window holes, and caves. Abstruse dikes and columnar basalts add more geological variety.

Except at high flows, this stretch is reasonably well-suited to intermediate boaters. It usually has enough water any month of the year. May normally has the highest mean flows, while September sees the lowest flows. In very low water (700 to 1200 cfs), anticipate encounters with rocks and seemingly endless shoals. Rafters and drift boaters should be prepared to do a lot of pushing, tugging, and cursing. Flows of about 2000 cfs are optimum for open canoes. Kayakers find flows of about 5000 cfs optimum. From 10,000 to 15,000 cfs, eddies become rare, the current is fast, and large standing waves develop into great rides for dories, rafts, kayaks, and expert canoers. At these volumes, swimmers would experience a long, cold endeavor to gain shore or reenter a craft. The trip is normally done with two nights of camping on the river, but at flows above 5000 cfs, this run can be a day trip.

The weather begins to warm up in June, but snow and rain are good possibilities in late May and early June. December, January, and February are very cold. The river can freeze during these months, but they are good times for observing winter populations of bald eagles and big game animals. In summer, shorebirds such as sandpipers and killdeer nest in the same areas that people use for camping. Be on the lookout for nests to avoid destroying them. Bear Creek seems to have the highest incidence of rattlesnake sightings, and occasionally a scorpion has been seen. Treat or boil drinking water, because streams originating beyond the canyon rim may be contaminated. These lower river sections receive heavy use. The carry-out method for solid human waste is preferred.

The put-in at Minam is at the confluence of the Minam River with the Wallowa River. The first 10 miles of the run are on the Wallowa River, which merges with the Grande Ronde River at Rondowa. The first 6 miles below Minam contain nearly continuous rapids. Below the put-in 1.5 miles is the Minam Roller, or Hatchery Hole. The roller develops at about 3000 cfs and

Deep in the whitewater (Martin Bauer)

becomes a great surfing and ender hole at about 5000 cfs. Beyond this volume, the roller becomes a boat eater and thrasher because of the pronounced backwash. This hole consumes swimmers, who may not surface until 30 feet downstream. This rapids is located on the first major right-side bend in the river and is recognized by several large basalt rocks on river left. At flows exceeding 5000 cfs, open boats should avoid the Minam Roller by holding to the right bank.

Minam State Recreation Area is at mile 2. Because of its campground, this is a popular alternate put-in. A mile farther down is House Rock Drop. The chute is to the left of a house-size boulder that fell into the river during construction of the railroad. The preferred route is close to the left side of the rock to avoid the large hole farther left.

At mile 5, Blind Falls, also called Vincent Falls, class 2 to 3, may surprise many boaters. A rock garden leads into a ledge that is difficult to see. Look for it 0.5 mile below railroad marker 42 after catching a glimpse of a powerline. A railroad bridge at mile 10 marks the confluence of the Wallowa with the Grande Ronde. Many nice campsites exist for many miles below here. Sheep Creek Rapid occurs at mile 12. At mile 20, the long, heavy rapids among rocks is sometimes called Martin's Misery.

Many other rapids, some of which lead into headwalls, occur between here and Wildcat Creek. Just below Wildcat Creek, the unpaved road from Troy crosses the river on the Powwatka bridge. Two unimproved take-outs are available on the right, above and below the bridge. Another alternate take-out, with sanitary facilities, is found 0.5 mile downstream from the bridge on the left opposite Mud Creek. The 8 miles to Troy are somewhat slower than the upstream miles. The unimproved take-out is on the right at the Green Bridge (foot-traffic only) at Troy.

More detailed information can be found in *Wildwater Touring,* by Scott and Margaret Arighi, and in *Oregon River Tours,* by John Garren (see Bibliography).

Hazards

The Minam Roller can swamp or flip boats at high water. Blind Falls (Vincent Falls) is difficult to see when approaching. It develops a keeper hole at low water. It and Sheep Creek Rapid should be approached with caution or scouted. Most of the rapids require more maneuvering at lower water. Sometimes rocks become decorated with twisted or broken canoes and ripped rafts.

Access

To reach the put-in from Interstate 84 in La Grande, take Oregon 82 north to Minam. The put-ins are near the store on the south (left) side of the river bridge at Minam. One of the put-ins is an Oregon State Parks and Recreation site; the put-in at the store is private, for shuttle patrons only. An alternate put-in is at Minam State Recreation Area about 2 miles downstream. This recreation area, with a campground, is at the end of a gravel road along the left bank of the river.

There are three, or more, routes to the take-outs. Go east on Oregon 82 to Enterprise, then take Oregon 3 north for 32 miles. Turn left at the Flora–Troy junction and follow the signs to Troy (about 2.5 hours driving time). The unpaved part of this route gets rough in spring and summer, slick when wet, and snow-covered with the onset of colder weather. A longer, 3-hour, mostly paved route goes similarly via Enterprise to Oregon 3 and Washington 129 to the bridge crossing the Grande Ronde at Boggan's Oasis café. Go upriver on Troy Road to Troy, the Mud Creek recreation site, or the Powwatka bridge. A third, mostly unpaved route to the Powwatka bridge is via the Wildcat Creek road, which can be rough, dusty, or muddy—and slow; ask the locals what they know. Shuttle service is available. Call the Minam Store (541-437-1111).

Gauge

Located at Troy. Currently available via the Internet (Grande Ronde at Troy gauge) (see Appendix A).

Gary Lane and T. R. Torgersen

215 Grande Ronde River Troy to Boggan's Oasis

Class: 2; 2+(3)	Length: 19.5 miles
Flow: 1400–3500 cfs; 5000–12,000 cfs	Character: canyon; roaded
Gradient: 17 fpm	Season: year-round

Below Troy, the lines of trees spilling over the canyon rim begin to withdraw from the more arid side slopes and the canyon becomes progressively steeper and drier. The brushy draws and grassy rimrocks are frequented by mule deer instead of the elk that are dominant upriver. Rattlesnakes are more common on this stretch. A few ranches are established along the river, connected by a road that parallels the run for the entire distance. A café and a small park with outhouses greet boaters at Boggan's Oasis in the state of Washington.

Hazards

High flows create some interesting waves and strong headwall crosscurrents. Such places are accompanied by surging boils and large whirlpools that may require some heavy stroking to avoid.

Access

To reach the put-in and for shuttle services, see the Wallowa and Grande Ronde Rivers: Minam to Troy run.

The take-out is at Boggan's Oasis café and lodge on Washington 129/Oregon 3 between Enterprise, Oregon, and Lewiston, Idaho. The highway winds steeply down to the bridge that crosses the Grande Ronde at the café. The infamous Rattlesnake Grade claws its way tortuously out of the river canyon from here. A good all-weather route to the Powwatka bridge and Troy strikes westward, upstream, immediately off the north end of the river bridge.

Gauge

Located at Troy. Currently available via the Internet (Grand Ronde River at Troy gauge) (see Appendix A).

Gary Lane and T.R. Torgersen

216 Grande Ronde River
Boggan's Oasis to Snake River (Heller Bar)

Class: 2(4); 3(4)	Length: 27 miles
Flow: 1400–3500 cfs; 5000–12,000 cfs	Character: valley desert
Gradient: 17 fpm	Season: year-round

Below Boggan's Oasis, the canyon becomes increasingly arid and devoid of coniferous forest. Semi-desert vegetation, characterized by hackberry trees and prickly pear cactus, become common. This river run is not known for its inviting campsites. Overnighters in the canyon rarely fail to encounter a rattlesnake, scorpion, or black widow spider.

At low water, a few class 2 rapids occur. At high water, several class 2 and 3 rapids accompany and some very large, powerful eddies. The Narrows, class 4, is toward the end of the run and is considerably more difficult than the other rapids. The Narrows is located 21.4 miles from the put-in or 5.5 miles below Slippery Creek, a major tributary that enters from the left. The approach is marked by a big natural X-like form on the left, one bend above the rapids. Some imagination must be used to see the X Look a little above eye level on an open hillside near the apex of the bend. The appearance of powerlines as the river bends right warns of The Narrows below.

Irregular ledges and volcanic debris that contort the river as it flows through a cut in solid basalt create the rapids in The Narrows. The Narrows normally has two sections. The upper section is a long set of irregular waves that give a roller-coaster ride. The second section is about 100 to 150 yards farther downstream, where most of the river funnels left to form a large, cresting, back-curling wave. The size of this curler varies widely with water level, but it has eaten many a craft. At flows above 10,000 cfs or so, additional cresting waves develop immediately below the curler. These waves can become the nastiest part of The Narrows. The take-out is at Heller Bar on the Snake River, 0.3 mile below the confluence with the Grande Ronde.

Hazards

The Narrows, class 4, is considerably more difficult than the other rapids. Be on the alert for rattlesnakes when scouting.

Access

The put-in, with its self-issue permit station, is at Boggan's Oasis, where Washington 129 crosses the Grande Ronde (see the Grande Ronde River: Troy to Boggan's Oasis run). This put-in is a partially improved Washington Fish and Game Department recreation site. An alternative put-in is at Shumaker, about 8 miles downstream from Boggan's Oasis. Obtain local knowledge to get to the steep, rough road that will get you to Shumaker from the top of the north side of the canyon.

To reach the take-out, drive north on Washington 129 to Asotin, then upstream along the Snake River to the Heller Bar boat ramp. Shuttles can be arranged through Boggan's Oasis (509-256-3372).

Gauge

Located at Troy. Currently available via the Internet (Grand Ronde River at Troy gauge) (see Appendix A).

Gary Lane

217 Snake River
Hells Canyon Dam to Heller Bar

Class: 3(5)	Length: 78 miles
Flow: 6000–60,000 cfs	Character: desert canyon; roadless
Gradient: 9 fpm, PD	Season: year-round

Typically a pool drop river, the Snake allows plenty of time to retrieve flipped boats and swimmers below the major rapids, if the water flows are between 6000 and 8000 cfs. The rapids can usually be negotiated by the average boater. Skilled river runners find tremendous challenge as the water level increases and the big drops become bigger, the water pushier, and the flow much faster. Biggest water is encountered at about 20,000 cfs; above this level, the rapids begin to wash out slightly while strong eddy lines and currents begin to develop. Flows in the spring and early summer can easily reach 60,000 cfs at the put-in and may double after the Salmon enters at 61 miles from the put-in.

Late spring trips are a real treat; the canyon is still green, the weather is usually pleasant. Summer is paradise: hot days and 70-degree water. Into late September and early October, the weather remains pleasant, the water cools a bit, and quick squalls can pop up. Year-round upstream winds can be encountered; it is best to boat in the morning to avoid them. Camping and hiking opportunities abound with large sandy beaches, more than 200 archaeological sites, and good trails. This area is protected by federal law, so do not disturb

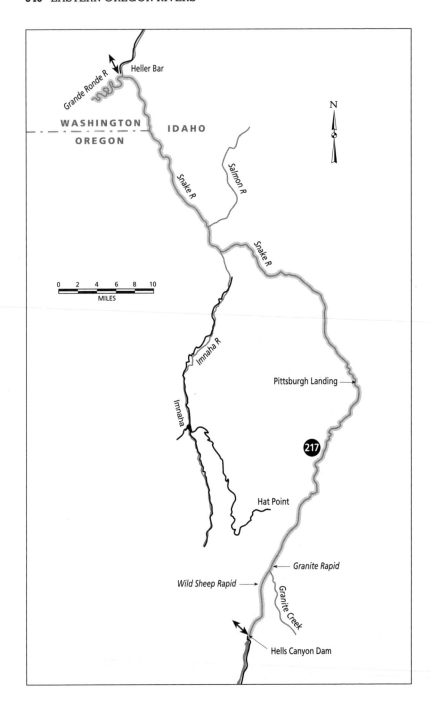

archaeological sites. More information can be found in *Idaho Whitewater*, by Greg Moore and Don McClaran (see Bibliography).

The two major rapids on the Snake can be run by intermediate boaters with a little guidance from skilled boaters. The first rapids is Wild Sheep, located not quite 6 miles from the put-in. Look for a large lone pine tree on the left and take out. A trail located up the left bank leads to a good scouting point. At low water, work either left or right of exposed rocks at the top before working to the center of the river for the final drop. The large diagonal waves from the left at the bottom can easily flip an 18-foot raft if not hit straight on.

Downstream about 2 miles is Granite Rapid. The best scouting is from river right where boaters can see the favored route: a tongue just right of center. Optional routes depend upon skill and size of boat. After Granite Rapid, many lazy miles of river with a few class 2 to 3 rapids, towering canyon walls, and possible wildlife sightings lie ahead.

Hazards

Wild Sheep and Granite Rapid have big waves and holes that can flip a large raft. Scout both. Beware of jet boats on the river, especially during the fall hunting season.

Access

The put-in is located just below the Hells Canyon Dam where a BLM ranger checks permits. The BLM can supply permit holders with a list of people who run vehicle shuttles, or you can run your own. From Interstate 84 in eastern Oregon, between Huntington and Ontario, take any of several exits to US 95 in western Idaho, and proceed north to Weiser. From Weiser, drive 31 miles north on US 95 to Cambridge, then turn left onto Idaho 71 and continue 29 miles to the dam.

To reach the Heller Bar take-out, return to US 95 and go north to Lewiston; cross the Snake River to Clarkston, Washington. Go south on Washington 129 to Asotin, Washington. At the light, bear left and continue upriver along the Snake to Heller Bar. The take-out is a very convenient concrete ramp with food and telephone available. An alternative to running the lower section of the Snake is to take out at Pittsburgh Landing, 31.5 miles downstream from Hells Canyon Dam.

To reach the Pittsburgh Landing take-out, return to US 95 and go north to White Bird. Cross the Salmon River and continue west on Deer Creek Road to Pittsburgh Landing.

Gauge

Currently available via the Internet (Snake River below Hells Canyon Dam gauge) (see Appendix A). The combined flow of the Snake and Salmon Rivers is given by the Snake River near the Anatone, Washington, gauge.

Ron Mattson

Owyhee River and Tributaries

218 East Fork Owyhee River
Garat Crossing to Three Forks

Class: 3+(6) P	Length: 73 miles
Flow: 600–6000 cfs	Character: desert canyon
Gradient: 11 fpm, PD	Season: snowmelt

The East Fork Owyhee takes you on a trip through history and geology in the remote desert canyons where Oregon, Idaho, and Nevada meet. There are mile-long stretches where sheer vertical walls adorned with hoodoos drop to the river. There are historic sites to visit and side canyons to explore. Bald Mountain Canyon is a superb hike. In some areas, it is possible to hike up to the canyon rim for spectacular vistas of the Owyhee Mountains. Birds abound, but boaters are unlikely to see another human soul. Because of the challenges and the remoteness, the trip requires solid class 3 paddling skills and thorough preparation for wilderness expeditions. There is a lot of flat water, particularly in the Bald Mountain reach and below the West Little Owyhee. Given the portages, six nights out is a comfortable time to allocate. While there is little or no competition for campsites, some stretches have few usable sites.

Most of the rapids are easy class 1 and 2 whitewater, with a few class 3 rapids. Owyhee Falls, class 6, about 29 miles into the trip, is a mandatory portage. Portage right at lower water, through the boulders, and put in just above a class 3 drop. At higher water, the more difficult left side portage must be used. A likely portage is 2 miles farther at Thread-the-Needle. This boulder choke is rated class 4 when the water goes over it, but at lower levels it is a sieve. There is a 3+ drop just above it. Cabin Rapid, located about 12 miles below the confluence with the South Fork, is a long class 4 drop. Scout from the house-size rocks river right. Cable Rapid, 2 miles below Cabin, is class 4, with the most difficult part at the very bottom. Again, scout right. On the left, 7 miles downstream, is the abandoned Five-Bar Ranch, which is worth a look.

The crowning glory is a warm spring located about 2 miles upstream of the take-out. It is truly a world-class spa. You cannot miss it, and you will have earned it. A left-side gravel bar provides a good camp just above the warm spring. There is more to know about this remarkable wilderness river than can be reported here. While planning, contact the BLM office in Boise, Idaho (208-384-3300) for maps and information about access, river conditions, and regulations on river use. The BLM website is also very useful (www.or.blm.gov/Vale).

Hazards

The two mandatory portages and two probable portages (Cable and Cabin Rapid) present difficulties. Use extreme care approaching the portage of Owyhee Falls; the water is fast. The canyon is in very remote desert country, some of the most remote in the Great Basin. Overland rescue would be difficult, but it would be made easier with use of a map of the primitive roads in the area, such as the DeLorme Idaho Atlas and Gazetteer. Purify water and watch for rattlesnakes.

Access

On BLM maps, the river is labeled as the East Fork of the Owyhee, and on other maps it is simply the Owyhee. Same river, same trip. Trips are likely to start in Jordan Valley, Oregon, the town nearest Garat Crossing and one providing a glimpse of Basque culture. Take Interstate 84 east into Idaho, turn south onto US 95, and continue 80 miles. Jordan Valley can also be reached from central Oregon via US 20 or US 395 to Burns. From Burns, take Oregon 78 southeast to US 95, turn left onto US 95 and continue 46 miles to Jordan Valley.

To reach the take-out from Jordan Valley and set up the shuttle, drive 2 miles east, turn right onto a secondary road, and proceed 37 miles south to Three Forks. (Three Forks is not a community.) The final 2-mile pitch down into the canyon is steep and rough. The take-out is possible without four-wheel-drive, unless it rains.

To reach the put-in at Garat Crossing, after setting up the shuttle, drive north on US 95, turn south on Idaho 78, and then south again onto Idaho 51 to Riddle. Beyond Riddle, near the East Fork Owyhee, turn right and proceed to Garat Crossing, Idaho, several miles west of the Duck Valley Indian Reservation. Garat Crossing is a gas pipeline crossing. Either slide your boats down from the rim or take one of the two possible tracks down to the river. A highly capable 4-wheel-drive rig is recommended for this part of the trip.

For more information on road conditions or to arrange a shuttle, inquire with Jordan Valley, Oregon driver Eva Materi (541-586-2352) or Caldwell, Idaho driver Kenneth Haylett (208-459-1292).

Gauge

Currently available via the Internet (Owyhee River at Rome) (see Appendix A). For a most enjoyable run, catch the river as it drops through about 1500 cfs. However, even 600 cfs is not too low to make this run. Optimum flows may occur as early as the first week of May or as late as the third week of June.

Dick Sisson, Paul Norman, and Alex McNeily

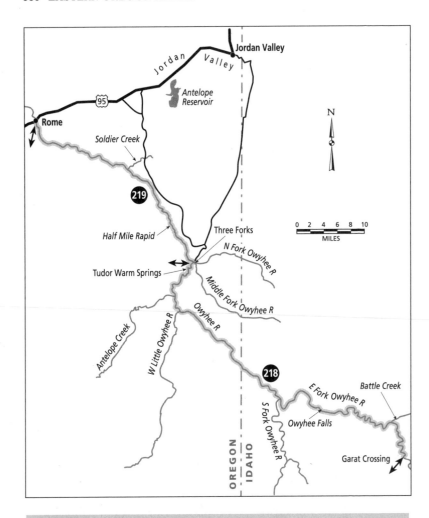

219 Owyhee River
Three Forks to Rome

Class: 4(5)	Length: 37 miles
Flow: 1200–8000 cfs	Character: inaccessible gorge; desert
Gradient: 22 fpm, PD	Season: snowmelt

The Owyhee River has cut a canyon as deep as 3000 feet down through volcanic rock. In many places the cliffs rise 1000 feet straight up from the river. The countryside is arid with little vegetation and no inhabitants. There are no access roads or trails between the put-in and take-out, although in a few places a person could climb out of the canyon in an emergency. The steepness of the cliffs and narrowness of the canyon provide a fascinating experience. The normal trip is two or three overnights.

In contrast to the pastoral scene at the put-in, numerous rapids lie downstream. Ample time should be allotted for the necessary scouting of rapids and for savoring the experience of isolation. Boaters may find hot springs, petroglyphs, and a large cave that makes an unusual camp shelter.

The weather in the bottom of the canyon can be oppressively hot in April and May, when this stretch is normally high enough to run. However, one should also be prepared for cool weather, cold water, and even snow flurries. The canyon has one of the densest rattlesnake populations in Oregon, so people may feel more at ease sleeping in tents. Camping areas are not nearly as plentiful here as on the Owyhee River: Rome to Leslie Gulch run or on most other eastern Oregon rivers. This river is becoming more and more popular.

At flows much over 3000 cfs, the river becomes very fast, but some of the rapids wash out. (For comparison, the Middle Fork of the Salmon, at the same flow, is considered easier than the Owyhee. Further information can be found in *Wildwater Touring*, by Scott and Margaret Arighi (see Bibliography.))

Three Forks, the put-in, is a slow-flowing pool. In 1.5 miles is Ledge Rapid, class 4. As the canyon narrows, the rapids pick up to class 2, and the Ledge is approached. The Ledge consists of several narrow chutes between boulders. Rafts have been wiped out there. Land near the base of large rocks on left and scout from the left. About 400 yards of class 4 boulder garden follow. In another mile, at the site of an abandoned sheepherders' cabin on the right, is a warm spring just downstream and a hot spring on the left 100 yards down. Several class 2 rapids appear in another 2.5 miles.

At mile 8.5, after several class 2 to 3 rapids, look for a bend to the right. Stop before the bend and scout Half Mile Rapid, class 4+. Some rafts have never reached beyond this nearly 0.5-mile-long rapids, which has an upper section and a lower section, with a short class 2 pool in between. Scout from the right. At low water, the lower section becomes extremely rocky; at any level, rafts have the tendency to get swept too far right and become lodged against boulders. About 100 feet upstream from the bottom of this rapid at rivers edge on the right bank is a large boulder (among many large boulders) with petroglyphs carved on its top surface. More than one group has sat on this boulder having lunch before noticing these rock carvings.

It is only a hundred yards to the next major rapids, Raft Flip Drop. Raft Flip Drop (mile 9), class 3 to 4, can be sneaked by kayaks on the left through the small left channel at high water levels, but rafts find a deceptively powerful roller at the bottom of the main chute that can flip a raft. In another 2 miles, several class 3- rapids run for 2 miles. A mile later, Subtle Hole (mile 14), class 3+, is longer than Raft Flip Drop. It leads into Bombshelter Drop, class 3, at mile 14+. A large cave on the left, just above river level, is a possible campsite. In a couple more miles are some fast class 3 rapids. A mile later is Finger Rock Rapid (mile 17), class 3. A small and a larger rock stick up at the head of the rapids. This is followed 1 mile later by several class 2 rapids.

Soldier Creek (mile 19) enters from the right, with an extensive gravel bar.

The next mile brings springs on the right and several class 3 rapids among boulders in a steep canyon located 100 yards above Widowmaker, with class 3 water leading to the rapids (mile 20.5), class 5. The approach to Widowmaker is identified by a 200-yard stretch of straight, narrow canyon. Ahead, the river seems to disappear among large boulders. On the right, a talus slope extends down to the river. As the flow of this run approaches 3000 cfs, Widowmaker appears ominous. At flows below 2000 cfs, competent boaters may run the class 3 rapids before stopping to scout Widowmaker, but all others should land on the right above the class 3 rapids. Although at levels below 1800 cfs, Widowmaker looks very tempting to kayakers, a portage is highly recommended. The portage is difficult on either side but is usually done on the right. It is possible for medium-size rafts to thread the chutes on the right. Skilled rafters run the right series of two chutes of the big drop. The drop from the class 3 rapids to the bottom of Widowmaker is about 20 feet, with Widowmaker itself about a 10-foot drop.

Numerous class 2 and some class 3 rapids characterize the next 8 miles. Small beaches occasionally dot the river banks. At mile 29 are class 2+ rapids; beyond, the canyon begins to open up. Several camping beaches and flat water can be found for the next 2 miles. The last rapids (mile 31), class 2, is followed by flat water to Rome, as the canyon rim fades away.

Hazards

This pool drop river is much more difficult than the gradient of 22 fpm implies. A number of class 4 rapids of varying length and one class 5 rapids await the boater. Because of the remoteness of the canyon and the extreme difficulty of hiking out, river conquerors must be conservative on this run. The road to the put-in becomes impassable after a rain. When scouting along the riverbank, be alert for rattlesnakes.

Access

To reach the put-in, see the East Fork Owyhee River: Garat Crossing to Three Forks run. From Rome, drive 16 miles east on Oregon 95 to a dirt road marked "Three Forks Road." Head south 35 miles, then descend to the river. The dirt road, especially the last mile, can be muddy and impassable.

The take-out is located about 0.2 mile upstream from the Rome bridge on US 95 on the east bank. A large parking area, boat ramp, and toilets are there. Shuttle service can be obtained in Jordan Valley (see the Owyhee River: Rome to Leslie Gulch run).

Gauge

Currently available via the Internet (Owyhee River at Rome) or call the River Forecast Center in Portland (see Appendix A). Although 1200 cfs is the normal minimum runnable flow, it has been run, with steep, rock-scraping drops, as low as 400 cfs.

Rob Blickensderfer

220 Owyhee River
Rome to Leslie Gulch

Class: 3(4)	Length: 66.5 miles
Flow: 1000–4000 cfs	Character: roadless; desert
Gradient: 15 fpm, PD	Season: snowmelt

This run on the Owyhee has an interestingly diverse landscape. The canyon in general is broad and shallow, although several stretches are narrow and steep-walled. The predominant basalts found in the upper canyon are interbedded with rhyolitic ash and sediments, which add various shades of white, red, green, and black to the canyon walls. Lambert Rocks are colorful badlands eroded from these sediments.

Because the Owyhee depends on snowmelt, the boating season is short and variable. It is usually runnable during April and May. Some years the season may extend into early June, while other years it may end by mid-May. The weather is also undependable, with temperatures ranging from freezing to 100 degrees Fahrenheit and higher. Be prepared for rain or drought. The normal trip is four or five overnights. The rapids on this run are mostly class 2, making it a nice river for intermediate kayakers and rafters. However, the few class 3 and 4 rapids and the remoteness of the river demand that experienced boaters accompany less skilled boaters. Additional information, including a river map, can be obtained from the BLM office in Vale (451-473-3144).

Beyond the Rome put-in 6.5 miles, Crooked Creek comes in on the left, marking the start of the canyon. The canyon opens for several miles; about 6 miles below Crooked Creek is Upset Rapid, class 3, followed by Bulls Eye, class 2 to 3. Artillery Rapid (mile 21.5), is a straightforward class 3. After the beautiful Lambert Rocks, Bogus Creek Falls is seen on the right at mile 27.5. Another 1.5 miles farther is class 3 Dogleg; after 2 more miles comes Whistling Bird Rapid.

Whistling Bird is preceded by a large rock wall upstream 0.5 mile on the left; a dry wash on the left, the rock face and slab on the right, and the noise of the rapids mark its location. Whistling Bird Rapid (mile 31), class 4-, should be scouted on the left by those unfamiliar with it. The current washes into a large slab that has fallen from the canyon wall, which should be avoided by pulling to the left.

In 2.5 miles, Montgomery Rapid (mile 33.5), class 3, is located in a steep-walled canyon after a left turn followed by a pool. It may be tricky for unsuspecting rafters at low water levels. The river drops and turns right, pushing boats toward a rock on the left. High water provides plenty of room to maneuver. About 2 miles below Montgomery Rapid is Nuisance Rapid. At low water (below 800 cfs), the right channel can be difficult for rafts. Just below Nuisance is Rock Dam Rapid. Most of the old dam has been washed away, but be careful at low water.

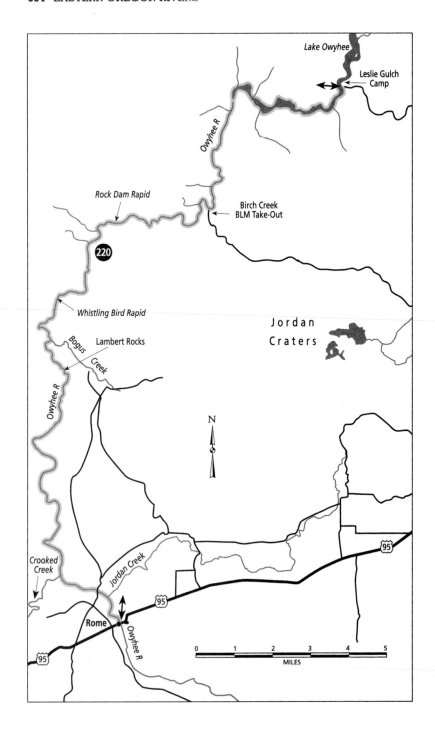

Lake Owyhee

Leslie Gulch
Camp

Owyhee R

Rock Dam Rapid

Birch Creek
BLM Take-Out

220

Whistling Bird Rapid

Jordan
Craters

Bogus Creek

Lambert Rocks

Owyhee R

N

Crooked
Creek

Jordan Creek

95

95

Rome

Owyhee R

95

0   1   2   3   4   5
MILES

After about 15 miles, boaters encounter slack water. A water wheel is on the right at mile 53.5. Lake Owyhee, an 8- to 12-mile flat stretch, is the toughest part of this run. In light rafts without a headwind, expect a minimum of 4 hours. Lazier folks (some might say smarter) may wish to arrange beforehand for a tow (see Access). Leslie Gulch (mile 66.5) comes in on the right where the lake bends left. Take out here.

Hazards
Scout Whistling Bird Rapid to avoid the large slab-rock; scout Nuisance Rapid at low water. Be prepared for changeable weather, as well as rattlesnakes.

Access
Shuttle service may be obtained from two sources in Jordan Valley: Eva Materi (541-586-2352) and Kenneth Haylett (208-459-1292). Haylett can also ar-

In the heart of the canyon, Owyhee River (Pete Giordano)

range for a tow along Owyhee Lake to the Leslie Gulch take-out. An alternate take-out that avoids the slack water on Owyhee Lake is the BLM boat ramp at Birch Creek at about mile 53.5 (just downstream from the water wheel).

Those wishing to run their own shuttle should take US 95 east to Jordan Valley and then north to the Succor Creek–Leslie Gulch turnoff about 18 miles north of Jordan Valley. The Birch Creek take-out is northwest of Jordan Valley and reached via US 95 and Cow Creek and Birch Creek Roads. To keep trip expenses down, obey the speed limit in Jordan Valley. From the turnoff, follow the signs to Leslie Gulch (approximately 26 miles) or to Birch Creek.

Gauge

Located at Rome. Currently available via the Internet (Owyhee at Rome gauge) (see Appendix A). A flow of 1000 cfs is considered minimum but has been floated as low as 400 cfs.

Dan Valens and Lance Stein

Coastal Surf Kayaking

Riding ocean waves in kayak, surf shoe, or surf ski is a thrilling form of whitewater boating that requires knowledge of ocean conditions, strong swimming skills, and suitable equipment. Rugged headlands, expansive beaches, and direct exposure to North Pacific ocean swells make the Oregon Coast one of the most spectacular surfing areas in North America. However, these same factors can produce hazardous ocean conditions that are subtle and unique to the Pacific Northwest. The following terms offer important safety tips for kayak surfing along the Oregon Coast. In addition to reading these sections, we strongly suggest that boaters unfamiliar with the ocean arrange initial trips with experienced wave riders.

Waves. Small spilling breakers in the 2- to 4-foot height range are ideal for beginning surf kayakers. Plunging breakers in the 6- to 8-foot height range can rip paddles from boaters' hands and pop spray skirts, forcing even the most skilled boater to swim for shore. Since larger waves break in deeper water, they also break farther from shore, leading surfers to greatly underestimate their size. For this reason, it is prudent to start surfing close to shore, and then move out gradually to the larger surf as true wave size is confirmed. Such an approach also ensures that surfers will observe the infrequent sets of very large waves (called "clean-up sets") before committing themselves to a thorough cleaning!

Beaches, Reefs, and Points. In their search for waves, surfers usually concentrate on beaches with offshore sandbars and reefs, as well as on points such as headlands and harbor jetties. These features cause swells to refract, or bend toward shore, and produce waves that break right or left along the shore, giving long rides to surfers.

Currents. Coastal currents can be wide and with velocities of several knots, twice the speed of a swimmer. They present a great danger to boaters out of their boats. **Rip currents** are particularly dangerous because they move out to sea a distance of 0.5 mile or more. Particularly strong rip currents occur alongside headlands and jetties. **Nearshore currents** are generated by shoaling waves that push water inshore from the breaker zone. Escaping water flows parallel to the shore in **longshore currents** and then heads back out to sea in rip currents, through gaps between offshore sandbars or reefs. Currents are intensified during conditions of large surf. The least hazardous "current" is the **undertow,** which is not really a current at all, just the backwash of a wave on a steep beach. The backwash dissipates a few yards from the beach face and is of little concern to experienced swimmers.

Rip currents heading out to sea can sometimes be identified by choppy surface water, turbid zones, or streaks of sea foam. Nearshore currents cover broad areas and can be difficult to recognize in the turbulent surf zone. Surfers and swimmers in the surf zone should keep an eye on fixed points on shore to see if they are drifting in a nearshore current. To get out of any current, swim or paddle perpendicular to the direction of current flow. In large surf, it might take 20 minutes or longer to swim out of a rip current and into shore. When an open-water rescue by other boaters is not possible, a tired or chilled swimmer should leave the boat and head for shore. Waves and wind will eventually put the boat ashore.

Equipment. Eskimos spent thousands of years developing the ultimate all-purpose sea kayak, from which modern kayaks have evolved. Flotation bags, support walls, and grab loops are necessary on today's boats. Boaters should use helmets and wear belted life jackets that cannot be pulled up over the shoulders by turbulent waves. Most important, a full wetsuit or drysuit is essential for safe boating in cold coastal waters where large surf can force boaters to take long swims. For winter kayak surfing, a hood and booties are worthwhile additions to the full wetsuit or drysuit.

Paddling Out and Dropping In. Conflicts or collisions sometimes occur between kayak surfers and board surfers. These conflicts can be avoided if kayakers adhere to the following rules of wave etiquette.

When paddling out to the breaker zone, surfers should paddle off to the side of other surfers who are catching and riding waves. The surfer who is closest to the breaking part of the wave has the right-of-way over others riding the wave face. Other surfers trying to catch the wave should back off to avoid dropping on the surfer who is already in position. Unlike the protocol at the favorite play wave on the local river, no well-ordered lineup of boaters is waiting to catch waves out in the surf zone. Thus, all boaters must make a conscious effort to share waves and to avoid catching waves that might propel them into other surfers. In addition, most board surfers are not used to surfing with kayakers, so give them plenty of room.

Good waves, mates!

Curt Peterson, Rick Starr, and Dale Mosby

coastal access overview (16 areas)

		Surf Area	Comments
NORTH COAST	221	Columbia River South Jetty	Just south of the Columbia River South Jetty	Provides some of the longest rides to be found on Oregon waves.
	222	Seaside Cove	Immediately south of Seaside; north of Tillamook head	A rocky bottom and potential long swims can make Seaside Cove a poor choice for inexperienced surfers.
	223	Cannon Beach and Arch Cape	Oswald State Park (Indian Beach); Cannon Beach; Arch Cape	Very popular with beginning board surfers.
CENTRAL COAST	224	Short Sand Beach	Oswald West State Park	Very popular area; 0.5 mile hike to beach.
	225	Cape Meares	Immediately north of Cape Meares	Long way out from shore.
	226	Cape Kiwanda	Just south of the tiny headland Cape Kiwanda	Popular area with hang gliders and fishermen.
	227	Gleneden Beach	Gleneden Beach County Park	Getting in and out of the surf zone can be difficult.
	228	Otter Rock	Southside of Otter Rock	Waves are formed over a wide range of conditions at Otter Rock, but rarely break with consistently good form.
	229	Yaquina Head Cove	Just south of Yaquina Head off US 101, about 4 miles north of Newport	Some of the most consistently ridable surf on the central coast.
	230	Yaquina Bay South Jetty to South Beach	1 mile south of Yaquina Bay bridge	Many surfers have frightening stories of getting caught in the south jetty rip current during large winter surf.
	231	Siuslaw River South Jetty	Just south of the Siuslaw River South Jetty	When the surf is large in the winter, ridable waves break between the jetties.
SOUTH COAST	232	Winchester Bay South Jetty	About 5 miles south of Reedsport	Perhaps the finest jetty beach break to be found on the Oregon Coast occurs south of the Winchester Bay South Jetty.
	233	Bastendorff Beach	Between the Coos Bay South Jetty and a small headland 1 mile south of the bay mouth	The beach breaks here are ridable over a wide variety of ocean swell and tide conditions, but paddling out is difficult in large winter surf when clean-up sets close out-rip current lanes.
	234	Lighthouse Beach	Beyond the Bastendorff Beach turnoff just before Sunset Beach	Probably the most popular beach in the Coos Bay area.
	235	Sunset Bay	About 3 miles south of Charleston	A tiny cove that offers small waves when other breaks are closed out by large storm surf.
	236	Port Orford	Between Battle Rock and Humbug Mountain, south of the tiny port of Port Orford	Some of the beach breaks form over a shallow rocky bottom.

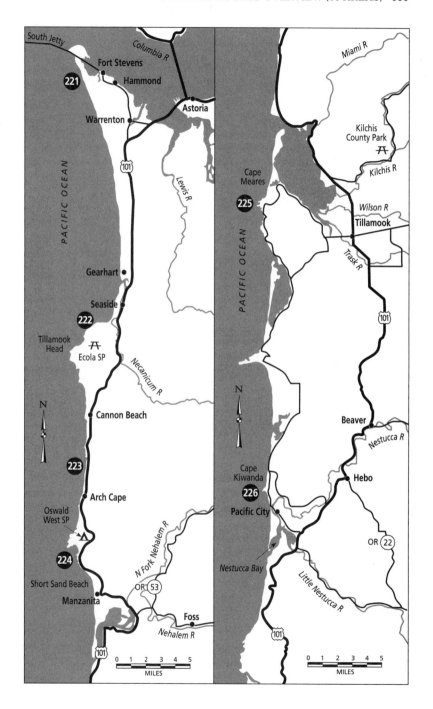

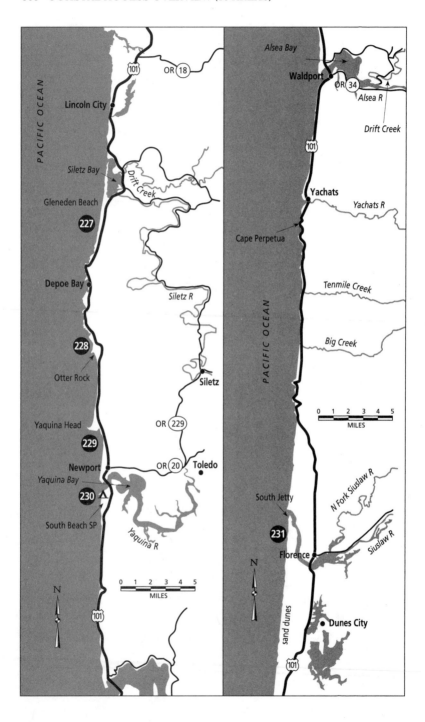

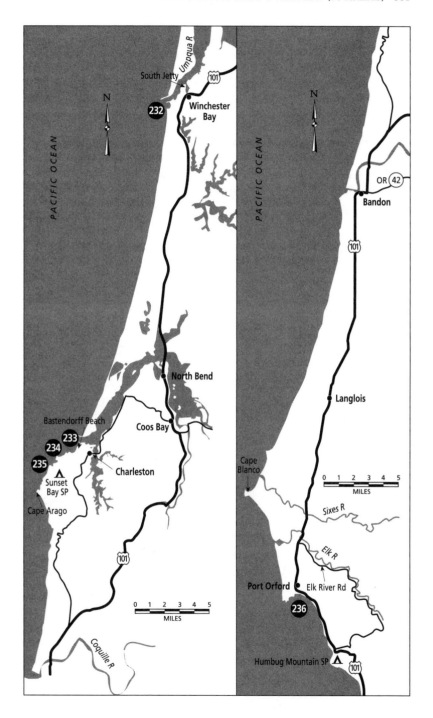

other rivers to explore

The runs in this section include a few gems, many good runs, a few marginal runs and a couple nightmares. Many of the runs have poor access, numerous logs, have only recently been run or are extremely difficult. Many of these runs involved a lot of exploring by dedicated boaters looking for new challenges. There are many rivers still unexplored by boaters. Have fun.

REGION 1: NORTH COAST RIVERS

Alsea River, North Fork: Upper Section to Fish Hatchery

Class: 3+(4+)	Gradient: 57 fpm	Length: 7 miles

This upper section of the North Fork Alsea is a good run. Unfortunately the shuttle is confusing and long. A 20-foot waterfall is about 0.25 mile below the put-in bridge and should be run on the right to avoid a hidden pothole in the center at the top of the falls. The middle section has fun class 3 rapids and one class 4 to 4+ ledge. The fish ladder at the hatchery has been run. Lots of good play throughout the run.

Little Boulder Creek: Little Boulder Creek to North Fork Siletz

Class: 5	Gradient: 300 fpm	Length: 3.6 miles

This tiny tributary of Boulder Creek has several waterfalls that are difficult to scout and portage. Also prone to wood hazards. The last half of the run is on Boulder Creek (class 3).

Clatskanie River: Upper Section to Swedetown

Class: 2(3)	Gradient: 70 fpm	Length: 6 miles

Coal Creek: East Fork to Harmony Drive

Class: 3(4)	Gradient: 100 fpm	Length: 4.5 miles

Long flat stretches separated by fun 5- to 10-foot ledges. Houses close to the river ruin what would otherwise be nice scenery. Scout the two-step waterfall halfway through the run.

D River: Source to Pacific Ocean

Class: 1	Gradient: 50 fpm	Length: 0.5 mile

World's second shortest river.

Five Rivers: 10 Miles to Mouth

Class: 1	Gradient: 12 fpm, PD	Length: 10 miles

Lake Creek: Triangle Lake to Fish Creek

Class: 5	Gradient: 162 fpm	Length: 1.7 miles

Naselle River, North Fork: Quarry to near Brock Creek

Class: 3	Gradient: 35 fpm	Length: 5 miles

Interesting river with flat sections separated by short, tight gorges. May require a long hike to the put-in if road is gated.

Nehalem River: US 26 to Spruce Run Park

Class: 1 to 2	Gradient: low	Length: 5 to 8 miles

This run features peace and quiet, nice scenery, and easy rapids combined with good surfing that should entice both beginners and intermediates.

Nehalem River, North Fork: Fish Hatchery on Oregon 53 to Boat Ramp

Class: 2 to 3	Gradient: 32 fpm	Length: 5 miles

Nestucca River: 1 Mile below Elk Bend Campground to Rocky Bend CG

Class: 3	Gradient: medium	Length: 6 miles

Continuous run with small rocky drops, some larger ones about halfway through the run. River is away from the road at some points.

Rock Creek: 5 Miles to Siletz River

Class: 2-	Gradient: unknown	Length: 5 miles

Salmonberry River, North Fork: Salmonberry Road to Salmonberry River

Class 3+(5)	Gradient: 125 fpm	Length: 3.5 miles

This run makes a nice alternative put-in for a run on the main Salmonberry River. Fun boulder gardens characterize the first 2.5 miles of the run. There are two class 5 drops in the last mile that can be portaged on the left. The scenery is good throughout the run.

Scappoose Creek: Above Bonnie Falls to Above Scappoose

Class 3(4)	Gradient: medium	Length: 4 to 6 miles

Small boulder gardens and one runnable 15-foot waterfall set in a semi-urban setting.

North Fork Siletz River: Valley of the Giants to Above Boulder Creek

Class: 4	Gradient 200 fpm

Continuous fast water. A good level is 9 feet on the Siletz gauge.

South Fork Siletz River: Valsetz Dam Site to North Fork Siletz

Class: 3 to 4	Gradient: 86 fpm	Length: 4 miles

The hardest rapid is the rocky drop just below the lake at the put-in. Great play at high water. The minimum level is 8 feet at the Siletz gauge.

Siletz River: Sam Creek to Old Mill Park

Class: 1	Gradient: 10 fpm, C	Length: 10 miles

Sweet Creek to Siuslaw (near Mapleton)

Class: 5	Gradient: 500 fpm (1 mile)	Length: 2 to 4 miles

This amazing creek drops about 500 to 600 fpm during one 0.25-mile stretch. Slides, falls, and chutes punctuate this run. Has great access for scouting, photographing, etc., with a walkway along the cliff. To get there, drive to Mapleton and take Sweet Creek Road, which follows the Siuslaw, downstream of Mapleton on the river left side. Drive about 12 miles on Sweet Creek Road to a park on the right, the take-out. Hike up the creek and behold.

Wilson River, Upper Devils Lake Fork: Deo Creek to Oregon 6

Class: 3+	Gradient: medium	Length: 2 to 3 miles

Continuous rapids through trees with occasional logs.

REGION 2: SOUTH COAST RIVERS

Chetco River: Slide Creek to South Fork

Class: 4	Gradient: 46 fpm	Length: 26 miles

2-mile carry to put-in.

Coquille River, North Fork: Uppermost Bridge to Bridge Above Moon Creek

Class: 3	Gradient: 40 fpm	Length: 13 miles

Coquille River, East Fork: 3 Miles East of Dora to Bridge on Gold Brick Road

Class: 3(4)	Gradient: 30 fpm	Length: 3.3 miles

Coquille River, Middle Fork: Bear Creek Campground to Bridge West of Camas Valley

Class: 3(4)	Gradient: 45 fpm	Length: 5 miles

Coquille River, South Fork: Natural Falls Section

Class: 5	Gradient: 235 fpm, PD	Length: 0.8 mile

Flow: 1 to 3 feet (painted gauge on pillar of 16-mile bridge); about 1.7 optimum (corresponds to about 1000 to 2000 cfs on gauge at Powers).

Pioneered in the mid 1980s, this run is a class 5 classic. One could only wish it was longer, closer to your backyard, and perhaps had some runnable waterfalls thrown in for good measure. From the put-in (a 0.5-mile easy downhill hike) to the take-out, boaters are confronted by a series of perhaps 12 class 5 drops through huge mossy boulder jumbles among old growth Douglass fir and Port Orford cedar.

The action begins immediately below the base of the thundering 85+-foot cascade of Coquille Falls. In the first drop, most of the flow plows into a fairly nasty boulder sieve, but there is a good sneak over a 5-foot ledge on far right. Below here the river drops 20 to 30 feet in a hundred yards and is the most difficult stretch. If you are not having fun, it is best to bushwack back upstream and chuck your boat uphill to your vehicle. If you are feeling good, you should be up for the rest of what the South Fork is going to throw at you. As always, out-of-control boating or swimming would be bad news; be safe.

Steve Stuckmeyer

Floras Creek: Bridge at Confluence of South Fork to Bridge 1.5 Miles from US 101

Class: 5 P	Gradient: 44 fpm	Length: 7.8 miles

Very flat for the first 6 miles. Very difficult and dangerous 0.5-mile gorge. Flat for the remainder of the run after the gorge.

Goose Creek: Near Saddle Mountain Road to South Fork Smith River

Class: 4(5)	Gradient: 90 fpm	Length: 5.5 miles

This classic run winds its way through a deep, spectacularly scenic canyon with lots of small drops and several unforgettable class 4 to 5 rapids. Easy scouting, a pool drop character, and crystalline water in a pristine setting make this creek well worth dipping a paddle into.

Jason Rackley

Hurdygurdy Creek: Bear Basin Road to Big Flat Road

Class: 4 to 5	Gradient: medium-high	Length: 6 to 7 miles

Hurdygurdy Creek is a steep, remote tributary of Northern California's South Fork of the Smith River. This is a very remote run, especially the part in the steepest part of the canyon. Once boaters enter the Devils Gap, they have no option but to hike downstream if something goes awry—the road swings impossibly far away from here to the other side of Gordon Mountain, so come prepared for anything.

Jason Rackley

Lobster Creek: Deadline Creek to Rogue River

Class: 4	Gradient: medium	Length: 4 miles

Millicoma River, East Fork: Bridge 19 Miles Above Allegany to Bridge at Little Creek

Class: 5	Gradient: 150 fpm	Length: 6.3 miles

Millicoma River, West Fork: Trout Creek Road to Henrys Falls

Class: 2+	Gradient: 53 fpm	Length: 4.5 miles

Sixes River: Bridge at Locked Gate to Sixes River Recreation Site

Class: 2(3 to 4)	Gradient: 37 fpm	Length: 5 miles

Smith River, South Fork: Upper Sections

Class: 5   Gradient: high   Length: 3 to 5 miles

REGION 3: SOUTHERN OREGON RIVERS

Big Bend Creek to Steamboat Creek

Class: 4(5)   Gradient: unknown   Length: 3 miles

Boulder Creek: 3 Miles Above North Umpqua to North Umpqua

Class: 5   Gradient: high   Length: 3 miles

Steep creek with many drops. Unfortunately, a forest fire has deposited many logs in the creek, essentially making the run unrunnable.

Champion Creek: 1 mile Up from Brice Creek Confluence

Class: 5+, T   Gradient: 300 fpm   Length: 1 mile

Technical boulder bashing with one runnable 20-foot waterfall and a couple of other ledges.

Fish Creek: unknown

Class: 5 to 5+   Gradient: high   Length: 3 miles

Jenny Creek: Near Copco Road to Iron Gate Reservoir

Class: 5 P   Gradient: high   Length: 5 to 6 miles

Small desert river with a couple of big waterfalls and several miles of continuous class 4 to class 5 rapids. The shuttle is very long and confusing.

Little River: NF 165 to White Creek Campground

Class: 4(5) P   Gradient: 120 fpm, C   Length: 7 miles

Great little creek run if you can catch it with a good flow. A fair amount of wood is usually in the upper part. Many fun, small ledges are sprinkled throughout the run as well as some good boulder gardens. The second half of the run is very scenic and contains a fun 10-foot waterfall.

Rock Creek: Northeast Fork to North Umpqua

Class: 3 to 4 P   Gradient: medium

Middle 6 to 7 miles are flat. Last mile is class 4.

Reynolds Creek: 3 miles above Steamboat Creek

Class: 5(6) Gradient: 300 fpm Length: 3 miles

Steamboat Creek: City Creek to Steamboat Falls

Class: 2+(4) Gradient: medium Length: 10 miles

REGION 4: UPPER WILLAMETTE AND MCKENZIE DRAINAGES

Big River: 7 miles Above Coast Fork Willamette to Coast Fork Willamette River

Class: 3 Gradient: medium Length: 7 miles

Blue River: Mann Creek to Quentin Creek

Class: 4(5) Gradient: 240 fpm Length: 1.5 miles

Brice Creek: Cedar Creek Campground to Layng Creek

Class: 3 Gradient: 75 fpm Length: 4.5 miles

Coal Creek: 4 Miles Above Middle Fork Willamette to Middle Fork Willamette

Class: 3 Gradient: medium Length: 4 miles

Fall Creek: Delp Creek to Gold Creek

Class: 4 T,P Gradient: 67 fpm Length: 2 mile

Class 2 to 3 water for 0.7 mile, then an easy 11-foot falls. Right after the falls, the creek enters a mile-long tight gorge that can be best described as a logjam hell.

Horse Creek: Trailhead Bridge to 7 miles Above NF 2638 Bridge

Class: 3(4) T Gradient: 114 fpm Length: 3.5 miles

Unlike Lower Horse Creek, this section is a fairly continuous flush with few logs. Mainly class 2 to 3 with one class 4 at Castle Creek.

Horse Creek: 7 miles Above NF 2638 Bridge to NF 2638 Bridge

Class: 2(3) Gradient: 67 fpm Length: 7 miles

Class 1 to 2 with one class 3. Numerous logjams, sweepers, and other dangers.

Junetta Creek: Curran Creek to Layng Creek

Class: 5 T,P	Gradient: 180 fpm	Length: 1 mile

Slow, meandering class 2 water with lots of fallen alder for 0.7 mile, then the creek drops 160 feet for the remaining 0.3 mile. Right under the main road bridge is a fun 12 foot falls.

Layng Creek: Junetta Creek to Layng Creek Work Center

Class: 2	Gradient: 60 fpm	Length: 3 miles

Easy class 2 to 2+. Take out above the manmade 6 foot ledge. A third mile above Junetta Creek is a complex, unrunnable 20+ foot falls followed by a short class 4 boulder garden. Above the falls the creek is a braided, log-filled mess for several miles.

Little Fall Creek: Gate on Little Fall Creek Road to Pengra Road Bridge

Class: 3	Gradient: 25 fpm	Length: 6 miles

A small, narrow tributary of Fall Creek. Mainly class 2 with two class 3 ledges within the first 1.5 miles. The last 2 miles are on Fall Creek and include the class 3 rapid just downstream of the Pengra Road covered bridge.

Lookout Creek: Bridge 2.5 miles Above Blue River Reservoir to Blue River Reservoir

Class: 3 to 4	Gradient: medium	Length: 2.5 miles

McKenzie River, East Fork: 3 miles Above Cougar Reservoir to Cougar Reservoir

Class: 4+(5) T,P	Gradient: 240 fpm	Length: 3 miles

Continuous class 4 boulder gardens with one class 5 located right after a huge logjam/landslide.

McKenzie River: Clear Lake to Carmen Reservoir

Class: 5(P)	Gradient: unknown	Length: 2 miles

This short section of river might be a fun late-season creek run, but for most folks it is simply a scenic hike. Hazards include two huge waterfalls (50+ feet each) that have been run but are definitely not recommended, and a 20-foot sliding falls that drops into an unrunnable logjam. If you are not planning on running the two falls, bring your hiking boots instead of your kayak.

McKenzie River: Carmen Reservoir to Trail Bridge Reservoir

Class: 2/3 P	Gradient: Medium	Length: 6 miles

Do not be lured into trying to boat below Carmen Reservoir. After a mile or two, the little water not diverted by Carmen Reservoir simply disappears into the lava and you are faced with a long hike down to the blue pool below the now dry Tamolitch Falls. Below the pool are 2 to 3 miles of very trashy (but probably runnable) class 2 whitewater until Trail Bridge Reservoir.

Mosby Creek: Gate on Mosby Creek Road to Waldon

Class: 1+(2+)	Gradient: unknown	Length: 4.5 miles

North Fork of the Middle Fork Willamette River: Waldo Lake to the Aufderheide Drive (NF 19)

Class: 5/6 P	Gradient: 270 fpm	Length: 7 miles

Huge drops and even bigger logs and logjams. Extreme boating at its best and worst.

North Fork of the Middle Fork Willamette River: NF 1944 Bridge to the Miracle Mile

Class: 3 P	Gradient: 55 fpm	Length: 11 miles

Mainly class 2 water interspersed with limbo logs, logjams, and other hazards. All but one of the class 3 rapids is created by logs/logjams.

Packer Creek: Entire run

Class: 4+	Gradient: unknown	Length: 3 miles

Salt Creek: Salt Creek Falls to NF 5884 Bridge

Class: 4+(6) T,P	Gradient: 193 fpm	Length: 6 miles

Class 5 to 6 for the first 0.33 mile. Around a blind corner is an 80+-foot falls, which is a tough portage. Below this, the creek mellows to class 3 with a few class 4 drops. The last 0.75 mile is a nonstop class 3 to 4 slalom. The 6 miles below the take-out bridge to the Salt Creek: McCredie Springs to Kitson Springs Road Bridge run is shallow, braided, and log-infested.

Separation Creek: Trail to Horse Creek

Class: 4 P	Gradient: 155 fpm	Length: 4 miles

Wood, wood, wood! And 25 portages in 4 miles.

Sharps Creek: Staples Creek to Row River

Class: 2(3)	Gradient: 37 fpm	Length: 7 miles

Staley Creek to the Middle Fork Willamette (above Hills Creek Reservoir)

Class: 4(5)	Gradient: 115 fpm	Length: 3 miles

Swift Creek: Bridge to the Middle Fork Willamette

Class: 5	Gradient: high	Length: 3 miles

Logs, logs, logs. . . .

REGION 5: MID-WILLAMETTE VALLEY

Blowout Creek: Cliff Creek to Detroit Lake

Class: 4	Gradient: 93 fpm	Length: 3.5 miles

Canal Creek: to Quartzville Creek

Class: 4	Gradient: 152 fpm	Length: 2.5 miles

One sloping 15-foot waterfall and one class 4 boulder garden.

Canyon Creek: Elbow Creek to Owl Creek

Class: 4(5) P	Gradient: 250 fpm	Length: 3 miles

Very small with wood.

Cedar Creek: Forest Road 2207 Bridge to Shady Cove Campground

Class: 5(5+)	Gradient: 133 fpm	Length: 5 miles

Steep, continuous boulder gardens with several demanding waterfalls. Amazingly, all the drops have been run. At high water, it can be extremely difficult to stop above several of the waterfalls. Many good boaters only run this creek once.

Elkhorn Creek: 3 Miles Above Little North Santiam to Little North Santiam

Class: 5	Gradient: high	Length: 3 miles

Steep rapids, big boulders, and several portages set in a remote gorge. The put-in involves a 1000-foot hike down a cliff.

French Creek: to Breitenbush River

Class: 4(5)   Gradient: 200 fpm   Length: 3 miles

Adequate flow when the Breitenbush is at 1700 cfs.

Henline Creek: to Opal Creek Trail

Class: 5   Gradient: high   Length: 1 mile

Many ledges and waterfalls set in a tight gorge. Some of the rapids have shallow landings and difficult entrance moves.

Indian Prairie Creek: 1 mile Above Thomas Creek to Thomas Creek

Class: 5   Gradient: high   Length: 1 mile

Steep rapids set in a tiny creekbed.

Little Luckiamute River: Sams Creek to Falls City

Class: 4   Gradient: 92 fpm   Length: 3 miles

Mostly flat with some wood hazards with one short class 4 section in the middle.

Little North Santiam: Mill Falls (Opal Creek Wilderness) to 0.5 Mile Above Gate

Class: 5   Gradient: high   Length: 2.5 miles

Fun boulder gardens with a couple of harder rapids that are difficult to scout and portage. Be careful of the tight rapid about 0.5 mile into the run and the dangerous slot a little over halfway into the run. Requires a 2.5-mile hike to the put-in at Mill Falls. Most boaters combine this section with the Little North Santiam River (Opal Creek): Old Mine to Three Pools run.

Little North Santiam: Three Pools to Salmon Falls (Opal Gorge)

Class: 5   Gradient: unknown   Length: unknown

Contains a vertical-walled class 5 gorge with difficult scouting.

Luckiamute River: 12 Miles from Kings Valley Highway (Oregon 223) to 6.7 Miles Above Oregon 223

Class: 3 to 4+ C,PD   Gradient: 1 mile at 150 fpm   Length: 5.3 miles

Continuous, technical water for a mile with a few ledge drops scattered downstream. Scout the major drops from the road at mile 11.4 above Oregon 223. The take-out below the big ledge rapid at mile 8.2 above Oregon 223 is recommended.

Luckiamute River: Helmick Park to Willamette River
Class: 1   Gradient: 1 fpm   Length: 14 miles

Marion Creek: Below Marion Lake to North Santiam
Class: 4   Gradient: medium   Length: 3 miles

Wood, wood, portage around a big waterfall, wood, wood. . . .

McDowell Creek: Majestic Falls to Logging Road
Class: 4 to 5   Gradient: 225 to 275 fpm   Length: 2 miles

Many fun ledges and one 10-foot waterfall. The 30-foot waterfall at the put-in has been run, but it has a shallow landing. At high water, the creek gets very continuous.

North Santiam River: Pamelia Creek to Bruno Mountain Road
Class: 3   Gradient: medium   Length: 3.8 miles

A good addition to the Bruno Mountain to Detroit run. The road is away from the river for much of the run, giving it a wilderness feel. Watch for wood which often collects 0.5 mile below put-in.

Packer's Gulch: Packer's Gulch Road Bridge to Quartzville Creek
Class: 4+   Gradient: 140 fpm   Length: 1 mile

Quartzville Creek: Freezeout Creek to Greg Creek
Class: 4+(5)   Gradient: unknown   Length: 3.3 miles

Sardine Creek: 1 mile Above Big Cliff Reservoir to Big Cliff Reservoir
Class: 5 to 5+   Gradient: high   Length: 1 mile

Sardine Creek is one of the best pure steep creeks that Oregon offers. This run has it all: big, technically demanding waterfalls; huge, mind-bendingly steep boulder gardens; and a sky-high 320 fpm average gradient that is guaranteed to keep hardcore steep creekers coming back for more. Access is easy, but catching this run with water in it is a considerable challenge. All the run can be scouted from the road, but you will not remember half of it when you are on the river. Several of the rapids have severe pin potential, so be sure to set safety and scout if you are not familiar with the run.

Soda River: Taylor Creek to South Santiam River

Class: 4- P   Gradient: 133 fpm   Length: 1.2 miles

Fun, slidey ledges.

South Santiam River: House Rock Campground to Soda River

Class: 3+(5)   Gradient: 120 fpm   Length: 2 miles

Has a big, steep rapid with two waterfalls and lots of debris in the middle.

Swift Creek: 2 Miles Above North Santiam to North Santiam

Class: 4   Gradient: high   Length: 2 miles

Logs with some rapids formed by logs.

Wiley Creek: Middle Bridge to South Santiam River

Class: 2(4)   Gradient: 30 fpm   Length: 5 miles

Willamina Creek: Blackwell Park to Yamhill River

Class: 1(3)   Gradient: 20 fpm   Length: 5 miles

Yamhill River, South Fork: Sheridan to Amity–Bellevue Road

Class: 1   Gradient: 4 fpm, C   Length: 11 miles

REGION 6: LOWER WILLAMETTE VALLEY AND CLACKAMAS RIVER

Butte Creek: Butte Creek Falls to Boy Scout Camp

Class: 3+(5) P   Gradient: medium   Length: 8 miles

There is a 25-foot runnable waterfall at the put-in. This is followed by 80- and 25-foot waterfalls. For the next 6 miles, the river has many good class 3 rapids. The last mile has a couple of harder rapids, including a narrow class 5 rapid at the take-out.

Clackamas, North Fork: NF 4610 to 3.75 Miles Above North Fork Reservoir

Class: 4(5)   Gradient: medium   Length: 3 to 3.5 miles

Lots of wood in a tiny streambed. Includes an 18-foot waterfall followed by a 6-foot ledge and two other ledge drops. In 2002, 30 portages around wood.

Delph Creek: Porter Road to Eagle Creek

Class: 3(4)	Gradient: medium	Length: 2 miles

Elk Lake Creek: Welcome Creek to East Fork Collawash

Class: 5 P	Gradient: medium	Length: 2 miles

This run is a mixed bag. The river below Welcome Creek is pretty mellow with a couple of boulder gardens and some flat water. Halfway into the run, a great 20-foot waterfall is preceded by a fun sloping ledge drop. After this waterfall, the river enters a beautiful gorge with one class 5 rapid and a difficult portage around a big sloping ledge with a logjam at the base. The remainder of the run is mostly flat but pretty.

Molalla, Nasty Rock Fork: Second Bridge Above Copper Creek to Copper Creek

Class: 4(5)	Gradient: medium	Length: 2 miles

The first 1.5 miles are small with three tight rapids. The third rapid is a 25-foot waterfall that has been run. Below the bridge is one tight rapid. The river then eases to class 3 for the remainder of the run.

Molalla, Table Rock Fork: Gorge

Class: 5	Gradient: medium	Length: 1 mile

This short run has several fun, tight drops. Only recommended at low flows. All drops should be scouted.

Pine Creek: 2 Miles Above Molalla River to Molalla River

Class: 4+	Gradient: high	Length: 2 miles

Tiny streambed with most of the good stuff in the last 0.5 mile.

Silver Creek: Below North Falls to Lower North Falls

Class: 5	Gradient: medium	Length: 2 miles

Five runnable waterfalls are in this short section. Access is limited as the entire run is contained within Silver Falls State Park, and there are strict rules prohibiting foot traffic on the banks of the creek. North Falls is unrunnable. Keep a low profile and treat the park rules with respect.

REGION 7: COLUMBIA GORGE

Eagle Creek: 6 Miles Above Historic Highway to Historic Highway

Class: 5(5+)	Gradient: high	Length: 6 miles

This run has become increasingly popular with expert kayakers in the last few years. Many big waterfalls and some other hard rapids are set in a spectacular gorge. Boaters must hike the entire distance to whatever put-in they choose. Getting out of the gorge can be difficult.

Gordon Creek: 1 mile Above Sandy River to Sandy River

Class: 4	Gradient: medium	Length: 1 mile

Hood River, East Fork: 10 Miles South of Town of Mount Hood to 5 Miles South of Mount Hood

Class: 4+	Gradient: unknown	Length: 5 miles

Hood River, East Fork: 6 Miles Above Parkdale to Bridge at Parkdale

Class: 4	Gradient: unknown	Length: 6 miles

Hood River, East Fork: Bridge at Parkdale to Dee

Class: 3(4)P	Gradient: 120 fpm	Length: 7 to 8 miles

Hood River, West Fork: NF 18 Bridge to Lake Branch Fork

Class: 3(5)	Gradient: medium	Length: 1.5 miles

Interesting gorge with many fun, small ledge drops. Fantastic scenery. Tough class 5 rapid and nasty boulder garden just above the take-out.

Little Sandy River: NF 14 to Dam

Class: 5 P	Gradient: high	Length: 10 miles

This run is currently illegal because it has been included in the Bull Run Watershed Management Area. Hopefully, access will return sometime in the future. When it becomes accessible again, it will be good to know that this is one of the best class 5 runs in northern Oregon.

The run begins with continuous boulder gardens in a tiny streambed. After portaging a 30-foot waterfall, the river gets wider and ledges and small waterfalls are separated by very steep, tight boulder gardens. Wood is often present in the rapids and pin spots abound. The last 3 miles are significantly easier than the upper river. The take-out involves a 1.5-mile hike up 800 vertical feet to the road.

Little White Salmon River: Lava Creek to Fish Hatchery

Class: 5	Gradient: high	Length: 2 miles

Easier than the classic run downstream, this run has plenty of action along with some interesting gorge scenery. Begins with class 3 and builds to class 5 for the last part of the run. Scout the tough boulder garden and falls just above the take-out.

Panther Creek: 1 mile Above Wind River to Wind River

Class: 4+	Gradient: high	Length: 1 mile

Steep, continuous, technical rapids. Only drawback is that the run is so short. Joins the Wind River upstream of The Flume (the Wind River, Washington: High Bridge to Columbia River run).

Trout Creek: Hemlock to Wind River

Class: 4	Gradient: medium	Length: 3 miles

Wind River, Upper, Upper: Above Falls Creek to Mineral Springs Road

Class: 3 to 3+(4)	Gradient: 90 fpm	Length: 3.5 miles

This section of the Wind River is a fun alternative to some of the harder runs downstream. The fun class 3 to 3+ rapids are set in a tiny gorge. Toward the end, before the gradient decreases and the gorge ends, is a tougher rapid. The gorge can get pretty wild with high water.

Zig Zag River: Toll Gate Campground to Sandy River

Class: 3+ T	Gradient: 108 fpm, C	Length: 3.2 miles

The first 0.5 mile is very tight. Then the run opens up for its remainder. The second half of the run is mostly class 2.

REGION 8: CENTRAL OREGON RIVERS

Squaw Creek: NF 1514 Bridge to Gauging Station South of Sisters

Class: 4+ P	Gradient: high	Length: 6.5 miles

Good quality rapids are set in a small creekbed with a lot of logs. Severe consequences result from missing the line of many of the rapids.

Deschutes River: Lower Benham Falls to Slough Camp

Class: 3+	Gradient: 60 fpm, C	Length: 1.5 miles

Short class 3+ section in the beginning eases to class 2, then flat.

Deschutes River: Slough Camp to Dillon Falls

Class:1	Gradient: 2 fpm	Length: 2.5 miles

Be sure to take out before Dillon Falls (class 5).

North Fork of the Crooked River: Deep Creek Campground to Paulina Highway Bridge

Class: 2+(P)	Gradient: 38 fpm	Length: 28 miles

White River: Oregon 35 Bridge to Barlow Crossing

Class: 5 to 6	Gradient: high	Length: unknown

White River: below White River Falls to Deschutes River

Class: 3	Gradient: medium	Length: 2 miles

REGION 9: EASTERN OREGON RIVERS

Imnaha River: Imnaha to Cow Creek

Class: 2(3)	Gradient: 65 fpm	Length: 12 miles

Imnaha River: Cow Creek to Eureka Bar (Snake River)

Class: 3(4)	Gradient: 65 fpm	Length: 12 miles

Requires taking out at Heller Bar on the Snake River.

Joseph Creek: Cougar Creek to Cottonwood Creek

Class: 4/5	Gradient: high	Length: unknown

Joseph Creek runs through largely private or leased land and is very isolated. If water in the Imnaha River is brown (i.e., 2800 to 3500 cfs), the water in Joseph Creek will be at a runnable level. The USFS portion is designated "Wild and Scenic" and deserves it.

Lostine River: Williamson Campground to Picnic Area

Class: 5	Gradient: high	Length: 3.5 miles

The water is crystal clear and very cold. An enjoyable level is 325 cfs. The run is remote and beautiful. The first half of the canyon is technical continuous class 3 at around 150 fpm. The last half is steeper with class 4+ to 5- boulder drops peppered throughout continuous whitewater and an 8- to 10-foot waterfall. At least one mandatory log portage and several logs that may need portaging.

South Fork Owyhee River: YP (Petan) Ranch to East Fork Owyhee River

Class: 3   Gradient: unknown   Length: about 30 miles

Run at flows from 250 to 3000 cfs.

West Little Fork Owyhee River, Anderson Crossing to Owyhee River

Class: 1(5)   Gradient: unknown   Length: about 30 miles

About 95 percent easy, 5 percent extremely difficult through narrow boulder-choked passageways, syphons, suck holes, and undercut amphitheaters.

Williamson River: Klamath Marsh (Kirk Bridge) to Williamson River Campground

Class: 3(4)P   Gradient: 46 fpm   Length: 6.5 miles

The Williamson River is in beautiful country that is not frequented by boaters. The run begins in the outflow from Klamath Marsh. The vertical drop is 300 feet and includes five waterfalls between 15 and 30 feet high, all but possibly one unrunnable, which makes this run an interesting combination of boating and rock climbing. However, for that certain kind of boater, the challenges of the remaining drops and the unique beauty of the canyon may compensate for all those portages.

Put in at the rubble dam just upstream from Kirk Bridge. If there is enough water to float the first 100 yards under the bridge and around the bend, enough water is present for the rest of the run.

Steve Cramer and Dan Parker

index

Abiqua Creek, 204
Alsea River, 60

Big Butte Creek, 116
Blue River, 151
Breitenbush River, 189
Brice Creek, 126, 130
Bull Run River, 237
Butte Creek, 205, 213

Calapooia River, 162, 166, 168
Calapooya Creek, 106
Canton Creek, 98
Canyon Creek, 173
Central Oregon Rivers (routes),
   281–314
Chetco River, 77
Christy Creek, 137
Clackamas River, 225, 226, 228, 230,
   231, 232
Clear Creek, 224
Coastal Access Overview, 358
Collawash River, 215, 217
Columbia Gorge (routes), 233–280
Copeland Creek, 96
Cow Creek, 89, 91
Crabtree Creek, 176, 177
Crooked River, 285, 287

Deschutes River, 291, 294, 295, 296,
   297, 298, 300, 301, 303, 304, 306,
   308
Devil's Lake Fork Wilson River, 42
Donner und Blitzen River, 328
Drift Creek (Siletz tributary), 56
Drift Creek (Alsea tributary), 61

Eagle Creek, 223
East Fork Hood River, 248, 250
East Fork Owyhee River, 348

Eastern Oregon Rivers (routes), 315,
   356
Elk River: Butler Creek to Fish Hatchery,
   75

Fall Creek, 140, 141, 142

Grande Ronde River, 334, 335, 337,
   338, 339, 343, 344
Grave Creek, 117
Grays River, 34

Hills Creek, 133
Hood River, 251

Illinois River, 122

Jackson Creek, 86, 87
Jarbidge River/Bruneau River, 332
John Day River, 322, 324, 326
Jordan Creek, 47

Kilchis River, 40
Klamath River, 310, 311
Klickitat River, 254, 255, 256, 257

Lake Branch Fork Hood River, 245
Lake Creek, 64
Layng Creek, 131
Little Klickitat River, 252
Little North Santiam River, 190, 192,
   193
Little White Salmon River, 265
Lower Willamette Valley and Clackamas
   River (routes), 201–232

Marys River, 162
McKenzie River, 153, 154, 155, 156,
   157, 158
Metolius River, 282

Middle Fork Rogue River, 115
Middle Fork Smith River, 80, 81, 82
Middle Fork Willamette River, 144, 146
Middle Santiam River, 186, 188
Mid-Willamette Valley (routes), 160–200
Mill Creek, 168, 170
Mohawk River, 160
Molalla River, 208, 209, 210, 212, 213
Moose Creek, 172

Nehalem River, 35
Nestucca River, 50
Nohorn Creek, 213
North Coast Rivers (routes), 33–65
North Fork Clackamas River, 220
Eagle Creek, 222
North Fork John Day River/John Day
    River, 316, 318, 321
North Fork of the Middle Fork
    Willamette River, 138, 139
North Fork Rogue River, 108, 111, 112,
    114
North Fork Siletz River, 51
North Fork Smith River, 79
North Fork Trask River, 48
North Fork Wilson River, 43
North Santiam River, 195, 196, 197,
    198, 199
North Umpqua River, 100, 101, 103,
    105

Other Rivers to Explore, 362
Owyhee River, 350, 353

Powder River, 330

Quartz Creek, 151
Quartzville River, 184, 185

Roaring River, 218
Rock Creek, 271
Rogue River, 119, 120
Row River, 131, 132

Salmon Creek, 135
Salmon River, 235
Salmonberry River, 38

Salt Creek, 134
Sandy River, 238, 239, 240, 241, 243,
    244
Siletz River, 53, 54, 55
Silver Creek, 202
Siuslaw River, 62
Snake River, 345
South Coast Rivers (routes), 67–84
South Fork Alsea River, 57
South Fork Coos River, 70
South Fork Coquille River, 71, 74
South Fork McKenzie River, 148
South Fork Smith River, 82, 83
South Fork Yamhill River, 171
South Santiam River, 180, 182
South Umpqua River, 91, 93, 94, 95
Southern Oregon Rivers (routes),
    85–124
Steamboat Creek, 99
Stebbins Creek, 272

Table Rock Fork of the Molalla River,
    207
Thomas Creek, 178, 180
Trask River, 49
Trout Creek, 267
Trout Lake Creek, 258
Umpqua River, 106, 108
Upper Willamette and McKenzie
    Drainages (routes), 125–160

Wallowa River/Grande Ronde River, 340
Washougal River, 276, 277, 278, 279
West Fork Hood River, 247
West Fork Millicoma River, 68
West Fork Washougal River, 274
White River, 288, 289, 290
White Salmon River, 260, 261, 263, 264
Wiley Creek, 175
Willamette River, 147
Wilson River, 44, 45
Winberry Creek, 143
Wind River, 268, 270

bibliography

Arighi, Scott, and Margaret Arighi. *Wildwater Touring: Techniques and Tours.* New York: Macmillan Publishing Company, 1974.

Bechdel, Les, and Slim Ray. *River Rescue: A Manual for Whitewater Safety.* Boston: Appalachian Mountain Club, 1997.

Bureau of Land Management. *Owyhee and Bruneau River Systems Boating Guide.* BLM/ID/GI-95/006+8350. Year unknown.

Campbell, Arthur. *John Day River: Drift and Historical Guide.* Portland, Oregon: Frank Amato Publications, Inc., 1980.

Carrey, Johnny, Cort Conley, and Ace Barton. *Snake River of Hells Canyon.* Cambridge, Idaho: Backeddy Books, 1979.

DeLorme Mapping Company. *Idaho Atlas and Gazetteer.* Freeport, Maine: DeLorme Mapping Company, 2000.

DeLorme Mapping Company. *Oregon Atlas and Gazetteer.* Freeport, Maine: DeLorme Mapping Company, 2001.

Garren, John. *Oregon River Tours.* Beaverton, Oregon: The Touchstone Press, 1979.

Jackson, Eric. *Whitewater Paddling: Strokes and Concepts. Kayaking with Eric Jackson.* Mechanicsburg, Pennsylvania: Stackpole Books, 1999.

Jones, Philip N. *Canoe Routes of Northwest Oregon.* Seattle: The Mountaineers, 1982.

Moore, Greg, and Don McClaran. *Idaho Whitewater: The Complete River Guide.* McCall, Idaho: Class VI, 1989.

Nealy, William. *Kayak: A Manual of Technique.* Birmingham, Alabama: Menasha Ridge Press, 1986.

Quinn, James M., and James W. Quinn. *Handbook to the Klamath River Canyon.* Medford, Oregon: Educational Adventures, Inc., 1983.

Quinn, James M., James W. Quinn, and James G. King. *Handbook to the Deschutes River Canyon.* Medford, Oregon: Educational Adventures, Inc., 1979.

———. *Handbook to the Illinois River Canyon.* Medford, Oregon: Educational Adventures, Inc., 1979.

———. *Handbook to the Rogue River Canyon.* Medford, Oregon: Educational Adventures, Inc., 1978.

Schwind, Dick. *West Coast River Touring: The Rogue River and South, Including California.* Beaverton, Oregon: The Touchstone Press, 1974.

State of Oregon, Oregon State Parks and Recreation Branch. "Willamette River Recreation Guide." Salem, Oregon: Oregon Parks Department, 1976.

Tice, Kevin Keith. *The Rogue River Guide.* La Crescenta, California: Mountain N' Air Books, 1995.

Walbridge, Charles, and Wayne A. Sundmacher. *Whitewater Rescue Manual: New Techniques for Canoeists, Kayakers, and Rafters.* Camden, Maine: International Marine/Ragged Mountain Press, 1995.

appendix a

RIVER FLOW INFORMATION

California/Nevada River Forecast
Center
www.cnrfc.noaa.gov/

California River Information
Center
800-952-5530

Dreamflows
www.dreamflows.com/flows.php

National Weather Service River
Forecast Centers
www.nwrfc.noaa.gov/misc/rfcs.cgi

Northwest River Forecast Center
www.nwrfc.noaa.gov/
503-326-7401

Oregon State Parks and Recreation
800-551-6949
For camping reservations, call:
Reservations Northwest
800-452-5687

Pat Welch's Flow Page
levels.wkcc.org/?P:Oregon.html

USGS Real-time River Flow
waterdata.usgs.gov/nwis/rt

Washington State Department of
Ecology
fortress.wa.gov/ecy/wrx/flow
/regions/state.asp

appendix b

WHITEWATER BOATING ORGANIZATIONS

Lower Columbia Canoe Club
17005 NW Meadowgrass Drive
Beaverton, OR 97006
www.l-ccc.org

Northwest Rafters Association
PO Box 19008
Portland, OR 97219
www.nwrafters.org

Oregon Kayak and Canoe Club
PO Box 692
Portland, OR 97207
www.okcc.org

Oregon Ocean Paddlers Society
PO Box 8712
Portland, OR 97207-8712
www.oopskayak.org/

PDXkayaker
www.pdxkayaker.org/

Southern Oregon Kayakers
kayak.coosweb.com

Willamette Kayak and Canoe
Club, Inc
PO Box 1062
Corvallis, OR 97339
www.wkcc.org

about the editor

Pete Giordano has been rafting and kayaking the rivers of Oregon, as well as other rivers across the United States, for more than 10 years. Pete owns Blue Sky Whitewater Rafting, Inc., a rafting company based in Estacada, Oregon, that operates guided rafting trips on a variety of rivers throughout Oregon. He has personally kayaked or rafted nearly all the runs in this book and has explored many other rivers in the state. In his spare time, Pete can be found perusing topographic maps in the hopes of finding more rivers to kayak.

THE MOUNTAINEERS, founded in 1906, is a nonprofit outdoor activity and conservation club, whose mission is "to explore, study, preserve, and enjoy the natural beauty of the outdoors. . . ." Based in Seattle, Washington, the club is now one of the largest such organizations in the United States, with seven branches throughout Washington State.

The Mountaineers sponsors both classes and year-round outdoor activities in the Pacific Northwest, which include hiking, mountain climbing, ski-touring, snowshoeing, bicycling, camping, kayaking and canoeing, nature study, sailing, and adventure travel. The club's conservation division supports environmental causes through educational activities, sponsoring legislation, and presenting informational programs. All club activities are led by skilled, experienced volunteers, who are dedicated to promoting safe and responsible enjoyment and preservation of the outdoors.

If you would like to participate in these organized outdoor activities or the club's programs, consider a membership in The Mountaineers. For information and an application, write or call The Mountaineers, Program Center, 7700 Sand Point Way NE, Seattle, Washington 98115; 206-521-6001.

The Mountaineers Books, an active, nonprofit publishing program of the club, produces guidebooks, instructional texts, historical works, natural history guides, and works on environmental conservation. All books produced by The Mountaineers fulfill the club's mission.

Send or call for our catalog of more than 500 outdoor titles:

The Mountaineers Books
1001 SW Klickitat Way, Suite 201
Seattle, WA 98134
800-553-4453
mbooks@mountaineersbooks.org; www.mountaineersbooks.org

The Mountaineers Books is proud to be a corporate sponsor of Leave No Trace, whose mission is to promote and inspire responsible outdoor recreation through education, research, and partnerships. The Leave No Trace program is focused specifically on human-powered (nonmotorized) recreation. Leave No Trace strives to educate visitors about the nature of their recreational impacts, as well as offer techniques to prevent and minimize such impacts. Leave No Trace is best understood as an educational and ethical program, not as a set of rules and regulations.

For more information, visit *www.LNT.org*, or call 800-332-4100.